THE DOME OF EDEN

The Dome of
EDEN

*A New Solution to the Problem
of Creation and Evolution*

STEPHEN H. WEBB

CASCADE *Books* • Eugene, Oregon

THE DOME OF EDEN
A New Solution to the Problem of Creation and Evolution

Copyright © 2010 Stephen H. Webb. All rights reserved. Except for brief quotations in critical publications or reviews, no part of this book may be reproduced in any manner without prior written permission from the publisher. Write: Permissions, Wipf and Stock Publishers, 199 W. 8th Ave., Suite 3, Eugene, OR 97401.

Cascade Books
An Imprint of Wipf and Stock Publishers
199 W. 8th Ave., Suite 3
Eugene, OR 97401

www.wipfandstock.com

ISBN 13: 978-1-60608-741-1

Cataloging-in-Publication data:

Webb, Stephen H., 1961–

    The dome of Eden : a new solution to the problem of creation and evolution / Stephen H. Webb.

    viii + 366 p. ; 23 cm. —Includes index.

    ISBN 13: 978-1-60608-741-1

    1. Bible and evolution. 2. Evolution—Religious aspects—Christianity. 3. Good and Evil. 4. Theodicy. I. Title.

BS659 .W43 2010

Manufactured in the U.S.A.

Contents

Acknowledgments vii

Introduction 1

one   The Theory That Would Not Die 13

two   Re-Trying Scopes:
What Machen Would Have Done to Darrow 69

three   Three Rival Theories and the Problem of Natural Evil 92

four   The Five Theses 139

five   Karl Barth on the Edge of the Gap 181

six   The Dome of Domes Divides the World 209

seven   Could Jesus Have Been an Octopus?
(Duns Scotus Replies to Darwin) 246

eight   An Ethics of Pets vs. the Darwinian Sublime 296

nine   The Nature of Naturalism 324

Conclusion 349

Index of Names 363

Acknowledgments

I used the rough draft of this book as the main text for a class on creation and evolution that I taught in the fall of 2008 at Wabash College. I told my students to treat it like any other book, and they did. They read it critically and discussed it thoroughly, even though the author was standing right before them and rewriting the text as they spoke. They pushed me hard, and for that I gratefully dedicate this book to them. My student assistant, Chris McCauley, was as helpful as he was tolerant of my disorganized office. Owen Anderson read an even earlier draft with a very helpful eye. A conversation with my student John Torma inspired the title of chapter 7. I am in Matt Halteman's debt for letting me try out some of my ideas for the inaugural lecture in his Animals and the Kingdom lecture series at Calvin College in January 2008. His hospitality was utterly gracious. I received no institutional support for writing this book or, come to think of it, my last two books either. Indeed, the stories I could tell! Nonetheless, I am grateful for everything.

Introduction

I am proposing a new theory about the relationship between the Christian doctrine of creation and the Darwinian theory of evolution. The biblical theology of creation and the Darwinian account of evolution are both theories, and there are also theories about how those theories relate to each other. The kind of theory I am presenting here is of that latter sort. That is, I am not trying to prove creation or disprove evolution. Instead, I am assuming that God created the world and that evolution occurs. Admittedly, I am more confident in the arguments for the belief that God created the world than the arguments for Darwin's theory of evolution, but I do not deny that evolution on some level is a biological fact and that Darwin's theory has much to recommend it. Nonetheless, I will raise many objections to Darwin's theory in these pages, not because I reject the idea that evolution happens, but because I think Darwinism has weaknesses that can be best brought to light by a proper understanding of the relationship of evolution to the Christian doctrine of creation.

A theory of the relationship of evolution and creation is required by the exigencies of Christian faith, but it is also made necessary by the kind of theory Darwinism is. I will argue throughout this book that Darwinism is a theory that naturally seeps into religious theories about God and creation. I used the image of "seep" in that sentence intentionally in order to indicate just how easily Darwinism can spill over its scientific banks and threaten to flood every other account of the natural (and supernatural) world. I do not think that this danger is exclusive to Darwinism. On the contrary, all scientific theories abhor a cultural vacuum, in that they are expressed, elaborated, defended, and applied in the language and assumptions of the culture from which they are born. Nevertheless, Darwinism is markedly immersed in its social setting, just as it is particularly aggressive in invading and colonizing other fields of knowledge.

Notice that I am not saying that scientific theories are nothing but the product of their historical and social context. I am not defending a postmodern perspective that would reduce the sciences to an artificial construction, making them a figment of our collective imagination. The scientific method is reliable and good and is not limited in its use to the so-called natural sciences. Even theologians base their beliefs on a logical analysis of the evidence. Nevertheless, scientific theories do not float around in an ethereal space of scholarly privilege high above the religious questions, metaphysical assumptions, and moral implications that shape every human encounter with the world.

Because it is so tightly harnessed to non-scientific language and assumptions, Darwinism inevitably does more work than its designers might have envisioned. My whole book, in a way, is a gloss on the words Pope Benedict XVI delivered, when he was a Cardinal, at a 1985 symposium on "Evolution and Christianity": "Today a new stage of the debate has been reached, inasmuch as 'evolution' has been exalted above and beyond its scientific content and made into an intellectual model that claims to explain the whole of reality and thus has become a sort of 'first philosophy.'" Consequently, "when natural science becomes a philosophy, it is up to philosophy to grapple with it." Darwinism presents a crisis to Christianity that is made possible by the uncoupling of physics from metaphysics. When cultures abandon the hard work of elaborating a coherent intellectual worldview, science, with its countless impressive successes, will push forward to pick up the slack. The particularly pernicious question that evolution raises is whether reason stands at the beginning of nature or stands out at the end of evolution as nature's way of playing a practical joke on us. As Pope Benedict put it in a 2006 conference, "what is fundamentally at stake is regaining a dimension of reason that we have lost."[1]

Regaining reason does not require, nor does my book provide, a harmonizing of evolution and creation. There are countless attempts at that, most of which begin with one side of the debate and only then reach out to the other side just enough to please nobody. Harmonizers that begin with evolution typically add just enough religion to make

---

1. Quoted in Christoph Cardinal Schönborn, ed., *Creation and Evolution: A Conference with Pope Benedict XVI in Castel Gandolfo*, trans. Michael J. Miller (San Francisco: Ignatius, 2007) 9, 10, and 161.

Introduction

evolution more palatable but not so much that religious skeptics would feel threatened by it. Theologians and scientists alike pursue this strategy, granting Darwinism its full range of claims while supplementing evolution with an overlay of religious meaning, as if the sole point of religion is to cover up the ugly truth of the struggle for life with some existential exhortations and sentimental consolations. Harmonizers who begin with a defense of the literal meaning of Genesis are just as unconvincing. They pry open the days of creation described in Genesis just wide enough to permit some evolution to squeeze through but not wide enough to do justice to the study of biology or to persuade Darwinians that Genesis has anything to contribute to their theory. Harmonizers of both varieties do little more than convince their own side that they can stay on that side without taking the other side seriously.

A theory about the relationship of evolution and creation is different from the attempt to harmonize them because a theory will inevitably change or challenge each side. My theory will be harder on evolution than it is on creation, but it will stretch theology as well as chasten science. My analysis of the doctrine of creation, for example, will put Christ front and center in order to make sense of certain aspects of evolution, but it will do so in a way that challenges some conceptualizations of that doctrine. My fidelity to the details of Genesis will most likely risk not being faithful enough for some and too faithful to others. I want to chasten Darwinism because I think it goes too far in its explanatory range and ambition and eliminates too much evidence in its focus on random genetic change and natural selection. Thus I will pose moral and philosophical challenges to Darwinism that will entail, at the same time, specific scientific objections and reservations. (I use *Darwinism* as an abbreviated way of referring to the currently dominant theory of evolution, which is a confluence of Darwin's original emphasis on natural selection and the struggle of life with the genetic revolution that took place in the early twentieth century.)

I realize that most of my readers will think it absurd that a theological argument can pose a credible intellectual challenge to a scientific theory, but if Darwinism entails various moral, metaphysical, and religious implications, then challenging those implications will affect Darwinism itself. If the clothes make the man and you ask the man to change clothes, you've changed the man as well. Stripping Darwinism bare of all of the cultural accretions it has gathered over the course of its tumultuous but fantastically successful career is a noble task, but it is hard and maybe even impossible to know where Darwinism ends and its implications and consequences begin. Darwin's many defenders exploit this fact by taking the offensive when religion, morality, or philosophy get in the way, but they turn to the defensive when they are accused of stepping over their scientific boundaries into the realm of speculation and ideology.

The dynamic of attack and retreat is what I call, in chapter 1, the rhetoric of the good and the bad Darwinian cop. The bad cop says Darwinism will explain everything you once took for granted and thus change everything you believe. If you offer good arguments why Darwinism cannot do this and then suggest that it follows that there must be something deeply wrong with Darwinism, the good cop will condescendingly explain that Darwinism is only a scientific theory and you should not get so upset about it. Take, for example, the Darwinian theory of religion. When it suits them, Darwinians claim to demystify religion, account for morality, and render metaphysics redundant. When critics sound the alarm and respond with an arsenal of elaborate objections, the bad Darwinians point to the good Darwinians, huddled in their laboratories, as evidence of how harmless and benign their theory is. I am overstating the situation, but only a little bit. I have had conversations with bad Darwinians who have sung the praises of the boundless explanatory power of their theory, while I have had conversations with good Darwinians who have told me that the bad Darwinians should not be taken seriously because they are not true scientists. When I report this to the bad Darwinians, they politely point out that the good Darwinians are not theorists and thus are blinded by the narrowness of their research. When I challenge the bad Darwinians on their theory, they remind me that Darwinism is a science and therefore I, a non-scientist, have no business pretending to know what they are talking about.

I am condensing many conversations I have had over the years for rhetorical effect, but there is no exaggerating the impact of Darwinism in higher education today. Darwinism is making a bid across the academic fields to become the unifying theory of the natural and human sciences, and, as such, it seeks to explain every aspect of animal (includ-

Introduction

ing human) behavior. If that is what Darwinism is, then it is only fair to let theologians and philosophers raise objections to the Darwinian program. Unfortunately, when faced with criticism, many Darwinians fall back on their specialized qualifications and denounce anyone without the proper professional credentials. More problematic, Darwinians like to erect a high wall of separation between religion and science so that they can keep religion out of their sacred grove, even as they feel perfectly free to walk through the gate that opens only from the inside.

One solution to this problem is to ignore Darwinian theorists who take scientific findings too far. The problem with that approach is that scientific theories are meant to be all-encompassing, and this one in particular is hard to ignore. In any case, I am of the opinion that the bad Darwinian cop is more right than the good one. Darwinism is a grand theory, and it should be allowed to put its best foot forward before being attacked and wrestled to the ground. It is only prudent to take the most aggressive Darwinians at their word. This is no time for theological complacency. Nonetheless, Darwinism needs to be approached as more than just a pesky cultural menace. Darwinism is an elegant, profound, and far-reaching research program, capable of replicating itself in any intellectual environment, so any theory about it has to be just as advanced. There is no sense in pretending that there can be an easy theological response to the problem of evolution.

The most popular criticism of Darwinism goes by the name of the intelligent design movement, which is an attempt to refine scientific and mathematical protocols for the discernment of evidence that at least some aspects of biological evolution are the product of design, not chance. Many people today assume that any critic of Darwinism must be a card-carrying member of the intelligent design movement. Perhaps I just don't know where to sign up, but I am actually more of a fellow traveler than a full blown booster, because I criticize Darwinism in a way that is different from the intelligent design community. Nonetheless, I have learned much from intelligent design theorists, as will be clear throughout this book. I agree with intelligent designers that Darwinism cannot provide a complete and coherent account of the formation and development of life. The intelligent design community speaks deeply to the basic human intuition of the purpose and planning that is, for most people, abundantly discernible in the natural world. Intelligent designers wager that if design makes theological sense, it should make a difference for the sciences as well. Design theorists thus challenge not only the study of biology but also the very definition of science. That is why this movement is so controversial. Power and prestige is at stake in what our society deems worthy of the scientific label. The usual Darwinian response is to argue that design cannot be detected by science, because science cannot prove or even lend credence to religion. This strikes me as a circular argument that has the further limitation of being a case of special pleading. It tries to separate science and religion on the basis of definition, not argument or analysis. I think intelligent designers are right to challenge a narrow view of science, that is, the tight boundary that most scientists (but very few philosophers) draw around science in order to protect it from philosophical and theological scrutiny.

Where I differ from intelligent design theory has to do with what theologians call the problem of natural evil. Intelligent design theorists attempt to ground design in a loving and all-knowing designer, but what about animals that are designed to kill each other? I define the problem of natural evil at the beginning of chapter 3, but briefly put, I do not think intelligent design takes the downside of nature—plagues, parasites, and predation—as seriously as it should. Figuring out how to detect design in nature is, I think, an important and potentially viable project, but nature's design leads to suffering, cruelty, and profligate death as well as increasing biological complexity. Pain is a necessary component of life, of course, but the sheer amount of pain in the world is, for many critics of religion, a major strike against the existence of a good and loving God. Explanations of why God permits evil in the world go by the name of theodicies, and theodicies are as complex as they are controversial. Some theologians argue that we simply do not know enough about the ways of God to account for evil, and, in any case, any attempt to rationalize evil ends up justifying it and thus belittling the plight of evil's victims. I disagree. I think theologians have a responsibility to provide an account of natural evil that makes sense of both the goodness of creation and the struggle of evolution. A theodicy is thus a necessary element in any attempt to reconcile creation and evolution. Intelligent design theory is not primarily a theological movement, but if nature is not what God meant it to be—if, that is, nature is fallen in some way, as Genesis suggests—then it follows that intelligent designers have an obligation to integrate a theodicy into their theory. That is, they must distinguish between design attributable to God's good intentions and design that goes awry from God's original plan.

Religiously literate defenders of Darwinism are very adept at using the theological problem of natural evil to their own advantage. They are eager to point to the bizarre and gruesome features of nature as evidence against the idea of an intelligent designer. It is an easy game to play: pick a shocking example of an animal that eats its young or sustains itself by pretending to be of benefit to another and ask, "Why would God create the world in such a way?" This is the common Darwinian retort to the intelligent design community. Ernst Mayr, one of the greatest biologists of the twentieth century, demonstrates the pervasiveness of this line of argument in an informal survey he conducted of his Harvard University colleagues who were fellow members of the prestigious National Academy of Sciences. "It turned out we were all atheists," he reported. "I found that there were two sources." One source was a skeptical mindset that might be related to their vocational disposition. As Mayr's colleagues repeatedly told him, "Oh, I became an atheist very early. I just couldn't believe all that stuff." The other source was the abundance of evil in the world. As his colleagues put it, "I just couldn't believe that there could be a God with all this evil in the world." Mayr concluded, "Most atheists combine the two. This combination makes it impossible to believe in God."[2] Mayr thinks this is an intellectually honorable position and reports his findings as if they make immediate and overwhelming sense. They don't. Mayr's colleagues appear to disbelieve in God because they think that only the natural world is worthy of serious investigation, yet they appear to believe in evolution because they think that they have sufficiently considered whether belief in God can make sense of the natural world. That is, they use a theological argument to support their scientific position even though their scientific position leaves no room for theology, and, by their own admission, they do not understand or read any theology. Perhaps the best spin we can put on Mayr's survey is to say that his colleagues are merely reacting to their own discoveries about the merciless battles of the species—battles

---

2. Quoted in Edward J. Larson, *The Creation-Evolution Debate: Historical Perspectives* (Athens, GA: University of Georgia Press, 2007) 51.

that violate our basic moral intuitions about how the world should be, if it were to be the kind of place created by a good God. Nature's grotesqueries make Darwinians shudder too frequently to permit them to take nature as a gift from God.

Another example of how Darwinism simultaneously makes and undermines theological arguments can be found in debates about junk DNA. Many Darwinians argue that biological flaws in nature not only prove evolution but also disprove intelligent design. If God designed nature, Darwinians argue, then why do so many organisms have so much DNA that contributes nothing to their biological make-up? Does God enjoy littering genomes with junk? Darwinians argue that junk DNA—non-coding sequences that do not produce proteins—demonstrates the haphazard way nature evolves, with organisms carrying excessive baggage that they would have discarded long ago if God had been planning their itinerary. Interestingly, this debate has taken a turn in recent years with scientists discovering new uses for DNA that they previously thought were just going along for the ride. It turns out that sequences of DNA in humans that appear useless actually control everything from stem cells to the opposable thumb. Whatever the outcome of these ongoing findings, it is interesting for my purposes to observe how Darwinians must struggle like the rest of us with a moral interpretation of nature. Whether nature is wasteful or productive, haphazard or planned, a gift or a burden, we cannot refrain from passing judgment on what nature is and what God should have done to make nature meet our own needs and expectations. The Darwinian description of evolution tends to echo the theological language of the fall, but it does so only to enable Darwinians to reject the idea that evolution is designed by a good and all-knowing deity.

Darwinians are right, in my view, to emphasize the wanton cruelty and apparent senselessness of evolution, but they are not right to think that this disproves the idea of an intelligent and beneficent designer. Instead, it points to the need for a post-Darwinian retrieval of the Genesis teaching about nature's fall. Bringing together the fall and evolution, however, can easily result in sloppy theology, because it is tempting to assign everything that is wrong in the natural world to the fall. R. J. Berry, a Christian and a professor of genetics, has articulated this complaint in his 2003 Gifford Lectures: "Some Christians interpret

Introduction

any facts which they find morally difficult as 'results of the fall' (such as 'nature red in tooth and claw' or the enormous number of human fetuses which spontaneously miscarry)."[3] No straight line can be drawn from the fall to evolution, although much can be said about how a Christian view of nature illuminates the moral dimension of evolution.

I try in this book to reach the bottom of the mystery of natural evil by following it all the way through both Darwinism and intelligent design, neither of which can provide it with a coherent foundation. If the natural world is fallen, as the Bible and Christian tradition teach, then the story of the fall found in Genesis, brief and befuddling as it is, must cast a penetrating light on the long history of biological evolution, but it must also challenge any conception of the universe as optimally designed. Randomness and design clash in the battle between Darwinians and intelligent design theorists, but both groups miscalculate just how morally loaded the concept of design (and its counterpart, luck) really is.

Darwinians rightly describe evolution as a struggle, but I want to suggest that this struggle takes place on more than just the natural plane. Intelligent designers rightly follow the signs of design to their source in a supernatural designer, but those signs can be misleading and easily misread. While any discussion of life cannot be complete without speaking of design, not all designs have the same ultimate purpose or the same ontological status. There is evil in the world, both natural and human. Consequently, both Darwinians and intelligent design theorists need a fuller account of the different kinds of purpose in nature and the role they play in our moral imagination.

Showing sympathy to the intelligent design movement is enough to get most books taken out of the production lineup at an academic press, but I also want to confess how much I have learned from scientific creationism. Scientific creationists, who are too often confused with intelligent designers, are often unfairly shunned by those theologians who blithely disregard evolution as a problem for Christian faith. Creationists are right to find Darwinism and Christianity incompatible, and they are right to look to Genesis for an alternative to Darwinism. My theory about the relationship between creation and evolution is

---

3. R. J. Berry, *God's Book of Works: The Nature and Theology of Nature* (New York: T. & T. Clark, 2003) 231.

based on an absolute trust in the Bible, and I have been inspired by the commitment of creationists to the proposition that Genesis gives a true account of the creation of the world. The Genesis account of the Garden of Eden for me holds more truth than we can possibly know, and I think we are only beginning to discover what it has to teach us about the origin, limits, and consequences of evolution. Nonetheless, Genesis does not preclude all forms of biological evolution, and neither can it be harmonized with evolution by simply filling in a few blanks in the text.

The first chapter constitutes an overview of the problem of evolution. It lays out my reservations, complaints, criticisms, and exasperations with Darwinism. Anyone writing about Darwin should come clean about what he or she "really thinks," so in this chapter I pull together a critical overview of the whole Darwinian enterprise. My main concern is to show how Darwinism, more than most scientific theories, is intimately dependent upon various moral, philosophical, and theological assumptions. Telling the story of life is a project in which every discipline has a stake, including theology. True, letting every discipline have a seat at the evolutionary table would make for a very crowded and noisy gathering. Biologists will want to sit at the head of the table and call for some order, but so will philosophers and theologians. Unfortunately, nobody has a plan for the seating arrangements. The problem, of course, is that academic disciplines in the rarefied atmosphere of higher education have become separate cultures sustained by diverse social practices and publicly enforced norms. Crossing disciplinary boundaries is a transgressive act that leaves behind the familiar shores of comforting credentials and habitual methodologies. Nevertheless, there are also constant calls for interdisciplinary work and broader scholarly conversations. Darwinism, I argue in chapter 1, is an aggressively colonizing discipline that swallows up adjacent modes of inquiry without altering its inner core. The rhetoric that some Darwinians use to protect their field from counterattacks should not be taken too seriously. Philosophically inclined Darwinians are right to press the implications of evolution for religion, but theologians are also right to insist that religious faith has something to say about biology as well.

I am convinced that only an historical perspective can explain why Darwinism is frequently cosseted and protected from theological

Introduction

and philosophical critique. In chapter 2 I try to tell the story of how Darwinism became such a divisive issue within the Christian church and why it is tragic not only for Christian unity but also for the unity of knowledge and the common good of public education. Darwinism has always relied on ancillary modes of thought to flesh out its details and uphold its assumptions. In this chapter I argue that the eventual triumph of Darwinism in the twentieth century was facilitated by liberal theological optimism and idealism associated with a now-dated belief in inevitable social progress, which is ironic given how Darwinism today is used to undermine any idea of purpose or progress in nature or history. The alignment between biology and the liberal Protestant establishment sheltered Darwinism from theological and philosophical scrutiny. The decline of the mainline Protestant churches as well as the maturation of evangelical and conservative forms of Christianity provides a new opening to reconsider Darwinism's relationship to morality and metaphysics as well as the relationship of evolution to the Genesis account of creation.

The next five chapters are theological. Chapter 3 is methodological in that it lays out the three most common attempts to reconcile evolutionary theory and the Christian doctrine of creation. I argue that these models fall short for a variety of reasons, but especially on the issue of natural evil. Chapter 4 is the heart of the book because it contains my solution to the problem of evolution in five theses. Readers who want to skip ahead and start arguing with me right away should start with this chapter. Chapter 5 shows that Karl Barth, the great Swiss theologian, came very close to anticipating many aspects of my theory. This chapter is not only meant to give my position some credentials in the world of academic scholarship, but is also intended to shed some new light on Barth by bringing out some of his provocative ideas on creation that are rarely discussed. Chapter 6 analyzes in depth the most important of my five theses—the one concerning what many translations of the Bible call the firmament, which God created to separate the waters (Gen 1:6–8). From this thesis I draw the name for my theory as a whole, the Dome of Eden theory. Chapter 7 also elaborates one of my theses. It constitutes a defense of the biological uniqueness of the human species by appropriating the teaching of John Duns Scotus on the Primacy of Christ. Achieving clarity about the priority of Christ provides the metaphysical foundation for the many convergences in evolution that have become the subject of the work of Simon Conway Morris. Bringing Scotus together with the problem of evolution also demonstrates the value of the univocity theory of religious language and leads to other surprising theological conclusions.

The final two chapters lay out some of the implications of my theory while comparing it to Darwinism. Chapter 8 develops a biblical account of animals in opposition to the Darwinian experience of nature's "natural" violence. Chapter 9 argues that Darwinism is committed to a self-contradictory form of naturalism. This naturalism, I argue, poses the greatest intellectual threat not only to the salvation of souls but also to the future of humanity. I know that sounds apocalyptic, but that does not mean it is not true.

one

The Theory That Would Not Die

Darwin's account of evolution is just a theory, but what a theory! There have been controversial scientific theories in the past, but never one that has raised so many deep and conflicting questions about such a broad range of moral, religious, and philosophical issues. Copernicus comes to mind as having had a similar cultural impact, but even he remains in a distant second place. Copernicus put the sun at the center of the solar system, humbling the earth, but Darwin put chance and struggle at the center of life, humbling humanity. Darwin cuts closer to the bone.

Many scientific theories take a few generations to achieve widespread acceptance. Good scientific theories settle into human consciousness by proving their predictive power, but the more startling and counterintuitive they are, they more they need to have their moral, religious, and philosophical implications tested as well. If truth is one and we are able to know the truth, then the more we investigate any scientific theory, the more it should cohere with the rest of our true knowledge. In fact, one of the chief criteria for judging the validity of a scientific theory is its ability to triumph, no matter how slowly, over the intellectual obstacles that even the strongest minds erect. Darwin's theory appears to violate this general pattern. The longer it survives, the more it shows signs of aging.

To its critics, Darwin's theory requires a leap of the imagination that makes it something less than hard science. The simple thesis that all forms of life have evolved from a single organism by means of genetic mutation and natural selection suggests an epic tale that only the greatest of poets could narrate. Even Darwin's staunchest supporters can admit that describing biological evolution is a work of art as well as science. As Simon Conway Morris, one of the leading biologists in the world, states,

"Of all the sciences, perhaps the richest in metaphors is biology."[1] What else would one expect when dealing with the overwhelming complexity of the history of life? Morris goes on to state that evolutionary biology is "much closer to metaphysics than it often cares to acknowledge."[2] Morris is a world-class scientist, but he is also a Christian, which might help account for his sense of the incompleteness of Darwinism and the need to keep pushing for richer, more multi-causal explanations of biological phenomenon. His description of biology's relationship to philosophy certainly sets him apart from scientists who think that metaphysics—the study of the basic foundational assumptions entailed in the pursuit of knowledge—is little more than conceptual poetry. Scientists are the products of the most specialized of educations, so it is understandable if they get nervous when they are told that their subject matter cannot be disciplined by their professional guild alone. We live in such a splintered world that the mastery of even one small subset of a scholarly field is a lifelong pursuit. It is hard enough to get a grasp of the Darwinian theory as a whole, let alone its various connections to other ways of examining the world. It must be frustrating for any Darwinian to hear that any explanation of evolution, if it is to be complete, must reflect on and account for the metaphysical, moral, and poetic dimensions of biology, but the fact that a bit of news makes someone feel uncomfortable is not a good argument for rejecting it.

The comparison of Darwinism with poetry and metaphysics should make poets and metaphysicians nervous as well. Poets are as precise in their use of language as biologists are often very vague, and metaphysicians analyze any and every assumption until they reach bedrock principles, while Darwinians can leave their assumptions undisturbed by the demands of conceptual clarification. Short of a genius like Darwin himself, who could write beautifully and was well immersed in the philosophical and theological issues of his day, evolutionary theory

---

1. Simon Conway Morris, "Evolution and Convergence: Some Wider Considerations," in *The Deep Structure of Biology: Is Convergence Sufficiently Ubiquitous to Give a Directional Signal?* ed. Simon Conway Morris (West Conshohocken, PA: Templeton Foundation, 2008) 46–67, at 46. For theological reflection, see Graham J. O'Brien, "A Theology of Purpose: Creation, Evolution and the Understanding of Purpose," *Science & Christian Belief* 19 (2007) 59–74.

2. Morris, "Evolution and Convergence," 61.

appears destined to depend on other disciplines to reach its goal of a comprehensive and complete account of living organisms.

Perhaps nowhere is the mixture of science, poetry, and metaphysics more evident than in descriptions of how life came to be. Darwin's defenders sometimes separate biological from chemical theories of evolution, but if Darwin's theory is to live up to its billing, it should go a long way toward accounting for the origin as well as the development of life. Evolution, in other words, must go all the way back if it is to shed light on how far we have come. Chemical evolution (also known as abiotic chemistry) is the branch of science devoted to this inquiry. It was founded on the premise that organic compounds can be synthesized by the right inorganic mix. In 1952, Stanley Miller, a graduate student in chemistry at the University of Chicago working in Harold Urey's lab, began experimenting with various pre-biotic (pre-life) soups in order to prove this premise. When the media picked up on word of his success, Darwinians savored their triumph. Miller was able to produce amino acids by animating a few water, carbon, and nitrogen molecules with an electric shock. If the building blocks of biology could bubble up from a prehistoric broth, then it was reasonable to conclude that Darwin was right to have dispensed with God's assistance in explaining the mystery of life.

But what if Miller was wrong? Although Miller's experiment is still celebrated, taught, and reported in scientific textbooks, most chemists were convinced by the 1970s that the earth's earliest atmosphere was nothing like Miller's recipe. In other words, Miller's result, and not just the ingredients, was cooked. In an attempt to prove that Miller's energies were not wasted, chemical evolutionists have created one scenario after another, each getting shot down in turn. The closer scientists look at the origin of life, it seems, the harder it is to figure out. In 1988, Klaus Dose, a leading prebiotic researcher, summed up the quest: "More than 30 years of experimentation on the origin of life in the fields of chemistry and molecular evolution have led to a better perception of the immensity of the problem of the origin of life on Earth rather than its solution. At present all discussions on principle theories and experiments in the field either end in stalemate or in a confession of ignorance."[3] The hype surrounding Miller's experiment should have

3. Klaus Dose, "The Origin of Life: More Questions than Answers," *Interdisciplinary*

faded into a chastened acknowledgment of failure. Instead, it remains, in the words of Jonathan Wells, a molecular biologist, one of the icons of evolution.[4] It symbolizes the hopes of the evolutionary community rather than the reality of their research.

Rather than confessing the futility of trying to fathom the origin of life, some scientists resort to poetic mythology. Richard Fortey, for example, uses language straight out of a horror movie to set the stage for evolution. "You might say that our atmosphere, and the possibility of life itself, was the consequence of a vast, terrestrial flatulence risen from the bowels of the Earth." The primordial broth from which the first cell emerged was, in this graphic image, a messy waste of accidental confluences and churning contradictions. Fortey's scatological metaphor is not only graphic but also fitting, given how the Darwinian struggle for survival so carelessly squanders life. Fortey, a senior paleontologist at the Natural History Museum in London, also mixes theology with his poetry when he says that the primordial Earth, far from being an appetizing soup capable of nourishing life, resembled "the medieval idea of Hell."[5] Other scientists, like Francis Crick, the co-discoverer of the structure of the DNA, turn to the plots of science fiction movies by proposing that the elements of life might have been deposited on the Earth by a meteorite or, perhaps, an extraterrestrial source.[6] Darwinian scientists have become so socialized in secularism's rejection of the supernatural that they would rather attribute the origin of life to space travel than to God.

Science Review 13 (1988) 348; quoted in Thomas Woodward, *Darwin Strikes Back* (Grand Rapids: Baker, 2006) 118.

4. Jonathan Wells, *Icons of Evolution: Science or Myth?* (Washington, DC: Regnery, 2002) ch. 2. For Wells's response to his critics, see "Critics Rave Over Icons of Evolution," online: www.Discovery.org.

5. Richard Fortey, *Life: A Natural History of the First Four Billion Years of Life on Earth* (New York: Vintage, 1997) 32 and 44. The idea that something hellish is at the origin of life is popular among Darwinians. Paul Davies writes, "The record of the genes suggests that [the common ancestor of all life forms] lived deep beneath the Earth's surface, at a temperature well above 100° C, and probably ate sulphur." *The Fifth Miracle: The Search for the Origin of Life* (New York: Touchstone, 1999) 165.

6. Francis Crick, *Life Itself: Its Origin and Nature* (New York: Simon and Schuster, 1981). For an excellent reflection on how Crick's atheism impacted his science, see Mary Steyn, "The Twentieth Century Darwin," *The Atlantic Monthly* (October 2004) 206–7.

Figuring out how something as complex as a cell could have emerged from simple chemical conditions could drive anyone to desperate speculations. Fazale Rana, who earned his PhD in biochemistry from Ohio University, has written a book detailing the features of the cell that point toward a creator, rather than natural selection.[7] He makes a cumulative case, rather than relying on a single biological puzzle, to carry the weight of his argument. A cumulative case for any position depends as much upon rhetoric as it does logic, because piling on example after example will never reach the high requirements of scientific proof. Indeed, cumulative cases against Darwinism sometimes seem to be little more than blockades thrown up against a battalion of road building trucks designed to plow right through the hardest material. Rana delights in dwelling on the disappointments, rather than the successes, of Darwinian explanation, which makes his book one-sided, but his three-fold argument is worth taking seriously. First, he examines biochemical systems that appear to require each other—like ribosomes that make proteins and yet are made from proteins—and thus could not have arisen sequentially. Second, he looks at the fine tuning of the cell, with structures and activities that depend on a precision that is hard to calculate, let alone imagine from a Darwinian perspective. Finally, he examines various biochemical systems that have relatively independent evolutionary trajectories and yet are structurally, functionally, and mechanically identical. This is called convergence, which is the subject of Simon Conway Morris's work, and it is a topic that I will return to in chapter 7.

Even mentioning Rana's name in the same sentence with Morris will cause some readers consternation, because Morris is Professor of Evolutionary Palaeobiology at the University of Cambridge, while Rana works for Reasons to Believe, an "international science-faith think tank" founded in 1986 to defend the scientific credibility of the Bible. Morris has received numerous awards and honors from his peers, while most biologists do not even consider Rana to be a member of the scientific community, even though he has published papers in peer-reviewed scientific journals. Institutional affiliations alone do not account for this disparity. Morris's research puts him in a class of the world's elite sci-

---

7. Fazale Rana, *The Cell's Design: How Chemistry Reveals the Creator's Artistry* (Grand Rapids: Baker, 2008). Also see Stephen C. Meyer, *Signature in the Cell: DNA and the Evidence for Intelligent Design* (San Francisco: HarperCollins, 2009).

entists, while Rana is employed by an organization with a very specific religious, as well as scientific, agenda. Nonetheless, Morris has avoided controversy, for the most part,[8] by pushing *as a Darwinian insider* for a broader understanding of the role of purpose in nature, while Rana has been more aggressive in arguing that the biological evidence leads by means of inference to the hypothesis of an intelligent designer. Both scientists, however, demonstrate how Darwinism needs to be broadened to make room for theological argument.

Theology, of course, is immersed in difficult and speculative mysteries of its own, so a science free of theological mingling has the advantage of not being encumbered by unwieldy and time-consuming exchanges. Nonetheless, many people continue to find evolutionary theory itself to be nearly as mysterious as the processes it seeks to describe. The cell operates according to an instruction manual known as the genome, which is the sum total of its genetic parts. The genome is an information system unlike any designed by human hands. The human genome encodes and transmits information according to such precise specifications that the minutest changes, according to John Sanford, a retired genetics professor at Cornell University, are more likely to produce "backwards evolution" of decay and decline rather than growth and creativity.[9] Most organisms are constructed so that each gene typi-

---

8. Accounts of his clash with Stephen Jay Gould can be found on the web. Robert A. Foley is one of his most thoughtful critics. See "The Illusion of Purpose in Evolution," Foley's contribution to *The Deep Structure of Biology*.

9. J. C. Sanford, *Genetic Entropy and the Mystery of the Genome* (Lima, NY: Elim, 2005). Sanford's comment on the face of it looks reasonable and well-informed, but it is actually quite scandalous, because he is referring to what is often called the problem of entropy and evolution. The Internet is full of websites making the case that entropy and evolution are contradictory processes. The second law of thermodynamics states that, because energy becomes diffuse over time, all physical systems in the universe have a tendency toward disorder, with less useful energy at the end than the beginning of the process. To many people this raises a fundamental suspicion: how could the world have been winding down all this time (since the big bang) while, at the same time, biological processes were becoming more complex. Outside of the Web, this question is rarely taken seriously, perhaps because it is just too puzzling. On the Web, this debate is not only endless but also intimidating to those of us (and I mean to include myself) who do not have advanced degrees in the sciences. People of faith are especially vulnerable to verbal abuse if they go out on a limb about issues that even scientists have a hard time understanding. The intellectually curious, however, need not tackle physics in order to understand the problem of increasing complexity in evolution. That problem is best seen in the cell, not the entire cosmos.

cally affects multiple characteristics, so that a change in one nucleotide in one gene will alter many different systems in that organism. Even genetic changes that are beneficial for one aspect of the organism will almost certainly be less than beneficial for other aspects. Successful evolutionary adaptation must be the product of a combination of multiple, simultaneous, and specific changes, with the likelihood of success exceeding odds so great that they are hard to calculate. And this roll of the dice must come up lucky millions and millions of times over the course of a few billion years.

Evolutionary biologists accept these odds and take their chances by struggling to demonstrate how the genetic throw of the dice could have been so favorable without being rigged. This is a brave strategy, and science is one of humankind's noblest endeavors, but when does the pursuit of a theory turn reckless? When confronted with the odds against their position, Darwinians typically argue that life is like a gambler on a roll, and we are the jackpot that proves how lucky we are. Logicians call this the fallacy of the "appeal to ignorance," because it assumes that something must be true as long as there is no known explanatory alternative. The alternative to a Darwinian explanation of evolution, however, is not simply an appeal to God, because God cannot be used to solve gaps in our understanding of the causal chain that stretches across time. God is the manufacturer of the chain, not one its many links. Nonetheless, philosophers and theologians who are interested in biology have raised a number of crucial questions about what the causal chain of biology is made of, how far it stretches, and what ultimately supports it. Darwinians who treat their theory as a sufficient and complete description of evolution render it irremediable and rule out these question by an imperious wave of the hand. They are quite content to be bound to a chain of their own making.

Of course, there are Darwinians who are open to considering ways in which their research needs to be in dialogue with philosophy and theology (Simon Conway Morris is one of them), but since many are not, it seems acceptable to use the Darwinian label as a shorthand for biologists who think creativity in nature can be completely explained by natural selection and thus without any recourse to the divine. These scientists practice a form of "metaphysical naturalism," which means that they think every event has and only has material causes.[10] Not all Darwinians who bracket God in their research are necessarily atheists. Some are devout believers, but they do not let their religious beliefs get in the way of their scientific pursuits. They practice what is known as "methodological atheism," which is a fancy way of saying that they put aside the existence of God during their work hours for the sake of pursuing causation back down the line of preceding creatures to its material end. Scientists, it needs to be said, are certainly right to keep probing fundamental questions that do not give any hint of an easy answer. Darwin's critics, however, are just as right to insist that scientists should admit failed experiments and weak hypotheses. Darwin's critics do not want evolutionists to stop asking tough questions. Instead, the critics want to ask tough questions of their own. What if biological causation looks more like a web than a chain? What if causation comes from the top (the mind) as well as the bottom (matter)? And what if the more closely anyone looks into the origin and evolution of life, the more mystery they find?

The idea that Darwin might be wrong is the scientific equivalent of blasphemy, but scientific knowledge is not supposed to take the religious form of dogma. Physics once taught a gradual accumulation of matter in the formation of the Earth that contradicted the creation account in Genesis. Physics now teaches a big bang theory—the universe, neither eternal nor infinite, came out of nowhere nearly 14 billion years ago—that conforms to the Christian idea that the world began at a singular point in time. The image of a big bang begs the question of how the fuse was lit, and indeed, physicists are typically more open to discussing the theological implications of their theories than biologists. Reflecting on the scientific research that led to the big bang theory, the agnostic scientist Robert Jastrow wrote, despairingly, "For the scientist who has lived by his faith in the power of reason, the story ends like a bad dream."[11] The big bang is not what physicists were looking for, but it is a bad dream only for those who remain committed to the un-

---

10. For the argument that it is illegitimate to move from what is the case to the claim that the supernatural does not exist, see Conor Cunningham, "Trying my Very Best to Believe in Darwin, or The Supernaturalistic Fallacy: From Is to Nought," in *Belief and Metaphysics*, ed. Peter Candler and C. Cunningham (London: SCM, 2008).

11. Robert Jastrow, *God and the Astronomers*, second edition (New York: Norton, 1992) 107

breachable separation of science and theology. The big bang explodes the idea that matter is eternal, which is the crucial assumption of all forms of metaphysical naturalism (the position that nature is all there is). Theologians who treat religious faith as one language game among many others typically refuse to make theological hay out of the big bang on the grounds that scientific theories cannot tell us anything substantive about the divine. Even if the big bang demonstrates the necessity of a higher power, these theologians argue, it does not tell us what this power is or what it wants from us. The religious content of cosmological speculations, at best, is trivial, and at worst, leads to the God of Deism, distant and remote, not the God of Christianity. This is a good point, but an argument that reaches halfway toward a valuable conclusion is still a good argument. Finding confirmation (or at least *not* finding disconfirmation) for the Christian doctrine of *creatio ex nihilo* (creation out of nothing) is no small matter.

The big bang scenario also suggests that the conditions that kept the explosive aftermath from imploding into the nothingness from whence it came were so finely tuned as to defy the mathematical imagination. The significance of this astronomical tuning is one of the most hotly debated items in the philosophy of science. Theologians who are content to relegate religious beliefs to the subjective realm dismiss the importance of this debate. They think that making inferences about God from the evidence of physics is an example of what is called a God of the gaps argument. The God of the gaps argument uses God as a hypothesis in order to fill in the gaps of our scientific knowledge. The gap argument is not very religiously satisfying because scientific progress has a way of filling in those gaps with new discoveries, and once the gaps are closed, God is rendered irrelevant. The God of the gaps theory is thus a devil's bargain, because it wagers not that our knowledge will always have holes in it but that the holes it does have will always stay the same. Theologians are right to be skeptical of God of the gaps arguments, but skeptical theologians miss something about the theological significance of the big bang. The God of the big bang is not brought in at the last minute to cover up temporary holes in our knowledge. The fine tuning argument works only when the big bang theory is pursued rigorously and fully to the end of its mathematical implications. At its best, the fine tuning argument leads to a God who is the manufacturer of the causal chain, not a God who holds together its missing links.

Physics can shed light on the doctrine of creation, but an even greater task is discerning what science can tell us about the doctrine of providence (God's ongoing governance of the world). Theologians actually talk about two kinds of providence: special and general. Special providence is the name theologians give to God's specific and particular acts in the world, and it has fallen out of favor in modern theology. Critics of special providence argue that God would not create a world governed by natural laws and then violate those laws in order to influence or control natural events. They prefer to think of God working with or through, but not against, the laws of nature. Some theologians recently have argued that quantum mechanics answers this concern. In quantum mechanics, the atomic and subatomic levels of matter are not totally determined by natural processes that can be measured by a scientific law. If nature is not a closed, deterministic system, these theologians argue, then God can shape events without contravening the laws of nature.[12] In other words, natural causation is less of a chain that a series of discrete dots, and God is able to connect the dots in various ways without forcing them into new positions. Quantum mechanics, which plays a significant role in biology at the level of genetic mutations, might help us to conceptualize how God intervenes in nature in ways that are congruent with nature's own unpredictability, which is the problem of special providence, but what about general providence? General providence concerns how God sustains and directs all of history, not just how God intervenes in particular events. For evidence from nature related to general providence, theologians need to look at the problem of natural selection in biology, not quantum mechanics in physics. Does it make sense to say that God can be in charge of the

---

12. Ontological indeterminism is only one interpretation of quantum mechanics, but it is a fruitful one for theological considerations of science and providence. See the important essay by Robert John Russell, "Special Providence and Genetic Mutation: A New Defense of Theistic Evolution," in *Perspectives on an Evolving Creation*, ed. Keith B. Miller (Grand Rapids: Eerdmans, 2003) ch. 15. A number of theologians and philosophers have been involved in the "divine action project" that seeks to discern conceptual space for divine action in quantum mechanics. See Amos Yong, "Divining 'Divine Action' in Theology and Science: A Review Essay," *Zygon* 43 (2008) 191-200.

direction of nature as a whole by influencing or controlling the process of natural selection?

That theological question should put biology on the frontier of the most advanced thinking about God, humanity, and the meaning of history. That, in fact, is already happening. The relationship between biology and religion is one of the most exciting research topics in the academy today. Yet many Darwinians isolate their theory from theological explorations and philosophical criticisms as if they were making a last stand on the last hill left in a cosmic battle that brooks no compromise. Darwinians typically insist that the whole enterprise of biology—indeed, the very spirit of science—depends on a strict interpretation of Darwinism. The geneticist Theodosius Dobzhansky, for example, is famous for his remark that "nothing in biology makes sense except in the light of evolution."[13] I have heard this comment repeated many times with the word *science* substituted for biology. Either way, this remark conjures an apocalyptic scenario where the slightest breech in the wall separating religion and science will bring down the foundations of Western progress. Kenneth R. Miller, a professor of biology at Brown University, has sounded the alarm in the loudest possible way: "What is at stake, I am convinced, is nothing less than America's scientific soul."[14] Such comments prove that nothing in their training prevents scientists from falling prey to the temptation of baseless polemical exaggeration. Fortunately, cooler heads have put forth the argument that "teaching the controversy," in the words of Gerald Graff, would bring more students into the sciences by appealing to their passion for argument and their proclivities toward rebellion and skepticism.[15] In any case, since macro evolution (evolution that produces new species over great stretches of time) is not an observable feature of living organisms, the functioning of those organisms can be studied without much reference to Darwinian theory. Moreover, medical and pharmaceutical schools do fine without maintaining departments in evolutionary science.

13. Theodosius Dobzhansky, "Nothing in Biology Makes Sense Except in the Light of Evolution," *American Biology Teacher* 35 (1973) 125–29.

14. Kenneth R. Miller, *Only a Theory: Evolution and the Battle for America's Soul* (New York: Viking, 2008) 16.

15. Gerald Graff, "To Debate or Not to Debate Intelligent Design?" *Inside Higher Education*, Sept. 28, 2005. Online:
http://www.insidehighered.com/views/2005/09/28/graff.

If Darwinism is to go unchallenged in the science classroom, and Christian theology is to be excluded from the rest of the curriculum, then public education will of necessity indoctrinate students in the worldview of metaphysical naturalism, which is hardly a good way to go about promoting critical thinking. Nonetheless, Darwinians have been so successful in defending the domino view of Darwin's importance—if Darwin goes, so goes everything that is good in Western civilization—that many people find it easier to imagine chance rather than intelligence guiding natural history. As the Victorian writer and Christian apologist G. K. Chesterton once observed, "There is something slow and soothing and gradual about the word [evolution] and even about the idea."[16] The very sound of it (unlike the sound of the big bang, for instance) is soft and assuring as it rolls off the tongue: one thing leads to another, seamlessly, and all things are intimately related to each other. It conjures up the continuity of a good historical narrative rather than the trial and error testing of the natural sciences. It is also so vague that even its most precise usage must be placed in an historical context. As the historian of science Robert Richards writes, "The term 'evolution' is pregnant with its history."[17] One consequence of its vagueness is that Darwinians can claim with absolute conviction that evolution is purposeless while at the same time argue that evolution offers us a moral vision of the interconnectedness of all things—a contradiction I will interrogate in chapters 7 and 8.

The vagueness of much of the Darwinian vocabulary means that Darwinian theory is constantly being adjusted and amended, to the point where some biologists have called for a scientific revolution to overthrow the Darwinian paradigm altogether.[18] The culture of higher education, however, rewards practitioners who stay within the acceptable boundaries of knowledge, not revolutionaries who want to move

16. G. K. Chesterton, *The Everlasting Man* (New York: Dodd, Mead, 1925) 3.

17. Robert J. Richards, *The Meaning of Evolution: The Morphological Construction and Ideological Reconstruction of Darwin's Theory* (Chicago: University of Chicago Press, 1992) 167.

18. See Douglas H. Erwin, "Darwin Still Rules, but Some Biologists Dream of a Paradigm Shift," *New York Times*, June 26, 2007. Online: http://www.nytimes.com/2007/06/26/science/26essay.html?ref=science. For an example of a biologist who has broken from orthodox Darwinism, see Brian Goodwin, *How the Leopard Changed Its Spots: The Evolution of Complexity*, second ed. (Princeton: Princeton University Press, 2001).

the boundaries around. In today's university, fields of study are sequestered in tightly segregated departments that zealously protect their interests like feudal lords driving off bandits. The result is that the life of the mind is fractured beyond repair. Gone are the days when higher education was held together by the common pursuit of universal truth. Nowadays, anything goes beneath the banner of academic freedom. Rather than setting the standards of intellectual debate, university administrators keep the peace by making sure that professors from different departments do not "interfere" with each other by challenging each other's presuppositions. Without a culture of rigorous interdisciplinary debate, it is no wonder that laboratory scientists can take any criticism of their work personally. Why should philosophers and theologians be permitted to look over the shoulders of scientists working with test tubes and microscopes all day? Many biologists play by the rules of academic non-interference by trying to limit evolution to laboratory or fieldwork, but no matter how hard they try their theory inevitably escapes to run wild through our cultural landscape. Evolution tells us a lot about who we are and what life means. Discussing it in a neutral and level tone, which is the style most commonly associated with the *hard* sciences, does nothing to domesticate its unruly impact on every aspect of human self-understanding.[19]

Of course, many biologists blame the cultural noise evolution generates on ignorance, prejudice, or well-intentioned but simple-minded misunderstandings. Others, not content to keep their peace, go on the attack. Much of the rhetoric from these philosophically inclined scientists and Darwinian philosophers sounds like the game of "good cop and bad cop." Aggressive Darwinians insist that evolution is a complete and universal theory that illuminates every aspect of life. Yet when critics push them on the implications and consequences of their views,

19. Scott L. Montgomery, in *The Scientific Voice* (London: Guilford, 1996), laments the loss of linguistic sophistication in scientific literature and "feels that beneath its poise of rational dignity, scientific discourse has come to embody a certain distrust and fear of language" (33). The proliferation of jargon is evidence that science has left behind the realm of common human experience. Montgomery notes that this was not the case for Darwin (see 104–5). One of the problems with evolutionary theory is that its founder spoke in terms that reflected and raised the general questions that plague human existence while biologists have inherited that theoretical framework and yet speak in hushed technical tones that hide or obfuscate evolution's broader ramifications.

the good Darwinian cops retreat to the laboratory or their fieldwork and claim they are misunderstood. The bad Darwinian cops warn you that everything you think you know must be rethought (and much of it discarded) from an evolutionary perspective. The good Darwinian cop assures you that everything you cherish will mostly stay the same.

The baddest Darwinian cops (and I am using that slang intentionally, because they think of themselves as daring and fearless) are Richard Dawkins and Daniel C. Dennett. Dawkins, a British Darwinian who teaches at Oxford, has an especially bleak view of life. He defines biology (somewhat ascetically) as the science that resists the temptation of invoking design to explain natural phenomena. He thus sets the ground rules for his debate with believers so that he wins at the outset by the power of definition. To his credit, he says that nobody could have been an intelligent atheist before 1859 (the year Darwin's *Origin of Species* was published), but he thinks that it is impossible to be an intelligent theist after 1859.[20] (One could just as easily say that nowadays you can be a Darwinian without being an atheist, but you cannot be an atheist without being a Darwinian.) These bad Darwinian cops are bold where Darwin was meek: in his autobiography, Darwin connected religious belief to an inherited instinct, like a monkey's fear of snakes, but he deleted the passage when it was published.[21]

Dawkins's bleakness stems from his deeply atheistic worldview. He is convinced that organisms are nothing more than conduits for their DNA, and thus nature is absolutely indifferent to the happiness of individual creatures.[22] Dawkins gave this worldview scientific credibility by formulating the famous catchphrase of "selfish genes" (genes that are not junk, though even junk DNA could be considered selfish because it manages to get carried along by functional genes). The idea of selfish genes amounts to a biological conspiracy theory: we are pawns at the hands of microscopic implanted bugs that apparently know more about us than we do. If that sounds too strong, just read the preface to the 1976 edition of *The Selfish Gene*, where he writes, "We are survival

---

20. Richard Dawkins, *The Blind Watchmaker* (New York: Norton, 1986) 1 and 5–6.

21. Janet Browne, *Charles Darwin: The Power of Place* (New York: Knopf, 2002) 433–34.

22. Richard Dawkins, *A River Out of Eden* (New York: Basic, 1995) 111–55.

machines—robot vehicles blindly programmed to preserve the selfish molecules known as genes."²³ Evolution is blind, but genes, it seems, are perfectly clear sighted. Dawkins has managed to smuggle direction and purpose into the backdoor of biology after kicking it out the front door. Genes, it seems, know their client's interests and how to look after them better than a public relations agent for a Hollywood movie star. This is the kind of theory that just begs to be debunked. As the Christian novelist Marilynne Robinson has wryly commented, "Finding selfishness in a gene is an act of mind which rather resembles finding wrath in thunder."²⁴ Dawkins, in other words, is a bad theologian posing as a provocative scientist.

Nonbelievers too can be amazed at Dawkins's paranoid worldview, as with the Australian philosopher David Stove's retort, "Genes can be no more selfish than they can be (say) supercilious, or stupid." People can be selfish, of course, but according to Dawkins they are supremely so when they have children, because they are trying to do nothing more than pass copies of their genes to another generation. Dawkins believes this even though there is no evidence that species who share a higher proportion of their genes with their offspring make for less selfish parents. Evidence aside, Stove again has a cutting reply. "Multiplying copies of oneself is a very different thing from multiplying pictures or statues of oneself."²⁵ Why would anyone, outside of a science fiction novel, want to achieve self-duplication? Making a copy of me will not add a single minute to my lifespan, nor is it obvious that a copy of me

23. Richard Dawkins, *The Selfish Gene* (New York: Oxford University Press, 1989) v. For a rather bizarre invocation of the divinity of genes, see John C. Avise, *The Genetic Gods: Evolution and Belief in Human Affairs* (Cambridge: Harvard University Press, 1998): "They mastermind our lives, influencing our physical appearance, health, behavior, even our fears and aspirations. They constitute our material reason for being—for eating and sleeping, warring and loving, hating and caring, forging relationships—for procreation. To them we owe our existence" and so on (3).

24. Marilynne Robinson, *The Death of Adam: Essays on Modern Thought* (Houghton Mifflin, 1998) 49.

25. David Stove, *Darwinian Fairytales: Selfish Genes, Errors of Heredity, and Other Fables of Evolution* (New York: Encounter, 1995) 175 and 174. When Darwinians talk about self-replication, they would do well to study the idea, well defined and elaborated by theologians, of the relationship between the Father and the Son in the Trinity. Theologians have developed a sophisticated understanding of the difference-within-sameness that encompasses the Father's begetting of the Son—a sophistication that makes Darwinian talk about copies look pretty simplistic and even foolish.

will give me much pleasure, given how much of a burden I usually am to myself. Wouldn't it be easier just to erect a statue of myself, if I am so concerned about my posterity? Besides, children are hardly copies of their parents. If they were, people would probably not want to have any, since most people hope their children will be better, and better off, than they are. Selfishness, far from being the cause of parenting, is what deters many people from having children in the first place. Yet Darwinians continue to promote selfishness as the crucial motivating factor behind evolution, as if it were an unproblematic emotion capable of explaining all of life's secrets.

Such objections do not deter Dawkins, who is convinced, in circular fashion, that the logic of evolution makes no sense without the concept of selfishness and that the pervasiveness of selfishness can be understood only in the light of evolution. At least Dawkins does not back down from the political implications of his position. "A human society based simply on the gene's law of universal ruthless selfishness would be a very nasty society in which to live. But unfortunately, however much we may deplore something, it does not stop it being true."[26] He sympathizes with those who want to build a better world, but he wants them to understand that they will not get any help from nature. This is an admirable sentiment, I suppose, but it is hard to know where the hope for a better world comes from if our genes control us like pagan gods with their contradictory and violent impulses.

Daniel C. Dennett, professor of philosophy at Tufts University, is as hard hitting as Dawkins. Polemically, he uses the term *brights* to designate secular atheists, and often rails against the dark ages of Roman Catholic influence over Europe. Dennett gets excited about the philosophical implications of Darwinism because evolution has been so often neglected by professional philosophers. He is surely right to insist that, "The Darwinian Revolution is both a scientific and a philosophical revolution, and neither revolution could have occurred without the other." He is more controversial, but no less right, when he describes evolution as a "universal acid." This adolescent metaphor comes, sure enough, from a fantasy that used to amuse Dennett when he was a schoolboy. He dreamed of an acid that would eat through everything and, consequently, would be impossible to contain. His point is that Darwinian

---

26. Dawkins, *Selfish Gene*, 3.

analysis knows no limits. "Much of the controversy and anxiety that has enveloped Darwin's idea ever since can be understood as a series of failed campaigns in the struggle to contain Darwin's idea within some acceptably 'safe' and merely partial revolution."[27] Dennett's language is colorful, but he is only saying what many Darwinians believe, even if they are usually more discrete.

Dennett's critics think that he takes Darwinism to an extreme, but it is more accurate to think of Dennett as a rigorously consistent Darwinian. Sometimes, of course, it is only by seeing what a position looks like when it is consistently held that the position's contradictions become apparent. Dennett is consistent in applying Darwinism to everything, but he is not consistent in what he thinks will be the result. Dennett thinks Darwinism entails left-leaning liberalism because this theory eats away at conventional morality and religious dogma. Of course, as any reader of old comic books knows, the inventor of universal acids always gets eaten by his own invention; Dennett does not pause to consider how his evolutionary philosophy escapes this fate. A universal acid will burn all the way down, debunking the debunkers along with everyone else. He cannot throw Darwinian acid in the face of the defenders of traditional morality while thinking that he can avoid getting any in his own eyes. Or if he does think that, he is blinded by his own rhetoric.

In a recent book, *Breaking the Spell*, Dennett berates religion for a host of crimes and inconsistencies.[28] To substantiate these charges, he capitalizes on the idea of *memes*, a concept that was first developed by Dawkins. Memes pass along information from one generation in a human society to the next and thus determine our social identity just as genes determine our personal identities. Genes, of course, are essential for life, but most memes are not, which is why we can imagine doing without some memes altogether. Dennett and Dawkins both think that religious memes have been maladaptive for human progress. Religion is thus like the flu—crowds effortlessly pass it on without knowing what they are doing. If religion is so bad for us, however, why do people keep

---

27. Daniel C. Dennett, *Darwin's Dangerous Idea: Evolution and the Meaning of Life* (New York: Simon & Schuster, 1995) 21 and 63.

28. Daniel C. Dennett, *Breaking the Spell: Religion as Natural Phenomenon* (New York: Viking, 2006).

spreading it to the next generation? After all, variations that do not benefit individuals are wiped out in the next generation. As Darwin wrote in *The Origin of Species*, "we may feel sure that any variation in the least degree injurious would be rigidly destroyed."[29] Why haven't Christians, with all their talk of love and forgiveness, simply died out? The simple answer to that question is to say that religion helps people think that life is worthwhile and that there is hope for the future, but Dennett and Dawkins think religion does this under false pretences. The hard answer to why religion survives, then, can only be that self-deception is inherently beneficial. That is, every known human society up to modern times survived and replicated itself because it was able to deceive its members about the value of life by means of religious delusions.

Religion is nothing but a pack of useful lies, according to Dennett and Dawkins, lies that were necessary only until modern science and technology came along to give our lives a better meaning. To make this argument persuasive, Dennett and Dawkins must explain two things. First, they must explain how human beings could ever know anything true about themselves, since they portray self-delusion as so useful that it is built into human nature. Second, they must explain how science and technology are not themselves a self-delusive meme that fools us into thinking that life is more meaningful than it is. In other words, if self-delusion is such a successful survival strategy, how can we know when we are deluding ourselves, and how do we know that Darwinism itself is not as deceptive as any religion? Indeed, this is a general problem for Darwinian explanations of human behavior: if every belief is more or less useful, and the utility of a belief counts against its being true, then no belief can be true, including the belief that every belief is more or less useful. (Or you can try to figure out whether you could ever know the truth of this proposition: "All beliefs are self-delusive except the Darwinian belief that all beliefs are self-delusive.") Could it be that Darwinism itself is a meme, a kind of virus that, once set loose, takes advantage of our biological inclinations in order to convince us that we are nothing more than those very inclinations? If so, then perhaps it is Darwinians, not genes, that are truly selfish.

If these philosophical puzzles are not bad enough, Darwinians must also solve the moral puzzle of how our selfish genes ended up

---

29. Darwin, *Origin of Species*, 130–31.

producing a saint like Francis of Assisi, or, if one wants to be less dramatic, how a meme like Roman Catholicism, which requires its best trained believers to be celibate, could ever have conquered the Western world. Indeed, how could Christianity have created the social and intellectual conditions that made somebody like Darwin (or Dennett and Dawkins) possible? If Christianity really were a powerfully deceptive meme, wouldn't it have done a better job of making sure that nobody discovered the theory of evolution?

All of these perplexing speculations and unavoidable questions are the stuff that fuel late night college conversations, but they seem never to have occurred to Dennett and Dawkins, who are too busy demolishing all of our cherished beliefs to be introspective about their own. Just when one is ready to think the worse of Darwinians, however, a good cop comes around to assure you that there is no cause for alarm. George Levine is a good example of a good Darwinian cop. A Victorian scholar who has written extensively on Darwin, he makes the case for a kinder, gentler Darwin in his recent book, *Darwin Loves You*. Levine tries to link Darwin to the love of nature and respect for humankind by telling us how exciting it was for him when he first read Darwin and how excited Darwin himself was about his discoveries. His book is full of words like enchanting, thrilling, lovely, and fascinating. Just as sophisticated Marxists used to try to save their arguments by distinguishing themselves from their crass brethren, Levine rejects the "vulgar" Darwinism of Dennett and Dawkins. He argues instead that there are no necessary connections between Darwinism and anti-religious reactionary politics. From the postmodern perspective, Darwinism can mean whatever you want it to mean, and clearly, it has been a meaningful experience for Levine.

Levine admits that his book is not a historical study of Darwin or a philosophical study of the moral implications of Darwinism. Instead, "I am looking here for an attitude, a state of mind and feeling."[30] He even admits that he is open to the charge of whitewashing Darwin in blatant disregard for the historical record. The obsessive attempt to find Darwin innocent of every negative social implication is so common among Darwinians that it functions as a kind of mantra of the bio-

---

30. George Levine, *Darwin Loves You: Natural Selection and the Re-Enchantment of the World* (Princeton: Princeton University Press, 2006) xvi.

logical sciences. Levine is typical in distinguishing between Darwinism proper and Social Darwinism, which is the name given to those who draw conservative—and sometimes reactionary—political conclusions from Darwin's theory. This distinction functions to protect Darwin from the charge that he was at least partially responsible for the rise of both extreme capitalism and authoritarian fascism. This rhetorical maneuver enables Darwinians to reject their critics not by examining their arguments but by insisting that they are aiming at the wrong target. Like a rigged carnival game, whatever target the critics hit is always the wrong one.

Social Darwinism was a term coined in the early years of the twentieth century and popularized by the New Deal liberal historian Richard Hofstadter in the 1940s. Hofstadter was trying to turn back the positive influence that Darwinism had on the laissez-fair capitalism of Gilded-Age America. Hofstadter wanted to give a label to that connection in order to dismiss it as a fundamental misunderstanding of evolutionary theory. He thus attributed the positive connection between evolution and capitalism to the nineteenth-century philosopher Herbert Spencer (1820–1903), who actually coined the phrase "survival of the fittest" and applied Darwinian theory to political thought. Social Darwinism makes sense only within the very specific context of a liberal-progressive critique of capitalism. It is a term that "would have baffled Darwin. In Victorian England, scientists took for granted that biological facts mattered for social theory and policy."[31] Darwinians used to be much more open about their belief that the human species has advanced to its high status in nature only through a struggle that culled the weak in mind and body. It is this belief that leads Dennett and Dawkins to argue that Christianity has exercised a counter-selective pressure on evolution and thus will itself some day be rendered extinct by evolutionary forces. Nonetheless, Dennett, Dawkins, and Levine are loath to equate Darwinism with Social Darwinism, and for a very good reason. If Darwin was a Social Darwinian, and Social Darwinians are aggressive capitalists and cultural elitists, then public support for Darwin, especially among those who are liberally inclined, will erode—and it is

---

31. Diane B. Paul, "Darwin, Social Darwinism and Eugenics," in *The Cambridge Companion to Darwin*, ed. Jonathan Hodge and Gregory Radick (Cambridge: Cambridge University Press, 2003) 224.

just that group, the liberally inclined, that Darwinians appeal to when they set out to smash the superstitions of religion.

What sets Levine apart from Dennett and Dawkins is his postmodern willingness to abide in this obvious contradiction. Thus, he both acknowledges and ignores the connection between Darwinism and unfettered capitalism. "No doubt," Levine confesses, "there *is* a clear connection between Darwin's science and rampant, dog-eat-dog capitalism."[32] Levine thinks that the Social Darwinians are right about Darwin's impact on history but that Darwin can just as easily be re-aligned with a different morality today. In order to persuade his readers that his position is not inconsistent, he repeatedly appeals to the emotions, not reason. Much of his book is taken up with comments about how he "feels a sympathetic fondness" for Darwin, how Darwin felt a "deep affection for his family," and how Darwin's outlook on the world was "vital and creative."[33] Like many Darwinians, he wants to convince the reader that secular humanists can be optimistic about the existential questions that plague humankind. The only way he can do this is by turning Darwinism into a religion, what we can call *Sociable* Darwinism, to distinguish it from *Social* Darwinism.

Everyone needs a hero now and then, but Levine turns his book into an embarrassing example of hero worship. He so badly wants to make Darwinism sociable that he thinks, as indicated by the title of his book, that Darwin loves everybody. His love for Darwin blinds him to the fallacy of his argument: he thinks that if he proves that Darwin's motives, while he was destroying traditional religious values, were sincere and compassionate, then Darwin can be excused of any bad outcomes of his theory. All that he has proven, of course, is that Darwin was a great writer. Darwin infused his books with a love of discovery as well as a poetic sensibility, but passion and poetry are not the stuff of natural selection. The best conclusion about Darwin that comes from this book is that Darwin's rhetorical practices were out of sync with his actual theory. That is, his writing style and moral vocabulary were still in debt to Romantic ideas about beauty and Christian ideas about compassion. He launched the theory of evolution, but he did not grow up immersed in its worldview. He made the world Darwinian, but Romantic poetry

32. Levine, *Darwin Loves You*, 10 (italics his).
33. Ibid., 138, 202, and 222.

and Christian morality protected him from the worst consequences of his own theory.[34]

Of course, Darwinians like Levine are free to speak poetically and sentimentally about nature, especially when they are trying to inspire their students to study biology. They are also free to use compartmentalization as a strategy for keeping their theoretical commitments and personal moral preferences from conflicting with each other. Nonetheless, critics are also free to question their consistency when they want to be aggressive debunkers when it comes to Christianity and soft-hearted humanitarians when it comes to New Age spirituality. Compartmentalization allows Darwinians to have it both ways. They believe that the struggle of life rules out all Christian talk of self-sacrifice and forgiving your enemy, while common ancestry and dependence on the environment translate into a beautiful and life-affirming ethos. In fact, it is not clear what Darwinism affirms other than the study of Darwinism itself. From the Christian point of view, the study of nature is an exercise in gratitude and awe, but it is hard to picture what a purely Darwinian study of nature would feel like. You can feel surprise at a chance event, but not awe and reverence. What would you be admiring, other than your own insightful perception? Darwinian theory, like any good theory, might be intellectually satisfying to those who can appreciate its intricacies and challenges, but that very same theory makes beauty an illusion of adaptation, not an experience of the transcendent. To be enlightened by Darwin is to understand that what we think is beautiful is actually a trick of our genetic make up.[35] What attracts us in the beautiful is the prospect of our survival, not any properties that objectively inhere in the object of our desire. When Darwinians call nature beautiful, they are really talking about the power they experience from mastering their environment. If Darwinians are right, then

---

34. For the best argument about Darwin's continuity with romanticism, see Robert J. Richards, *The Romantic Conception of Life: Science and Philosophy in the Age of Goethe* (Chicago: University of Chicago Press, 2002).

35. For a good discussion of this issue, see Anthony O'Hear, *Beyond Evolution: Human Nature and the Limits of Evolutionary Explanation* (Oxford: Clarendon Press, 1997) ch. 7: "Beauty and the Theory of Evolution." For one of the best books on the aesthetic implications of the cosmological argument, see Benjamin Wiker and Jonathan Witt, *A Meaningful World: How the Arts and Sciences Reveal the Genius of Nature* (Downers Grove, IL: InterVarsity, 2006).

they too must be controlled by their genes, and that puts the beauty of evolution in the eye of the beholder indeed.

If Dennett and Dawkins are the bad Darwinian cops and Levine is a good Darwinian cop, then David Sloan Wilson, distinguished professor of biology at Binghamton University, plays both roles in the same book. In *Evolution for Everyone*, he laments the specialization in higher education that keeps Darwin's theory from being applied to every field of knowledge. He is, he says, an "evolutionist without any qualifiers." This might sound threatening, but he reassures his readers that "the basic principles are easy to learn," and indeed they are. You pick a topic, whether it pertains to individuals, society, or culture, and you ask how it has changed over time in a given context. Then you try to figure out whom or what gained an advantage by the change. "Just about anyone," he enthuses, "can become an evolutionist by learning to think like Darwin."[36] This book is indeed an idiot's guide to evolution.

Several of the Darwinians he praises are not even scholars of any kind, let alone biologists. Wilson tells the story of Margie Profet, a woman who never studied biology, dropped out of school to find time to think, and ended up winning a MacArthur foundation "genius" award for her evolutionary theory of pregnancy sickness (morning sickness as it is usually called). When she started thinking about pregnancy sickness, she realized that nobody had applied Darwinism to it. She gathered some statistics and discovered that women who experience sickness in pregnancy are less likely to miscarry than women who do not. So she naturally theorized that pregnancy sickness is the body's way of telling women to be careful about what they eat. Pregnancy sickness, in Darwinian words, is a biological adaptation aimed at helping women and their babies survive pregnancy! And she did all of this by "stitching her argument together from past studies that were conducted largely for other purposes."[37] It was that easy.

Wilson's other favorite example is the story of one of his students, named Matt, who was bored with college until he discovered how easy and exciting it was to be a Darwinian. Matt took Wilson's advanced course on evolution that was for undergraduates and graduate students

---

36. David Sloan Wilson, *Evolution for Everyone: How Darwin's Theory Can Change the Way We Think About Our Lives* (New York: Delacorte, 2007) 1 and 20.

37. Ibid., 78.

when he was only a first year student. He was a jock in high school and not academically inclined, but he was so self-assured when he got to college that he thought he could master anything. Many first year students are like this, but rather than finding out that he had more to learn than he could ever have imagined, Matt found out that he could imagine anything by learning a few simple Darwinian principles. He thrived in Wilson's course by focusing on the biological origin of laughter. Like Profet, Matt discovered that little had been written about laughter from an evolutionary perspective. His conclusion about laughter was as predictable and banal as Profet's theory of morning sickness: "Laughter is an especially effective mechanism for causing members of a group to feel the same way at the same time."[38] During his junior year, he wrote an article outlining this theory with Wilson that was accepted—no joke!—in the *Quarterly Review of Biology*.

If evolution really is for everyone, then it should be applied to Wilson himself, of course. Evolutionary theory can explain his enthusiasm for evolution by the fact that his environment—teaching awards, journal publications, great book blurbs—has been so encouraging. At what point, however, does this mania for applying evolutionary theory become maladaptive? "One of my tall claims," he writes, with a touch of modesty, "is that an evolutionist such as myself can waltz into a new subject (such as religion) and teach something to the experts whose factual knowledge is far greater than I can ever hope to achieve." So what is religion? "My main hypothesis was that religious groups are products of cultural group selection and are indeed like bodies and beehives."[39] Wilson tests his hypothesis by examining Calvin's leadership of Geneva, and finds full confirmation. "I discovered that Calvinism was

38. Ibid., 179.

39. Ibid., 74, 237, and 243. For his full length treatment of religion, see David Sloan Wilson, *Darwin's Cathedral: Evolution, Religion, and the Nature of Society* (Chicago: University of Chicago Press, 2002). Wilson, like a lot of Darwinians, is trying to find an evolutionary substitute for religion: "Part of the religious temperament is to imagine a future vastly better than the present. In purely scientific terms this means finding a new cultural structure that is as miraculous in our eyes as Christianity was to Justin [the Martyr]. I do not know if such a structure exists, but can anyone prove that cultural evolution has already run its course, that all symphonies have been written and all structures built? I think not" (218). Even Darwinians believe in miracles. But also get this comment on forgiveness: "In the context of evolutionary models, retaliation is absolutely essential to keep the wolves at bay. To retaliate can be divine" (194).

essential for the viability of the city." Once again, Darwinism has led to the discovery of the obvious.

Like Levine, Wilson wants evolution and beauty both, even though evolution reduces every human ideal to its biological utility. Wilson treats beauty as a problem to be solved, not an experience to be cultivated and cherished, but he puts a new spin on the typical Darwinian solution. Rather than arguing that beauty is useful, he argues that everything "that is regarded as valuable is also regarded as beautiful." In other words, the useful is beautiful. He offers two examples of this maxim. First, he thinks that we value landscape paintings because we "love to surround ourselves with water, lush vegetation, and open spaces dotted with trees" (116). Forests are useful; thus we think paintings of them are beautiful. Second, Abraham Lincoln, who during his lifetime "was regarded as hideously ugly," has been "made beautiful by his nonphysical qualities."[40] Lincoln was valuable to his country, which is why we revere his features. If we extrapolate from these examples we can see how absurd they are. According to his first example, people who live in the country would be the greatest collectors of pastoral paintings. According to his second, John Merrick, who was known as the Elephant Man, a disability that he handled with inimitable courage and dignity, should be considered one of the most handsome men of his time. As for Wilson's maxim, it might be true that we value everything we regard as beautiful, but a moment's pause will convince anyone that we do not think that everything we value is beautiful. I can make a list of the things I value right now as I write this: my computer, the table it sits on, the coffee cup that holds my pens and pencils, even the book that Wilson has written, which is prompting these thoughts. None of these things would I call beautiful.

These confusions do not stop Wilson from being an evangelist for the good news of evolution. "Creationism," he writes, "fails as a theory in part because it is so unhelpful. Does anyone know God's will for burying beetles?" The beetles he refers to routinely commit infanticide, and Wilson implies that this is beyond the reach of theological explanation. Why would a perfectly good and wise God create a world where some animals have to eat their young in order to survive? Wilson thinks the answer to this question is obvious: God would not do any such thing,

---

40. Ibid., pp. 17, 116, and 123.

and with God out of the way, the only explanation left for such behavior is Darwinian. The problem with this line of analysis is that it ignores what Christians actually have to say about beetles that eat their young. If Wilson is going to argue that it makes no sense to believe that God makes baby-eating beetles, then he should at least pause to consider what theologians say about this kind of problem, and it turns out they have quite a lot to say about it. The behavior of Wilson's beetles is an example of what theologians call the problem of natural evil, and it is a problem that has been treated by the brightest minds in the history of Western civilization, but you would never know that from Wilson's jibe. I will define and investigate this problem in chapter 3, but I want to observe here that Wilson's Darwinian explanation of the beetle's bizarre behavior is not as profound as he thinks it is. His explanation comes down to this: "At the same time that they are nurturing some of their offspring, they are munching on others until they have reduced their brood to a size appropriate for the carcass" that they are consuming.[41] Eating their young helps beetles deal with scarce food resources. This seems like a plausible explanation, but notice how far it comes from being a scientific law. It has no predictive value, since scientists cannot tell which species will develop this trait or why it is not more common given the widespread scarceness of resources, so it works only in hindsight, as an explanation of a trait that has already been observed.

The statement, "The environment selects some beetles to eat their young," serves a function in biology similar to the function the statement, "Nature is fallen," serves in theology, but there are significant differences. Biologists argue that their statement is merely descriptive. That is, it is neutral in terms of any moral judgment or evaluation of the beetle's behavior. Theologians by contrast happily acknowledge that their statement is clearly normative. Christianity teaches that nature is not what God intended it to be, and thus nature alone cannot be a guide to moral behavior. On the face of it, then, theology seems to depend upon a moral vision of nature while biology appears to accept nature for what it is, without imposing any norm on it. That distinction between normative and neutral modes of inquiry, however, hardly does justice to biology. When ecologists talk about ecosystems, for example, they make judgments about what constitutes human interference and

41. Ibid., 25 and 23.

they provide reasons for restoring those systems to an earlier state. Even when Darwinians talk about competitive advantages they are using morally loaded language drawn from human moral activity (just ask any liberal critic of capitalism whether competition is a morally neutral behavior). Of course, biologists will claim that they try to strip their language clean of moral terms, but that is just the point: they can't. Nature is too complex, mysterious, and too much a part of us to ever be described in a satisfactory way without the aid of moral terminology. Darwinians prove this proposition every time they defend evolution, because they are making a moral judgment about a natural process.

Wilson is a good example of how thoroughly Darwinism is infused with morality. He thinks evolution is good for everyone. It might be objected that he is talking about evolutionary theory, not evolution itself, but his argument renders that distinction irrelevant. Evolution has created us, he argues, with the skill to understand nature. That skill is good; therefore, we should be grateful to evolution. This follows from the claim, which is inherent in Darwinism, that evolution is always beneficial for the biological survivors, because, by definition, natural selection has rewarded them with more life, while biological losers are not around to lodge any protests. It follows that evolution itself, and not just the study of it, is good—or at least good for us.

Nonetheless, there is an ambiguity in the title of Wilson's book, *Evolution for Everyone*. Is evolution *for* everyone in the sense that evolution is a benefit for every single human individual or is evolution only *potentially* beneficial to everyone since it is ongoing and there are in our midst today some who are not making the best of their struggle for existence? The idea that evolution is good for every single human is plainly untrue (presumably, natural selection sacrifices some human individuals to their species, just as it sacrifices beetle babies for the greater good of beetledom), while the idea that evolution is only potentially good for us implies that evolution is of little significance, since we can make of it what we want. If, unlike other animals, we can make evolution work for us, then we should define ourselves according to freedom and rationality rather than our genes. In that case, evolutionary theory might be *bad* for us, because it cannot account for the rationality that sets us apart from the evolutionary process.

The Dome of Eden

One of Wilson's chapters is entitled, "How I Learned to Stop Worrying and Love Genetic Determinism." Though we are hardwired, he says, to distinguish between friends and foes, biologists now know enough about natural selection to offer advice about how to achieve world peace. "In principle, it is possible to completely eliminate violent conflict by eliminating its preferred 'habitat,' regardless of how rare or common it has been in the past." He admits that a shared value system is a prerequisite for world harmony, but he thinks that "pluralism can be enshrined as a virtue and its suppression punished," since "virtually any value system can be stabilized by rewards and punishments, as long as it is agreed upon by consensus." If this leaves the reader thinking that Wilson embraces fascism as a way of enforcing pluralism in order to insure global order, he corrects that impression by arguing for the power of art to take the place of religious values. He is especially taken with the power of dance. "Could we establish world peace if everyone at the United Nations showed up in leotards?"[42] He thinks the answer is obviously yes.

And so the story goes, with the good and bad Darwinian cops taking turns interrogating religion with such a confusing mixture of kindness and cruelty that nobody notices that they have no warrant for religion's arrest. The good Darwinian cops assure you that evolution can be taught in public schools as a set of facts that does not need theological or philosophical scrutiny. The bad Darwinian cops think evolution cannot be taught without making a good, even if implicit, case for atheism. Bad Darwinian cops take inordinate glee at the prospects for a thoroughly Darwinized curriculum and the wreckage it would cause for traditional moral and religious beliefs. Good Darwinian cops call this wreckage "critical thinking." The bad cops think religion is wrong, while the good cops think religious is okay as long as it does not get in the way of science. Neither will listen to religious objections to their arguments, because they insist that religion has nothing to contribute to evolutionary theory. No wonder parents do not know what to do when their kids come home spilling out countless questions about evolution that their science classes have raised but will not let them discuss.

---

42. Ibid., 285, 293, and 294.

A thoughtful response to Wilson might be that he has strayed out of his biological niche in the intellectual world.[43] Nonetheless, his search for new environments to apply Darwinian theory is very much a part of the evolution of Darwinism. After the Scopes Trial, which I will discuss in chapter 2, put a long halt to public criticisms of Darwinism, Darwinians became less anxious about the relevance of their theory for cultural and moral issues, but with the resurgence of evangelical Christianity in the past several decades some Darwinians have tried to take back American culture. Many scientists, needless to say, would be quite happy to restrict Darwinism to biology, but what if that restriction is not itself scientific? What if the bad cops are right—that evolution makes truth claims about everything? If so, then randomness and strife are the foundation for the highest human ideals as well as the lowest organic life forms, but that raises a problem for the future flourishing of Darwinian theory. What parents would want their children being taught that Darwinism explains not only speciation but also compassion, honesty, and self-discipline?

Perhaps Wilson's ambition, which lies at the heart of Darwinism, has inadvertently demonstrated how empty evolution is. If it is this trivial when applied outside of biology, why would we non-biologists imagine that it is deeper when it is restricted to biology? One cannot help but suspect that if evolutionary theory looks absurd, simplistic, and circular when applied to something as complex as religion, then it might look the same way when applied to biological organisms. We can put this point in a syllogistic form for the sake of convenience and handy usage. If evolution is true, then it is true about everything; but if it is true about everything, then we are doomed to live in a world without truth, beauty, and goodness. If we are not so doomed, then evolution is not true about everything, and if evolution is not true about everything, then there is good reason to think that it is not true about anything.

Probably the most disturbing and radical moral implication of Darwinism has to do with death. Death was given new life by Darwinism, one could say, because the death of countless living beings, from the

---

43. The argument that the Darwinians I have examined are neither good scientists nor good philosophers is best presented in Karl Giberson and Mariano Artigas, *Oracles of Science: Celebrity Scientists versus God and Religion* (New York: Oxford University Press, 2007).

The Dome of Eden

perspective of evolution, is the necessary condition for the production of superior species. Darwin detailed the cruelty of nature in chapter 3 of *The Origins of Species*, which he titled, "Struggle for Existence." Most of this chapter is typical bad cop fare about the bleakness of nature, but he ends it with a kindly thought, as if he wanted to reassure his readers that they need not take him literally. "When we reflect on this struggle, we may console ourselves with the full belief that the war of nature is not incessant, that no fear is felt, that death is generally prompt, and that the vigorous, the healthy, and the happy survive and multiply." With this good cop comment Darwin reveals his metaphysical and, one can only call it, religious motivations in developing his theory. Evolution is consoling because we who stand atop it can congratulate ourselves for surviving. Death is just another way of saying life, and cruelty is the best form of kindness.

If religion is defined as the way in which humans deal with death, then the tendency to promote Darwinism to the status of a religion began with Darwin himself. Even if he did not treat his theory as a religion, he certainly treated it as an alternative to religion, which suggests that he thought it was on the same conceptual level as religion. Throughout the *Origins*, Darwin argues that belief in a gracious and good God is incompatible with the overwhelming amount of suffering we find in nature. Darwin did not believe in God, but he was certain that if God existed, God would not have permitted so much suffering in the world.[44] Darwin was dealing with what theologians call the problem of natural evil, and theological solutions to this problem usually draw from the doctrine of the fall to account for the suffering and strife of nature. Darwin had no interest in the particularities of specific theological doctrines, but he was very interested in the broad outlines of theological debates. He lived in a Christian age, and he thought like a theologian. He sought an explanation for death and suffering that could undermine by mimicking religious faith. In the penultimate sentence in *Origins*, he writes, "Thus, from the war of nature, from famine and death, the most exalted object which we are capable of conceiving, namely, the produc-

---

44. For one of the best treatments of the influence of theodicy on Darwin's thought, see Cornelius G. Hunter, *Darwin's God: Evolution and the Problem of Evil* (Grand Rapids: Brazos, 2001).

tion of higher animals, directly follows."[45] All the death and suffering of billions of creatures is worth it because we are the result.

Darwin loves you indeed! For Darwin, evolution loves the fit, the healthy, and the strong, and it loves them because they have overcome all odds in the struggle to pass on their genes. And when Darwin looks at nature, what does he love if not the wasting of life that is necessary for a few to win the right to life? Perhaps it is wrong to say that Darwin discounts beauty and goodness, because in these passages we see that Darwin has redefined the beautiful and the good. For Darwinians, death is both natural and good, because the pitiless and gruesome squandering of animal life is the means by which nature profligately spends its resources in order to invest in the chosen few. For Christianity, death is the enemy that was unleashed by sin, defeated on the cross, and, Christians hope, will be overcome in the end time. In the ancient world, pagans thought death was natural, and thus they tried to meet it with either resignation or courage, but they did not think it was good. Christians, in contrast to both pagans and Darwinians, try to meet death with hope because they think that death, being contrary to God's plan for all of creation, is not only profoundly unnatural but also deeply empty of any lasting meaning.

During his lifetime, Darwin did his best to obfuscate the nihilistic implications of his thought—perhaps, biographers always speculate, out of respect for the piety of his wife—and his defenders argue that Darwin cannot be held accountable for what some of his followers made of his theory. Many practicing scientists especially like to insist that moral (or immoral) implications have little or nothing to do with Darwin's theory. Nonetheless, the trend among biologists who like to philosophize and philosophers who study biology is to argue that no strong line can be drawn between evolution as a science and evolution as much more than science. Evolution is one of those theories that will not quit until it has explained everything. It is disingenuous, then, for scientists to extend natural selection to cover everything from the origins of music to sexual preferences and then to be offended when theologians argue that Darwinism develops a theory of morality that is pernicious and pitiful. If the philosophical and theological implica-

---

45. Charles Darwin, *The Origin of Species and The Descent of Man* (New York: Modern Library, 1936) 62 and 374.

tions of evolution are wrong, then Darwinism has not succeeded in its explanatory endeavors. If it cannot successfully account for everything it tries to explain, then it is only reasonable to question its major presuppositions.

Darwinism certainly can be softened in its presentation, but it remains a theory hard in social implications and cultural consequences. It takes courage to be a consistent Darwinian, just as it takes faith to be a Christian. Few scientists have been as honest about this as Michael R. Rose, professor of evolutionary biology at the University of California, Irvine.

> Particularly with respect to the clash between Darwinians and their persecutors, no evolutionary biologist can claim objectivity. Too often we feel like we are clinging to a mountainside, the winds of controversy blowing around us. This has led many of us into confusion and equivocation. Some of us dissimulate, and pretend that evolution is some benign force in the world. Bromides about evolutionary progress have deformed our popular writings. We are cowards too often, and when not, usually foolhardy.[46]

The theory of evolution is designed in such a way that it is fated to be a cultural icon as well as a model of biological explanation.

The idea of evolution is part of a cultural struggle that, ironically, looks something like the Darwinian description of the evolutionary process itself. The Darwin debates have mobilized a variety of interest groups into a strenuous competition over who gets to define the meaning and purpose of life. Darwinians want religion out of the science classroom, even if their theory cries out for religious examination. Some conservative Christians want equal time for the Bible in biology class, even if it means squeezing the Bible into a classroom where it will be out of place, while others want scientists to teach the theory of Intelligent Design. Meanwhile, few public schools are equipped to deal with these theological and philosophical issues in any meaningful manner, especially given the intellectual atmosphere of religious relativism and secular humanism that pervades the educational establishment.[47]

---

46. Michael R. Rose, *Darwin's Spectre: Evolutionary Biology in the Modern World* (Princeton: Princeton University Press, 1998) 4–5.

47. As I write these words, the New York Times reports that the Florida Department of Education modified its science standards to mandate the teaching of evolution be-

Something has to give, but nobody wants to compromise, and so far, no single position has been able to climb to the top of the contender's heap. Even if one position in the debate is most fit for survival, it is not clear who or what is doing the selecting. The issues are too complex for the media to do more than entertain us with a circus of contradictory claims and contentions, and universities are too politicized to provide the proper forum for disinterested deliberation. Without any obvious way of mediating the conflict, political muscle is often called in to determine the outcome. Thus, lawsuits abound, though the issues are too riddled with philosophical assumptions for competent legal judgment. A culture war is better than a civil war, but deciding this conflict by waging campaigns over local school board elections does little to advance the arguments on either side. No position will please everyone, but if there is no position that can account for the reasons behind the different points of view, then the cultural stalemate will continue while the politics get worse. At the end of the day, the question of the origin of life is too important to let politicians settle it by negotiating a compromise. Nothing less than the truth will do.

Nonetheless, having said all of this (and I will raise more questions about Darwinism throughout this book), I do not want to deny that evolutionary theory has had many impressive scientific successes. Evolution has moral consequences that cannot be countenanced by most people and most societies, but as a working hypothesis it has plenty of evidence in its support. Evolution happens. The world is very, very old. This book does not deny that basic claim. The theory of evolution has more holes in it than most biologists are willing to admit, but it also has a lot of explanatory power. Much of its power comes from its simplicity and elegance. Like Marx's sweeping reduction of economic history to class conflict or Freud's speculations about the sexual conflicts of childhood that control the development of adult behavior, Darwin holds out the promise of a complete explanation of the mysteries of life that will revolutionize all of our ways of thinking. Marx and Freud were masters of suspicion, undercutting common sense and traditional

---

cause it is "the organizing principles of science," which would be a surprise to most physicists and many chemists. The same article talks about "supposed" weakness of evolutionary theory and implies that a mistrust of evolution will inevitably jeopardize student trust in the "basic power of science." Amy Harmon, "A Teacher on the Front Line as Faith and Science Clash," *The New York Times*, August 24, 2008, 1.

morality alike. They challenged what most people took for granted—in the case of Marx, that private property is a prerequisite for personal responsibility, and in the case of Freud, that people are rational and free rather than under the control of unspoken sexual impulses. Darwin too undermines common sense and traditional morality by depicting the development of life as a pointless race for biological supremacy.[48]

Marxism, Freudianism, and Darwinism all have troubling moral implications and consequences, but Marxism was brought low by economists and psychoanalysis was uprooted by advances in psychology. Neither was particularly damaged by the complaints of moral theologians. The fate of Darwinism too will be decided, most likely, by other scientists, not those who stand outside the credentialed community of biological insiders. Nonetheless, it is possible that the moral problems of Darwinism indicate empirical and conceptual conundrums that will be hard to solve. Indeed, while orthodox Darwinians like Dennett and Dawkins have been much in the news recently, other scientists, as well as many philosophers of science, are finding holes, gaps, and fissures in evolutionary theory that might be hard to fill with the dogmas of orthodox Darwinism.

On its surface, the Darwinian research program is really not that hard to describe. The Darwinian formula begins with a struggle for survival among organisms as they compete for ecological resources. It adds to that struggle a variation in the traits that organisms pass on to succeeding generations. This variation is due solely to random genetic mutations. Then Darwinism argues that environmental factors favor some traits over others. This is the work of what Darwinians call natural selection. These favored traits, which enable an organism to survive and flourish in a particular ecological niche, spread throughout a given population of a species. The Darwinian formula extrapolates this process of adaptation on a micro level within a species (which is observable in nature) to the macro level of the creation of new species (which has never been observed by science). When a new type of organism evolves, frequently in isolation from the larger population, to the point of be-

---

48. Marx and Freud have been long discredited by better economic and psychological theories. Of the giants of modern skepticism, only Darwin remains. If one were to be suspicious of these masters of suspicion, one might suspect that Darwin is so staunchly defended today because he provides the last best rationale for a materialistic view of life.

coming unable to interbreed with its original group, then a new species has formed. Imagine this process beginning with the simplest organism and stretching out over billions of years and you have a portrait of how every creature we see is descended from a common ancestor.

It all seems simple enough until you start asking questions. Natural selection is often employed by Darwinians as if it indicates something that is active and creative, but it is really nothing more than "a process of elimination."[49] Putting the word *natural* in front of selection might cut off debate about supernatural forces working in evolution, but it does not really add anything to the word *selection*. The word *selection* denotes an intentional activity, so it is, given Darwinism's rejection of all purpose in nature, a misnomer for whatever it is that Darwinians are talking about. Darwinians often talk about natural selection being blind, but that just reinforces the fact that selection is not quite the word they are looking for if it has to be so dramatically qualified. After all, a blind agent doing something is still an agent acting for a reason (acting, that is, purposefully). Perhaps what the Darwinians really mean is that selection is blind, deaf, and dumb, although even that is not quite correct.[50]

---

49. Ernst Mayr, *What Evolution Is* (New York: Basic, 2001) 117. Also see Matthew C. Haug, "Of Mice and Metaphysics: Natural Selection and Realized Population-Level Properties," *Philosophy of Science* 74 (2007) 431–51.

50. There is precious little empirical evidence for natural selection. One of the success stories of Darwinism is the study of the changing size of the beaks of soapberry bugs. See for example Scott P. Carroll and Christin Boyd, "Host Race Radiation in the Soapberry Bug: Natural History with the History," in *Evolution* 46 (1992) 1052–69. The authors begin by admitting that most "phylogenetic patterns have their origins obscured in history, so that much of what we believe about their evolution comes from inferential analysis alone" (1053). I think this is an understatement, but it points to the fact that much or most of biology is based on inferential reasoning, not empirical evidence. Indeed, they go on to say that, "Direct empirical studies of evolutionary change over more than a few generations are very rare" (1053). Of course, few critics of Darwinism deny that evolution occurs on the level that these authors are describing— beak sizes will change as bugs migrate to new ecological niches. (These bugs have slender, tubular beaks that reach through fruit walls to the seeds, in order to suck them dry. When bugs migrate, they find different fruit to suck, thus putting pressure on beak sizes to vary accordingly.) The question is whether natural selection drives these changes and whether these changes are sufficient to account for speciation. Many problems stand out with this article. First, and perhaps most critically, the variation in beak lengths preexisted the migration of bugs to new ecological niches. In other words, natural selection in this case was selecting among preexisting variations in a

The Dome of Eden

Even if we can conceive of a selection process that is not intention-given population. Natural selection did not create anything new. Second, the authors themselves state that they do not know to what extent the variation in beak lengths were attributable to long distance immigration (in other words, longer beaked bugs moved into and mixed with bugs with shorter beaks that themselves had moved into areas where longer beaks were more useful) or other factors beyond natural selection. "The novel beak length distributions... most likely result from rapid genetic changes. ... An alternative explanation is that long distance migrants with pre-adapted beak lengths colonized" these areas (1062–63). The best they can say is that, "While we cannot directly trace the historical movement of bugs in the U.S. or from any more distant sites, several forms of evidence argue against long distance immigration as an important factor in establishing" the changes (1063). This is hardly exact scientific language and does not do much to build confidence in the authors' conclusion. Third, the authors say that natural selection was a "predominant force" (1064—whatever that means) but not the only or maybe even not the main factor involved in these evolutionary changes. Genetic drift could be a major factor (genetic drift is just a fancy biological term for the idea that many genetic changes occur that have no specific environmental cause and make no specific contribution to the reproductive success of the organism in question). Indeed, after discussing genetic drift, they write, "Thus we return to selection as the major factor behind the soapberry bug's rapid changes in beak length on new hosts" (1065). So now natural selection has been demoted to a "major factor," which is again unspecified. Fourth, there are way too many variables to control in this or any other similar "experiment." As the authors say, "This is not to argue that beak length will eventually perfectly match fruit size in all host races. First, selection exerted by the insects on fruit morphology may result in the continued evolution of the plants...." (1065). As the animals evolve, so do the plants in their environment. How does natural selection work if the pressures being put on organisms are themselves pressured to change by the evolving organisms? This calls into question the very idea of any gene centered formula for natural selection because the organism's environment is as active as the gene is. Fifth, and most fundamentally, these changes in beak size do not produce new species. "How independent have the new host races of the soapberry bug become as evolutionary entities?" (1066). The populations were still, at the end of the day, interfertile. Sixth, for true speciation to occur, the same tenuous process of beak selection would also have to happen simultaneously and in some sort of coordination with changes in other features such as body coloration and food preferences. But of course there is no coordination of changes; it would be lucky indeed if the newly beaked bugs also went through evolutionary changes that resulted in other distinctions that added up to true speciation. This is where intelligent design comes in: Beaks serve a purpose, and their sizes can change according to the size of the fruit they suck. But what was the point of the little juts of material that began to accumulate at the end of the bug's face before it was a beak? What did the beak do before it was long enough or complex enough to suck fruit? Why was it selected for, when it added nothing to the reproductive success of the bug? Biologists do have speculative answers to these kind of questions, but they can only posit a prior function for the precursor of the beak. This just puts off the problem of how something can grow from point A, where it has function A, to point B, where it has function B, when, in between those two points, it has no function at all, and thus has no reason to be selected by nature.

al or purposeful, what is it that is being selected—groups, individuals, genes, or some combination of all three? The issue of what natural selection targets (which is again a purposeful term) is so complicated that biologists have come up with a technical term, *phenotype*, to explain how natural selection weeds out the unfit. Unfortunately, phenotype is hard to explain because it refers to the totality of an individual, including its shape, biochemistry, physiology, and even its behavior. The phenotype of an organism is the product of the interaction of its genotype (its genetic material) with its environment. In an attempt to keep the focus on genes as the target of natural selection, Dawkins has developed the concept of the extended phenotype. The extended phenotype is the effect genes have on the world at large through that gene's effect on the individual body that carries it, including the behavior of that body.[51] Dawkins is stretching an already convoluted term in order to maintain his gene-centered view of life. Whatever the wisdom of piling up qualifications of an already burdened term, the problem is that the genetic mutations that are selected for fitness are protected by a thick mattress of factors that makes evolution even more improbable than it appears. Natural selection, which is blind, has to hit a target that is buried deep beneath anything that natural selection could see, if it could see.

The fossil record also stubbornly refuses to cooperate with Darwinian assumptions. If evolutionary process really is as gradual as Darwin hypothesized, fossils of transitional forms should be more common, but instead they are incredibly rare. Rather than finding transitional forms, paleontologists ordinarily find representatives of species that show only what can be considered transitional characteristics. As the philosopher Robert Koons explains, "Given that the forms of life found in the fossil record are more numerous and variegated that those we find alive today, it is not at all surprising that we should find fossil forms that are 'intermediate' in some vague sense between living forms. What we don't find is the kind of continuous, seamless web of transformation of adaptive structures that would be needed to confirm the truth of Darwinism."[52] The Darwinian literature is full of tips

---

51. Richard Dawkins, *The Extended Phenotype: The Long Reach of the Gene*, rev. ed., (New York: Oxford University Press, 1999).

52. Robert C. Koons, "The Check is in the Mail: Why Darwinism Fails to Inspire Confidence," in William A. Dembski, ed., *Uncommon Dissent: Intellectuals Who Find Darwinism Unconvincing* (Wilmington: ISI, 2004) 4. Some biologists are abandoning

for how to answer critics who raise this question. The most common tip is the argument that small populations are most likely to produce transitional fossils from one species to another, and thus these fossils will be exceedingly rare. Whatever the merits of this argument (it is counterintuitive at least, since mutations that survive are by definition more prevalent than those that do not), the fact is that the fossil record more closely comports to the idea of a sudden appearance of species (sudden according to geological standards of time) rather than their gradual evolution.

Discontinuity of biological forms strikes many critics of Darwinism as the best interpretation of the fossil evidence. This is especially true of the Cambrian explosion, the big bang of speciation, which continues to baffle Darwinians. Virtually all animals living today trace their lineage to this spectacular event, 550 million years ago, when all of the major body plans of animals suddenly appeared on the world's stage. How evolution could have been so creative in such a geologically brief period of time is unclear, if not downright mysterious. Darwin himself recognized this phenomenon as one of the chief objections to his theory of gradual biological change over millennia. Stephen Gould was so frustrated by the fossil record that he formulated the theory of punctuated equilibrium, which replaces Darwin's image of a ramp of continuous evolution with a staircase of bigger steps. Although evolutionists struggle to come up with new explanations for biology's big bang—spinning ever-new theories to patch up the original one—the Cambrian explosion continues to shadow their best efforts. When pushed by critics to explain their failure, Darwinians often respond that the alternative (that is, a theory of evolution that makes room for God working through nature) is so impossible to conceive that Darwinism simply must be right.

Doubtless, many more significant and exciting empirical discoveries are on the horizon for Darwinism, but even wrong theories (ether comes to mind) can produce persuasive evidence. Empirical discoveries thus cannot compensate for questionable presuppositions and conceptual ambiguities, and Darwinism has plenty of those. In fact, the empirical problems with Darwinism, serious as they are, pale in

---

the gradual change model of evolution in favor of what Eugene V. Koonin calls the big bang model. See Koonin, "The Biological Big Bang Model for the Major Transitions in Evolution," *Biology Direct* 2:21 (2007) n.p. Online: http://www.biology-direct.com/content/2/1/21.

comparison to its conceptual muddles. Perhaps most disturbing is the way that Darwinism raises fundamental problems with regard to the scientific method. Debates abound about the precise formula, if there is one, of the scientific method, but predictability is usually one of its ingredients. Even Darwin's staunchest supporters admit that a lack of predictive value is one of their theory's strongest weaknesses. For example, Ernst Mayr, an accomplished scientific practitioner as well as a philosopher of science, states that, "Probably nothing in biology is less predictable than the future course of events."[53] Unexpected outcomes emerge in evolution all the time, and novelty is by definition hard to predict. Predictions in biology are about as accurate as, and far less useful than, forecasting the weather.[54] While Mayr concludes from this admission that predictability must not be a valid requirement for scientific research, it is just as credible to wonder whether a scientific theory that does not tell us anything about the future can be very certain about the past.

If a scientific theory cannot generate good predictions, then it should at least be testable. Testability, for philosophers of science, has more to do with being able to falsify, rather than prove, a scientific theory. If you try your best to set up experiments to falsify a hypothesis and fail, then you accept it, at least for the time being. This is how the famous philosopher of science Karl Popper described the scientific method, and he found Darwinism failing the test. Although Popper later backed down from his rejection of Darwinism as a science, his initial skepticism remains persuasive to many critics. Natural selection is not a scientific law, like the law of gravity. Popper argued that natural selection actually comes close to being a tautology (a tautology is a claim that is true by definition, like "It is what it is" or "Dumb people are not smart"). Thus, the "law" of natural selection claims that organisms that best fit their environment propagate the most offspring, but this is true by definition. (If you define fitness as the ability to leave the most offspring, then saying that organisms that leave the most offspring best fit their environment does not tell you anything informative. It is like saying that all tables are tables or that survivors are the ones that

---

53. Ernst Mayr, *Toward a New Philosophy of Biology: Observations of an Evolutionist* (Cambridge: Harvard University Press, 1988) 33.

54. Ibid., 20–21.

survive.) Popper, by the way, did not reject Darwinism. He just did not think it was pure science. He called it "a most successful metaphysical research program."[55]

Popper was right to back off his argument that natural selection is a tautology. Tautologies explain nothing, but Darwinism has demonstrated significant explanatory power. Nonetheless, Popper's suspicions about the causal adequacy of natural selection have been deepened and developed by many other philosophers. The main problem can be put generally: imagining how an organism might evolve from one state to another is not the same thing as proving that it actually happened that (or any other) way. Indeed, any account of how A became B is not falsifiable if, no matter what new evidence comes to light about how hard it is to go from A to B, the details of the account can always be altered to fit the new evidence. In other words, if you know the beginning and ending of a story and are determined to get the main character from the one to the other, and if you are the least bit ingenious, you will have no difficulty in finding a narrative path that gets the job done.

Likewise, arguing that some evolutionary pathway must be true because there is no known alternative explanation is hardly a good argument. How can you ever know that you have ruled out all of the alternatives? Of course, the absence of proof does not mean Darwinians are wrong (proof might be right around the corner), but it does not mean that they are right either. Besides, a passionate conviction that evolution simply must be true given the lack of proof for the possible alternatives can lead to intellectual sloth in acknowledging Darwinian explanatory failures. It can also attenuate intellectual curiosity, especially when it comes to the alternative of positing a purposeful designer.

Few Darwinians have been more sophisticated in their self-reflections than Mayr, who has been called "the Darwin of the twentieth century" for his work on biodiversity. That makes his confession of Darwinian causal inadequacy significant. "Every organic system," he writes, "is so rich in feedbacks, homeostatic devices, and potential multiple pathways that a complete description is quite impossible." That sounds as if Darwinian explanation is besieged with too many causal

---

55. For his recantation and his own summary of his earlier position, see Karl Popper, "Natural Selection and the Emergence of Mind," *Dialectica* 32 (1978) 339–55. For a discussion of Popper in the context of evolution, see Robin Attfield, *Creation, Evolution and Meaning* (Burlington, VT: Ashgate, 2006) ch. 3.

factors, but Mayr admits that the problem is much worse than that. "In dealing with a complex system," he writes, "an explanation can hardly be considered very illuminating that states: 'Phenomenon A is caused by a complex set of interacting factors, one of which is b.' Yet often that is about all one can say."[56] That is a stunning statement. Life is so complicated that the best of our theories cannot isolate the determinative causal factors behind biological change.

A complicated process is not purely random or chaotic, of course, but there is no *prima facie* reason to reject the idea that we cannot completely explain or understand a process complicated enough to end up with us. Species become more complex over time, but as Niels Henrik Gregersen points out, there is no law of complexification. "Not even a future Theory of Everything," Gregersen suggests, "that is, a theory uniting the four known forces of gravity, electromagnetism, weak and strong atomic forces, would be able to explain the perplexing particulars of evolutionary history." Gregersen, Professor of Theology at Copenhagen University and an expert on religion and science, notes that natural selection seems to have very little to do with the physical organization of matter (which is why physics and biology have little to do with each other), and he suggests that the laws of biology should be seen as "higher-level generalizations rather than as laws in the strict sense of universal and prescriptive laws."[57] Biologists work with laws, but their laws have lots of exceptions, which makes it very difficult to discern what kind of laws they are.

Philosophical defenders of Darwinism sometimes shift the blame for Darwinism's methodological problems to the scientific method itself. They begin with the historical observation that the traditional formulations of the scientific method were based on physics and chemistry and thus were not meant to apply to biology. They then divide into two basic camps. One camp argues that the scientific method needs to be reformulated in order to account for biology's distinctiveness. Causality, for example, might be reformulated as a plural phenomenon with no single definition and no universal rules, and physics might be

56. Mayr, *Toward a New Philosophy of Biology*, 34 and 29. Also, see D. M. Walsh, "The Pomp of Superfluous Causes: The Interpretation of Evolutionary Theory," *Philosophy of Science* 74 (2007) 281–303.

57. Niels Henrik Gregersen, "The Complexification of Nature: Supplementing the Neo-Darwinian Paradigm?" *Theology and Science* 4 (2006) 6.

displaced from its foundational role as providing the final explanations for all natural phenomena. The other camp argues that biology is an autonomous field with its own rules and methods but still a part of the broader scientific enterprise. Biology cannot be reduced to physics, nor should it be; the sciences are diverse but equally important and valid. There is no unity of the sciences beyond a gentleman's agreement not to interfere with each other. Where physicists talk about laws, biologists talk about statistical and probabilistic generalizations, and where the harder sciences advance through new discoveries, evolutionary theory makes progress through the clarification of concepts, ideas, and terminology. Natural history is aptly named because it is similar to the way that historians investigate the human past.

Whether or not the whole enterprise of science needs to be reconceived to make room for biology, it is clear that biology has a dose of interpretive artistry not commonly found in physics and chemistry. The Darwinian interpretation of nature is not merely literary or subjective, of course. It falls somewhere in between the narrative-oriented study of history and the scientific laws of physics and chemistry. Darwinism does not simply tell a story, because it combines a narrative mode of explanation with generalizations based on inductive observation and deductive hypotheses.[58] Calling Darwinism an interpretation of nature is thus not meant to dismiss it in a crude manner. Not all interpretations are the same, and many philosophers have argued that good interpretations of anything follow rational rules and procedures. Indeed, the study of interpretation is itself a field of philosophy called hermeneutics. Hermeneutical philosophers tend to think of the act of explaining something as more like constructing a plausible narrative than discerning universal and rigorously definable laws. Philosophers debate the causal adequacy of narrative as a mode of explanation, and Darwinism

---

58. See David L. Hull, "Central Subjects and Historical Narratives," in *History and Theory* 3 (1975) 253–74, as well as his *The Metaphysics of Evolution* (Albany, NY: SUNY Press, 1989). For a defense of the compatibility of narrative explanation with deductive scientific laws, see Mary B. Williams, "The Logical Skeleton of Darwin's Historical Methodology," in *Proceedings of the Biennial Meeting of the Philosophy of Science Association* 1 (1986) 514–21. In his book, *Mystery of Mysteries: Is Evolution a Social Construction* (Cambridge: Harvard University Press, 1999), Michael Ruse examines the way Darwinism has always been in debt to various cultural, historical, metaphysical, and religious assumptions, and in the last chapter he tries to distinguish between pure Darwinism and cultural imports.

can no more be reduced to narrativity than it can be reduced to the laws of physics. Nonetheless, its narrative mode of explaining the origin of life will inevitably clash with the narrative of the Bible. As much as it wants to be (and is) a scientific theory, Darwinism is also a sweeping and dramatic story of where life comes from and what life means. For this reason, evolution is, as the philosopher of science Mary Midgley unequivocally states, "the creation myth of our age."[59] Midgley does not mean that it is a myth in the sense of a set of beliefs that are obviously untrue. She means that it is a myth in the sense of being a powerful explanatory strategy that has shaped the consciousness of the modern imagination in ways that we have hardly begun to explore.

One should not rush to the judgment that these methodological problems, which doubtlessly worry philosophers more than most scientists, render Darwinism bankrupt. Ernst Mayr, for example, raises these philosophical puzzles precisely because he thinks they can be solved, at least some day in the future. The solution he foresees, however, pertains primarily to conceptual clarification rather than the traditional means of empirical breakthroughs. The need for conceptual clarification in Darwinism stems from the vagueness of many of its most foundational terms. Take, for example, the title of Darwin's famous book, *The Origin of Species*. It is utterly misleading. Many have joked that Darwin explained the evolution of species but left out their origin. That is, natural selection works on organisms that struggle to survive. It cannot explain how life itself began. One could also joke that Darwin explained the origin of evolution but left the species out. That is, Darwin not only failed to explain how life came to be, but he also made the concept of species so fluid that it became nearly useless. Before Darwin, species were considered ideal kinds or types, so that individuals were classified according to how closely they approximate an abstractly defined form. Darwin actually never settled on a definition of species, but modern biologists define a species as a population that is exclusively capable of interbreeding and producing fertile offspring. Without a general and uniform category representing all of its members, however, all we are left with is particular individuals and their variable relations to others and their environment. Since populations of related individuals are always in transition, species as such do not really exist. We see species in

---

59. Mary Midgley, *Evolution as Religion* (New York: Routledge, 2002) 33.

nature only because we see a snapshot of biological time that precludes us from taking the long view.

Randomness is another vague Darwinian term, and it is usually thought to be the hardest Darwinian puzzle to solve, but randomness just might be one of those concepts that is as unstable as the thing it tries to denote. Books, articles, and websites carry on an interminable argument about whether random phenomena are an indication of the limits of our knowledge or an ontological aspect of nature itself. There is general agreement that randomness does not necessarily mean uncaused, but the agreement stops there. Critics charge that randomness cannot give rise to complex biological forms, while evolutionists argue that the role of randomness in evolution is woefully misunderstood. Simply defined, "If a process is random, then different possibilities have the same (or nearly the same) probabilities."[60] Given this definition, natural selection does not operate randomly. The environment "selects" those traits that have the greatest chance of survival. Randomness does occur in evolution, however, on the level of genetic mutations. Mutations are random in that they do not occur because they might benefit an organism. Even here, however, critics must be careful. Different mutations are not equally probable, or conversely, some mutations are more likely than others. Nonetheless, genetic mutations are random with respect to their impact on their organism and its relationship to its environment. More fundamentally, the direction of evolution is random according to orthodox Darwinism, but is this the same kind of randomness that pertains to genetic mutations? Randomness is hard to pin down in Darwinism because it is not clear that it is being used in a univocal manner, even though it permeates the whole system of explanation.[61]

Randomness is related to the problem of teleology, which lies at the foundation of Darwinian conceptual confusions. The challenge Darwinism makes to teleology is worth some careful inspection. Any discussion of teleology usually begins with Aristotle, who was a biologist as well as a philosopher. Indeed, Aristotle thought you could not study biology without doing philosophy. It has become common in

---

60. Elliott Sober, *The Philosophy of Biology* (Boulder: Westview, 1993) 36.

61. See Robert L. Millstein, "Discussion of 'Four Case Studies on Chance in Evolution': Philosophical Themes and Questions," in *Philosophy of Science* 73 (2006) 678–87.

recent work on Aristotle to reject the idea that he attributed purpose to the cosmos as a whole. He kept his level of analysis focused on the goods that specific types of things pursue.[62] Whatever Aristotle thought about the cosmos as a whole, he clearly thought that living organisms could not be described with reference to matter alone. All organisms, for Aristotle, have not only an efficient cause (the factors or motions that immediately precede them) but also a final cause (or *telos*) toward which they aim. No explanation of any organism can be complete without reference to how and why that organism acts for a particular end. Indeed, final causation has an explanatory priority over efficient causation because the order and regularity of nature cannot otherwise be explained. Aristotle entertains the idea that nature does not act for a purpose but finds "it is impossible that this should be the true view." He engages philosophers who put chance, which he defines as an "accidental cause," at the heart of nature, but he seems to think that it is impossible to avoid thinking about nature in terms of the language of purpose and benefit. Organisms act for the sake of something, and knowing that for which they act is essential to understanding the organism. (This does not mean that all organisms are conscious of their aims!) Nature exists in a state of change that is not random or pointless; all motion has a goal, just as, in Aristotle's metaphysical terminology, every substance has its own proper function and end.[63]

Debates about Aristotle and teleology continue, but there is no debate that Christianity turned Aristotle's teleology into an account of the way God's plan pervades the entire world. Theologians under the influence of Aristotle portrayed a world where things are pulled by their purpose in life as well as pushed by their near contemporaries. Christians believed that God, as the final end of all striving, is the ultimate source of this pulling. From this perspective, all of nature is a theater displaying God's glory, or to change the metaphor, nature has a dimension of divine depth. It was not until the Protestant Reformation taught Christians to read the Bible for its plain sense rather than its

---

62. See Monte Ransome Johnson, *Aristotle on Teleology* (Oxford: Clarendon, 2005).

63. Aristotle *Physics* II.8, in *The Complete Works of Aristotle*, ed. Jonathan Barnes (Princeton: Princeton University Press, 1984) 1:339–41.

symbolic depths that people began reducing causation to only one dimension.

Modern science broke from Aristotle's rich and layered understanding of causality by limiting causation to a relationship between an event and its immediate, contiguous antecedent (what Aristotle called efficient causation). Nevertheless, the question of whether purpose can ever be completely expunged from our understanding of nature is one of the hardest in philosophy today, and appeals to Darwin's authority does not make that question any easier to answer. Immanuel Kant was one of the first modern philosophers to attempt a conceptual analysis of the study of biology, and he puzzled over the problem of purpose in nature long before Darwin came on the scene. In the *Critique of Judgment* (1790), Kant argued that any investigation into living organisms must assume a teleological causality (that is, agents acting for a reason), because life can never be reduced to a purely mechanistic explanation. This holds not just for the actions of creatures but also for the anatomical parts of an organism, which must be imagined, Kart argues, as fitting together according to an overall plan or design. For Kant, each part of an organism is both the end of a physiological process and the means of achieving a physiological function. For example, a bird's wings, feathers, and hollow bones work together to promote flight, and without that end in mind, the configuration of these parts does not make any coherent sense. Living things, according to Kant, are not like found objects or human inventions; their parts fit together for the purpose of the whole, and that whole—the living creature—must be assumed to be capable of acting (partaking of purposeful activity). Finally, Kant takes it for granted that purposeful activity or organization can be understood only by reference to an intentional designer or creator.

Nonetheless, Kant also argued that the final causation (to use Aristotle's language) of teleology has no legitimate place in scientific explanations. Science must explain living creatures by forging a causal chain of previous events, that is, by following time step by step into the immediate past, and science must treat that causal chain as if it were generated and held together by some kind of mechanism. Biology thus must be mechanistic if it is to have any predictive and universal value. The upshot of this analysis is an unsolvable dilemma for biology. Biology must assume the very thing (purpose) that it at the same time must exclude from its investigations. That is, biologists must "treat organisms *as if* they were teleologically regulated, as if the idea of the whole, its design, operated to organize the parts, to cause them to develop toward certain ends."[64] Simply put, we can never escape using teleological language and assumptions when we think about living creatures, but we cannot prove that living creatures are the product of purposeful action. Biology, Kant concludes from this inquiry, can never be a full or complete science. Biology gives us empirical patterns and regularities in nature, but it can never give us a complete and exhaustive analysis of what living creatures are.

Kant was trying to demonstrate why finding purpose in nature seems so built into human nature.[65] Kant was an idealist who located purpose in our minds rather than in things themselves, but by the end of the eighteenth century it was common to attribute purpose directly to natural phenomenon. William Paley's *Natural Theology*, published in 1802, was the last great portrait of a purpose-filled universe. He surveyed nature and found evidence of design wherever he looked. Not just design, but the most complex interconnections of beneficial relationships demonstrated, to his satisfaction, that the evidence for divine planning was overwhelming. Darwin occupied Paley's old room at Christ's College in Cambridge during the 1820s, and he studied Paley's book assiduously. While older scholarship on Darwin portrays him as the antithesis of Paley, newer work has revealed a much more dependent relationship. As Arthur McCalla writes, "Darwin used design language in the *Origin of Species* and elsewhere in order to subvert the design argument by replacing miraculous intervention with natural process."[66] The philosopher Tim Lewens agrees, explaining that "The evolutionary process bears deep similarities to the process of intelligent design. It is these deep similarities that explain and justify the appearance of

---

64. Richards, *Romantic Conception of Life*, 236. Also see Philippe Huneman, ed., *Understanding Purpose: Kant and the Philosophy of Biology*, North American Kant Studies in Philosophy (Rochester, NY: University of Rochester Press, 2007).

65. For a discussion of studies that document how children naturally perceive purpose in nature, see Justin L. Barrett, *Why Would Anyone Believe in God?* (New York: Rowman & Littlefield, 2004) ch. 3.

66. Arthur McCalla, *The Creationist Debate: The Encounter between the Bible and the Historical Mind* (New York: T. & T. Clark, 2006) 106.

the same vocabulary in both domains."[67] Where Paley discerned God, Darwin detected natural selection, but both men were moved and inspired by nature's contrivances, even though they disagreed about what was doing the contriving.

Paley thought all organisms were perfectly adapted to their environment by God's design. Early in his career Darwin agreed about the first part of that claim but had doubts about the second. In fact, Darwin used the language of "perfect" adaptation right up to the point when he wrote chapter 6 of *On the Origin of Species*, where he speaks of relative adaptation.[68] From the perspective of his mature work, perfect adaptation is a religious vestige in Darwin's thought, a carry over of the idea that nature is marvelous and awe-inspiring because it is internally driven to a harmonious and complete interlocking of all of its parts. Darwin eventually tried to discard this theological baggage, even though it worked to his advantage, since the language of perfect adaptation opened the door for the first attempts by liberal theologians to put a theistic spin on his theory.[69] Regardless, even imperfect or relative adaptation is ambiguous, since it preserves something of Paley's idea of the purposive dimension of nature. The concordance of the *Origin* shows that Darwin used teleological terms like end, final cause, purpose, useful, and utility dozens of times.[70] One of Darwin's favorite ways of explaining adaptation in non-theological terms was to talk of the act of gaining an advantage, but such an act cannot be understood or described outside of a teleological framework: something is striving for something else in order to gain an advantage. Not all actions are purposeful (there are accidental or purely passive actions, for example,

---

67. Tim Lewens, *Organisms and Artifacts: Design in Nature and Elsewhere* (Cambridge: MIT Press, 2004) 3. Lewens defends Darwinism but admits that "biology is in an awkward position: it makes free with a vocabulary of design, even though modern biology recognizes no intelligent designer as the artificer of the species" (2).

68. See the important work of Dov Ospovat, *The Development of Darwin's Theory: Natural History, Natural Theology, and Natural Selection, 1838–1859* (Cambridge: Cambridge University Press, 1981).

69. See the fine discussion of how perfect adaptation influenced Aubrey Moore, arguably the father of theistic evolution, in Richard England, "Natural Selection, Teleology, and the Logos: From Darwin to the Oxford Neo-Darwinists, 1859–1909," in *Osiris*, 2nd series, 16 (2001) 270–87.

70. P. H. Barrett, D. J. Weinshank, and T. T. Gottleber, *Concordance to Darwin's Origin of Species* (Ithaca, NY: Cornell University Press, 1981).

although some philosophers argue that such actions should not be called actions in the strictest sense of that term), but a living creature that acts for its own benefit (or for any other reason) is indeed acting purposefully.

Darwin was not a philosopher, and certainly not a Kantian, but he was actually quite aware of the problem that his main concept, natural selection, actually suggests that nature is an agent intentionally selecting traits for some higher purpose. A passage from the *Origin* is worthy quoting in full:

> In the literal sense of the word, no doubt, natural selection is a false term; but who ever objected to chemists speaking of the elective affinities of the various elements?—and yet an acid cannot strictly be said to elect the base with which it in preference combines. It has been said that I speak of natural selection as an active power or Deity; but who objects to an author speaking of the attraction of gravity as ruling the movements of the planets? Every one knows what is meant and is implied by such metaphorical expressions; and they are almost necessary for brevity. So again it is difficult to avoid personifying the word Nature; but I mean by Nature, only the aggregate action and product of many natural laws, and by laws the sequence of events as ascertained by us. With a little familiarity such superficial objections will be forgotten.[71]

Darwin's wishful thinking came true. This "superficial" objection has been forgotten, rather than resolved. Metaphors are used so systematically in biology that Darwinians have forgotten that they are metaphors. Nietzsche once defined all concepts as metaphors about which we have forgotten that they were metaphors, but he did not mean this as a compliment to concepts.[72] Today, Darwin is praised for the poetic qualities of his prose, rather than interrogated for the philosophical ambiguity of his terminology. Even when he is trying to be clear, however, Darwin hedges his bets by suggesting that a teleological view of nature is "almost necessary." If it is necessary, then how can Darwinism try to portray evolution as without purpose, and if it is not necessary, then

---

71. *Origin of Species*, 1882 edition, 63.

72. See Friedrich Nietzsche, "On Truth and Lying in an Extra-Moral Sense" (1873) in *The Portable Nietzsche*, ed. Walter Kaufmann (New York: Vintage, 1982).

why does Darwin continue to use purposeful language, as he does so a few pagers later:

> It may metaphorically be said that natural selection is daily and hourly scrutinizing, throughout the world, the slightest variations; rejecting those that are bad, preserving and adding up all that are good; silently and insensibly working, whenever and wherever opportunity offers, at the improvement of each organic being in relation to its organic and inorganic conditions of life.[73]

Just because Darwin warns us in advance that he is using a metaphor does not make the problem of the metaphorical nature of Darwin's language any easier to evaluate. Qualifying selection with the word natural does not change the fact that there is a whole lot of teleology going on here. It can hardly be claimed, then, that ascribing evolution to intelligent design introduces teleology into evolutionary theory. It introduces a different teleology, but some form of teleology is already there.

Some scholars argue that Darwinism will always contain traces of the Christian worldview it tried to erase, like a vestigial appendage that the scientific body cannot quite shake off. From this perspective, Darwin was the last of the natural theologians, not the father of secular humanism. Steve Fuller, for example, calls Darwin a "recovering creationist."[74] Darwinism is trapped by what it struggles so hard to overcome.

Schools of thought swing from one extreme to the other on this debate, so perhaps it is best to see him as a transitional figure. That is the position of David Kohn, who argues that Darwin facilitated more strident versions of secularism by translating theological language into non-religious terms. Kohn represents the social construction school of the history of science. That is, he thinks that scientific theories can only be understood by putting them in their historical context, and that "if any science was socially constructed it was Darwin's." Natural theology is thus "constitutive and regulative to the formation of Darwin's science." Darwin kept his language about adaptation ambiguous because he was negotiating a complex position on the relationship of religion

---

73. *Origin of Species*, 65–66.

74. Steve Fuller, *Science vs. Religion? Intelligent Design and the Problem of Evolution* (Malden, MA: Polity, 2007) 35.

and science. He preferred a sanitized to a radical materialism and never fully resolved his struggle with Christian faith. Consequently, his theory is inherently ambiguous. He was, in Kohn's own ambiguous words, "profoundly teleological and yet profoundly non-Providential." Kohn concludes that Darwin's theory "unslips the scholastic knot of God and purpose by translating the self-evident Christian myth of purpose into the self-evident scientific myth of evolving function. Thus it secularizes, and captures without loss of potency, the core ideological justification of capitalism: what works in nature works in society."[75] In other words, Darwin is able to cast off a providential interpretation of teleology only be clinging to the capitalist justification of life's struggles. Even this conclusion, though, shows how convoluted Darwinism can be. Justifications of capitalism were thoroughly enmeshed (and arguably still are) in theological debates about the purpose of competition and the qualified goodness of material scarcity. Wherever Darwin turned, he found religion. How could it have been otherwise in Victorian England?

Darwinians today might be willing to admit that these theological problems were a part of evolutionary theory in the nineteenth century, but what about today? Is Darwinism not liberated from such teleological considerations? Some biologists are aware of the problem of the persistence of teleological terminology in Darwinism. David Sloan Wilson, for example, raves about the social organizations of genes, because he thinks this demonstrates that cooperation, not competition, lies at the root of nature. "The concept of organisms as societies," he writes, "is more than just an arresting metaphor." He approves of an article entitled "The Social Gene," by the Harvard biologist David Haig, that uses the following words to describe genetic interactions within a single organism: "allegiance, binding agreements, cabal, cajole, cheat, clique, coalition, coercion, collectives, commons, conspire, contractual arrangement, corrupt, deceit, egalitarian, exploitation, factions, fair play, firm, fraud, free-riders, gangster, huckster, institutions, licensing, lottery, manipulate, marketplace, misappropriate, monopoly, motivation, open society, parliament, partnership, payoffs, police, politics, protection racket, rogue, sabotage, security system, self-interest, social

---

75. David Kohn, "Darwin's Ambiguity: The Secularization of Biological Meaning," *The British Journal for the History of Science* 22 (1989) 218, 218, 220–21, and 221.

contract, squabbling, steal, strategists, surveillance, swindle, team, trade, transaction costs, and unauthorized."[76] Our cells are evidently as organized as we are, and they have all the problems of a post-industrial nation-state. In spite of Wilson's approval of this language, many scientists will insist that these terms are indeed *just* metaphors. But if you strip the metaphors from biology, what would you have left? The answer is not just "not much" but quite possibly "nothing at all." Even the least colorful of scientific papers routinely describe parts of organisms as agents undertaking actions for a goal.

Dawkins's concept of selfish genes is another obvious example of how biologists ascribe purpose to nature in their words even as they deny that purpose in their theory. One can attribute design to a beneficent deity or to blind and selfish genes, but either way one has appealed to a purposeful designer. Selfish acts, after all, are goal-directed, and all actions must have an agent that performs them, which is why Darwinians spend so much time personifying genes. Genetics has thus come full circle back to Paley. It goes without saying that genes are not consciously purposeful, but purposeful activity does not necessarily require consciousness. Animals act purposefully, even though they may or may not be conscious of their actions. Yet wouldn't it just be a lot easier to attribute purpose to God, rather than genes? Those who are mystically inclined might be willing to entertain the hypothesis, associated with process philosophy, that consciousness goes all the way down in nature, but most people will have a hard time believing that. Those more metaphysically realistic will say that selfishness is just a fancy way of describing what Darwin called the struggle for life, but there is no struggle unless there is a struggle *by* something *for* something else. Note too that one can ask this question without returning to yet another mystical idea—that of a vital force embedded in nature distinct from physiochemical forces. Vitalism is making a come back these days with new age philosophies that promote alternative medicines that balance and harmonize bodily energy. Vitalism is a tempting alternative to scientific reductionism and materialism, but rather than imagine nature as magically imbued with a mysterious spiritual essence, the truly robust alternative to Darwinism is intelligent design, which follows our intuitions of a purposeful nature to their logical conclusion.

76. Wilson, *Evolution for Everyone*, 136–37.

The question is whether Darwinians can coherently think that the purposeful activity of evolution is not purposeful in any meaningful way. It is easy to dismiss metaphorical images of a ladder of evolution or of humanity as evolution's crown, since those metaphors are (for Darwinians, anyway) obscure remnants from the age of Christian faith. Nonetheless, unless biologists tell us how to read their own favorite metaphors (or give us a way of translating their metaphors into non-metaphorical language), who is to say which metaphors are best? Life is dynamic, and biology is the study of the mechanisms that make life move, but for Darwinians, life biologically understood is not going anywhere. Yet organisms must be misinformed, because each living thing struggles for more life, even if adding meaningless life to meaningless life will never add up to any meaning. Life is ultimately purposeless, but organisms (or genes) are determined to maximize their life at the greatest possible price anyway. Organisms struggle for life because, evidently, they do not know how pointless it is. Consequently, higher organisms must develop strategies to keep this knowledge hidden from them, or else evolution would just run out of steam.

Perhaps the best that can be said about the core metaphysical commitment of Darwinism is that it has something to do with the purposelessness of the useful, or put another way, teleological action that is without purpose.[77] The portrait of nature as a massively purposeless squandering of life in the service of selfishness so deep that it operates on a molecular level unconscious of its own depravity is not theologically neutral. Mayr tries to escape this quandary by distinguishing between teleomatic processes and teleonomic processes.[78] A teleomatic process follows a scientific law without any goal in mind. The examples Mayr gives are the law of gravity and the second law of thermodynamics. Something falls or something hot cools down whether it wants to or not. A teleonomic process, by contrast, is controlled by a goal that is built into the process. The growth of an adult from a fertilized zygote is the result of a program that initiates and causes that development. Mayr

77. This is, in a way, the position of James G. Lennox, who argues that Darwin is so often misunderstood on teleology because he invented a new kind of teleology, one that fits no previously known philosophical scheme. Lennox, "Darwin was a Teleologist," *Biology & Philosophy* 8 (1993) 409–21. Also see John Beatty, "Chance Variation: Darwin on Orchids," *Philosophy of Science* 73 (2006) 629–41.

78. Ernst Mayr, *Toward a New Philosophy of Biology*, 44–48.

argues that biologists use teleological language because they are dealing with teleonomic, not teleomatic processes. In other words, evolution as such is not goal-directed, but the programs built into organisms, and the processes by which these programs came into existence, are.

Mayr's position is an example of how Darwinians use new technical terminology to muscle their way through intractable conceptual puzzles. That is, he shifts the problem of understanding how biologists can be teleological in their practices but anti-teleological in their theory to the even greater problem of defining what a program is. The result is an increase in confusion rather than clarity. Any talk about biological systems being operated by programs is obviously metaphorical, being drawn from the world of computers. The world of computers is, in turn, a human world full of purposeful activity. To his credit, Mayr realizes the mess he has gotten himself into. To the philosopher who wonders how programs can direct behavior that is only apparently teleological, he replies, "Alas, all the biologist can tell him is that the study of the operation of programs is the most difficult area of biology."[79] In nonbiological language, programs get something done because they are designed by an intelligent agent. If Mayr is using this language in a metaphorical fashion, then it is his responsibility to either tell us what he really means or explain why his theory is trapped in metaphors.[80] Even thinking of biological programs as machines is no help, because machines are designed for a purpose. It seems we are stuck with purpose in our language no matter how hard Darwinians work to obscure purpose in nature, but if we cannot describe nature without inscribing it with purpose (Kant's dilemma), how do we know that there is a nature beyond our language that is not purposeful?

That Darwinism is so in debt to apparently interminable philosophical disputations should cause anyone studying biology to wonder whether Darwinism is a complete or adequate account of biological change. Yet if Darwinism is so theory-laden, and its theory is saturated with theological ideas and perforated by philosophical puzzles, then it is unfair to police the scientific boundaries of Darwinism by charging

79. Ibid., 50.

80. Mayr states, without explanation, that "the origin of a program is quite irrelevant for the definition" (49) and defines programs "in such a way as to avoid drawing a line between seemingly 'purposive' behavior in organisms and in man-made machines" (49).

theologians and philosophers with trespassing. Indeed, the theory of evolution is a battlefield in America's culture wars because the boundaries of science in this instance are so clearly unmarked. The problem is not just that theologians and philosophers challenge Darwinism but also that evolutionary theory itself has no set boundaries. Darwinism is a totalizing theory, so that it would be appropriate to speak of evolution*ism* if that term were not so awkward. If evolution is a theory with boundary problems, then Christians need to do more than just politely request that Darwinians keep to their side of the religion/science divide. Nonetheless, this does not mean that Christians must reject evolution altogether. Rather than simply figuring out where to draw the line separating evolution and creation, theologians must develop a critique of what it is about Darwin's theory that is so misguided. Theologians should be as careful and nuanced in their treatment of Darwin as they have been in their criticisms of Marx and Freud.

Like most problems in life, it is easier to see what should *not* be done than what should be done. The temptation of the Christian Right to reject evolution altogether is much bemoaned by scientists and academic theologians these days, but the temptation of the Christian Left to baptize evolution is, arguably, a more seductive and dangerous risk. By baptizing evolution, I mean the tendency of many liberal Christians to accept evolution as "the way God made the world." This might seem like a fairly insignificant surrender in only one small skirmish in the culture wars of the twenty first century. After all, evolutionary scientists are a highly organized and culturally powerful force in our society, operating with the full support of the federal and state governments. So why fight them? The problem is not just that one surrender leads to another, eventually wearing a broad path down from the heights of theological knowledge along which one can easily slip to the very bottom of secular atheism. Evolution is not just one step along this slippery slope; it *is* the slippery slope. If evolution is how God speaks the world into being, then God's voice is seductive and violent, because evolution works to draw creatures against each other by promising more life for the strong (the well-adapted) at the expense of the weak (the ill-adapted). Evolution, Darwin says, is random and violent. Any attempt to envision this process as the direct will of God will have a domino effect on every other Christian doctrine.

The Dome of Eden

Darwin has done more than any single individual to throw the weight of modern culture against religion. Even for millions of otherwise devout Christians, Darwin has left the impression that the Bible's authority is on shaky ground. No task for theology is more pressing than to affirm, once again, the ongoing veracity of the Bible, especially the absolute truth of the Genesis account of creation. Genesis is not only true; it also provides us with the most radical critique of Darwin imaginable. I have no desire to read Genesis anew in order to update it from the perspective of evolution. On the contrary, I want to read evolution in a radically new way from the perspective of Genesis. Genesis, I am wagering, speaks the truth about evolution that evolutionary theory itself could never anticipate and can never disprove. God speaks the same truth through the Bible to all people at all times, but the way we hear God's Word is shaped by our historical and social context. The truth God speaks is powerful enough to dispel the delusions and destroy the idols of any age, but those delusions and idols vary from one period to another. Throughout history, Christians have often been unprepared to understand the fullness of God's Word. Darwin forces us to look again, and ever more closely, into the abundant riches of the biblical revelation.

two

Re-Trying Scopes:
What Machen Would Have Done to Darrow

Once upon a time, evolution was unassailable in America. Darwin's theory did not start out that way, and it has lost much of its luster in recent years, but in the middle of the twentieth century Darwinism looked like it was designed to last forever. Darwinism survived a very bumpy scientific start in its first several decades but went on to win the most decisive cultural clash of the century. If the Darwinian theory of evolution were a person, not a theory, we would consider him (most decidedly *him*) lucky. Darwinism is the scientific version of the classic rags to riches story. Darwin had bet the farm on the idea that chance and struggle were at the heart of life, and by the middle of the twentieth century he seemed to have won.

The scientific odds were against Darwin in the early years because his theory was as inadequate and incomplete as it was elegant and ambitious. In the first decades of the twentieth century the details of what came to be called Neo-Darwinism were still being worked out, so that scientific skepticism about evolution was not uncommon.[1] His contemporaries were most concerned about his neglect of the inductive method, because he based his theory on speculation more than observation. As Harvard biologist Ernst Mayr admits, "When he published the *Origin*, he actually did not have a single clear-cut piece of evidence for the existence of [natural] selection."[2] Proponents could be overzealous in piecing together the fossil evidence, as was the case of a diagram, popular in scientific textbooks in the 1920s that showed a linear devel-

---

1. See Peter J. Bowler, *The Eclipse of Darwinism: Anti-Darwinian Evolution Theories in the Decades around 1900* (Baltimore: Johns Hopkins University Press, 1983).

2. Ernst Mayr, *What Evolution Is* (New York: Basic, 2001) 121.

opment of the horse, only to be overturned by later scientific evidence in the 1940s.[3]

Natural selection was supposed to explain why organisms with favorable traits were more likely to survive and thus pass on those traits to the next generation, but Darwin did not know why mutations occurred or how mutations were inherited. That huge gap in his theory would be filled only when the work of an obscure Central European monk named Gregor Mendel (1822–1884) became widely known in the early part of the twentieth century. Mendel's work laid the foundation for the study of genetics, but it still took several decades for scientists to figure out how to synthesize it with Darwinism. The result, called Neo-Darwinism, or the modern evolutionary synthesis—though it is common practice to shorten Neo-Darwinism simply to Darwinism, as I have done in this book—did not gain a consensus of scientific support until the publication of Julian Huxley's book, *Evolution: The Modern Synthesis*, in 1942

Mendel paved the way for a restoration of Darwin's scientific reputation, but Scopes made Darwin a cultural hero. John Scopes, a high school biology teacher, was the defendant of the famous trial that bears his name, but the real target was traditional Christianity and its high regard for the authority of the Bible. When Tennessee passed a law against teaching evolution in public schools, the American Civil Liberties Union announced that it would provide free legal services to anyone willing to challenge it. Dayton, Tennessee, was a town down on its economic luck, and one of its civic leaders argued that a trial would help put it on the map. The town fathers agreed and asked Scopes, who had been filling in for the regular biology teacher during a sick leave, to volunteer to be charged for violating the new law.

Scopes said yes, and the rest was history—but it was hotly contested and heavily manipulated history. Long before talking heads dominated every political debate, the 1924 trial was all about spin, and the pro-evolutionary forces were able to keep the trial spinning for decades as a warning to anyone who might dare to challenge Darwin. The Darwinian side was led by H. L. Mencken, the satirist and social critic, and Clarence Darrow, America's greatest defense lawyer. Both men were zealous crusaders against religion. They saw an opportunity to use

---

3. Wells, *Icons of Evolution*, ch. 10.

Scopes to drive a wedge between those who were on the side of science and those who cast their lots with "bigots and ignoramuses," as Darrow put it.[4] They also saw an opportunity to bring down a populist politician, William Jennings Bryan, who was nearing the end of a prolific but stormy career.

Darrow learned his atheism from his father, who was an avid reader of Darwin and passed on a fervent anticlericalism to his son. Like many secularists, Darrow was influenced by Andrew Dickson White's *The Warfare of Science* (1876), which was, according to the Scopes historian Edward Larson, "responsible for much of their thinking about religious bigotry and intolerance."[5] Although many evangelical and conservative Christians were inclined to accept some form of evolution at the turn of the twentieth century, even if not Darwin's emphasis on randomness and combat, White argued that Christianity was trying to destroy science and that Darwin represented the last hope for a final victory of reason over superstition. Darrow took White seriously and saw his chance to score a significant victory by attacking Bryan.

Bryan was known as "The Great Commoner" because he yearned for a world that respected ordinary people enough to let them run it. Good politics were not possible, he thought, without good people. He was a progressive and an evangelical, a combination that strikes many people today as unlikely, though progressive politics in the nineteenth century was unthinkable without evangelical ideas and energy. Populism as a political movement can easily degenerate into the prejudices of the masses, but Bryan was a high-minded populist, and it was Christianity that elevated his political goals. That is why he was a vociferous critic of capitalism and militarism, both of which he linked to Darwinism. Always an optimist, he never met a social problem that a political agenda, backed by a well-organized moral crusade, could not solve. Christians had a responsibility to disparage Darwinism because "science, as well as the Sabbath, was made for man."[6] Like many evangelicals, he was worried about the rise in popularity of the eugenics movement. First articulated by Darwin's cousin, Francis Galton, eugen-

---

4. Edward J. Larson, *Summer for the Gods: The Scopes Trial and American's Continuing Debate over Science and Religion* (New York: Basic, 2006) 6.

5. Ibid., 21.

6. Ibid., 42.

ics used Darwinism to legitimate the goal of improving the human race by controlling heredity. Far from improving humanity, Bryan thought Darwinism led the cultural elite to treat the masses with contempt. Bryan argued that Darwinism reduced humans to beasts in order to treat them like cattle. Bryan was also worried about recently published research that argued that primates had become humans through hunting. He thought Darwinians were replacing the Christian law of love with a law of violence and hatred. This was too much for a man who had resigned as secretary of state under President Woodrow Wilson in protest over Wilson moving the country toward war. Bryan could no more sympathize with Darwinism than he could with militarism in Europe, much of which was justified, at least in Germany, by appeals to the evolutionary ethos.

Bryan was hardly anti-scientific. Darwin's theory was taught at Illinois College during Bryan's student days there, and there is no record of his objecting, but he was more enthusiastic about the study of the classics. He learned how to present himself in public by studying the speeches and the rhetoric of the great men of the past. No political peer had the same vocal power that he so effortlessly exercised. Yet he witnessed a great transformation in public education that left him deeply disturbed. During his youth, education was an essentially moral enterprise, training students to be responsible citizens and principled contributors to society. Schools could do that because there was a social consensus on the need for a Christian foundation for education. Schools were supportive of the values students brought with them to the classroom. All of that was changing by the 1920s, with evolutionary theorists leading the way.[7] Evolution drove a wedge between biblical morality and public education. Traditional Christians first resented and then began actively protesting its instruction in public schools. Many educators did not welcome the competition and began pushing back. Public education was becoming more a matter of passing on the worldview of the cultural elite than the preservation of the ancient truths of Greece, Rome, and Israel.

---

7. Much has been written on the transformation of American education in the middle of the twentieth century. For my analysis, see Stephen H. Webb, *Taking Religion to School: Christian Theology and Secular Education* (Grand Rapids: Brazos, 2000) 77–81, and ch. 6.

Re-Trying Scopes

Bryan went to Dayton to defend the local control of schools and the right of state legislatures to pass laws pertaining to the responsibility of teachers to their local communities. He believed in what we would call character education today, and he had an abiding trust in ordinary people to best judge what values their children need to learn. Bryan was convinced that Darwinism was a threat to these freedoms because it undermined morality as much as it contradicted the Bible. Nations must be strong spiritually if they are to flourish politically, just as individuals must be confident that their lives have significance beyond the flux of haphazard biological accidents.

Always the politician, Bryan kept his focus on America as a unique moral enterprise. The survival of democracy, he was convinced, depends on the idea that humans are unique because they are created in God's image. His lectures, *In His Image*, are a forgotten theological classic, although more than one hundred thousand copies were sold in 1922, the first year of their publication. Those lectures and the Scopes trial came near the end of his life, but Bryan's principled objection to Darwinism was consistent throughout his career. As he declared in one of his most popular lectures, "The Prince of Peace," Darwinism is a "merciless law by which the strong crowd out and kill off the weak."[8] Some evolutionary philosophers now openly embrace variants of this position, but many scientists continue to deny that evolution has any cultural or social implications. They insist that it is simply a neutral description of natural biological processes. Evolutionary theory, however, is too all-encompassing to permit such a modest disclaimer. At stake in evolutionary debates are the uniqueness of humanity and the relevance of the gospel ethic of love and forgiveness.

Bryan believed in inspiring and consoling rhetoric, but Darrow believed in self-interested strategy. Darrow waited until the last day of the trial to pull a surprise by calling Bryan to the witness stand. Bryan was vain about his public speaking skills, but he was not a quick-witted debater like Darrow, and Darrow knew it. Darrow grilled him on the Bible stories that are the hardest to explain from a scientific point of view. Darrow asked about Jonah and the whale, Noah's flood, Adam's rib, and whether Joshua made the sun stand still. Darrow asked not a

---

8. Michael Kazin, *A Godly Hero: The Life of William Jennings Bryan* (New York: Knopf, 2006) 140.

single question about the topic of the trial. In fact, he went out of his way to avoid evolution and its perplexities, because he knew that attacking the Bible would be easier than explaining Darwin. He posed as a sincere and somewhat incredulous interlocutor of the Bible, but his intention was obvious. He wanted to ridicule Bryan by making him look foolish for taking every biblical passage literally. Bryan, who was effective in using the Bible to promote his progressive causes, had never thought in any systematic way about the various problems involved in interpreting the Bible. He was a politician, not a theologian. Yet the problem with his response to Darrow was not his literalism but his lack of creativity in showing how the Bible can speak to concerns about evolution without losing its voice. More fundamentally, he could not articulate the wrongness of a progressive reading of Darwinism because he himself was so committed to the progressive cause. More traditionally conservative Christians, beginning with Bishop Samuel Wilberforce in 1860, understood that Darwinism was a threat to Christianity not because it upholds capitalism and militarism but because it entails a pessimistic, reductive naturalism. Bryan was aiming at a target that was of his own making.

Darrow's target was also hand-made, but it had a better market. Darrow was trying to make Bryan look foolish not to the secular, cultural elite, who needed no convincing that the Bible was outdated, but to the emerging Protestant elite, who needed prodding to denounce one of their own. Darrow was no Christian, but he knew that his brand of militant secularism could flourish only if it adopted the rhetorical tactics of religious modernists. Likewise, liberal Christians needed Darwin to seal their triumph in the twentieth century. There was nothing inevitable or necessary about the liberal displacement of conservative Christianity among the American Protestant elite. Throughout the nineteenth century, evangelical Christians had occupied the seats of power in most public institutions as well as in churches and seminaries.[9] By the 1920s, liberal Protestants were making a dramatic bid to control the seating arrangement of American culture. If they were to establish themselves as keepers of American culture, they needed an

---

9. For a good history of this conflict, see George Marsden, *The Soul of the American University: From Protestant Establishment to Established Nonbelief* (New York: Oxford University Press, 1994).

issue to prove just how cultured they were. Their credentials consisted of the claim that they provided a bulwark against the dangers of fundamentalism. If the debate about evolution had been primarily over the interpretation of Scripture, it would never have gained such national prominence. At stake was social power and cultural prestige.

Conservatives (soon to be called fundamentalists) reacted to this liberal surge to dominate the national culture by trying to retain local control of public schools. They battled Darwin because they were worried about who controlled the schools. As Larson explains, "Darwinism did not become a fighting matter for many fundamentalists until it began to influence their children's education in the twenties."[10] Few teenagers went to high school in the nineteenth century, but public education expanded dramatically in the first part of the twentieth. These trends were especially pronounced in Southern states like Tennessee, where conservative Christians struggled to maintain what they thought was a distinctively Christian culture against the secularism and materialism of the North.[11] Northerners thought the Southerners just did not understand Darwin, while Southerners thought the Northerners just did not understand the relationship between religion and education. Southerners tended to identify religion with the social cohesion and cultural traditions that Darwinism most deeply threatened to undermine. Liberal Protestants, meanwhile, exercised an almost religious zeal in their efforts to reconcile Christianity with modern progress, which they took to be exemplified by the theory of evolution. From a sociological perspective, liberal Protestants were facilitating a mass conversion to the cultural norms and rational assumptions of the secular cultural elite. That is why liberal Protestants reacted to fundamentalists with scorn and antagonism. Even in their retreat, biblical literalists were standing in their way.

The battles were intense because the winner in this cultural war got to draw the boundaries of acceptable public speech, which would determine the leadership of the schools, the media, and politics for several generations. Not surprisingly, then, liberal Protestants charged

---

10. Larson, *Summer for the Gods*, 23.

11. See Charles A. Israel, *Before Scopes: Education and Evolution in Tennessee, 1870–1925* (Athens: University of Georgia Press, 2004), and the insightful review by Jonathan R. Baer in *Journal of Religion* 85 (2005) 665–66.

traditional Christians with uncivil conduct in their refusal to compromise with modernity. To be precise, liberals found fundamentalists guilty of the social equivalent of treason. Fundamentalists betrayed the American ideal of freedom by obstructing scientific endeavor. More menacingly, fundamentalists had turned their backs on the rational spirit that defines the modern world. What they had really done, of course, was to reject the optimistic attitude toward progress that had become a secular substitute for religion among the cultural elite. From the liberal perspective, their punishment fit their crime. For rejecting the scientific spirit of progress, they were cast out of any institution having to do with education. They were left behind and forgotten by those segments of America that believed that the coming kingdom would be the better world that humans could create. After Scopes, Darwin became a symbol of modernity, and anyone who rejected Darwin was in danger of being held in contempt by the court of public opinion.

How had Christianity in America become so bitterly divided? Like any war, claims about who fired the first shot are controversial and hard to prove. Nevertheless, it is still important to examine the decisions and strategies that culminated in the defeat of conservative Christians at Scopes. The historian J. David Hoeveller has traced one significant strand of the rise of liberalism back to Darwin. "In the United States Darwinism helped shape the intellectual contours of modern liberalism and progressive politics. And, perhaps surprisingly, Darwinism, sometimes by inspiring fear of its implications, gave rise to a generation of liberal theologians who reshaped American Protestantism."[12] My use of the word liberal here, which follows Hoeveller's lead, needs some qualification, because the terms *liberal* and *conservative* have changed over the years, Moreover, scholars have pointed out that it was sometimes orthodox Calvinists, with their commitment to an orderly cosmos ruled by unchanging providence, who were anxious to elaborate on the connections between God's sovereignty and natural selection. Nonetheless, the theologians who were most excited about Darwin were the ones who believed in modernity's march of progress and the need for the church to keep up with the pace that nature set.

---

12. J. David Hoeveller, *The Evolutionists: American Thinkers Confront Charles Darwin, 1860–1920* (Lanham, MD: Rowman & Littlefield, 2007) ix.

Gary Dorrien has demonstrated in his magisterial history of liberal theology that the key decade in the liberal Protestant appropriation of evolution was the 1890s. Dorrien's example is the liberal theologian Henry Ward Beecher, who gushed about the positive religious significance of Darwin's theory in his book, *Theology and the Evolutionist* (1897). "It would be difficult to find anywhere," he wrote, "a nobler statement of the profound mystery of life than is to be found in the writings of Darwin, Huxley, and Herbert Spencer."[13] Like many of his contemporaries, Beecher did not grasp the bleakness of Darwin's view of nature. He certainly was not alone in failing to distinguish between Darwin and Darwin's most popular expositor, Herbert Spencer (1820–1903), who developed an entire philosophy based on the survival of the fittest that is called Social Darwinism. It was common in the latter part of the twentieth century for scholars to argue that Spencer misunderstood Darwin and that Darwin's ideas, properly understood, could not possibly lead to Spencer's philosophy. That caricature of their relationship is changing. According to the philosopher Anthony O'Hear, for example, "It is not at all clear whether much, except tone, separates the social views of Darwin and Spencer."[14] Indeed, Darwinism has come around to Spencer's passions by being very eager to apply Darwin to social problems, and that makes Spencer look prescient, not perverse. In fact, Spencer talked about evolution years before Darwin, and Darwin was as much of a closet Spencerian (he happily adopted the phrase "survival of the fittest" from Spencer) as Spencer was an avowed Darwinian. A recent biography has made the case that Spencer was a more subtle thinker than the caricatures of him as a stalwart supporter of unfettered capitalism suggest.[15] Subtle or not, he is unduly neglected for his role in both preparing the way for Darwin and also systematizing Darwin's political and economic instincts.

In terms of a distinction I used in the first chapter, Beecher was a good Darwinian cop, while Spencer had and still has, unfairly or not, a

13. Beecher is quoted in Gary Dorrien, *The Making of American Liberal Theology: Imagining Progressive Religion, 1805–1900* (Louisville: Westminster John Knox, 2001) 318.

14. Anthony O'Hear, *Beyond Evolution: Human Nature and the Limits of Evolutionary Explanation* (New York: Oxford University Press, 1997) 135.

15. Mark Francis, *Herbert Spencer and the Invention of Modern Life* (Ithaca, NY: Cornell University Press, 2007).

very bad reputation. With allies like Spencer, Darwin needed a boost, and he got it from the liberal Protestant establishment, which realigned him with the forces of social progress and optimistic humanism, rather than the forces of ruthless competition associated with Spencer.[16] Darwin made some gestures at limiting evolution to the study of biology, even though its expansion into all realms of study was built into his theory from the start, but it was liberal Christians, as historian Peter J. Bowler has documented, who should get the credit for turning his theory into a cosmic doctrine of human self-congratulations.[17] It is often thought that Darwin overthrew the argument for God's existence from the design of nature, but in reality he opened the door for liberal theologians to use Darwin to complicate and revise that argument for their own ends. More specifically, liberal theologians made Darwin accessible and acceptable by associating his theory with the idea of progress.

William Paley thought that everything in nature fit together in a miraculous way. Paley was not interested in *how* God designed the world; the important thing was to convince his readers *that* God designed the world. Nature is well-designed, Paley thought, because God wanted it that way. Paley took some of the mystery out of nature with his detailed analyses of its interlocking parts, but he did this only because he wanted to show how miraculous nature is. In a way, Darwin never abandoned the universe of Paley's discourse. One historian has noted that "Darwin was preoccupied with design . . . throughout his

16. For a survey of positive theological uses of evolution, see James R. Moore, *The Post-Darwinian Controversies: A Study of the Protestant Struggle to Come to Terms with Darwin in Great Britain and America, 1870-1900* (Cambridge: Cambridge University Press, 1979). Also see Claude Welch, *Protestant Thought in the Nineteenth Century: 1870-1914*, vol. 2 (New Haven: Yale University Press, 1985) 204-11. Like many scholars who discuss this period, Moore notes that Christians of more orthodox leanings were the ones most likely to try to accommodate Darwin. "The Darwinians to a man remained closely in touch with established theological traditions" (303). I concede this point, but it only makes sense that theologians who wrestled with Darwin were deeply committed to Christian faith and were trying to figure out how Darwin complements, rather than denies, that faith. These men were not liberals in the sense of being secular liberals, but they did pave the way for what came to be known as Protestant liberalism. Also see Jon H. Roberts, *Darwinism and the Divine in America: Protestant Intellectuals and Organic Evolution, 1859-1900* (Madison: University of Wisconsin Press, 1988).

17. Peter J. Bowler, *Monkey Trials and Gorilla Sermons: Evolution and Christianity from Darwin to Intelligent Design* (Cambridge, MA: Harvard University Press, 2007).

life" and that "his relationship to the idea of intelligent design in the world was consistently ambivalent."[18] Another has written that "The design doctrine of natural theology was changed rather than destroyed by Darwin because his theory was based on the idea of order in nature."[19] Because the design argument was not dependent on any particular description of the designer, it was compatible with many different worldviews. Darwin wanted to out-design Paley by showing how the parts of nature fit together in a way that was more elaborate and complex than any theologian had previously imagined. He demonstrated that previous theories of nature's design were insufficiently scientific because they attributed design to divine intervention rather than making design a nearly miraculous property of nature itself. The idea that nature itself prefers perfect adaptation provided an opening, as I pointed out in chapter 1, for providential interpretations of evolution. For example, Asa Gray, the most important American botanist of the nineteenth century, became a staunch supporter of Darwin only after he reconceptualized natural selection as a form of providential teleology.

Many liberal theologians were quick to follow Gray's lead. They embraced Darwin in part because they drew a parallel between God's relationship to nature and the proper way the elite should govern society. They interpreted Darwin to mean that the complexity of nature is the means, not the impediment, to God's plan. Darwin helped them to get rid of the cumbersome idea of special creation, which argued that everything is created by God in its own particular way. The concept of evolution helped liberal theologians see how God uses gradual processes that, appearances notwithstanding, eventually bring out the best in the world. Liberal Protestants were thus able to revive the doctrine of providence on the basis of an evolutionary worldview that covered both nature and history. This was a genuine theological accomplishment, but it came at a high price. Theologians who embraced evolution as the natural process through which divine providence works found themselves in an odd position. Any argument meant to limit evolution to biology was an attempt to limit God! If evolution is how God works,

---

18. Neal C. Gillespie, *Charles Darwin and the Problem of Creation* (Chicago: University of Chicago Press, 1979) 86.

19. William E. Phipps, *Darwin's Religious Odyssey* (Harrisburg, PA: Trinity, 2002) 172.

then it must be how God works through all levels of creation, from the simplest organisms to human beings and the cultures we create. Evolution could not be exalted high enough, because it is the way of divinity. It follows that even religion—and God too, of course—must be subjected to Darwinian analysis.

Liberal theologians not only insisted that evolution must have universal, indeed, cosmic application. They also insisted that it must be benevolent with regards to human destiny, if not to any other species. Belief in the inevitable progress of history was deeply rooted in the nineteenth century, and liberal Christians were quick to recruit Darwinism as further proof of the perfectibility of human society. Some scholars have argued that Christians turned to the idea of progress in the nineteenth century as a form of psychological compensation for all the changes and challenges that were besieging Christianity. Old traditions were dying in the face of massive economic and social changes. Rather than mourn these losses, liberal Christians celebrated change as the essence of Christian faith. Progress replaced providence as liberals abandoned the doctrine of original sin and other impediments to an optimistic view of history. Devotees of progress refigured obstacles as opportunities for reform and advancement. This is where Darwin became important. Everyone knew that nature was full of pain and death. Darwin, liberals decided, demonstrated how natural evil is only a preliminary for greater goods, because out of the struggle for life came us! Liberals thus provided evolution with all the credentials it needed to be widely accepted in Western society.

If these claims seem exaggerated, then go to any small Protestant liberal arts college that bought the best books of the day in the late nineteenth century, as did mine, and ponder the excitement with which liberal church leaders greeted Darwin. Take John Fiske (1842–1901), for example. He wrote more than thirty books on the spiritual genius of evolution. His masterpiece, *Outlines of a Cosmic Philosophy* in two volumes, builds up to the conclusion that evolution gives us "not Atheism or Positivism, but a phase of Theism which is higher and purer, because relatively truer, than the anthropomorphic phase defended by theologies."[20] In other words, we cannot imagine that a personal God

---

20. John Fiske, *Outlines of Cosmic Philosophy Based on the Doctrine of Evolution*, vol. 2 (Boston: Houghton, Osgood & Co., 1878) 412.

would create the world through evolution, but that is good, because it forces us to abandon old fashioned ideas about God as a personal being making personal demands upon us. God is an abstract principle of creativity, not the One who is best identified in the person of Jesus Christ.

In another book, Fiske gives us very clear statements about the universality and benevolence of evolution. On its universality: "From man's origin we gather hints of his destiny, and the study of evolution leads our thoughts through Nature to God." On its benevolence: "Toward the spiritual perfection of humanity the stupendous momentum of the cosmic process has all along been tending. That spiritual perfection is the true goal of evolution, the divine end that was involved in the beginning." And Fiske explains how evolution helps us to come to terms with our otherwise troubling observations of the operations of evil in nature: "As we recognize in the universal strife and slaughter a stern discipline through which the standard of animate existence is raised and the life of creatures variously enriched, we become to some extent reconciled to the facts. Assuming, as we all do, that the attainment of higher life is in itself desirable, our minds cannot remain utterly inhospitable towards things, however odious in themselves, that help toward the desired goal."[21] This is a theology of sacrifice that is exactly backward to Christianity, which asks us to sacrifice for others. Fiske looks at the countless lives sacrificed for our benefit, and he says amen.

Or take Henry Drummond (1851–1897), a Scottish naturalist who responded to Darwin with the aptly titled, *The Ascent of Man*. For Drummond, "Nothing is in finer evidence as we rise in the scale of life than the gradual tempering of the Struggles for Life." Its slow amelioration is the work of "the reign of Love which must one day, if the course of evolution holds sway, be realized." The struggle for life is actually a lesson in being kind to others! Furthermore, evolution is a more spectacular act than the creation described by Genesis, because "a process of growth suggests to the reason the work of an intelligent Mind," not a magician.[22]

---

21. John Fiske, *Through Nature to God* (Boston: Houghton Mifflin, 1901) xii, 77, and 68–69.

22. Henry Drummond, *The Ascent of Man* (New York: James Pott, 1894) 35 and 37.

Lest it be thought that the baptizers of Darwin were all Protestant, the work of the Anglo-Catholic Aubrey Lackington Moore (1843–1890) deserves comment, because he did more than anyone to make Darwin welcome in the Anglican Church. Moore was a contributor to *Lux Mundi*, a book that became famous as the manifesto for progressive Anglo-Catholicism. Moore regretted the breakup of the medieval synthesis of science, philosophy, and religion. He saw in evolution the potential for a recovery of an integrated theology of nature. "Darwinism appeared and, under the guise of a foe, did the work of a friend.... Either God is everywhere present in nature, or He is nowhere. He cannot be here and not there."[23] Protestants had lost sight of a comprehensive vision of divine activity in nature because they had no philosophical tradition upon which to rest their faith. Moore thought Darwin could do for theology in the modern era what Aristotle had done for theology in the Middle Ages.

The transitional figure between these English and American religious leaders of the 1890s and the liberal Protestant acceptance of Darwin in America by the 1920s is John Dewey. Dewey was the most famous, productive, and influential American philosopher of the first half of the twentieth century. Although he repudiated institutional religion, he was intensely invested in reconstructing a vaguely spiritual sensibility to sustain the public morals needed in a time of massive social transformations. He provided the intellectual substance for liberal Protestantism, even though, or perhaps because, he rejected traditional Christianity. In an important lecture given in 1909, "The Influence of Darwinism on Philosophy," he set the agenda for the progressive interpretation of evolution that continues to this day. He was completely uninterested in theology, so he saw the significance of Darwin in terms of its impact on epistemology, not faith. He was enthusiastic about the potential for treating the mind as an instrument of adaptation. In Darwin he saw evidence of "a new intellectual temper" that would lay "hands on the sacred ark of absolute permanency." This new temper is old hat in academic circles today, where it is called social construction. For Dewey, moral and religious values are useful only insofar as they advance social interests, which are determined by the confluence of

---

23. Charles Gore, ed., *Lux Mundi: A Series of Studies in the Religion of the Incarnation* (London: John Murray, 1902) 73.

humanity and its ever changing environment. Philosophy after Darwin must forswear "inquiry after absolute origins and absolute finalities in order to explore specific values and the specific conditions that generate them." The new, post-Darwinian logic must make a radical break from the past. "Old questions are solved by disappearing, evaporating, while new questions corresponding to the changed attitude of endeavor and preference take their place." The point of philosophy is not to contemplate the eternal truths but to develop "a method of moral and political diagnosis and prognosis."[24] Philosophy should serve social progress, which alone is sacred.

All of Dewey's subsequent work developed these thoughts, but he had no need to continue reflecting explicitly on Darwin. By the 1920s, to pick back up on Dorrien's history, the idea that the evolution of nature confirms the liberal conviction in the inevitability of historical progress was so widely taken for granted that Darwin was hardly mentioned by liberal theologians or philosophers.[25] That is, Darwinism was assumed, not argued for. This was especially true after Scopes, which ended the debate only to begin the accusations and incriminations. After Scopes, liberals only bothered to talk about Darwin in order to defend him when fundamentalists went on the attack. Protestant liberals did not share the conservative worry that the idea of universal common descent detracts from human dignity and uniqueness. They were willing to replace human uniqueness with an ethic of situational connectedness, drawing from Darwin to argue that no organism stands alone and that even the value of human beings should be measured by the ecological whole. Here was proof, they argued, that nature, without any miraculous interventions on behalf of God, can come up with increasingly complex species and, eventually, human beings. If nature has gotten us here so far, then only imagine how much further social programs and government agencies can get us. Evolution seemed to confirm liberal optimism about the future, trust in the accumulative effect of gradual change, and hope for social perfection.

24. John Dewey, "The Influence of Darwinism on Philosophy," in *John Dewey: The Middle Works, 1899–1924*, vol. 4: *1907–1909*, ed. Jo Ann Boydston (Carbondale: Southern Illinois University Press, 1977) 3, 10, 14, and 13.

25. For Gary Dorrien's observation that Darwin was taken for granted by liberal theologians by the 1920s, see his *The Making of American Liberal Theology: Idealism, Realism, and Modernity, 1900–1950* (Louisville: Westminster John Knox, 2003) 9.

The Dome of Eden

The great irony of this story is that what Darwin gives, Darwin can also take back. Liberal theologians promoted Darwinism as proof of their belief in historical progress and their optimism about human nature, but Darwinian scientists responded by insisting that evolution is purposeless and void of direction or inherent meaning. Darwinism began its career in America as an ideology enabling the ascendancy of optimistic and rationalistic Protestant elite, but it is ending its career shaking the foundations of both hope and reason. As John G. West has documented in a magisterial work, the lasting impact of Darwinism in America is the dehumanization of society as experts increasingly treat humans as self-interested animals bent on their own glorification. Clarence Darrow, in the year before the Scopes trial, defended the notorious killers Leopold and Loeb on the grounds that Darwinism demonstrated that "every human being is the product of endless heredity back of him and the infinite environment around him."[26] So much for Bobby Franks, the victim, and so much for human freedom and responsibility! Of course, a whole host of intellectual movements have contributed to the decline of Protestant liberalism, and, increasingly in these fragmented times, these movements are vigorously contested, but Darwinism, for the cultural elite, is still treated as if it were untouchable. To put Darwin on trial, as Phillip Johnson has recommended, would open up too many painful issues that Scopes was supposed to have closed.[27]

A growing chorus of conservative voices is demanding a retrial, in the hope of reversing the original verdict, and there are even signs that many liberals are beginning to see their alliance with Darwin as a pact with the devil, if this alliance had not forced liberals to give up any belief in the devil. Liberals are having second thoughts about Darwin because evolutionary philosophers have taken a decided turn to the right. Evolutionary theorists like Steven Pinker call for a new era of social thought based on a tragic vision of human history and a chastened recognition of the permanence of human nature.[28] Human behavior that

26. John G. West, *Darwin Day in America: How Our Politics and Culture have Been Dehumanized in the Name of Science* (Wilmington, DE: ISI, 2007) 46.

27. More than anyone else, Phillip E. Johnson's work has opened the door to the most recent flood of criticisms of Darwin. His first book was *Darwin on Trial* (Chicago: Regnery Gateway, 1991).

28. Steven Pinker, *The Blank Slate: The Modern Denial of Human Nature* (New

has taken eons to develop, the new conservative Darwinians argue, cannot be changed by social programs or sincere exhortation. Everything from war and competition to basic gender differences are built deeper into human nature than liberal optimism could ever fathom. It is hard to know what to make of the liberal values of tolerance, equality, and mutual understanding if we are shaped, in the words of a recent book by two biological experts, by "mean genes."[29] What is the future of liberalism if Darwinians now teach us that people are basically not nice—and that we have little hope of making people better by treating them more nicely? Evolution conveys such a dark and dreary view of human nature that one is tempted to say that Darwin's theory has brought the doctrine of original sin out of retirement. We are programmed, it seems, to frustrate and foil our own best ideals of what we think we should be.

Conservative Darwinians are a helpful correction to the odd way that many liberals continue to think that Darwinism supports the optimistic and progressive aspects of secular humanism. It is doubtful, however, whether "Conservatives need Charles Darwin," as Larry Arnhart writes, as much as Darwin needs conservatives.[30] Arnhart wants conservatives to end the culture war against Darwin by recruiting him for their side. While I agree that Darwinism should lead everyone to recognize that the perfectibility of human nature is a modern myth (the return of Pelagianism, an ancient Christian heresy, to be more precise) that has been a source of great evil in the world, I am skeptical about the potential for a Darwinian conservativism. Darwinism is an equal opportunity debunker, which is something liberals could not see when they were using evolution to browbeat their enemies, the fundamentalists, throughout the twentieth century. Conservatives should not make the same mistake by returning the favor. Liberals and conservatives are opponents in their interpretation of the Bible, but evolution is the enemy of both.

York: Penguin, 2003).

29. Terry Burnham and Jay Phelan, *Mean Genes: From Sex to Money to Food: Taming Our Primal Instincts* (New York: Penguin, 2000).

30. Larry Arnhart, *Darwinian Conservativism* (Charlottesville: Imprint Academic, 2005) 1. For the best criticisms of this position, see Carson Holloway, *The Right Darwin? Evolution, Religion, and the Future of Democracy* (Dallas, TX: Spence, 2006) and John G. West, *Darwin's Conservatives: The Misguided Quest* (Seattle: Discovery Institute, 2006).

Darwinism does have moral implications, as I argued in chapter 1, but those implications are surely corrosive of the best intentions of both liberalism and conservatism. Debates about a Darwinian politics are inevitable, given Darwinism's status as a comprehensive theory of life, but also interminable, given the shifting definitions of left and right and the vagueness of Darwinism itself. What is not uncertain is Darwinism's intentions with regard to Christianity. What would have happened if Christians had turned to criticizing Darwin rather than each other? Historians sometimes play the game of imagining what history would have been like if a major event had turned out differently than it did. Making up stories about alternative worlds in which, say, Hitler won the war is not only a matter of scholarly fun. It is also a matter of looking into the past to see what might have been and thus what still could be for the future. I do not want to retry Scopes, but I do want to close this chapter with a counterfactual reflection on one of the great losers of theological history.

J. Gresham Machen (1881–1937) was one of the most insightful theologians of the twentieth century, but since much of his insight concerned the dangers of liberalism, he has ended up excluded from the canon of theologians that is taught in seminaries and universities. His most famous book, *Christianity and Liberalism* (1923), made him the intellectual leader of the conservative rebellion against the rising tide of liberalism. He does not discuss Darwin in that book, but the way he describes liberalism leaves little doubt about how he understood Darwin's influence. The chief trait of liberalism, Machen argues, is the attempt to break down the barriers between God and man. God, for liberals, is a word that refers to what is going on in the world, not outside of it. "We find ourselves in the midst of a mighty process," Machen imagines liberals thinking, "which manifests itself in the indefinitely small and in the indefinitely great—in the infinitesimal life which is revealed through the microscope and in the vast movements of the heavenly sphere."[31] Machen thought liberals began by denying the doctrine of original sin and ended by believing that historical progress here below could take the place of preaching salvation in heaven above.

---

31. J. Gresham Machen, *Christianity and Liberalism* (1923. Reprinted, Grand Rapids: Eerdmans, 2002) 63.

Re-Trying Scopes

According to Machen, liberals tend to translate supernatural claims into natural ones. If you want to think like a liberal, think social justice when you hear the word heaven and think about the human spirit when you hear the word God. In this way, Machen argued, liberals abandoned the historic truth claims of Christianity for a humanistic approach to life's questions and an aesthetic appreciation of religious symbols. Religion is an indirect way of talking about those aspects of our environment that we cannot directly understand. Machen calls this approach naturalism, and he argues that it "is not content in occupying the lower quarters of the Christian city, but pushes its way into all the higher reaches of life; it is just as much opposed to the philosophical idealism of the liberal preacher as to the Biblical doctrines that the liberal preacher has abandoned in the interests of peace."[32] In other words, Machen understood that Darwinian naturalism might begin by attacking traditional views of the Bible but it would not be satisfied until it also attacked the liberal values of tolerance, equality, and mutual understanding. Machen knew, long before Dennett admitted it, that Darwinism bites any hand that feeds it.

Actually, Machen never rejected the basic ingredients of Darwin's theory. His position was nuanced. He was not very worried about the idea that humans descend from lower life forms. Instead, he defended the Genesis account of creation because he thought miracles were central to Christian faith. The debate over miracles was intense and disruptive during Machen's lifetime. Darwin had taught liberals that God is present in nature as a guiding force that works according to the laws of science. God is the source of all that is good in the world, but God works toward the good from within nature, not without. Liberal theologians decided that God works through history in the same way. Just as nature began with mere matter and ended up with rational and self-conscious creatures, history begins with primitive societies and is moving in the direction of greater cultural forms of justice and morality. The point is that God does not contradict the natural processes of evolution or the social processes of history. God is present in nature and history, but God does not tower over them and intervene to change their course. Machen argued that this position denied God's majesty and freedom and overestimated human goodness. That is why Machen

32. Ibid., 6.

thought the Genesis account of creation was so important. If God did not create the world supernaturally, as Genesis reports, then God does not stand outside of natural and historical processes. And if God does not stand outside of nature and history, God cannot intervene into this fallen world in a miraculous fashion, in which case there is no hope for our salvation.[33]

What would American Christianity be like today if Machen's ideas had triumphed among the theological elite? What would have happened if Machen, and not William Jennings Bryan, had gone to Dayton Tennessee to debate Darrow? Speculating about this counterfactual possibility is just that, speculation, and Christians with a strong sense of providence probably should not dabble in creating alternative histories to the one history God has given us to live. Nonetheless, debating counterfactual scenarios does remind us that history is the record of human error and that God frequently works toward our good in spite of, not because of, the decisions we make. The liberal-conservative divide in Christianity at first hurt conservatives more than liberals, but in the long run it has clearly hurt liberals more than conservatives. Liberal theologians have forgotten how to fight for the principles of their faith, and their victory at Scopes was, in retrospect, the beginning of a series of capitulations to modernity that look a lot like defeat.

Bryan responded to Darrow's hard Darwinism with a soft idealism, as if good thoughts alone can stop a bully. In fact, Darrow was not only a bully to Bryan but he also defended bullies, most famously Leopold and Loeb. Bryan had nothing but disdain for Darrow's disingenuous defense of these heartless killers, but he was even more appalled by the impact Darwin (along with Nietzsche: the two were often read in conjunction in these years) could have on young minds. This was further evidence, he decided, that local communities have the right to regulate what students read and learn. Bryan, ever the political progressive, was always looking for ways to protect the young and vulnerable. He thought Darwinism was the harbinger of competitive capitalism and cultural elitism and wanted to mount a resistance from

---

33. D. G. Hart explains how liberals used evolution to bolster their view that God works through historical processes to bring about the righteous kingdom and thus God has no need of miracles in *Defending the Faith: J. Gresham Machen and the Crisis of Conservative Protestantism in Modern America* (Phillipsburg, NJ: P. & R., 1994) 103–4.

the standpoint of the marginalized and oppressed, a perspective that liberals would later come to embrace. That is why he was in Dayton. He did not think that schools should be forced to subsidize teaching that subverted the highest ideals of solidarity and compassion. This strategy let Darrow portray him as a foolish and self-righteous innocent who avoided the hard evidence of the real world of Darwinism. Bryan's position was in fact too complex for Darrow to handle, which is also why *Inherit the Wind* had to treat him as such a stereotype. The fact that the stage production of that movie is still performed all across the country is evidence of how the cultural elite remain ensnared by their prejudices and baffled by Bryan's foresight. Bryan was more worried about the moral than the biblical consequences of evolution, though morality and the authority of the Bible were closely associated in his mind. He was a defender of the common man and traditional values, traits that *Inherit the Wind* manages to turn into fodder for ridicule.

Machen would have chosen a strategy that countered Darrow at his Darwinian core. He would have met Darrow's hard Darwinism with the equally hard cross of Christ. He understood that the battle over evolution affects every aspect of Christian belief, but he was especially concerned that the liberal Protestant appropriation of evolution portrayed human nature in such a positive light that it denied the doctrine of original sin. He would have defended the traditional Christian depiction of humanity as both depraved but also uniquely chosen among all creatures to embody the image of God, and he would have warned about the consequences of taking our measure of God from nature and its bitter struggles. He would not have let evolution become a wedge issue dividing Christians, because he would have used it as a wedge issue dividing the world into those who believe in the God above and those who are left with nothing to stand on except the struggle below.

The allure of imagining a different debate at the Scopes trial is especially poignant because Bryan actually asked Machen to come to Dayton Tennessee to testify. Machen declined the invitation. As his biographer explains, "His decision not to testify at Dayton indicated that despite his commitment to historic Christianity he was still attached to the world of the university."[34] Machen wanted to be respected in the academic community, and he knew that if he sided too strongly against

---

34. Hart, *Defending the Faith*, p. 85.

The Dome of Eden

Darwin he faced expulsion from that world. He earned just enough of his sense of social status from the academy to decline an invitation that could have changed the course of Christian history—for let no one be fooled that Machen would have preserved Darrow's dignity while utterly destroying his arguments.

Ironically, Bryan lost the debate against Darrow because he was too liberal, not because he was too conservative. In fact, his most recent biographer calls him "a great Christian liberal."[35] Bryan's commitment to Christianity stemmed in large part from a sentimental understanding of morality. He was a literalist about the Bible, but even more important in his thinking was a moral literalism with regard to the ethic of love. He lived during the period that preceded the great split between those Christians who put their hope in the coming of social justice and those Christians who put their hope in the afterlife. He wanted it both ways, but his passion for political reform put him firmly on the side of those who think that love can be translated into transformative domestic and foreign policy. He was decidedly out of step with the emerging premillennialism of his evangelical brethren (the belief that the second coming will happen suddenly and after a period of social disarray), harkening back instead to the nineteenth-century postmillennial dreams of a perfect society (the idea that Christ's kingdom can be gradually achieved through the Christianization of the social order). Bryan fervently wished that all people could learn to get along with each other, and he thought the Bible told them how.

After Scopes, Bryan's fellow idealists abandoned his distinctive blend of faith and politics like wreckage on a highway to a decidedly different destination. The media began portraying conservative Christianity as a threat to American freedoms, and Bryan was depicted as the point man of fundamentalist intolerance and ignorance. The combination of theological conservativism and political progressivism that Bryan represented became the evolutionary equivalent of a malfunctioning genetic mutation, as liberals and leftists began their long march away from the people of small town America who were so devoted to this common man. Bryan's battle with evolution cost him his rightful place in history, and that battle sent conservative Christians to the cultural sidelines as they lost their leadership roles in all levels

---

35. Kazin, *Godly Hero*, 305.

of American education. Scopes turned what should have been a much needed debate into an intellectual scapegoating, but the trial's victim was not just Bryan. Scopes was an utter disaster for all Americans, even the defenders of evolution, because their theory was subsequently set aside as a sacred cow that could not be touched by theological or philosophical criticism. Darwinism became an ideology, which postponed the trial of public rational debate that would be needed to determine its ultimate standing in American society.

three

Three Rival Theories and the Problem of Natural Evil

Any good theory about a difficult topic should answer established questions that rival theories raise but cannot answer on their own. A good theory opens new perspectives on old issues by bringing disparate material together in a surprising and productive way. A good theory should also raise new questions that the alternative theories never even imagined. One way a good theory challenges alternative theories is by explaining the inadequacies of their presuppositions. Thus, before plunging into my own theory, I will summarize and analyze the presuppositions of the three principle alternatives. Since I think the strength of my theory lies in how it deals with the problem of natural evil better than these alternatives, I will first define natural evil and then, after examining these three theories, return to the problem of natural evil to show how these three rival theories come up short in dealing with this problem.

Technically speaking, natural evil is any undeserved harm experienced by any self-conscious individual not caused by a human agent. That definition, however, is deceptively simple, because this category is notoriously ambiguous and easily used in indiscriminate ways. First, it can be used to refer to things that happen in nature only to the extent that they have a direct and disastrous impact on humans, such as earthquakes or tsunamis. Earthquakes, from this perspective, are not evil in themselves but they can be the cause of evil when entire cities are destroyed and untold damage done to human lives. Second, it can be used to denote the way humans can upset the balance of nature (through pollution, for example). Third, it can be used to refer to things not caused by us in nature that seem evil regardless of their effect on us, like the extinction of entire species or the suffering of a prey being devoured by its predator. I will be using the term in the third sense, that is, to refer to the suffering of non-human animals.

Probably the best place to start in explaining natural evil is to distinguish it from the category of human evil. There are three elements to human evil: first, a perpetrator whose motivation defies the rational calculations of self-interest; second, an action that insults our sense of human dignity; and third, victims who cry out for justice. Natural evil typically does not include the first of these elements, an evil agent, but it does include the other two, disturbing actions and vulnerable victims. The victims of natural evil are generally taken to be humans, as in cases where disease, earthquakes, or wild animals take human lives; but to better distinguish natural from human evil I will focus on non-human animals, to the extent that they can suffer and are conscious of their suffering. Notice that the category of natural evil does not necessarily attribute evil to nature as a whole. It indicates, rather, events in nature that strike us with the same force of wrongness as evil caused by humans. Human evil challenges our understanding of what it means to be human, while natural evil challenges our understanding of what nature is, although, since we are a part of nature, natural evil also forces us to ponder the murky depths of the human heart.

Because there are no evil agents in natural evil, some philosophers and theologians think that it does not make sense to talk about natural evil at all. Actually, there are an increasing number of theologians willing to consider the way animals can be said to make moral decisions.[1] I am inclined to think that it is wrong to hold wild animals responsible for their behavior. Lions, for example, act out of an instinct for survival, not the desire to be cruel. Domesticated animals are another story, though when these animals are cruel, it is usually only because cruel humans have forced them to be that way. Regardless, granting that animals cannot be evil does nothing to mitigate the argument that animals can be the victims of evil. My position is that just because a lion is not

---

1. The best statement of this position can be found in a recent essay by Celia Deane-Drummond, drawing on the work of Marc Bekoff, "Shadow Sophia in Christological Perspective: The Evolution of Sin and the Redemption of Nature," *Theology and Science* 6 (2008) 13–32. She argues that if some scientists think animals exhibit latent virtues, then they also must have latent vices. She then takes this position one step further by arguing that tendencies toward good and ill are actual forms of morality relative to the world that animals occupy.

intentionally cruel when it eats its prey does not mean that the lamb does not suffer inordinately when the lion eats it. Essential to my position is the contention that the higher animals (mammals at least) have a level of self-awareness that makes them susceptible to moments of suffering and anguish that is not totally dissimilar to what we humans are able to experience. Some skeptics will object that what appears to be evil in nature is only an anthropomorphic misinterpretation wherein we project our own feelings of moral badness onto the natural world. The problem with this objection to natural evil is that it takes a single truth—that we often project human traits and feelings onto the animal world—and expands it to the point where animals as individuals with desires and needs quite like our own disappear.

The claim that animals can and do suffer needs to be carefully qualified if it is to be taken seriously outside of the animal welfare and animal rights communities. Animals do not worry about the future, mourn the past, or have anxiety about the present in the exact same way that humans do, so animal suffering is not equivalent in degree or, perhaps, even in kind to human suffering. It is also true that we can overreact to animal suffering, imagining it to be worse than it is. When wild dogs disembowel their prey, their victims undergo a severe state of shock that must lessen their suffering. Moreover, carnivores often attack sick prey, thus bringing a swift end to an animal that otherwise might have suffered an even worse death of slow starvation and painful disease. It is wrong to say that the life of most animals defies the Christian witness of a God who loves creation, but if even some animals lead such lives, what are we to say about God's love for the world? I think it is a fairly incontrovertible claim that animals can suffer in ways that make us cringe and motivate us, when we are able, to intervene to alleviate their suffering. If evil is a level of anguish that prompts us to think that we should do whatever we can to make it stop or go away, then animals clearly can be subjected to evil just like humans.

Just as theologians and philosophers debate the intelligibility of attributing moral agency to animals, they also debate the intelligibility of attributing evil to nature in as a whole. After all, evil is something that seems out of the ordinary to us, a level of badness that strikes us as horrendous or terrifying, and nature is nothing if not natural. What happens in nature does so according to the impersonal laws discovered by science. Nature is just the way things are, so it cannot be good or bad. Some theologians have been quick to employ this position—that "nature is just the way things are"—to do battle with the idea that God should have made a world quite different from the one we occupy. They argue that if God wanted rational creatures that are free to obey or disobey the divine plan, then God was limited in the kind of world God could have created. An even stronger version of this argument is that there are metaphysical as well as scientific constraints to the way God could have created any world.

The idea that our world is the only kind of world God could have created suggests that God should not be blamed for any evil we find in it. A number of theologians have defended this position. Thus Peter van Inwagen argues that Christians should be skeptical about their ability to imagine alternative worlds where high-level sentient creatures exist without physical suffering. The universe as we know it produced us only through the process of evolution, and it is hard to imagine how evolution could take place without a great deal of suffering. "One important thing that is known about the evolution of the universe into its present state is that it has been a very tightly structured process," he writes. "Only in a universe very much like ours could intelligent life, or indeed life of any sort, develop by the operation of the laws of nature, unsupplemented by miracles. And the natural evolution of higher sentient life in a universe like ours essentially involves suffering, or there is every reason to believe it does."[2] Likewise Christopher Southgate argues that much of human evil is explainable by reference to our free will but natural evil is intrinsic to nature and thus not really evil at all. As Southgate writes, "I hold that the sort of universe we have, in which complexity emerges in a process governed by thermodynamic necessity and Darwinian natural selection, and therefore by death, pain, predation, and self-assertion, is the only sort of universe that could give rise to the range, beauty, complexity, and diversity of creatures the Earth has produced."[3] He calls this the "only way" argument. Michael Corey

---

2. Peter van Inwagen, *The Problem of Evil* (New York: Oxford University Press, 2006) 119. He writes, "I am convinced that the teaching of the Bible is that the natural world is and always has been, apart from the effects that fallen human beings have had on it, just as God made it" (132).

3. Christopher Southgate, *The Groaning of Creation: God, Evolution, and the Problem of Evil* (Louisville: Westminster John Knox Press, 2008) 29.

adds a new twist to the "only way" position by speculating that God created the world through evolution in order to challenge us intellectually and spiritually. "For by making it seem as though a mindless natural process was ultimately responsible for creating the biosphere, evolution furthers God's purpose in the world by substantially increasing the epistemic distance between Himself and humanity." Evolution keeps the question of our origin ambiguous, forcing us to take the leap of faith. "Unfortunately," Corey admits, "this requires the suffering of billions of innocent creatures in order to be effective, because it is this very suffering that makes evolution appear to be a viable alternative to the doctrine of creation."[4] Evidently animals suffer so that we might wonder why they suffer and thus be tempted by God into thinking that there might be good reasons against believing in him.

Theologians who argue that this world is the only world that God could have created run the risk, in their attempt to justify God's relationship to natural evil, of portraying the world as thoroughly and necessarily evil. That is, if there is no possible world that God could have created that would have been without evil, then the very existence of matter is thoroughly saturated in and inseparable from evil. If evil is built into nature, however, it is God who put it there. Actually, the charge that nature is evil comes up most frequently in discussions of entropy, the second law of thermodynamics, which demonstrates how disorder inevitably increases in the universe. If disorder is built into nature, then is not nature our enemy, rather than our friend? The economist Jeremy Rifkin thinks so. He portrays the law of entropy as a supremely irreversible threat to our survival. "We are so used to thinking of biological evolution in terms of progress. Now we find that each higher species in the evolutionary chain transforms greater amounts of energy from a usable to unusable state. . . . The higher the species in the chain, the greater the energy flow-through and the greater the disorder created in the overall environment."[5] No theologian has explored the connection between entropy and evil more thoroughly and carefully than Robert John Russell, founder and director of the Center for

4. Michael A. Corey, *Evolution and the Problem of Natural Evil* (Lanham, MD: University Press of America, 2000) 156.

5. Jeremy Rifkin, *Entropy* (New York: Bantam, 1981) 55. Also see Quentin Smith, "An Atheological Argument from Evil Natural Laws," International *Journal for Philosophy of Religion* 29 (1991) 159-74.

Three Rival Theories and the Problem of Natural Evil

Theology and the Natural Sciences at the Graduate Theological Union in Berkeley, California. After drawing several correlations between the two, he concludes that entropy is one of the physical preconditions of evil. "Although the characteristics of entropy and evil do not give direct support to one another, if evil is real in nature, entropy is what one would expect to find at the level of physical processes."[6] Russell's conclusion about entropy is actually similar to my position on evolution: evolution is not evil, but if evil is real in nature, then evolution is what one would expect to find in biological processes.

The temptation to equate evolution with evil is understandable because Darwinian descriptions of nature echo the Christian account of the fall. When Darwinians talk of selfish genes, it is hard not to think of original sin. Nonetheless, equating nature with evil runs counter to the Christian tradition, most notably the claim found in Genesis that nature is good. If nature were evil, then we could not trust our five senses let alone any scientific discoveries, and we could not even trust our own bodies, which Genesis tells us were made from the "dust of the ground" (Gen 2:7). Moreover, what reason would we have to intervene and prevent animal suffering or clean up ecosystems after natural disasters? What "good" would we be doing if there was nothing good to be saved?

Historically speaking, the groups that have equated nature and evil have always been treated as heretics by orthodox Christians. These groups, like the Manicheans and the Cathars, have a dualistic metaphysics, which means that they divide the world into spiritual and material substances and attribute matter to the creation of Satan. The Christian teaching that the material world is a gift to us is a better interpretation of the way most people experience nature. It is hard, if not impossible, to condemn nature because we owe whatever goods we possess to its support and sustenance. As long as we value ourselves, we are rationally compelled to acknowledge the goodness of nature at least to the extent that nature benefits us. That seems like an uncontroversial point. After all, poets, environmentalists, and people out taking a walk in the woods praise nature all the time. Notice, however, that if it makes sense to

---

6. Robert John Russell, "Entropy and Evil," *Zygon* 19 (1984) 465. Also see P. R. Masani, "The Thermodynamic and Phylogenetic Foundations of Human Wickedness," *Zygon* 20 (1985) 283–320.

praise nature, it should not be absurd to find some aspects of nature that do not live up to that praise. Commending nature and judging parts of nature to be evil are complementary speech acts. Perhaps this is just another way of saying that we can never be neutral with regard to nature. That is the conclusion that the philosopher Mary Midgley reaches in an important essay on this topic. "There is no way in which we humans can resolve the difficulty of finding an appropriate emotional attitude to the cosmos that we live in by simply refusing to have any such emotional attitude. We cannot take up a relation to the entire world around us which is purely cognitive . . . because we ourselves are part of it."[7] If we have a moral relationship to ourselves we will have one to nature as well.

To do justice to natural evil from a Christian perspective, an increasing number of theologians have tried to reinterpret nature's violence in terms of the Christian notion of sacrifice.[8] These theologians argue that the category of sacrifice is the key to understanding the universal features of religion as well as the moral character of the natural world. Just as all ancient religions practiced sacrifice in one form another, these theologians argue, nature itself is "cruciform," that is, it takes the form of sacrifice. Christianity demonstrates the meaning of sacrifice by revealing how God draws life out of suffering and hopelessness. The death and resurrection of Jesus Christ, we could say, is repeated throughout the drama of evolution, in the way that one generation has to give way to the next and sometimes entire species must be sacrificed to another. Nature thus speaks to us in the form of a parable about the redemptive power of sacrifice. Whether through entropy or evolution, nature is analogous to the incarnation, in that it shows how sacrifice is not just the meaning of the life of Jesus but also the key to understanding the entire cosmos. The problem with this position is that it seems to endorse or rationalize suffering by equating it with the redemptive action of Christ on the cross. Suffering and death in evolution are necessary for the development of new species, but addressing that suffering with the language of sacrifice makes it look noble and necessary.

7. Mary Midgley, "Criticizing the Cosmos," in *Is Nature Ever Evil? Religion, Science and Value*, ed. Willem B. Drees (New York: Routledge, 2003) 23.

8. See, for example, Holmes Rolston, "Kenosis and Nature," in *The Work of Love: Creation as Kenosis*, ed. John Polkinghorne (Grand Rapids: Eerdmans, 2001) and John F. Haught, *God After Darwin: A Theology of Evolution* (Boulder, CO: Westview, 2008).

Three Rival Theories and the Problem of Natural Evil

The word that theologians need to avoid in discussing natural evil is "necessary." Reinhold Niebuhr's famous phrase that summed up the Christian tradition on sin—that evil is inevitable but not necessary—should be applied to natural evil as well.[9] Suffering is intrinsic to evolution, but if suffering is necessary then God must have intended it, which suggests that either God is evil or evil is really good. Robert John Russell has advanced the most creative argument against the necessity of suffering in evolution. The new creation promised by the Bible and instantiated by the resurrection of Jesus Christ, he says, demonstrates that natural evil cannot be necessary for life. Russell calls the resurrection of Jesus "the first instantiation of a new law of nature."[10] Darwinism is the old law that will not just pass away but be replaced by the new law of grace. When Christ rules creation, creation will still have rules, but they will most assuredly not be the rules of random changes and ceaseless strife.

Throughout this book I will use *natural evil* to refer to aspects of nature such as plague, predation, and parasitism (the three P's!) that have a significantly deleterious impact on non-human animals. (It would probably be more accurate to speak of *evolutionary evil*, but that severs the modern discussion of biology and evil from the long tradition of speaking about natural evil. Continuity in terminology is important because Darwinism refocuses the problem of evil but does not create it from scratch.) Used in this way, the concept of natural evil presupposes the capacity of some non-human animals to experience not just pain but suffering, which can be defined as an experience of intense pain that is disproportionate to any benefit or gain that we might attribute to the animal. In other words, natural evil is not just the experience of pain or death, for those are necessities of life, given that all biological processes involve the physical limitations of disruption and decay that eventually bring those processes to an end. What is unavoidable might be tragic, but it is not ordinarily considered evil, just as that which is necessary to advance an agent's interests might be regrettable, but is not ordinarily considered evil. Not all animal death is lamentable, since many animals

---

9. Reinhold Niebuhr, *The Nature and Destiny of Man*, vol. 1: *Human Nature* (New York: Scribner's, 1941).

10. Robert John Russell, "Natural Theodicy in an Evolutionary Context: The Need for an Eschatology of New Creation," in *The Task of Theology Today*, ed. David Neville and Bruce Barber (Hindmarsh, Australia: ATF, 2005) 121–52.

The Dome of Eden

have little or no awareness of themselves as distinct individuals with their own interests and desires. Nonetheless, if even a fraction of animal death is lamentable, then that is a problem for any thinking human being, since it raises the question of our responsibility toward animals and our attitude toward nature in general.

Contrary to some theories of evil, then, I hold that the problem of evil is a problem for everyone, atheist and theist alike. Indeed, Darwin himself was driven to the idea of evolution precisely because he took this problem so seriously. "I cannot persuade myself," he wrote in a letter to the American naturalist Asa Gray, "that a beneficent and omnipotent God would have designedly created the Ichneumonidae with the express intention of their feeding within the living bodies of caterpillars."[11] He was referring to a wasp that lays its eggs in a caterpillar, which she paralyzes but does not kill, so that her larva can have fresh meat when they hatch. Macabre details like this led Darwin to look for natural laws, not benevolent intelligence, as the source of nature's designs. As far as I know, scientists to this day do not know whether the caterpillar is merely immobilized or anesthetized, so we do not know if the caterpillar feels any pain as it is eaten alive. If Darwin were consistent in trying to imagine what God would or would not do in creating nature, he would have to praise God for designing a painless death, rather than blame God for this little bit of wanton cruelty. Darwin, however, was not interested in the specificities of theological argument. He was responding to pain and suffering in nature in a way that we all share, even atheists. Nonetheless, I admit that natural evil is an especially difficult problem for those who believe in a perfectly loving God, since love is nothing if it is not the strong desire to ameliorate the suffering of the loved one.

Animal suffering that is evil is, to use a category that is frequently employed in these discussions, *excessive*.[12] It is excessive both in terms of its intensity and its disutility. Some pain that animals experience is not useful, but if it is trivial we would not call that evil. Likewise, pain that is beneficial for an animal can be intense, but if it advances an animal's interests, we do not call it evil. Suffering that is excessive goes be-

---

11. Quoted in Southgate, *Groaning of Creation*, 10.

12. For an earlier attempt to define excessive or gratuitous suffering, see William Hasker, "The Necessity of Gratuitous Evil," *Faith and Philosophy* 9 (1992) 23-44.

yond both what is necessary and what is beneficial. Suffering that is not excessive is natural, which is another way of saying that it is not evil. We judge something in nature to be evil, then, when we think that natural processes have departed from their regular patterns to wreak havoc on living creatures that are dependent on those processes.

But how do we know when animal suffering is excessive? From the animal's point of view, any pain is probably too much pain, but I am using *excessive* in a more specific sense than that. When a dog gets bitten by a flea, or when we squash the flea, or when we put a flea collar on our dog to get rid of the fleas, there is, few would doubt, some experience of pain going on. However, few would suggest that this situation is evidence of natural evil. Of course, specifying when pain becomes excessive to the point of causing suffering is an impossible endeavor, but isn't that the nature of suffering? When someone is suffering, they experience an intensity of discomfort that defies rational measurement. That this is a subjective experience that is hard to objectify is an essential part of the suffering. If suffering becomes sufficiently intense, it renders the sufferer mute, and any degree of suffering is hard to communicate in exact detail or careful terms. Suffering puts the sufferer beyond the community of the non-sufferers, which is why suffering is a problem in the first place.[13]

We can never define excessive suffering in any precise or detailed way, but there are ways to refine and clarify the concept of natural evil. It is indicated, I want to suggest, when there are three factors present in our response to animal suffering. First, natural evil, as with evil in human affairs, is indicated by the uneasiness of our response. When we see animals suffering in grave ways, we respond with a level of sympathy, discomfort, and even disgust that is not completely incomparable to how we respond to signs of evil in human affairs. Our response tells us that something is fundamentally wrong. We are horrified and indignant.

Second, natural evil is indicated when we intuitively sense that we, or someone, should try to set things right. Evil of any kind calls forth not only moral judgment but also an obligation to intervene. Evil

---

13. For a nuanced discussion of suffering that complements my own, see Wesley J. Wildman, "The Use and Meaning of the Word 'Suffering' in Relation to Nature," in *Physics and Cosmology: Scientific Perspectives on the Problem of Natural Evil*, ed. Nancey Murphy et al. (Notre Dame: University of Notre Dame Press, 2007) 53–66.

violates our sense of justice and demands rectification. This does not mean that we *can* intervene to stop evil. Evil, by its very nature, is a level of harm that we cannot control. Frequently, in the face of evil, we are forced to cry out for someone, anyone at all, to intervene, because the individuals who witness evil are often rendered mute or impotent by its immensity. This is true of natural evil as well. Changing the course of events in nature can be even harder—and it is frequently impossible—compared to taking responsibility for evil situations in human affairs. Nonetheless, if there is such a thing as natural evil, it too should lead us to wish that we, or someone, could try to set things right. Evil, after all, is the sense that something is not as it should be, which implies that things could and should be otherwise.

Third, natural evil is indicated when we experience a serious violation of what we consider to be of ultimate importance in life. For people of faith, that means their understanding of God, because God is the source of all that is good and thus the measure of what falls short of the good. Indeed, many people of faith think that only God can rectify or redeem evil, so that the experience of impotence in the face of evil becomes, paradoxically, an experience at the same time of God's power and providence. Of course, how people imagine God varies significantly, and some people do not believe in God at all, but notice that in my definition, it is not necessary to believe in God to ponder natural evil. It is only necessary to have a sense that one's highest ideals are being violated in a way that calls for outrage and judgment. It might be something as simple as the sacredness of life or something more complex like our identification with all living beings, but natural evil is something we cannot stand by and observe objectively and dispassionately. We are forced to respond because the evil is not only striking a lowly victim but also challenging our highest values. Theism makes the problem of natural evil both worse (by highlighting its contrast to a God of love) and better (by extending the hope of redemption and reconciliation to the natural world), but even an atheist has to ponder what kind of moral values can survive a world that is immersed from the ground up in events of such a troubling caliber.

Theistic Evolution

Perhaps the simplest and most popular way to deal with the conflict between evolution and Genesis is the model known as *theistic evolution* (hereafter TE). Actually, there is a simple and a more complex version of this model. I will call the simple version the *addition model* and the more complex version the *dimension model*. The addition model is easy to explain and seldom developed in detail by theologians or philosophers, because it makes no demands on either Christians or Darwinians. This position accepts everything that biology says about evolution as a fact. It adds to these biological facts the idea that evolution is a process that is under God's ultimate control. The addition model, as its name suggests, is an attempt to add theism to evolution without subtracting anything from evolutionary theory. Sometimes theologians will refer to this model as an attempt to "baptize" evolution, but that is a misleading analogy. When someone is baptized, they are asked to change their life by renouncing their old loyalties and accepting a new master. One might say that addition TE accepts two masters, but it is probably more accurate to say that it accepts evolution as the master and theology as the servant, because evolution is allowed to establish the rules and limits of God's engagement with the world.

Adding two numbers, it hardly needs to be pointed out, keeps them distinct even as they are combined, and that is the strength of the addition model. Many Christians sense almost intuitively that evolution is incompatible with the biblical portrait of God, and yet they might not want to challenge Darwin's theory for a variety of reasons. The addition model lets these Christians conceive of evolution as an instrument that God employs that does not reflect anything about God's nature. Evolution and Christianity add up to a worldview, but the sum is not greater than, nor does it modify, the parts. To better understand this position, change metaphors and think of evolution as a tool that God uses only when wearing protective gloves or as a creature that God handles with a bit of squeamishness. Addition TE lets Christians admit that evolution is not, on its surface, a very graceful or loving way to bring species into existence, so the model encourages Christians to try to separate God's plan for the world from the means by which he implements that plan. God can thus be shielded from the consequences of evolution. If evolution is simply a tool, then God does not get his hands dirty when he finesses the survival of the fittest. The problem with this view is not the distinction between the means and the end of creation, which is legitimate if somewhat abstract. The problem is that the means of God's creative act must reflect the end, if God is to be thought of as a coherent agent. In other words, if God designed evolution, then he must endorse it. If it is his tool, then it must fit his hands—if it is his creature, then it must do his bidding—and thus it must say something about what he is.

Christians who take the addition TE position point out that God can bring good out of every bad deed, and everything is ultimately under his authority. Both halves of that proposition are true, but they are untrue when they are combined together to legitimate evolution. God can bring good out of every bad deed, but God does not do bad things in order to bring out the good. Everything is under God's ultimate authority, but not everything works the way God initially planned. God permits or tolerates evil, for reasons we cannot fully comprehend. God has appointed creatures, and not just humans, with freedom, and God has decided to let the consequences of that appointment run their course. One of those consequences is human sin, which is so evident wherever you look that it hardly needs elaborating. Another is the struggle for life among non-human animals, which is a necessary by-product, according to TE, of the way God designed the universe.

The methodological weakness of this model needs to be spelled out more carefully. Addition TE relies on an absolute separation between facts and values that has become suspect in the philosophy of science as well as in hermeneutics (the study of any act of interpretation). Addition TE accepts evolution as a fact, but it does not accept the values that are associated with evolution. This can be confusing, because holders of this position typically sound like they accept all of evolution, but they don't. Instead, they imply that the facts of evolution can be separated from the theoretical and moral considerations of randomness and purposelessness. In other words, addition TE assumes that people can agree about facts without agreeing about what those facts mean. Thus, Darwinians think the facts point to randomness while Christians think the facts point to God's design, but those disagreements are merely a matter of different interpretations of the

Three Rival Theories and the Problem of Natural Evil

same set of facts. The problem with this position is that Darwinism is not about facts. In fact, Darwinism has precious few facts it can appeal to for empirical support of its theoretical assumptions. Darwinism is a thoroughly interpretive enterprise. Besides, facts in general are never just facts. We call something a fact when it fits in with a larger scheme of meaning. Something is a fact when it does not require us to adjust our values in order to acknowledge it. Facts and values, then, are more closely connected than addition TE allows.

The addition model tends to treat evolution and creation as two non-competing and incommensurable worldviews. Stephen Jay Gould formulated the classic expression of this position with his NOMA principle, which stands for "nonoverlapping magisteria."[14] The idea that biology and religion just represent two incomparable bodies of thought—they talk about different things in different ways—is meant to appeal to everyone but actually appeals to very few. The strength of dimension TE is precisely its insistence that science and religion cannot and do not contradict each other. If truth is one, as all monotheists believe, then science and religion must be compatible. More than being merely compatible, they must show a potential for convergence as they both seek to explore the ultimate dimensions of meaning.

Dimension TE grants evolutionary theory enormous credence but tries to locate religious meaning not in addition to it but as a deeper dimension of it. No thinker has been more closely associated with TE than Pierre Teilhard de Chardin (1881–1951), and he is the classic example of what I am calling dimension TE. A mystic, scientist, philosopher, and Jesuit, Teilhard developed a theological cosmology that placed evolution in the center of both biological and spiritual development. Controversial during his lifetime, he was the subject of a scholarly explosion of interest in the fifties and sixties, and continues to draw interest to this day. Prone to exuberant speculation about all things religious and scientific, Teilhard thought that evolution was the direct work of God in moving creation to the point where humanity and divinity can intersect in Jesus Christ. Enthusiastically, he laid down a new law of religious life, what he called the "imperative literally to love evolution." The implications of this law more than the law itself

---

14. Stephen Jay Gould, *Leonardo's Mountain of Clams and the Diet of Worms* (New York: Harmony, 1998) 269–83.

got him into trouble with the Catholic hierarchy. If God is the source of evolution, then God must be the source of evil, a conclusion Teilhard did not hesitate to embrace. "For evil appears inevitably with the first atom of being which creation releases into existence."[15] Original sin is so original that it begins with God's creation of the first bit of matter.

Although the Catholic Church condemned Teilhard's view of sin, the Church's official position on evolution as such has often been associated with theistic evolution. This is a serious misreading of Catholic teaching, and so a slight detour in this discussion is warranted. The magisterium did not take a formal teaching on Darwinism until Pope Pius XII issued *Humani Generis* in 1950. Pope Pius XII drew the line at the human soul, which is created directly and without mediation by God, and left open the question of the evolution of the human body from lower species. That position was left undisturbed until Pope John Paul II addressed the Pontifical Academy of Sciences on October 22, 1996. In that speech, he admitted, without mentioning Darwin by name, that "new findings lead us toward the recognition of evolution as more than a hypothesis." The media reported this comment as if the Pope was embracing Darwinism in a complete turnaround, but the story is far more complex than that. Not only had the Church not completely rejected evolution, the Pope was not completely accepting it either. In this address, the Pope did not say that evolution could not be criticized, and he did not identify evolution with God's creation of the world. In fact, he went on to say that, "Theories of evolution which, because of the philosophies which inspire them, regard the spirit either as emerging from the forces of living matter, or as a simple epiphenomenon of that matter, are incompatible with the truth about man."[16] The plural—"theories of evolution"—was intentional, as the Pope went on to say that "we should speak of *several* theories of evolution," opening the door to critiques of Darwin's particular theory. Pope John Paul II also left

---

15. Pierre Teilhard de Chardin, *Christianity and Evolution*, trans. René Hague (New York: Harcourt Brace & Company, 1969) 184 and 33. Of contemporary theorists, John F. Haught uses the metaphor of depth to talk about evolution and creation; I discuss his work in ch. 8.

16. Online: http://www.ewtn.com/library/PAPALDOC/JP961022.HTM. For a good survey of Catholic teaching about evolution, see George Sim Johnston, *Did Darwin Get It Right? Catholics and the Theory of Evolution* (Huntington, IN: Our Sunday Visitor, 1998), chs. 8–9.

open the question whether evolution could be finally and definitively separated from philosophical materialism.

John Paul II's successor, Pope Benedict XVI, weighed in on this issue when he was a Cardinal, and he has also been identified, quite unfairly, with TE. His comment that has been most quoted is, "We cannot say: creation *or* evolution, inasmuch as these two things respond to two different realities." These two ways of looking at the world must be complementary, he insists. But what is not often quoted is the remainder of his discussion. "But we must have the audacity," he argues, "to say that the great projects of the living creation are not the products of chance and error. Nor are they the products of a selective process to which divine predicates can be attributed in illogical, unscientific, and even mythic fashion."[17] So Pope Benedict XVI rejects the idea that chance is a cause of life, and he rejects the idea that theology can simply be added to evolution. That is what he means when he says that divine predicates cannot be attributed to evolution. What evolution does and who God is need to be kept separate. Pope Benedict XVI ends his discussion by insisting that living creatures point to reason and design as their source and origin.

Confusion and debate about what the Catholic Church teaches about evolution was ignited again when Christoph Cardinal Schönborn, archbishop of Vienna and general editor of *The Catechism of the Catholic Church*, tried to correct the impression that still lingered that the Catholic Church has no problem with Darwinism.[18] In an opinion

---

17. Pope Benedict XVI (Joseph Ratzinger), *"In the Beginning . . ." A Catholic Understanding of the Story of Creation and Fall* (Grand Rapids: Eerdmans, 1995) 50 and 56. Admittedly, Pope Benedict XVI can talk like a theistic evolutionist at times, as in a 1968 radio address: "The alternative: materialism or a spiritually defined world view, chance or meaning, is presented to us today in the form of the question of whether one regards spirit and life in its ascending forms as an incidental mold on the surface of the material world (that is, of the category of existing things that do not understand themselves), or whether one regards spirit as the goal of the process and, conversely, matter as the prehistory of spirit." Quoted in Christoph Cardinal Schönborn, ed., *Creation and Evolution: A Conference with Pope Benedict XVI in Castel Gandolfo*, trans. Michael J. Miller (San Francisco: Ignatius, 2007) 14.

18. *First Things* published several follow up essays by Cardinal Schönborn as well as several critical responses from Stephen M. Barr. For their exchange, see http://www.firstthings.com. Cardinal Schönborn expanded his remarks into a book, *Chance or Purpose? Creation, Evolution and a Rational Faith*, trans. Henry Taylor (San Francisco: Ignatius, 2007).

The Dome of Eden

piece for the *New York Times* on July 7, he wrote an impassioned rejection of Darwinism that surprised those Catholic theologians who want the Church to co-exist peacefully with evolution in a kind of non-aggression pact. More than his critics, Cardinal Schönborn takes seriously Darwinism's claim to offer a comprehensive account of the origin of life by means of randomness and struggle. On such a foundation, the Cardinal argues, the doctrine of providence cannot be built. Cardinal Schönborn argues that Darwinism was at its inception inseparable from a metaphysical materialism, so theologians should appropriate only the genuinely scientific, and not metaphysical, aspects of Darwin's theory. Cardinal Schönborn locates the space for this retrieval in neither science nor theology but in natural philosophy. The language of design is appropriate, he suggests, for a philosophical mediation of science and theology. He is thus reluctant to embrace all the ambitions of the intelligent design movement, which wants to reconstruct Darwinism within science.

Cardinal Schönborn's hope that natural philosophy can do the work of saving evolutionary theory from Darwinism when theology and intelligenct design have failed might be idealistic, but it represents Catholicism's commitment to a full, and fully philosophical, account of the truth. At some level, and in some way, science and religion must be complementary, because truth it one. This is a fundamental insight and an axiom for all theological responses to Darwinism, but the way in which it is typically implemented by dimension TE is fundamentally flawed. If Christian truths abide in a deep dimension within evolution, then why can only Christians discern that dimension? That is a question for epistemology, but TE raises even more troubling questions for theology. Viewing creation through the prism of evolution will inevitably subject Christian doctrine to the distortions of evolutionary theory.

The theological problems of TE can be discerned in a representative work of dimension TE by Jerry Korsmeyer, who is both a theologian and a physicist. Korsmeyer is a follower of process philosophy, which argues that God takes risks in the world by establishing future aims and goals for all creatures rather than providing a plan that he expects everyone to follow. The God of process philosophy is limited and vulnerable in his relationship to the world. This God works through persuasion rather than intervention and is thus well suited for the mechanisms of evolution. As Korsmeyer writes, "It is as though divinity labored to persuade, to lure creatures forward, creatures who sometimes responded to the invitation and sometimes did not." The 99 percent of all species that have ever lived and are now extinct, including, of course, the dinosaurs, evidently did not respond to God as they should have. God, however, cannot be blamed for these dead ends along evolution's path. "Evolution has demonstrated how God works in the world. Divinity has worked slow and well." Evolution has created us, Korsmeyer implies, so how could it be such a bad thing? We are not only the end result of evolution but also the beginning of a new stage, where we can work with evolution to shape the future and thus become "co-creators of values revealed and discovered."[19] We can become like God in this world by assuming divine power in responsible ways.

There are many disturbing aspects of this position, but perhaps the most worrisome is its treatment of natural evil. Dimension TE, as Korsmeyer makes clear, accepts the law of survival of the fittest as reflective of the will of God. Why would God work against evolution if evolution is how God works? In fact, God does no such thing, because the evolutionary process is the means by which God brings forth creative organisms that can choose to cooperate with the divine will. In the process view, God leads most species into the pitiless dead end of extinction (most species that have ever lived are extinct, so that evolution is extinction-driven) in order to give other species the opportunity to develop new skills and capacities. Christianity teaches that God exercises forbearance toward the glut of suffering in the animal kingdom, but there is a difference between forbearance and entrapment.

Process theologians make up for this picture of God by explaining that God feels the pain of those creatures that must be sacrificed for a great good. Moreover, even when God wants to persuade biological processes to follow a better course, his power is limited. Process philosophers believe that God is not omniscient and omnipotent. "God can't persuade a cancer cell from establishing itself and growing in a critical site in a human body, because such response is not possible for such

---

19. Jeffrey D. Korsmeyer, *Evolution and Eden: Balancing Original Sin and Contemporary Science* (New York: Paulist, 1998) 84, 86, and 86. For a similar development of theistic evolution, see Ted Peters and Martinez Hewlett, *Evolution from Creation to New Creation* (Nashville: Abingdon, 2003) ch. 7.

a cell."[20] God, evidently, has very limited powers of persuasion. This begs the question of how God could have had enough power to guide evolution in the first place, beginning with the development of the first cell, if God cannot even impede the progress of rebellious cancer cells. It is as if God created evolution only to find that evolution got out of control, leading to consequences that God had not anticipated. If God guides evolution, and organisms evolve only because they are pitted against each other in a struggle for resources that results in a variety of biological developments only some of which are successful, then isn't God responsible for the bad as well as the good that comes out of it?

I will return to the problem of natural evil at the end of this chapter, but for now, its consequences for dimension TE should be clear. By neglecting to distinguish between creativity and destructiveness in nature, dimension TE legitimates the cruelty of nature, which would include everything from cancer to predatory animals. Dimension TE thus credits God with countless instances of gruesome and gratuitous cruelty. This God might be the God of philosophy, but it is not the God of the Bible. Such a God would be the author of the most extreme winner-takes-all game ever devised. Not even the mercenary executives of a network reality TV program could invent a system like this, which feeds off of itself in a frenzy of buzzing, purposeless aggression. The root problem here is that TE does not recognize any role for Satan in the world. The God of TE is the source of both life-affirming growth and death-dealing corruption. God is both good and evil, which makes God unrecognizable according to life and teachings of Jesus.

Intelligent Design

The second model that is an alternative to my own is intelligent design (hereafter ID). ID is a growing scholarly movement that uses mathematical models to demonstrate that certain forms of organization, called specified or irreducible complexity, could not have come about by chance. Led by Phillip Johnson, Michael Behe, William A. Dembski, and Stephen Meyer, ID is actually one of the oldest ways of looking at the universe, even though it is articulated by the very latest theories of probability. Ancient Greek and Roman philosophers argued incessantly

---

20. Korsmeyer, *Evolution and Eden*, 107.

about the ultimate source of natural order. There were atomists, such as Democritus and Epicurus, who speculated about the creative possibilities of infinite space and eternal matter, but their influence in the West was eclipsed by Plato, who defended, particularly in the *Timaeus*, the idea that the world shows evidence of divine creation, and Aristotle, who revised Plato's position with a more "restrained teleology."[21] Beginning with the Enlightenment, these philosophical puzzles became once more the subject of great intellectual fascination, with long running debates about natural order and its relation to God. Darwin should be seen as the last, rather than the first, great challenger of the philosophical arguments for creation, or, as Keith Thomson puts it, Darwin was "the beginning of the end" of teleological interpretations of nature.[22] Darwin gave everyone the rudiments of a conceptual framework for understanding how the universe, with all of its complexity, could be the product of a combination of chance events. Prior to Darwin, one could almost say that ID was the commonsense view of nature (in the sense of universal as well as prima facie reasonable). After Darwin, the design framework continued to express the commonsense view of nature, but even professional theologians and religious studies programs ceased teaching the arguments of natural theology. Perhaps one reason that supporters of design arguments want to teach it as a science is the fact that natural theology has no other home in the secularized world of higher education.

The biggest complaint about ID is that it does not play by the rules of science, but ID theorists insist they are methodological minimalists, inferring the action of an intelligent designer only when the evidence fits a predetermined set of probability standards. Indeed, as easy as ID is to conceptualize in general, its mathematical details quickly become extremely difficult. Rather than arguing against it on its own ground, however, the response of the scientific community has been rancorous and vitriolic. As Dembski has lamented, most scientists have "adopted a *zero-concession policy* toward intelligent design."[23] Unsympathetic

21. David Sedley, *Creationism and its Critics in Antiquity* (Berkeley: University of California Press, 2007) 168.

22. Keith Thomson, *Before Darwin: Reconciling God and Nature* (New Haven: Yale University Press, 2005) ch. 13.

23. William A. Dembski, "Dealing with the Backlash against Intelligent Design," in *Darwin's Nemesis: Phillip Johnson and the Intelligent Design Movement*, ed. Dembski

scientists frequently try to silence ID with an overwhelming barrage of rhetoric rather than with argument and analysis. One of their standard rhetorical moves is to challenge the reputation and backgrounds of the ID defenders. They cast aspersions on the credibility of the ID community because it is full of devout Christians. Critics also claim that ID is not sufficiently scientific because they do not publish in peer-reviewed journals. ID supporters respond by pointing out that anyone who has worked in higher education knows how conformist scholars can be.[24] Besides, the argument about peer review is circular. If reputable scientific journals refuse to even consider ID papers because they assume that ID is not scientific, then the fact that ID papers are not accepted by reputable scientific journals cannot count as an argument against ID.

The idea that ID is tainted due to the religious beliefs of its defenders amounts to little more than an attack on the motives of the ID defenders, rather than a criticism of the ID arguments, and such attacks are usually not tolerated in the academy. Even if it were true that ID theorists were motivated by religious conviction, that would not diminish the rational force of their arguments. Even if it could be shown that the motivation in this case warped the reasoning, why not just show how the reasoning is warped, rather than worry about the source of the motivation? Secular liberals make similar (and similarly flawed) arguments about keeping religiously motivated policies out of the political arena. If facts are permitted to interfere with these charges, it is interesting that nearly all of the well known ID theorists came to their conclusions as a result of scrutinizing Darwinian imponderables, not from following a theological line of argument. Behe, for example, is a Roman Catholic who came to ID not by means of a midlife religious crisis or by direction from the Roman magisterium, but by a determined examination of anomalous data. In fact, Behe was a professor of biology at Lehigh University before he even began having doubts about Darwin. When Behe began reevaluating his training, he risked putting his career in

---

(Downers Grove, IL: InterVarsity, 2006) 86. For the best introduction to ID, see Dembski, *The Design Revolution: Answering the Toughest Questions about Intelligent Design* (Downers Grove, IL: InterVarsity, 2004).

24. See Frank J. Tipler, "Refereed Journals: Do They Insure Quality or Enforce Orthodoxy?" in *Uncommon Dissent: Intellectuals Who Find Darwinism Unconvincing*, ed. William A. Dembski (Wilmington, DE: ISI, 2004) 15–130.

jeopardy because he was not yet a full professor. Even today, after many scholarly achievements, his colleagues at Lehigh University are embarrassed by him. The Biology Department mission statement posted on the web reads, "It is our collective position that intelligent design has no basis in science, has not been tested experimentally, and should not be regarded as scientific." This is bad philosophy, if not poor collegiality, because many theories in science are not experimentally testable in any straightforward fashion.

Behe began to have second thoughts about Darwin during a long day in 1987 that he spent reading Michael Denton's *Evolution: A Theory in Crisis*, published in 1985.[25] He has described this day as the intellectual shock of his life.[26] Denton, a biochemist who has taught at several universities, also was not motivated by religion to undertake criticisms of Darwin. His book opened up the critical space for the kinds of questions that made ID possible, but Denton himself was not a creationist or a design advocate and, at the time, presented no theoretical alternative to the Darwinian paradigm that he so vigorously dismantled.[27]

Behe's newest book, *The Edge of Evolution*, is the most comprehensive formulation of ID yet. Only in the past few decades, Behe argues, has the state of genetic research reached the point where an informed judgment about Darwinism can be made. Darwinians are imaginative when it comes to speculating about the possible pathways that connect the stages of the development of an organism. Behe demonstrates how these theoretical constructions run into too many roadblocks in the real world of genetics. Behe shows that the closer you look at nature, the more complicated it gets. Changes at the molecular level require long jumps that cannot be traversed by random mutations. Behe locates the limits of evolution in the length of these steps.

Much of Behe's book tells the fascinating story of the epochal battle between the human and malarial genomes. Darwinians are fond of using the metaphor of an arms race to describe evolution. Behe

---

25. Michael Denton, *Evolution: A Theory in Crisis*, 3rd ed. (Bethesda, MD: Adler & Adler, 1986).

26. For information about Behe and the other leaders of ID, see the highly informative book by Thomas Woodward, *Doubts about Darwin: A History of Intelligent Design* (Grand Rapids: Baker, 2003). Also see Behe's contribution to *Uncommon Dissent*.

27. Denton has since developed his own alternative to Darwinism, which I discuss in ch. 5.

shows that our attempts to disarm malaria look more like trench warfare instead. In an arms race, each side (predator and prey) responds to the other by improving their position, which means that their relative positions remain the same, even as their individual performances improve. Gazelles that run the fastest will pass more of their genes along to the next generation, for example, resulting in faster gazelles overall, but the lions that chase them will do the same thing. Darwinians use this metaphor to illustrate how species advance even as their role in the predator-prey scheme remains the same. But what if the struggle of life looks more like trench warfare than an arms race? In trench warfare, anything goes for immediate gain. Species fight each other without any lasting improvements in their biological structures. "If the enemy can be stopped or slowed by burning your own bridges and bombing your own radio towers and oil refineries, then away they go. Darwinian trench warfare does not lead to progress—it leads back to the Stone Age."[28] This is exactly what happened in our attempt to disarm malaria. When chloroquine was first made widely available, it slowed down the spread of this tropical disease, but the malarial parasite soon evolved an effective defense against the drug. However, this battle did not result in a new and improved malarial cell. Instead, when chloroquine was no longer a threat, malaria reverted back to its old ways. Its protective mutations deteriorated; they did not create anything new.

Behe admits that mutations can result in biological advances when organisms adapt to their environment by taking tiny, incremental steps. When larger steps are needed, however, evolution does not have a chance. Behe locates the limits of evolution in the length of these steps. "The more intermediate evolutionary steps that must be climbed to achieve some biological goal without reaping a net benefit, the more unlikely a Darwinian explanation."[29] In his previous book, *Darwin's Black Box*, Behe compared evolution to the challenge of building a mousetrap and concluded that evolution was not up to the task. In this book, he talks about evolutionary pathways, and demonstrates how gradual and lucky the evolutionary assent must be. Rather than strolling randomly—like a drunkard, in a famous image of Stephen Jay

---

28. Michael J. Behe, *The Edge of Evolution: The Search for the Limits of Darwinism* (New York: The Free Press, 2007) 43.

29. Ibid., 104.

Three Rival Theories and the Problem of Natural Evil

Gould—through a minefield of obstacles, evolution appears to be a very sober process. When it is required to make progress by taking steps that increase in length, number, and agility, Darwinian theory breaks down. Without some kind of support, organisms that need to move forward in relatively brief time spans are more likely to stumble than advance. Or, as in the case of malaria, any successful step they take is just as likely to be followed by a step backward as by any forward progress.

Nonetheless, rather than demolish Darwinism, Behe wants to explore its limits, as his title indicates. He meets evolution half way by stating his agreement with scientists who posit a common ancestor for the lineage of all creatures. He also acknowledges that Darwinian theory can account for some aspects of the development of new species. He just doesn't think that random mutation and natural selection are an exhaustively complete description of the path life has taken. Evolution is such a sensitive topic for the scientific community that Behe will be dismissed as a fringe thinker, but the biological community would be foolish to do so. Behe does not think the edge of evolution is its undoing. He is a reformer, not a revolutionary. Behe wants to divide the Darwinian cake into small pieces so that he can be picky about what he's willing to ingest. Whether he has gotten to the bottom of Darwinism, he has shown that it lacks explanatory depth. Most importantly, he holds out the possibility that the progress of science, more than the claims of theologians, will undermine the dogmas of Darwin.

Behe's work is obviously above personal, if not scientific, reproach, but that does not stop the smear campaign. Critics not only make innuendos about the motives of individuals involved in ID, they also argue that the ID community as a whole is involved in an alarming conspiracy. They refer to this conspiracy as the wedge argument. There is nothing like a little bit of evidence to get a conspiracy theory going. Founded in 1990, the Discovery Institute is a non-profit public policy think tank that supports research in many fields, including ID. The Discovery Institute tries to influence science and culture through conferences, debates, and publications devoted to exposing the materialistic assumptions of much modern scientific practice and promoting theism as a better foundation for knowledge. In 1990 one of their early fundraising proposals was posted on the Internet and dubbed the "Wedge Document." Even if every ID theorist in the country read and signed this document, it would hardly constitute a dangerous threat to American democracy. Its main statement is that the idea that humans are made in the image of God is the bedrock of Western civilization and that materialism is incompatible with the progress and achievements in the West that were made possible by this Christian conviction. If this is a conspiracy, then Christianity itself is the guilty party.

In the minds of the critics, then, ID is merely a ruse for subverting the Constitution in order to get God back into public schools. This suspicion has received a boost from a recent United States federal court decision, *Kitzmiller v. Dover Area School District* (2005), which ruled that ID cannot be taught as an alternative to evolution. The District Judge, John E. Jones III, decided that ID is a religious, not a scientific, position. Consequently, he argued, requiring its teaching in public schools would violate the Establishment Clause of the First Amendment of the U.S. Constitution. This decision was unfortunate for a number of reasons.

First, the teaching of religion in public schools is not nearly so circumscribed by the Constitution as Judge Jones seems to think.[30] A vigorous democracy requires an openness to religion in public schools just as a thriving scientific community needs to be open to criticism of all kinds.

Second, impugning the motives for something is not the same thing as demonstrating its defective reasoning. Philosophers of science make a basic distinction between the context of a scientific discovery and the logic of its justification, a distinction the Judge seemed to ignore. A position like ID should be decided on its merits, not the alleged motives of those who stand behind it.

Third, even if ID involves some elements of what might be called theological reasoning, the case can still be made that it should be taken seriously in the science classroom. The Judge acted as if associating ID with some aspects of theological argumentation settled the matter, but

---

30. See Stephen H. Webb, "The Supreme Court and the Pedagogy of Religious Studies: Constitutional Parameters for the Teaching of Religion in Public Schools," in *Journal of the American Academy of Religion* 70 (2002) 135-57, as well as my response, in the same issue, to Randall G. Styers: "Rejoinder: Lowering the Wall: Taking Sides in the Religion and Education Debate," 169-71. For a critique of this decision, see David K. Dewolf et al., *Traipsing into Evolution: Intelligent Design and the Kitzmiller v. Dover Decision* (Seattle: Discovery Institute, 2006). For a secular atheist's position, see Thomas Nagel, "Public Education and Intelligent Design," in *Philosophy & Public Affairs* 36 (2009), 187-205.

this begs the question of what evolution is, as well as religion's role in raising questions about scientific theories. It is quite possible that evolution itself entails theological lines of argument (or anti-theological lines of argument, which, given the Supreme Court's strictures that schools must be neutral between religion and anti-religion, amounts to the same thing). If a scientific theory is ruled inadmissible in public schools if it has traces of religious argument, then the scientific community itself will be stifled in seeking new ways of looking at the world. As Steve Fuller argues, "Science and religion are not 'separate but equal' as the *Kitzmiller* verdict suggests, but rather are substantially overlapping modes of inquiry." Fuller, who testified against the ACLU witnesses at this trial, calls their absolute separation of religion and science tendentious and denies the argument that ID would be bad for science education. "This suspicion is historically unfounded. On the contrary," he writes, "design-based thinking fosters the context for scientific discovery."[31] ID is a religiously inspired project that plays by the rules of modern science. Modern scientists are suspicious of it for being religiously inspired, even though its convictions about the trustworthiness of a universal, rational order in nature and the sacred destiny of humankind to govern nature by knowing that order was the motivation and rationale for the rise of science in the first place. Whether the sciences can flourish with a different motivation and rationale is still an open question, but Fuller insists that definitions of what constitutes science should follow the evidence wherever it leads and not impose an abstract classification on messy practices in order to police what might be artificial boundaries.

Fuller is a sociologist who approaches this controversy from a purely historical, non-religious point of view. He thinks the conflict between Darwinism and ID is more social than cognitive, and the evidence supports this view. Critics vilify the ID community for sneaking theological assumptions into science, much as communists were once feared in America for their foreign ideas and divided loyalties. The critics do not know how wrong they are. ID theorists actually go the extra mile in keeping their faith out of their equations. They posit a designer only where evidence of design exceeds any reasonable probability of

---

31. Steve Fuller, *Science vs. Religion? Intelligent Design and the Problem of Evolution* (Malden, MA: Polity, 2007) 98 and 101.

a naturalistic explanation. William Dembski is especially careful in specifying what level and what kind of complexity justifies inferring an intelligent designer. He has developed an "explanatory filter" to test the probability that something has been caused by nature or by chance. One of his two PhDs is in mathematics (the other is in the philosophy of science, where he has been influenced by and has written about the French phenomenologist Michael Polanyi; he also has a masters of divinity degree), and though he is an elegant writer, his mathematical theory can zoom into the stratosphere. The point is that he sets the threshold of his probability theory extremely high so that his conclusions about design are always very conservative. Even with that threshold, he finds enough evidence for design in the universe to conclude that intelligence is an irreducible feature of reality.

If ID theorists are not pure scientists, it is because they mix up science and philosophy more than science and religion. ID theorists are engaged in a fairly old-fashioned metaphysical quest that harkens back to the origins of philosophy in the ancient sense of that term—the love of wisdom. What they bring to this quest is a very modern commitment to mathematical theories of probability. The critics complain that ID does not accept the naturalistic basis of science, but that is precisely the issue that is being contested, and it is not fair to reward victory in a contest to a side that refuses to compete on a level playing field. By being open to the theoretical possibility of an intelligent, purposeful designer, they are trying to prove that science has not earned its naturalistic presumption. Why should science shove God off the table before the quest for knowledge has even begun?

Another objection that Darwinians raise against ID is that it does not do justice to the problem of natural evil. It might seem like this is an objection that only theologians would formulate, but it is actually mounted most often by Darwinians. Jeffrey P. Schloss, Distinguished Professor of Biology at Westmont College, has pointed out how Darwinians hold not only waste, destruction, and the superabundance of death against the doctrine of creation but also "useless traits, clumsy design, or suboptimal function as a scientific argument against special design."[32] An example of this (not used by Schloss) can be found in the

---

32. Jeffrey P. Schloss, "Neo-Darwinism: Scientific Account and Theological Attributions," in *Back to Darwin: A Richer Account of Evolution*, ed. John B. Cobb Jr. (Grand Rapids: Eerdmans, 2008) 113.

Three Rival Theories and the Problem of Natural Evil

film *Flock of Dodos*, a documentary by Randy Olson that pokes fun at the intelligent design movement.[33] Olson goes to great lengths (and takes great pleasure) in demonstrating how rabbits eat their own poop. More scientifically put, rabbits produce a dropping called cecotropes that are produced in a part of the rabbit's digestive tract called the cecum, where they ferment in a way that makes them digestible. That rabbits have a macabre system for allowing them to benefit from food they cannot readily digest strikes Olson as an obvious falsification of the hypothesis of an intelligent designer. Perhaps, he muses, an unintelligent designer might produce an animal forced to eat its own poop, but surely not an intelligent one. Olson concludes that nature is too weird to have been perfectly designed. As Schloss explains, this charge is as unfair as it is ignorant, since intelligent design theorists use a criterion of irreducible complexity, not perfection or even optimality, to infer design from nature. ID theorists never argue that nature perfectly meets our human expectations of what is orderly or even palatable.

The objection to ID on the grounds of natural evil makes for a poor argument when it is stated in scientific terms but a good one when it is put into theological form. Theologians need to ask ID what kind of God their theory justifies and what kind of complexity their idea of God explains. In other words, ID theorists need a stronger theology of God and a more critical examination of evolution. As Schloss points out, the best response to Darwinians who harp on natural evil is to inform them that theologians actually provide reasons why evolution ends up with defective products. As Schloss puts it, from a Christian perspective "the very causal process [of evolution] appears deeply morally objectionable."[34] In other words, Darwinians point to flaws in nature to disprove theism, but theism anticipates such flaws by illuminating the way in which the evolutionary process itself is thoroughly flawed (from a moral standpoint).

Far from sneaking too many assumptions about religion into the sacred halls of science, then, ID does too little to sift through the kinds of inferences that should be made about God. ID, like all rational pro-

33. *Flock of Dodos*, written and directed by Randy Olson (New Video Group, 2006).

34. Schloss, "Neo-Darwinism," 115. Schloss also argues that if natural evil is a warranted argument against God, then "natural beneficence becomes an argument against neo-Darwinism, which cannot brook altruism" (115).

The Dome of Eden

grams that begin with nature, can draw a line of logic straight up to God, but it is careless concerning what it is trying to say about who God is and how God works. Too much significance is placed on the concept of design with too little discussion about the various kinds and purposes of design. Design is more than an aesthetic category. We appreciate anything that is well designed, but a well-designed crime, even when we give it our grudging admiration, is a design that we do not want to applaud or support. Notice that I am not accusing ID theorists of committing the error that is called "the God of the Gaps." The God of the Gaps is a God who is ushered into science only to fill in gaps in natural processes that cannot be explained by physical causation alone. ID theorists do not commit this mistake because they infer the handiwork of God only when the evidence—not gaps in the evidence—point in that direction. That is, they try to push the evidence as far as it will go in the direction of proving design, not randomness. True, what appears irreducibly complex today might, with further scientific advances, become reducibly complex tomorrow, but that does not mean that the category of irreducible complexity is empty and meaningless. Nevertheless, by beginning with complexity—any kind of complexity, as long as it is complex enough!—ID ends up subordinating the idea of God to a particular scientific method. The God that ID ends up with appears to help evolution over the hurdles that prevent one species gradually emerging from another. In fact, he seems like a servant of evolution, always there to provide the missing steps when evolution stumbles. Is God really so eager to aid the evolutionary process? Are there forms of complexity that God does not encourage and create? The intelligent agent ID describes is hardly the God who creates everything by the power of his Word. Rather, this is a God who gets the evolutionary ball rolling and then kicks that ball back into play when it gets stuck in the weeds. ID needs to have a coherent concept of the designer in order to know what kinds of design God would be involved in and why God intervenes when he does. An intelligent designer should not be conceived as subordinate to the category of design. If that is done, then God becomes the empty sign that is filled in by everything that natural selection cannot do on its own.

While ID risks subordinating God to its category of design, and thus drawing a limited and misleading portrait of God, it also gives away

Three Rival Theories and the Problem of Natural Evil

too much concerning evolution. ID portrays evolution as a process that works most of the time but occasionally needs a boost from a supernatural agent. ID thus accepts complexity as the target of Darwinian explanation, but while it examines whether Darwinism achieves its goals, it never questions the target itself. Complexity in Darwinian terms is but another name for the way nature selects those genetic mutations that confer a benefit for survival. Complexity can be considered elegant and even beautiful, but it is a product of a struggle that spells death and suffering. ID thus runs up against the problem of natural evil that also confronts theistic evolution. ID, to put it plainly, does not tell us what is wrong with evolution. Although it criticizes the explanatory completeness of evolution, it does not criticize the evolutionary process itself. It goes too far in accepting evolution on its own terms, up to the point of a level of complexity that defeats naturalistic explanation.

My criticisms echo a charge frequently made by ID's secular critics. Critics argue that design in nature is too clumsy to have been planned and executed by a perfect God. Design is often suboptimal, to use the technical term. Why are the retinas backward in vertebrate animals, for example? Surely God would not have done it that way! There is something to this criticism, although it is ironic that secular critics of ID stoop to a theological, not a scientific, argument against it. This argument is wrong, however, in trying to fathom why God would do something in a way that we deem less than perfect. God is free to arrange things in a way that baffles our sense of efficiency. Besides, nature is well designed, protecting us as much as it is testing us. This argument is right, nevertheless, in wondering why ID theorists want to make God responsible for everything in evolution. Although Christians believe that God is in ultimate control of the world, God is not necessarily the only supernatural agent shaping the course of evolution. If ID is willing to make inferences to a good intelligent designer, why can't it make inferences to an evil intelligent designer?

Intelligence, in other words, is a necessary but not sufficient condition for a supernatural and benevolent designer. There can be intelligent good designers and intelligent bad designers. Intelligence alone is a morally neutral category. Intelligence can be used for the good, in which case it is what we call wisdom, but intelligence can also be misused for the bad, in which case it becomes mere cunning and calculation. God is good and wise, but Satan is very intelligent as well as evil.

Nonetheless, I am sympathetic to the basic position of ID, which is the target of accusations from both fundamentalists, who think ID has gone too far in accepting evolution, and scientists, who think ID has not gone far enough in accepting evolution. The theoreticians of the ID movement have done more than any other group to elaborate the weaknesses of Darwinism. They are a courageous and brilliant bunch. Even so, Christians need to know not just where evolution pulls up short but also where it goes too far. Christians need to know that evolutionary theory is epistemologically weak, but they also need to know that the evolutionary process is morally ambiguous. Evolution is evidence that something is wrong in the world. The theologian's relationship to evolution must be more than a cheerleader (as in TE) or an enabler (as in ID). God is needed to make sense of evolution, but God judges evolution as well. Christians need a theory of creation that makes sense of why evolution is wrong as well as what about it is right.

Creation Science

The third and last model that I will discuss as an alternative to my own is young-earth creationism, which is often associated with a movement known as creation science (hereafter CS). Creation science in turn is sometimes divided into scientific creationism, which examines the physical evidence of creation without regard to the Bible, and biblical creationism, which lays out the details of Genesis 1–11. For my purposes, I will not make this distinction. The CS model is often ridiculed in the press and among educators, but I would wager that most of these scoffers have little knowledge about its details. CS is actually full of creative thinkers who are as adept and original in reading the creation account in Genesis as many biologists are in looking at nature for evidence of natural selection. CS is, in fact, a more complex and thus a harder-to-describe movement than is TE or ID. It accepts the same data base, the same set of evidence that Darwinians use, and argues that a different set of presuppositions will lead to a different interpretation of that evidence. Because much of the thinking of the CS community takes place on websites or in journals and publications not ordinarily

Three Rival Theories and the Problem of Natural Evil

read by academics, it is easy to stereotype CS and fail to come to grips with the strength and courage of its arguments.

Most people know CS, if they know it at all, for four basic beliefs. First, CS uses the genealogies of the Bible to calculate the age of the earth, which they estimate in the range of 6,000 to 10,000 years old.

Second, CS rejects the radiometric dating that puts the earth's age at roughly 4.5 billion years. CS proponents argue that the earth was surrounded by a water (or, more precisely, vapor) canopy that produced a benign atmosphere for the antediluvian (pre-flood) earth. The result was a greenhouse effect, making the earth a rain forest, rich in oxygenation. The first humans and animals would have been protected from harmful cosmic radiation, which accounts, they argue, for the long life spans of the Old Testament patriarchs as well as the incredible size, prior to the flood, of animals like the dinosaurs. Most importantly, this canopy, they surmise, would have reduced the radiocarbon in the high atmosphere, which falsifies radiometric dating techniques. These claims are fascinating, but they have the appearance of reading into Genesis anything that will contradict Darwin. I will return to the water canopy theory when I discuss my own theory of the dome in the next three chapters.

Third, CS believes that God created the world in six twenty-four-hour days, and that God created "each after their kind." Some CS theorists will admit that God created the basic forms of the species at this time, and that these forms can undergo some evolutionary development.[35]

Fourth, CS believes that Noah's flood not only happened but that it explains many of the geological features that scientists mistakenly interpret as evidence for an old earth. This is called catastrophism, which is rejected by the uniformitarian assumptions of modern science. Uniformitarians hold that geological change occurs so gradually that there are no differences between the processes that shaped the earth in the past and the processes that are at work today.

Perhaps the most problematic position that is sometimes associated with CS is the argument that God made the earth with the ap-

---

35. For a very sophisticated debate about the time of creation, see David G. Hagopian, *The Genesis Debate: Three Views on the Days of Creation* (Mission Viejo, CA: Crux, 2001).

The Dome of Eden

pearance of old age.[36] Most CS theorists attribute the old appearance of certain geological features like mountains and canyons to catastrophes that caused sudden changes in the earth. A minority hold the view that God created the world to make it look old to us, even though it is not. The lesson to be drawn from this is that God tests us by making evolution scientifically plausible but theologically dangerous. Precisely what features God planted in the earth to make it look old, however, is difficult to ascertain in the CS literature. Some CS theorists go so far as to argue that God created the fossils found in rocks. Henry Morris, one of the best CS theoreticians, disagrees. If God had created any indication of death or decay, he rightly argues, "This would be the creation not of an appearance of age but of an appearance of evil, and would be contrary to God's nature."[37] Morris contends that all fossils, because they witness to death as the consequence of sin, postdate the fall of Adam and Eve. Morris treats every possible conflict between evolution and creation as a problem to be solved by appealing to God's absolute power. That is how he solves the problem of why light was present on the first day, but the sun, moon, and stars were not made until the fourth day (Gen 1:16–19). He suggests that it is possible that God himself (through his creative power) was the source of the light waves that traversed space in order to provide light for the first three days.

Henry Morris is also convinced that scientific dating methods do not work because the fall produced structural changes in the cosmos. This argument is completely different from the "created with the appearance of old age" position because, rather than assuming the earth has always looked the way it does today, it proposes the idea that the earth was once radically different from the way it is now. Morris contends that the fall caused thermodynamic decay. That is, entropy, the second

---

36. The idea that the earth was created with all the appearance of ancient age was first systematically defended in the eccentric book by Philip Gosse, *Omphalos: An Attempt to Untie the Geological Knot* (London: John Van Voorst, 1857). A member of the Plymouth Brethren, his work was widely ridiculed. *The Genesis Flood* has not met similar derision because it was written for and has been limited to the fundamentalist community.

37. Henry M. Morris, *Scientific Creationism* (Green Forest, AZ: Master, 1985), p. 210. For a good discussion of Henry Morris and his background, see Karl W. Giberson, *Saving Darwin: How to be a Christian and Believe in Evolution* (San Francisco: HarperCollins, 2008) 130–37.

Three Rival Theories and the Problem of Natural Evil

law of thermodynamics, did not pertain to the Garden of Eden.[38] This appears impossible to believe, since Adam and Eve expended energy and destroyed energy in the plants they ate. Moreover, if entropy were absent in the Garden, matter would have been, for all practical purposes, eternal, since it would not have decayed in any way, and the eternity of matter is clearly excluded by the theological idea that God created the world out of nothing (*ex nihilo*).

Although some of their theories strike many of us as fanciful, it would be a mistake to see people like Morris as cranks. Indeed, I have found them to be visionaries who apply to scripture all the rules of consistent and logical argument. CS theorists force those of us not in the fundamentalist camp to ask the really hard questions about Genesis. The charge of literalism is often a dismissive rhetorical ploy that puts the literalist outside the community of rational inquirers, and this is not fair. I believe that the Bible, insofar as we have good translations of the original manuscripts, is indeed the Word of God, and that, as such, God meant every word. It is never misguided to take scripture so seriously that you hear each word, phrase, and sentence as God's direct speech to you. God is the author of the Bible in the sense that God speaks to us with these very words, if we read them in the right spirit (that is, with the aid of the Holy Spirit).

While I accept the evidence for an old earth, the best way for Christians to resolve the problem of evolution is to be faithful to Scripture, no matter where that fidelity leads. On that score, young-earth creationists model a close and creative reading of the biblical text. That is not such an easy feat. Creative readings of Genesis abound in the theological literature, but they often are not very close to the actual meaning of the text, while close readings of the text are often not very creative in providing context and historical background. The CS community is especially thoughtful when it comes to the limits of the purely symbolic reading of Genesis. A purely symbolic reading of Genesis has no boundaries to keep it from becoming very sloppy, and as a result, it typically leads down a slippery slope of disrespect for the authority of Scripture. CS is right to suspect that when Genesis is treated in a purely symbolic manner, its details become irrelevant to its meaning, and once

---

38. Henry Morris, *Biblical Basis for Modern Science* (Grand Rapids: Baker, 1984) 195–97.

that happens, it can be said to mean anything the reader wants. Theistic evolutionists, for example, have little reason to pay close attention to Genesis, because they think the truth about creation lies in evolution. For TE, Genesis adds some mythical coloring and some moral lessons to evolution, but the actual words of Genesis do not require careful dissection.

Nonetheless, symbolic readings of scripture are not necessarily alien to the meaning of Scripture, no matter how highly the reader connects that meaning to the infallible inspiration of the Holy Spirit. Sometimes, in other words, the context of a passage calls for a symbolic reading. CS reminds us that symbolic readings of scripture must be argued for on the basis of the details and integrity of the text. The symbolic interpretation should arise from a basic fidelity to the text and not from a desire to escape problems in the text.

CS is able to find new ways of following the truth of Genesis because it is driven by the urgency of meeting the challenge of Darwin. Unfortunately, this also means that CS theorists are tempted to read the text anachronistically as a response to Darwin. That is, they read Genesis through the grid of evolutionary theory. They stake the meaning of Genesis too closely to the questions raised by evolution and treat the Bible as if it were a fount of scientific information. The result is a mixture of radical insight and original interpretations marred by a tendency to treat Genesis as if it were an ancient scientific textbook. Even given this problem, CS encourages all Christians to make progress in understanding creation and evolution by keeping focused on the trustworthiness of the Bible.

Whence the Thorns and Thistles?

Variations and modifications of these models abound, but they are the basic strategies for reconciling the Christian teaching about creation with the Darwinian theory of evolution. Each model has strengths and weaknesses, and in the next chapter I will propose a new theory that, I hope, builds on their strengths and rectifies their weaknesses. I have already pointed out that TE and ID share a weakness in dealing with the problem of natural evil. That is precisely the problem that my own approach is most geared to handle, so I want to end this chapter discussing just how difficult that problem is. My basic assumption about how to deal with this problem is this: Any adequate theological account of evolution must explain how God is the source of everything good in nature without being directly or immediately responsible for natural evil. Put differently, a theology of evolution must explain the relationship between the Genesis portrait of a world devoid of death and suffering and the violence and cruelty that are so integral to evolution, and it must explain this relationship, in my view, while maintaining a high view of the authority of Genesis.

To its credit, CS takes natural evil more seriously than TE or ID. Indeed, while CS can be very creative when it comes to understanding modern science, on the issue of natural evil it does not deviate from theological tradition. CS has problems with its relationship to science, but now I want to examine the position it ordinarily takes on the problem of natural evil. If CS can make sense of natural evil, that would be a good reason to take its creation science more seriously. Like most of the Church Fathers, most CS theorists explain the suffering of animals as a consequence of God's punishment of Adam and Eve for their sin. The crux of the issue is whether this position makes sense. Is it reasonable, as well as biblical, to attribute animal suffering to human mistakes?

Before we can discuss the relationship between the human fall into sin and natural evil, we need to figure out what Genesis says about these things, but that is notoriously difficult to do. Of course, the problem of violence in nature is not just a problem for Christians, and it is not just a problem raised by Darwin either. Nevertheless, any attempt to read Genesis after Darwin sharpens this problem to the point where it becomes a conceptual sore spot in theology. The unavoidable place to start is with the story of Adam naming the animals, which suggests that they were already domesticated at the beginning of time—a suggestion, it goes without saying, that is completely at odds with evolution. One definition of a pet is an animal we do not eat (people keep all kinds of pets these days), and Adam did not eat animals in the Garden. Instead, God gave Adam and Eve all the vegetation of the Garden to eat. True, God gave Adam and Eve dominion over the animals (Gen 1:28), but immediately afterward God told them, "See, I have given you every plant yielding seed that is upon the face of all the earth, and every tree with seed in its fruit; you shall have them for food" (Gen 1:29). In the very next verse, God declares that He has given to all of the animals "every green plant for food" (v. 30). Both humans and animals, it seems, were vegetarian, which makes textual sense because there was no violence in Eden.[39]

Vegetarian lions make textual sense, but they can make biological sense only if the world as a whole was dramatically changed after the fall. That too is what the text seems to imply. After the failure of Adam and Eve to obey God, the whole world fell under a divine curse. I used the passive voice in that sentence because we should not jump to the conclusion that we know what God actually did to make the divine curse a reality. The serpent is actually the first recipient of God's curses. "Because you have done this, cursed are you among all animals and among all wild creatures," God declares. "Upon your belly you shall go, and dust you shall eat all the days of your life" (3:14). Some modern scholars think the whole point of the Eden story is contained in this curse, which, they argue, is intended to explain why snakes crawl on the ground. If so, it is a lot of story for such little payoff! These scholars buttress their argument by claiming that the teller of this tale would not have had access to any traditions about evil spirits possessing an animal or taking an animal form, but this seems like a stretch. Some ancient religions worshipped snakes or connected gods to them, and snakes were widely associated with the underworld. Genesis points in a different direction. As the Old Testament scholar André LaCocque points out, the Bible treats the snake as "an ambiguous hybrid being" that "transgresses boundaries of identity." While some ancient religions honor snakes as symbols of immortality, the Bible denounces them as dangerous and repulsive—"the impure animal par excellence."[40] Perhaps, though, pagan and biblical views are not so different as they might seem. The serpent promises wisdom and life in the one, but in the other these promises are unveiled as false and illusory. In any case, that the story of Eden has more at stake than the locomotion and diet of reptiles is indicated by the continuation of the curse: "I will put enmity between you and the women, and between your offspring and hers; he

---

39. From a literalist's perspective, there was no fire in Eden to cook meat with and a single meal of one animal would have wiped out the entire species.

40. André LaCocque, *The Trial of Innocence: Adam, Eve, and the Yahwist* (Eugene, OR: Cascade, 2006) 147.

Three Rival Theories and the Problem of Natural Evil

will strike your head, and you will strike his heel" (3:15). This passage is traditionally called the *protoevangelium*, which means the first proclamation of the Gospel, because the ancients thought it referred to the coming of Jesus (the woman's offspring) and his ultimate triumph over Satan. (This interpretation was reinforced by linking Gen 3:15 to Rev 12:1–6, which depicts a woman clothed with the sun in battle with a red dragon. Roman Catholics read this as a reference to the Virgin Mary.)

The CS position, as represented by Ken Ham, founder and president of the Answers in Genesis ministry and its Creation Museum (located near Cincinnati), resolutely rejects any intimation that the Garden of Eden was less than perfect in every way. It thus locates the fall of Satan after the seventh day of creation.[41] Sin and imperfection enter the world only after the fall of Adam and Eve. The divine curses, in this perspective, are the cause of actual changes in the world. The curse against the serpent, for example, is actually a curse against the entire animal kingdom, because the serpent represents animals, not Satan. The fate of the serpent is thus representative of the violence that will now saturate all of nature. CS defends this position in the light of the other curses, which seem to signal actual changes in the world. Eve is punished by painful childbirth and subordination to her husband, while Adam is sentenced to hard labor in working the land. The land is cursed because of Adam as well—"Cursed is the ground because of you," God says (Gen 3:17)—with the result that it now brings forth "thorns and thistles," (3:18), as if the earth itself is testifying to man's rebellion. As God tells Adam, "By the sweat of your face you shall eat bread until you return to the ground, for out of it you were taken; you are dust, and to dust you shall return" (Gen. 3:19). According to CS, this marks the first appearance of death in the Bible.

All of these changes are hard if not impossible for us to imagine, given the world as we know it today. The idea that the thorns and thistles suddenly appeared after the world in all of its fullness and complexity had already been created is hard, if not impossible, to reconcile with the most rudimentary facts of biology, but that merely means we need to rethink biology, as well as think harder about the biblical witness. Adam and Eve ate plants in the Garden, and presumably they cultivated those plants, but plants, according to Darwinism, compete with each

---

41. Ken Ham, *The New Answers, Book 2* (Green Forest, AZ: Master, 2008) 272.

The Dome of Eden

other for survival just like animals, and thorns are one of the many defensive systems that plants develop to gain an edge on their rivals.[42] From all that we know about biology, a garden without weeds is unimaginable, although someone might retort, isn't that just the point? Eden is paradise, which in this life *is* unimaginable. Nonetheless, even the unimaginable must be conceivable if theological issues are open to discussion, debate, and defense.

Thorns, death, and violence not only among animals but also between animals and humans—this is the state of affairs after the fall. Many traditional accounts of Genesis focus on the question why, rather than how, God changed the ground rules of humanity's relationship to nature. Some accounts argue that God created this state of affairs in order to punish Adam and Eve, while others emphasize rehabilitation as the motive, with God using these conditions to call humanity back to its original state of righteousness. Some have even argued that God permitted animals to go wild to provide humans with a contrast to virtuous behavior and a reminder that when we go bad we are returning to our animal natures. We cannot be humans, so this argument goes, without having an animal nature that we need to control, and thus we need to experience animals that behave in ways contrary to the most minimal notions of civilization.[43]

Upon closer examination, however, the *how* question seems more pressing than the *why*. Did the divine curses change the actual structure of the world, from its biology through its chemistry right down to its physics, or did those curses only change the way Adam and Eve experienced their environment? Were the changes ontological (a philosophical term that denotes the objective essence and entirety of something) or subjective? In other words, did God create thorns and thistles at this

---

42. Michael Pollan has argued that plants are aggressive in evolving traits that satisfy human and animal desires, because those traits enlist human and animal aid in their propagation. Flowers appeared during the Cretaceous period and spread with stunning speed, because animals were now attracted to plants in a reciprocal relationship. "Beauty had emerged as a survival strategy." *The Botany of Desire: A Plant's-Eye View of the World* (New York: Random House, 201) 108. Genesis speaks a similar truth: Our most fundamental relationship to plants is the appreciation of beauty. Thorns and thistles are evidence that nature is in rebellion against us just as we are in rebellion against God.

43. Stephen R. L. Clark toys with this explanation of natural evil in "Progress and the Argument from Evil," *Religious Studies* 40 (2004) 186.

point in the narrative, or did God tell Adam and Eve what they could expect now that they were in a state of exile? Was the divine curse an action that created something new, or was it an announcement of what Adam and Eve could expect as the consequence of *their* action? Did God permit weeds or did Adam just notice them for the first time, since he was being forced to work the land? And if God did not create thorns and thistles at this point in the narrative, where were they before Adam had to cut them down in order to prepare the fields for planting?

Most versions of CS assume an ontological account of the consequences of the fall. Ken Ham, for example, argues that some features of what he calls "defense and attack structures" were present before the fall, although they were not originally used for that purpose.[44] Animals had sharp teeth, but before the fall they used those teeth to chew on plants, not each other, since all animals were vegetarian in the Garden. Thorns, however, might have been present on bushes and trees in the Garden, but they did not pose a problem to humans or animals until the fall made agriculture both a necessity and a burden. Ham attributes these post-fall changes to genetic mutations and other alterations in God's original blueprint. Ham also finds support for the ontological view in the New Testament, most notably when the Apostle Paul writes that all of creation is "subjected to futility," in "bondage to decay," and is "groaning" for redemption (Rom 8:20–22).

The ontological view has serious scientific problems, but can it be reconciled with the Christian view of the nature of God? There are three good reasons to answer no to this question. First, the ontological-change position fails to meet modern standards of justice. Those standards dictate that punishment be limited to the perpetrators of a crime, and not anyone who happens to be associated with them but not their crime. The doctrine of original sin can be seen as a form of collective punishment, but it is one thing to say, as does the Apostle Paul, that in Adam all humans sinned (due, presumably, to the shared substance of human nature), and another to say that Adam's punishment was taken out on later generations of non-human animals. When my children do something wrong I do not punish them by making them watch me punish our dogs. That would be unfair to our dogs and unlikely to be an effective deterrent to my children. Another dictate of modern justice

---

44. Ken Ham, *The New Answers Book 1* (Green Forest, AZ: Master, 2006) ch. 21.

is to make the punishment proportionate to the crime. Thus, when my boys forget to tidy their room, I do not burn it down. That would be a vindictive overreaction and, as such, would confuse my children more than it would help them. Punishing animals for something Adam and Eve did would be like burning down the house for the crimes of its occupants.

Second, the ontological interpretation of the divine curses does not fit with the beginning of the Genesis creation story. According to Genesis, God created the world only once. If nature is full of thorns, violence, and death, and God created these aspects of nature only after the fall, then God must have created much, if not most, of the world in a second creative act. Why don't we hear more about this second creation? One could try to explain this second creation by arguing that it was the fall, and thus Adam and Eve that caused the ontological changes in the structure of the world, not God. That, however, confuses a cause with a reason. Even if their fall was the reason for these ontological transformations, only God could have caused these new conditions to come into being. Adam and Eve could not create thorns or force animals to eat each other.

Third, if God altered the course of natural history in order to impact human history, then God is responsible for that alteration. It is one thing to believe that God, in the kingdom to come, will make the lamb to lie down with the lion (Isa 11:6), but it is another to believe that God turned peaceful lions into predators who enjoy dismembering lambs just to teach us a lesson about the dangers of gluttony. The prophets of the Old Testament firmly believe that God will one day redeem all of nature, but they do not impute evil to God's direct activity. God is not the author of evil in any form or shape.

If these arguments are persuasive, then God did not create a bad world to replace the good one that preceded the fall. The failure of the ontological-change position thus gives credence to the idea that a subjective interpretation best fits Genesis. After all, the divine curses can be read as more descriptive than creative. That is, God is describing in these verses what will happen to Adam and Eve (and the plants and animals) now that they have disobeyed him. In the subjective interpretation of the divine curses, Adam and Eve do all the changing, not God or nature. God does not decide to start all over by changing the laws of nature, and nature is not recreated from the ground up. Nothing new is created, and what God originally created is not changed in any fundamental way. What changes is the attitude Adam and Eve take toward the world. Before the fall, they accepted everything as a gift from God. They were full of grace. After the fall, resentment, envy, and bitterness replace gratitude and joy. Adam tries to control the ground from whence he came, and the result is frustration, sickness, and death. Rather than appreciating animals, he now tries to exploit them, and ends up fearing them. Eve tries to use her sexuality to control Adam, and the result is also frustration, sickness, and death. The original human pair thus functions as a moral warning about what happens when every couple tries to master their situation and each other, rather than giving everything over to God.

The subjective view is appealing because it turns the Genesis story into just a story, and thus let's the reader off the hook of taking the details of Genesis seriously. That is also, of course, its weakness, because the Bible, for Christians, should place us on the hook, and it is only Jesus Christ than can get us off of it. Perhaps its strength and weakness is best seen in how it deals with death and the fall. Christianity has traditionally taught that death is not really a natural part of life, because it is not a part of the goodness of the created order. That at least seems to be what the Apostle Paul taught. "Therefore, just as through one man sin entered into the world, and death through sin, and so death spread to all men, because all sinned" (Rom 5:12). A straightforward reading of this verse suggests that death was not a reality prior to the fall. As the Catholic catechism states, "Death entered the world on account of man's sin," though the catechism clarifies this statement by saying that "death therefore was contrary to the plans of God the Creator" and applies this statement only to humanity.[45] That is, the catechism does not say that animals did not die until Adam sinned, although that possibility is left open. Subjective exegetes dispute this interpretation of Romans by arguing that Paul is talking about spiritual death, not bodily death. After all, Adam and Eve did not die immediately, Moreover, it is hard to imagine what it would have meant if Adam and Eve had not sinned and thus had lived in the Garden forever in their human form. Subjective

---

45. *Catechism of the Catholic Church*, 2nd ed. (United States Catholic Conference, 2000) 263 (1008).

exegetes thus take death as a symbol of divine judgment, the price we must pay for our rebellious tendencies—"For the wages of sin is death" (Rom 6:23). Moreover, subjective exegetes argue that the world into which death enters is not the world as a whole but the uniquely human realm. As evidence for this interpretation, they note that very few people argue that no plants "died" before Adam sinned, from which they conclude that death cannot be conceived as completely foreign to Eden. If the subjective view of the fall is right, then the fear of death, not death itself, is the penalty brought about by humanity's rebellion against God, the source of all life.

The subjective view of the fall has much to commend it, and it can inspire rich and deep interpretations of the Bible. Nonetheless, it will be rejected by any who, even if they are not literalists, are committed to a plain reading of the Genesis story. The subjective position tries to sweep the thorns and thistles under the carpet of symbolic speculation, and the result is just a little bit too neat and clean. It fails to do justice to the Bible's attempt to describe the radical newness of humanity's fallen situation. We can put the problem like this: If there were thorns and thistles in the Garden, wouldn't they have frustrated Adam and Eve before the fall? I am sure some readers are wondering whether a good method of interpreting Genesis should be rejected just because of an obscure detail like the thorns and thistles, which is the kind of topic that makes theologians with a low view of biblical authority cringe. Surely, I can hear them saying, there are more important things to talk about! Among academic theologians today, Genesis is a hotbed for debates about gender relations, not the cosmological implication of weeds. You are much more likely to find a discussion of the origin of thorns on the web than in a scholarly book. Nonetheless, it is a question that not only must be answered if Genesis is to be treated as the inspired Word of God, but it is also a question that will shape any close reading of the Genesis narrative. It is one of those questions that, the more you think about it, the more important it becomes. If there were no thorns and thistles in the Garden, and God did not simply create them after the fall, where were they all the time Adam and Eve were in paradise?

The subjective position also falls short in explaining the mystery of sin and the power of salvation. Simply put, if the fall is merely a matter of a changed attitude, isn't that something we can correct on our own?

Three Rival Theories and the Problem of Natural Evil

If all that is wrong with human nature is that we are a bit unhappy and easily frustrated, then we hardly need God to take on human form and die on the cross for us. A bit of therapy, some anti-depressants, and a vacation to a tropical island would do the job just fine. Indeed, the subjective view tends to deny the existence of natural evil altogether, because the disorder of nature is really all in your head! It follows that we should never complain about life because whatever exists is good and if we think something is wrong in the world we have only ourselves to blame. The subjective position is not only theologically unsatisfying. It is also scientifically obscure. What, after all, is the source of this changed attitude? Did God alter the chemistry of the human brain in order to make humans more impatient and anxious? That cannot be the case, because then the subjective position would be little more than a variant of the ontological position. Humans must have suddenly lost some of their perspective on life when they were kicked out of paradise. That is plausible, but it hardly constitutes a fall from grace. Losing perspective is more like one step down the moral ladder than a plunge into the bottomless darkness of original sin.

The best attempt to provide some conceptual specification of the subjective position can be found in the Roman Catholic teaching that Adam and Eve lived in the Garden in a state of original justice that included supernatural and preternatural gifts. Supernatural gifts in the Garden raised humanity above all of nature by uniting humans with the divine. Preternatural gifts elevated humanity in accord with human nature. The distinction is subtle but crucial for putting the best possible spin on the subjective position. The preternatural gifts are distinct from the supernatural because they strengthen, rather than completely surpass, humanity's natural capacities. These gifts enabled Adam and Eve to live a sinless life by ordering their bodies, wills, and minds toward God. The Catholic Church defines these gifts, which were lost in the fall, as bodily immortality, integrity between reason and the passions, and an infused knowledge regarding the natural law and the physical universe.

The category of preternatural gifts has great potential for helping to resolve the conflict between evolution and Genesis. Take the immortality of the first human pair as an example. From the Catholic perspective, human immortality was not something built into the physical constitution of the human body. Nor was it something that far surpasses anything we can ever imagine about the human body. Instead, it was a bonus, a gift, added to our nature in such a way as to strengthen what we already had. As a gift, immortality could be taken away without necessitating a radical biological change in the human species. To the naked eye, the loss of our immortality would not alter our physical appearance or make-up. Preternatural gifts, then, are not detectible by science; they do not show up in the fossil record. They can be granted and lost in a way that does not contradict the biological structure of our humanity. Catholic theologians thus are able to acknowledge a radical change in humanity after the fall (a very real loss of gifts that were once our own) that nonetheless does not fundamentally alter the essential or physical nature of human being. Whether this change should be called ontological or not depends on how ontological is defined (did humans experience a loss of some aspect of their fundamental being or only a loss of something that was always more than what they ordinarily experienced themselves to be?). Nevertheless, from this perspective the consequences of the fall were more than subjective but less than ontological in the sense of changing the rules of biology.

The category of preternatural gifts is important and helpful, but it does not directly address the question of the change in animal behavior or plant life, although one can speculate about expanding the gift of integrity to include the proper relationship between not only reason and the passions but also the human will and animal obedience. In other words, just as we lost our ability to hold our passions in check after the fall, we lost our ability to live harmoniously with the animals. Yet this takes us right back to the problem of blaming animal suffering on human fallibility. Even if we lost the gift to relate to animals, why did animals turns against each other and us? Why should animals suffer for something we have done?

One might speculate that animals too lost a gift of harmonious living after the fall, as indicated by the curse on the serpent. Thus the fate of animals would follow in parallel fashion the fate of humans. This is a tempting explanatory scenario, although it is not to be found in any Catholic teaching. There might be good reasons for its absence from the Church Fathers. If God granted animals certain gifts in Eden that are in accord with their biological nature (this is the definition, remember, of

Three Rival Theories and the Problem of Natural Evil

preternatural gifts), then that means that animals have a much greater capacity for moral agency than most people assume. If animals are predisposed to be in harmony with each other, why don't we see more evidence of that in nature? And why would God punish all animals on the basis of what one of them, the serpent, did? In the case of humanity, Christianity teaches that all humans fell in Adam and Eve because humans share a supernatural solidarity with them, as indicated by the idea that we are created in the image of God. Is there a similar solidarity that animals share with each other, and if so, what is it? Moreover, the serpent is portrayed in this story as a crafty creature that comes from outside the Garden. Genesis 3:1 tells us that he was "more crafty than all the other animals." What kind of animal was he? The serpent is a moral, if not biological, predator, so what is he doing here? Is the serpent even an animal at all, or, as much theological tradition teaches, Satan in disguise?[46] If the latter, then it makes no sense why God would punish animals for something Satan did. But then the question arises, where did the serpent come from, and how did he get into the Garden if the Garden was such a perfect place?

With the topic of animals, the subjective view of the consequences of the fall reaches its explanatory limit. If humans lost the gift of ordering the world, and animals did not change at all, then they would still have been as docile in their exile as they would have been in the Garden. And if God changed animals in order to punish humans for losing their gift of being in harmony with nature, how did he do it, and is that just? Perhaps the best we can conclude is that neither an ontological nor a subjective view of natural evil is compatible with either the biblical text or the facts of biology. That means we should either give up talking about the fall altogether or we need to return to Genesis to try to figure out how some combination of the two can be worked out in a reading of the text that takes all of its details with the utmost seriousness. That is what I will try to do in the next chapter. For now, let me make two preparatory points.

First, even biblical literalists can keep in mind both Eden's reality and its uniqueness. Eden is an ideal of a kind that we can know

---

46. For a comprehensive treatment of the emerging interpretation of the serpent as Satan, see Neil Forsyth, *The Old Enemy: Satan and the Combat Myth* (Princeton: Princeton University Press, 1987).

only in the most imaginative way. Second, the Bible portrays Eden as a particular place, not the whole of the earth. In other words, there were weeds on our planet, but not in the Garden. This is, by the way, what St. Augustine says. "But we should not jump to the conclusion that it was only then that these plants came forth from the earth. . . . For they might have grown elsewhere . . . to provide nourishment for certain animals, since some animals find soft dry thistles a pleasant and nourishing food."[47] The Garden of Eden was God's plot of land, established by divine mandate and protected from aggressive, non-native plants. This was the land God chose for the first human pair, just as God would later choose special land for the people of Israel and create a new earth for our paradise. There are animals in Eden, but there are also animals outside of Eden, and how those two groups relate to each other will help us solve the puzzle of evolution and creation.

---

47. Augustine, *The Literal Meaning of Genesis*, vol. 1, trans. John Hammond Taylor (New York: Newman, 1982) 94.

four

The Five Theses

In this chapter, I will present my theory about the relationship between the Christian doctrine of creation and the Darwinian theory of evolution in five theses. I have arranged these theses in this chapter to maximize their narrative flow and to demonstrate their logical connections. I take the name for my theory from the third thesis, the Dome of Eden, because it is probably the most striking part of my argument, but that thesis works only if it is taken as one step in a tightly connected series of claims.

To follow these theses, all the reader needs is an open mind and confidence in the absolute reliability of the Bible. This theory is for Christians, but since many Darwinians think that Christianity provides no plausible alternative to or explanation of Darwin's theory of evolution, and that this lack of an alternative is itself evidence for the truth of Darwin's interpretation of evolution, it should also be of interest to skeptical and secular Darwinians as well. In later chapters, I will show how my theory opens new avenues of thought on a variety of old debates. I call it a theory because it is more than just another reconciling scheme. Reconciling schemes are all too common in theology these days. Attempts to harmonize Genesis and science long preceded the provocations of Darwinism, but after Darwin harmonizing schemes became even more urgent and elaborate, especially among conservative, evangelical, and fundamentalist Christians. Reconciling schemes tend to take one side of the puzzle and trim it in order to make it fit with the other side. Liberal Christians have long rejected these schemes and tend to speak instead of building bridges between evolution and creation, a metaphor that demonstrates an effort to join two separate entities by a neutral device that keeps them safely separate. A theory, by contrast, will be transformative of both fields, and its application will extend well beyond the positions being bridged.[1]

Here is a quick summary of the five theses: First, the abrupt transition between the first two verses of Genesis indicates that something has gone terribly wrong in the world. Theology has traditionally blamed this wrongness on the fall of Satan. The thesis that Satan, one of the angels, fell from heaven before the creation of Adam and Eve is independent of the argument that there is a textual gap in the opening of Genesis. That is, one can hold to the fall of Satan without thinking that this fall is indicated by a gap in the Genesis text. Nevertheless, the textual gap makes for a striking defense of Satan's fall. It also sets up my interpretation of the result of that fall.

Second, the world that Satan fell into was not the Garden of Eden, which the Bible portrays as a specific place set aside by God for the demonstration of divine perfection. Satan fell into the world that we know as our own, not Eden, which we know only through biblical revelation. Satan enters into the Garden, but only after he has already begun battling God on earth. As a result of Satan's rebellion, nature becomes the scene for a struggle between good and evil long before the human heart becomes a similar battleground. God is not the source or cause of natural evil, but God does permit Satan to exercise a limited reign over nature. Evolution is rightly described in terms of conflict and strife because Satan made it that way, not God. (This thesis, by the way, is similar to the position defended by C. S. Lewis. He held that Satan corrupted the animal kingdom before the creation and fall of human beings.[2])

Third, Eden was a real place, but it was unlike any reality we have ever directly known. Notice that this thesis is not identical to the purely symbolic interpretation of Eden. When theologians talk about the symbolic value of Eden, they mean that Eden has value as a means of taking the measurement of human morality. From the symbolic perspective,

---

1. For an excellent discussion of what theology can contribute to evolutionary theory, see Antje Jackelén, "What Theology Can Do for Science," *Theology and Science* 6 (2008) 287–303.

2. See the able summary of C. S. Lewis's position in Leszek Kolakowski, *Religion: If There Is No God* . . . (South Bend, IN: St. Augustine's, 2001) 52. Also see Richard J. Pendergast's provocative essay, "Evil, Original Sin, and Evolution," in *The Heythrop Journal* 50 (September 2009) 833–45.

Genesis sheds light on what it means to be human, what it means to exercise power over nature, and what it means to be divided by gender, among other things. That makes the Garden story an example or illustration of more general and basic ideas, while I think that the Garden story is the singular foundation for every idea about humanity, morality, and nature. Nonetheless, the reality of Eden needs to be carefully demarcated; it was not real in the sense that we can plot its coordinates on the space-time continuum that we experience today.

Fourth, if Eden is a fundamentally real place, and if Satan tries to battle God in nature from the very beginning of creation, then there must be some reality that divides Eden from (the rest of) the world. Evil was already present in the world, in the guise of the serpent, when Adam and Eve were created, but evil had to cross into Eden in order to ruin God's plan. The logic of the Genesis narrative requires some sort of barrier that served to set Eden apart from the rest of the world. That is in fact what we actually find in the text. Genesis 1:6–8 says that God created a dome (sometimes translated as firmament) to separate the waters, under which God "let the dry land appear." What the dome is and what it does is so difficult to fathom that most readers skip over this verse, while most commentators suggest that the dome was just a fancy way for the writer of Genesis to talk about the sky. I will argue that the firmament can be construed as a shield or dome over Eden, and thus it was constructed to protect Eden from the impact of Satan's fall. Some readers will scoff at this view, but I think it makes the best sense of the text, and it certainly helps modern Christians make sense of evolution. It does not really matter, in the end, whether the dome was physical, metaphysical, or mythical. It is a long neglected but essential resource for any coherent reflection on natural evil. To put it in general terms, the Dome of Eden is the principle given to us by scripture that helps us to distinguish between what God intended for nature and the natural evil we see all around us.

Fifth, the reason for Satan's fall, to come full circle, is the same reason for creation as a whole, as well as the reason why human nature cannot be reduced to its biological components. God created the world because God the Father had already determined to take form in God the Son, and the form God the Father gave to the Son is the same form in which we were created. The world and all that is in it is a gift to the

Son from the Father. We are who we are because the Father wanted free creatures who could decide to share in the Son's love of the Father. Jesus Christ is the reason for the world, and we were created to be rational companions of him. God did not become incarnate as a response to the fall. God made the world in order to accommodate the incarnation. The cross was in response to the fall, but the incarnation is the revelation of what God determined to be from the very beginning. Satan is the great deceiver because Satan was jealous of Jesus Christ, the form that God the Father had determined to grant the Son. Jealousy, then, is the root of all evil, not power, pride, or greed. Satan could not worship God in a created form, and he could not abide by the fact that there were creatures that were granted an intimacy with the Son that he would never know. Indeed, one of the deceptions that Satan most thoroughly sows is the idea that God became human because we are at the center of the cosmos, not Jesus Christ.

In sum, Genesis portrays Eden as a real, localized place, which means that Genesis implicitly acknowledges a world outside of Eden. Satan fell prior to the creation of Adam and Eve, which suggests that the world outside of Eden was subjected to his manipulations and distortions. Satan was able to enter into the Garden under God's permission, but the fact that there was something like a serpent in the world is evidence that the nature outside of Eden was not running the course God had intended for it. Eden must have been protected from the outside world, which accounts for the role of the firmament (the dome) in Genesis. And humanity was created in the image of Satan's arch enemy, Jesus Christ, which is why Satan was (and is) so eager to make life for humans hellish. With regard to the puzzle of natural evil, God did not create wild animals after the fall, nor did God turn the tame animals of Eden against each other in order to punish Adam. Rather, the animals of the Garden were the prototypes of all animals, the metaphysical realities that Satan tried to mimic, replicate, and destroy in the battle over evolution.

Thesis One: The Textual Gap

The fall of Satan is an ancient tradition with biblical roots, but the evidence for it that most concerns the topic of this book is the so-called gap between the first two verses of the first chapter of Genesis. Alert evangelical readers will know immediately that I am talking about what is called the Gap Theory of creation. The Gap Theory refers to an interpretation of Genesis that is commonly used by apologists who try to harmonize the biblical account of creation with the theory of evolution, but it is not widely accepted even among evangelical and fundamentalist theologians. Discussions of the Gap Theory are more likely to be found on websites than in academic journals, and the names of prestigious theologians like Karl Barth, who I will discuss in chapter 5, are rarely, if ever, associated with it.[3] In practice, the Gap Theory is usually more of an observation than a theory. It simply observes that there appears to be a gap between the first two verses of the first chapter of Genesis. In the very first sentence of the Bible, we are told that God created the heaven and the earth. In the second verse, we read, "The earth was a formless void and darkness covered the face of the deep, while a wind from God swept over the face of the waters" (NRSV). Why does the earth, which has been created in verse one, appear to be lying in waste and darkness in verse two, and why is there a mysterious wind (commonly translated as spirit) hovering above it?

The Gap Theory argues that the troubling portrait of the earth in verse 2 is evidence of the impact of Satan's fall. In other words, there is more going on between these two verses than the text is telling us. Although the text passes over this gap in silence, it points to the terrible event of Satan's rebellion against God. Various biblical and other ancient sources describe or at least imply Satan's fall from heaven after the creation of the world and before the fall of Adam and Eve, but the claim that Genesis indirectly attests to this idea is highly disputed.[4] After all, the text passes over Satan's fall in a silence as mysterious as the wind that sweeps across the waters. Nonetheless, Gap Theorists insist that this abrupt transition speaks volumes about a huge gulf in God's plan for the world, a gulf that can be attributed only to Satan. If so, then Satan must have begun working against God some time prior to the events that take place in the rest of the Genesis account.

---

3. The classic work on the Gap Theory from the evangelical camp remains the very important book by Arthur C. Custance, *Without Form and Void* (Hamilton, Ontario: Doorway, 1989; first published in 1970).

4. See, for example, Gary A. Anderson, "The Exaltation of Adam and the Fall of Satan," *Journal of Jewish Thought and Philosophy* 6 (1997) 105–34.

There are many reasons why the Gap Theory is controversial. Some of them are exegetical, with scholars arguing that Gen 1:2 merely describes the earliest stage, rather than an interruption, of creation. This argument can be divided into two positions, which we can call the chaos and canvas positions. The chaos position argues that Gen 1:2 describes the formless matter that God created before going on to order it into a hospitable world. This position agrees with the Gap Theory that the world described in Gen 1:2 is menacing, but it insists that God created this chaos, perhaps in order to demonstrate that even disorder is under God's control. The canvas position denies that there is any menace in Gen 1:2. Instead, this verse describes a neutral stage or simply posits a precondition of creation, like a frame built for a picture before it is painted. It is creation before God gave the world its recognizable features, akin to a blank slate or empty canvas. Although the first position is closer to the Gap Theory than the second, both must grapple with the argument that Gen 1:2 is rife with mythological allusions to threatening waters and primordial violence.[5] The critic of the Gap Theory thus needs to explain why the writer of Genesis is using such loaded language to describe a relatively static reality (the world as it was prior to God's further creative activity).

Theological problems with the Gap Theory abound as well. Modern theology has not taken Satan very seriously as a causal agent, and even if it did scholars are trained to be suspicious of inferring strong conclusions from ambiguous textual evidence. The Gap Theory has also met with disapproval due to its frequent connection to what is sometimes called the Reconstruction Theory. The Reconstruction Theory holds that the six days of creation are really days of re-creation. A disaster occurred in the gap between the first two verses of Genesis that required

---

5. Alexander Heidel is often cited as a skeptic of mythological allusions in Gen 1:2, but he actually was much more neutral about the question: "There are those who seem to be convinced that Gen. 1:1—2:3 shows Babylonian traces, while others appear to be just as convinced that it does not. In my estimation, no incontrovertible evidence can for the present be produced for either side: I believe that *the whole question must still be left open*" (*The Babylonian Genesis: The Story of Creation*, 2nd ed. [Chicago: University of Chicago Press, 1951], 139 [his italics]). Heidel's main concern is to argue that Gen 1:2, even with its mythological allusions, does not call into question the presence of *creatio ex nihilo* in Gen 1:1. For a stronger attempt to reject mythological debts in Genesis, see David Toshio Tsumura, *Creation and Destruction: A Reappraisal of the Chaoskampf Theory in the Old Testament* (Winona Lake, IN: Eisenbrauns, 2005).

God to reconstruct what he had already made.[6] From the perspective of orthodox theology, the Reconstruction Theory grants Satan too much power and God not enough. It suggests that Satan could ruin creation, not just disrupt it, and that God had to redraw the providential map in response to Satan, changing his plan to get around Satan's roadblocks. Nothing in the Gap Theory, however, necessarily implies that God's creative activity in the Garden of Eden is a second attempt at creating the entire world. According to the Gap Theory, Gen 1:2 refers to the cosmos as a whole, but the story of Eden refers only to a specific, limited place. Thus, there is no logical reason why the Gap theory has to be linked to the Reconstruction Theory.

Still, the Gap Theory today would be little more than a curiosity were it not for its usefulness in dealing with the problem of evolution. Evolution challenges many aspects of Christian faith, but two of the most prominent debates concern the origin of natural evil and the proper reading of the Genesis narrative. Natural evil refers to the way the natural world, and not just human nature, departs from God's goodness. Simply put, the world we experience all around us does not much resemble the description of the Garden of Eden, where all creatures lived peacefully with each other and the first humans did not have to suffer in order to live off the land. Evolution enters the picture because it seems to suggest that sheer randomness and pointless struggle are built into the very fabric of nature, which means that nature could never have been as good as Genesis thinks God created it. Animals, according to evolutionary theory, have always been subjected to plague, predation, and parasitism, and though Christianity attributes the human condition to the actions of the first human pair, or, more abstractly, their exemplary misuse of freedom, it makes little sense, even from the most traditional theological perspective, to explain the suffering of non-human animals by referring to the choices humans once made.

Thus, evolution raises some troubling questions that intersect the problem of natural evil and the proper reading of Genesis. If non-human animals did not begin suffering, along with humans, after Adam and Eve were expelled from the Garden of Eden, does that mean God

---

6. For a description and critique of the Reconstruction Theory, see Hanri Blocher, *In the Beginning: The Opening Chapters of Genesis* (Downers Grove, IL: InterVarsity, 1984) 41–43.

created them to suffer, and if so, why does God call everything in the Garden good? One way to solve this problem is to interpret Genesis symbolically and accept evolution as the way God created the world. The Gap Theory responds to these quandaries by another route. Simply put, it changes the traditional location of natural evil in the Genesis narrative. Rather than placing the origin of natural evil after the fall of Adam and Eve, the Gap Theory places it after the creation of the cosmos and before the creation of the Garden of Eden, and the Gap Theory blames natural evil on Satan, not humanity. If Satan fell after God's initial act of creation, Gap Theorists reason, then that would account for natural evil and go a long way toward contextualizing the biological process of evolution. It might also help to maintain the integrity of this foundational scripture.

The idea that the Gap Theory can solve one of the most difficult problems in contemporary theology sounds too simple to be true, and it is too simple, but could some version of it be true? Any theory that looks like it was invented for the specific purpose of defending an outdated set of beliefs is going to be received with much skepticism, even though apologetics is a time-honored theological task. If this theory is to gain widespread credence, it will have to be connected in a systematic way to a broader set of traditional theological topics and concerns. In other words, just calling it a theory does not make it so. Recall that after recounting the decisive event of God creating the heavens and the earth, Genesis tells us that the earth was waste and void, with a foreboding darkness over the deep and a wind sweeping the water. Even if the Gap Theory is correct that this indicates the initial consequence of Satan's fall, which must have occurred sometime after or in conjunction with God's creation of the world, the theory does not tell us what Satan did after his fall, nor does it clarify the relationship of Satan's fall to the subsequent creation of the paradise in the Garden of Eden. We simply cannot cram everything we know about Satan's fall into this textual gap. That is both too messy and too convenient. We also cannot simply stuff everything we know about evolution into the gap as well. Evolution, if it is to be credited with the origin of species, is an extremely long process. Evolution did not occur in and only in the gap. Throwing evolution into the gap is a throwaway move that is unlikely to be very persuasive to most Christians, let alone professional theologians. The conceptual space opened up by the apparently abrupt transition from the first to the second verse of Genesis cannot possibly hold every biological fact of evolution. Nonetheless, it is still an important piece of the puzzle that lends credence to the other four theses.

Thesis Two: A Biological Interpretation of Spiritual Warfare

The important question for a theology of creation and evolution is not when Satan fell but rather what he did afterwards. The Gap Theory tells us that Satan fell, and it tells us that Satan fell soon after God created the world. But it does not tell us what Satan did after his fall. I want to propose that what Satan did after his fall is directly related to the phenomenon of biological evolution. I am not arguing that what Satan did is evolution per se. Evolution, as described by most biologists, is too creative to be attributed to an evil origin and too complex to be reduced to a single negative portrait. Evolution is constructive as well as deadly, cooperative as well as competitive. Yet I do want to argue that Satan's activity is very much connected to the cruelties in nature that Darwin tried to explain with his law of brutal competition and impassive selection. That is, Satan is as responsible for natural evil as he is responsible for moral evil, and evolution is to natural evil what freedom is to moral evil. Evolution in nature, like freedom for humans, is one of the battlegrounds upon which the struggle of good and evil takes place.

The fall of Satan is so often part of the package of the story of Adam and Eve that it is assumed to be directly recounted in the Genesis text. Obviously Satan did not fall in the sense of moving from an above to a below, but the spatial metaphor is appropriate, given the way we associate excellence with height and moral perfection with transcendence. In a way, a more vivid description of the fall of Satan would have been a fitting beginning of the Bible, because Satan's fall symbolizes the downward movement of sin in contrast to the ascension of Jesus Christ into heaven, which is the climax to his triumph over death. For that very reason, however, Satan's fall should not have been the focus of Genesis. The movement downward from God's abode to the creation of heaven and earth is not a movement into sin. God's condescension to create something outside of the divine life is a glorious act of absolutely free generosity. Throwing Satan into the beginning of the creation narrative would have given him a starring role, and given Satan's association with pride, it would have fallen into Satan's plan, not God's. Genesis was right to be discrete about Satan.

The idea that nature is full of evil in the form of suffering and violence will strike many readers as eccentric or perverse. Busy Americans love to take refuge in nature to enjoy its beauty and admire its ecological balance. The darker side of Darwinism has not survived our modern need to escape from human woes into the bounty of natural beauty. Moreover, many Christians these days simply do not have a very vivid sense of evil, whether moral or natural. Liberals tend to treat evil as the accumulative outcome of unjust social arrangements that create poverty and oppression, while conservatives tend to confront evil on a personal level, as the worldly pressures that impede the exercise of holiness. Conservatives have kept alive the tradition of an actual agent of evil, traditionally named Satan, but they talk about Satan most often in the context of the apocalypse, or the coming end of the world. It is what Satan does at the beginning, not the end, of the world that is the subject of my attention.

Without the fall of Satan, nothing about evolution, let alone Genesis, makes moral sense. Yet I have already noted how the Bible is reticent to reveal too much about the relationship between Satan's fall and God's creation of the world. The main character of the Bible is God, not the devil. Giving him too much attention would risk letting him steal the show. As all movie fans know, we cannot take our eyes off an evil character once he comes on the screen. Evil has a seductive power. Any portrait of evil takes the risk of glorifying it. Yet there is more to the Bible's reticence about Satan than that, and it is one of the benefits of my theory that it explains this reticence. If the fall of Satan is directly related to his work in evolution, then it makes perfect sense that God would have been reticent in revealing Satan's role in the beginning of the universe. God could not have included information to ancient peoples that was part of a scientific worldview that would not emerge for centuries to come.

The Bible, as Calvin often insisted, is an accommodation to the limits of our knowledge, and the story of creation must be the most accommodating revelation of all. Not only does God know more than we ever could or will, but also God knows things in a way that is different from our knowing. God knows from eternity, while we are planted squarely in time. The Bible is the whole truth of revelation, but it is not the whole truth about everything (it does not tell us how the steam engine works, for example). Yet even though the Bible does not tell us everything we can know about the world, it does tell us what is worth knowing, and it teaches us the wisdom we need to make sense of extra-biblical truth claims. The Bible, that is, plants seeds for further understanding, and on the topic of evolution, we have to study Genesis closely to bring those seeds to fruition.

The revelation of Genesis was given to us in part so that we would know that other, competing accounts of the origins of the world are false. Many ancient pagan mythologies depict an original violence at the heart of the world, with gods slaying each other and the world springing from their spilled blood. As the first book of the Bible, Genesis must get the true story of God's relationship to the world off to an unmistakably clear start. God alone is the creator of the world, and God brought the world into being out of a joy in the creative act. The world is good. It is not the product of violence, hatred and strife.

Some scholars argue that Satan's appearances in the Old Testament are so brief and obscure that he should be considered an invention of Christianity.[7] If so, it was an invention that the logic of faith made necessary. To blame God for the world's woes is the height of blasphemy, yet to blame nothing or nobody would be, in effect, to blame God. In point of fact, however, the fall of Satan has deep roots in Jewish tradition, especially in the Second Temple period (536 BCE to 70 CE). Much of the speculation about fallen angels centered on the story in Genesis 6 about "sons of God" who roamed the earth, mated with "daughters of humans," and initiated the wickedness that led God to send the flood. Jewish biblical commentators during the Second Temple period routinely interpreted this story to be about renegade angels. In her extensive survey of this material, Annette Reed has concluded that "virtually all Christian exegetes in the second and third centuries adopted the angelic interpretation of Gen. 6:1–4."[8] This position, she argues,

7. For this position, see Henry Ansgar Kelly, *Satan: A Biography* (Cambridge: Cambridge University Press, 2006).

8. Annette Yoshiko Reed, *Fallen Angels and the History of Judaism and Christianity: The Reception of Enochic Literature* (Cambridge: Cambridge University Press, 2005) 148. For comments on Augustine's position, see 221.

was more dominant among orthodox theologians—including Justin Martyr, Irenaeus, Tertullian, and Cyprian—than heretics. Augustine began the process of doubting this interpretation by arguing that the angels sinned only at a one-time event, at the time of creation, probably because he was worried about heretics who saw the fall of angels as a recurring pattern in history.

The New Testament affirms the fall of angels and connects their fall with the disorder of the natural world, especially the problem of disease. The book of Acts depicts the healing ministry of Jesus as a battle against Satan. Peter in a speech that succinctly summarizes the gospel notes "how God anointed Jesus of Nazareth with the Holy Spirit and with power; how he went about doing good and healing all who were oppressed by the devil, for God was with him" (Acts 10:38). Later in the same book the Apostle Paul accused a false prophet of being a "son of the Devil" who makes "crooked the straight paths of the Lord" (13:10), which suggests that Satan is twisting and distorting what God is doing in the world. When Herod defies God, he is struck dead and "eaten by worms and died," a punishment that also appears in 2 Macc 9:8–9, which suggests that our bodies were not meant for such violent treatment. Jesus could not have been clearer when he said that Satan "was a murderer from the beginning" and "the father of lies" (John 8:4). Satan is the author of violence, hatred, and strife.

If Satan was a murderer from the beginning, how far back do we have to go to find evidence of his handiwork? Evidently, wherever we find death and deception, no matter how early in the biblical, biological, and historical record, we find Satan.

In tracing the cause of violence back to Satan, it would be easy to exaggerate his role in the events that brought the world into being. Genesis does not bring Satan into the picture until the serpent enters Eden because Genesis does not want to give Satan any credit for what God has done. Satan is the author of evil, but because we see evil all around us, it is tempting to think that Satan has more power than he does. Satan can manipulate what God has created, and he can alter life forms through his mimicking of God's creativity, but Satan cannot create anything out of nothing, which is the theological lesson of the first chapter of Genesis. Satan can be creative when it comes to evil, but he is not the creator of the world.

The Five Theses

The most vivid and direct description of Satan's fall actually comes at the end, rather than the beginning, of the Bible, and this is as it should be. Satan is best thought of in terms of God's victory over him. By revealing Satan's full identity in the end of the narrative, the Bible is saying that Satan is fully known only in defeat. The important chapter regarding Satan in Revelation is the twelfth, which confirms the satanic identity of the serpent in Genesis and gives as the reason for Satan's fall his jealousy of the woman "clothed with the sun" (12:1) and her child. The Church Fathers interpreted this chapter to mean that God showed the angels his plan to have Mary give birth to the Messiah, which prompted Satan's rebellion. The great dragon wanted to "devour her child as soon as it was born" (Rev 12:4), which God prevented, but God did permit Satan's predatory rage to enter into the garden in the form, appropriately, of a snake. Mary is the second Eve, just as Jesus is the second Adam, so if Satan could not have Mary, he could at least try to get to Eve. Jesus, by ending Satan's reign, is a dragon-slayer, which is the truth behind the many beautiful legends about heroes battling dragons. Jesus passed his courage onto his disciples, who tamed snakes as evidence of their spiritual power (Mark 16:18). Indeed, the faithful are destined to have all things subjected "under their feet" (Heb 2:8, Ps 8:6).

Far from exercising authority over nature, humans are subjected to its contingencies, but that does not mean that the world as we experience it provides the best clues to what God originally intended (and what God has planned for us). Evolution works under a divine permission—as does everything that happens on earth—but evolution is in some sense a work of Satan, not God. Genesis portrays God creating the world immediately and without the need of any biological mechanism. That is not to say that God could not have created the world through some sort of process. It is just to say that God did not create the world through this particular process. Evolution leaves a trail in history that is marked by blood and anguish. It makes death the necessary precondition of life, since without death there would be no struggle to grab more of life, and there would be no room for new life forms. Evolution is the song of death. It is a powerful song, and not without its creative effects, but it is not the song the faithful will sing in heaven to the glory and praise of the Son. It is a song that could have been sung only by the Son's chief competitor. It is the terrible sound of Satan.

The astute reader might find echoes of my position in ancient heretical groups that made Satan into a kind of second God, nearly as powerful as the one true God. These groups, often grouped together under the label of "Gnostics," were rejected by orthodox Christians for granting too much power to Satan and not enough to God. They were given their name, which is taken from the Greek word for knowledge, because they claimed to have secret sources of divine revelation, and they loved to speculate about how the stars and various orders of angels control human destiny. There were many good reasons why the Church rejected them, but that does not mean that they were wrong about everything, or that we have nothing to learn from them. Gnostics took evil seriously. They took it so seriously that they could not imagine how God created the world. When Gnostics looked around themselves, they saw disease, natural disasters, and death in countless disguises. They thought that Satan must have created the natural world, while God created only our souls. They taught that our souls have become stuck in the material world, and only astrological speculation can open the way for the soul's escape from the body's trap. All of this is profoundly wrong, but there is something in it that is right. The world has come into being in a way that is under Satan's influence, while still being under God's ultimate control. But if that is true, then what about the world that God created and called good?

Thesis Three: The Unique Space and Time of Eden

On the one hand, the Tree of the Knowledge of Good and Evil planted in the center of the luxurious Garden of Eden indicates that this is no ordinary story. On the other hand, the mention of four rivers, two of which (the Tigris and Euphrates) were well known, indicates that this story is more ordinary than we might care to think. Eden is a story about everybody, and as such it tells us more about ourselves than about Adam and Eve. Yet Eden is also a singular story about one particular couple, and as such every detail counts. While theologians used to take every word of Genesis seriously, the flora and fauna of Eden hardly gets a second look today. For many contemporary theologians, the story of

Eden might speak of general moral truths, but it is just a story, not to be taken literally. Even the idea that Genesis is a story about the fall—a singular moment in time when something went terribly wrong with human nature—has been jettisoned by many theologians, who resist its implication of collective guilt and trace the origin of this doctrine to the anguished speculations of Augustine.[9] Even so, the attractive power of Eden is hard to deny, and the details of the Bible's descriptions of it, even from just a literary perspective, are worthy of serious attention. Unfortunately, however, its details will not matter for most people if its reality is but a dream. Moreover, if it is just a dream, how can it carry so much moral weight? Once the reception of the story of Eden begins treating it as little more than make-believe, it is hard to continue insisting that it provides the key to unlocking the secrets of the human heart. Can Eden be about us today if it was never about anyone in the past?

For most of Christian history, Eden was a source of creative literary mythologizing as well as serious theological moralizing. Most Christians could not conceive how something so important could be not physically real. People could accept the fact that Eden was inaccessible, but still, it had to be (or had to have been) somewhere. Alessandro Scafi, in a beautifully illustrated volume, has written the definitive history of various attempts to map paradise.[10] Some pre-modern theologians thought it could not be found because the flood had cut it off from the rest of the world, while others placed it at the top of the highest mountain, above the waters of the flood, but also beyond the reaches of even the bravest explorers. All agreed that paradise lay in the East, which served to inspire and embolden Christopher Columbus's exploratory voyages. Even when men could not find it, they drew their maps around it, using it as the ordering principle for how they envisioned the world.

Actually, Christian tradition has handled the reality of Eden with more subtlety than most people today realize. Origen, the most sophisticated early Christian theologian, set the stage for debates about Genesis by downplaying its physical reality. Actually, what Origen taught about Genesis was the subject of enormous controversy in the centuries fol-

---

9. See, for example, Patricia A. Williams, "Sociobiology and Original Sin," *Zygon* 35 (2000) 783–812.

10. Alessandro Scafi, *Mapping Paradise: A History of Heaven on Earth* (Chicago: University of Chicago Press, 2006). See the excellent review by Alan Jacobs, "In Search of Eden," *First Things* (February 2007) 26–30.

lowing his work and is still the subject of scholarly debate today. He was criticized by later theologians for spiritualizing details of Genesis through the allegorical method, but scholars today often doubt whether these criticisms were fair or accurate. Origen was particularly charged, interestingly enough, with spiritualizing the waters above the heavens that had been separated by the firmament (Gen 1:7).[11] After a careful study of this issue, Peter Bouteneff concludes, "Though he seems sure of what paradise is not, he never truly defines what it is."[12] Whatever Origen really taught about Genesis, his reputation was damaged by his speculations about Eden, and later theologians had to be careful not to go too far in dismissing its historical reality. Even so, as Bouteneff points out, some of the Church Fathers continued to treat Eden as a "parahistorical" reality, or, as in the case of Gregory of Nazianzus, "the space where the human person, endowed with free will, is given the substrate over which to exercise that freedom."[13] In other words, the material reality of Eden was such that it was the perfect medium of human freedom.

By the time of St. Augustine, theologians were applying a variety of interpretive strategies to Genesis. In his third and final commentary on Genesis, Augustine writes that it was common in his day to use one of three theories about Eden. "There is, first, the opinion of those who interpret the word 'paradise' in an exclusively corporeal sense. Then there are those who prefer to give an exclusively spiritual sense to the word. Finally, there are those who accept the word 'paradise' in both senses, sometimes corporally and at other times spiritually."[14] The third theory, Augustine writes, appeals to him. In other words, Eden is beyond our imagination, so its reality stretches our language, but only in the direction of truth. Augustine goes on to say that before turning to a figurative or symbolic interpretation of the text, we should try as hard

---

11. See the discussion in Peter C. Bouteneff, *Beginnings: Ancient Christian Readings of the Biblical Creation Narratives* (Grand Rapids: Baker Academic, 2008) 106-7. He might have interpreted the waters above to be angelic powers and he might have read this verse to be about our need to separate the good from the bad in our lives (and thus to have an "inner firmament" [178]).

12. Ibid., 110.

13. Ibid., 148 (these are Bouteneff's words).

14. St. Augustine, *The Literal Meaning of Genesis*, 2 vols., trans. John Hammond Taylor (New York: Newman, 1982) 2:32.

as we can to keep with the "proper sense of the events narrated."[15] The obscurities of Scripture should keep us humble, rather than making us rush to ridicule those who wrestle with them. Critics "full of worldly learning" who do not restrain themselves in scoffing at Scripture they do not understand "are like wingless creatures that crawl upon the earth and, while soaring no higher than the leap of a frog, mock the birds in their nests above."[16] The Roman Catholic catechism follows Augustine on this point by teaching that, "The account of the fall in Genesis 3 uses figurative language, but affirms a primeval event, a deed that took place at the beginning of the history of man."[17] Genesis reveals universal and basic truths through what is at times non-literal language, and yet the catechism insists that the story really refers to a primeval event. This is also the position of the important evangelical thinker Bernard Ramm.[18] Events are recorded by someone who was not a witness of them. Something happened more or less as it is described, but since we cannot know just how much more or less, we should err on the side of thinking there is more to the story than our modern skepticism leads us to expect.

Still, there is no getting around the fact that any straight talk about Adam and Eve, the gates of Eden, and paradise lost will strike many people today as little more than cheap tokens taken from the language of myth. There is some truth in this: Genesis has all the character of myth—which is exactly what one would expect if it were really true. I do not mean by that statement to imply that Genesis is an empty exercise in inventive rhetoric. I want to insist that Genesis is really true, even though its subject matter is set apart from the world as we know it. Genesis tells us what kind of world God gave to the first humans. I believe that the account of the Garden of Eden and all of its details are

---

15. Ibid., 2:34.

16. Ibid., 1:44.

17. *Catechism of the Catholic Church*, 2nd ed. (Washington, DC: United States Catholic Conference, 2000) 98, no. 390.

18. Bernard Ramm, "The Fall and Natural Evil," *Southwestern Journal of Theology* 5 (1963) 21–32. He says he agrees with the Scottish-Reformed theologian James Orr that Genesis "is authentic history but in oriental, allegorical, symbolic form" (21). Ramm by the way does not think thistles and thorns were created after the fall. Instead, man confronts them for the first time after he is "thrust out of the protective shelter of his Paradise" (23–24). Ramm does not say what that protective shelter was.

true. But this account is at odds with what we know from biology about the sequencing of life forms, the age of the earth, and the struggle of life against life. Genesis, however, is not at odds with the real world; evolution is. Genesis is counterfactual because it is at odds with Darwinism, but at the same time Eden reveals evolution to be *countercreational*.

The reason Genesis has something of the character of myth is that it is more, not less, real than the primary reality we most ordinarily know. We live in the fallen world, where natural resources are scarce, human greed is unlimited, and strife seems built into the nature of life. The Garden of Eden story will always strike us as myth because it *is* myth—of the most transforming kind. Myth can be defined as an untrue story, or it can be defined as the best and only way to preserve truths that are beyond our reach. Even if we accept the second of these two definitions, it sounds like we are assigning the Genesis story to the status of fiction, no matter how inspiring we think it might be. It is thus not quite right to define Genesis as a truthful myth, whatever that might mean. Instead, I want to suggest that Genesis is as true as we can expect any such account of the origin of the world to be. The problem with Genesis is not that it uses symbolic, metaphorical, or legendary images and ideas. The problem is that the world Genesis depicts is not the one you and I live in now. Eden is the world before, outside of, and in opposition to the struggle of species for survival. Genesis is a fantastic account of the world because the truth itself is fantastic, given that the world as we know it is dull and dreary in its brutal regularities. The Genesis narrative is unique, then, because it describes a place that was both in and not in our world. It is the place that gives the narrative its mythical and legendary qualities, not the other way around. What Genesis is describing could be described in no other way.

We typically think that the difficult thing is to imagine Eden as a real *place*, as our ancestors did, but it is actually much harder to imagine the temporality of Genesis, not its spatiality. Suppose that Eden was a real place, whatever that means, and then ask a simple question. How long did Adam and Eve spend in the Garden before their expulsion? Some early theologians taught that however long it was, it was not very long. After all, Adam and Eve were given the command to be fruitful and multiply, but by the time of the fall there were no children. This is not an irrelevant piece of information. As all parents know, children help us to measure time. By seeing our children grow and change, we know the days are passing us by. How did the first couple measure their days prior to the fall? Even if they had had children in the garden, they would not have had to worry about providing for them, since God was taking care of them. How long was each day in terms of the minutes we count by, and how long did those days seem to Adam and Eve? Was each moment perfect, and if so, how long did each moment last? To make these questions even harder to answer, we could say that the clock was not running in Eden, because death had not yet entered their world. Moments pass for us only because they slip into a past whose receding distance can be crossed only by the dim traces of memory, and they extend into a future that is bound by the inevitability of our demise. We exist always in the passing of time, along the thin edge of its nearly pointless present. Whatever Adam and Eve experienced, it must have been closer to the time of heaven than the time that binds us to death here on Earth.

Speculating about time in Eden is just that, but such speculations can still be enlightening. Time conditions our passage through the world more than space, since we can imagine standing still better than we can imagine stepping outside of time. That is, even when we are standing still, we are still moving through time. We can best imagine God's relationship to us, in a way, as being closer to our experience of space than our participation in time. Traditional theism teaches that God sees everything, past, present, and future, all at once. God's temporality is spatialized, one could say. God is not bound by time because God can move in and out of any particular space (this is God's omnipresence). Adam and Eve, I want to suggest, might have experienced time as a form of space. That is, time was something they could move in and out of without seeing their lives move backward beyond their reach or forward into the unknown. They could see the times of their lives like we might see the various objects of our room. As we move around a room and touch first a desk, then a chair and a stack of books and a painting, we do not feel like we have lost anything about ourselves or that we are in danger of disappearing into death. We are at home, comforted by the familiar and the settled. Time for Adam and Eve would have been no different, because their home was the home of homes, and everything in it had been given to them by God—and they did not face death.

If time in the Garden is difficult to measure and conceive, the same goes for time outside of the Garden. Time outside of the Garden was biological time, sometimes called deep time, and even secular Darwinians admit that the timeframe required for the stupendously slow evolution of species is so long that it exceeds our ability to picture it. The deep time of evolution stands outside of our temporal framework. We have nothing to compare it to. Like the frame of a painting that escapes our notice while we examine the artwork that it encloses, the time of evolution escapes our horizon when we look at what is actually going on in nature. Although we can attach numbers to deep time, that does not make it any more comprehensible. As much as modern humans take pride in discovering deep time, the time of evolution is no more real to us today that the time of the Garden. Both times resist being plotted according to our ordinary sense of chronology. Both times have a mythic dimension that transcends ordinary time. If each of these times is unique in their own way, then it also follows that they cannot be satisfactorily synchronized. To synchronize the events in each of these temporal fields, Edenic time and deep biological time, assumes that there is a third time—our time, the "real" time—that is the measure of all other times. Our time, however, is yet another time, hardly to be privileged as the only time, and since our experience of time is distorted by the fall, our time traps us in the immediacy of our personal lives and the relative brevity of human history. Our time is bound by the pace of human activity. It stands midway, perhaps, between the violent and faceless time of deep biology and the perfectly paced time of paradise, but it is no truer than these times and it permits no direct access to either.

Some theologians in the fundamentalist and evangelical camps have argued that the only way to preserve the literal truth of Genesis from the falsifying evidence of deep biological time is to interpret its days figuratively. Given the mythical elements of the Genesis story, the figurative interpretation of the six days of creation can be very appealing. Nevertheless, this argument promises more than it can deliver. The argument over whether the days of Genesis should be understood as twenty-four-hour days or long epochs misses the true character of Genesis altogether, just as the usual interpretation of Genesis as myth misses its real truthfulness. The figurative interpretation of the days of

Genesis is right, but for all the wrong reasons. The days of Genesis are not twenty-four-hour days, but that is not because they actually lasted several million years. If we could experience the time of the Garden, it would assuredly not be the same time we experience in the natural world, so it makes little sense to debate how long the days of Genesis lasted.

Theologians have long argued that God is eternal, and that eternity is not just another form of temporality, lasting for a very long time. Eternity has no duration, and as such it is closed off to our human experience, just as the gates of Eden were shut after the fall. Eternity is neither the extension nor the negation of time; rather, eternity is the fulfillment of time. We tend to think of eternity as an infinite amount of time, but God can enter into every moment of time because God stands outside of time. God is present and active throughout time because God's time is not our time. The time of the Garden of Eden is not the time of eternity, but it also is not our time. It is something in between. Eden is the time of God's most visible and active presence on earth short of the incarnation. It is, we could say, the time when God shared his time with humanity. In the incarnation, God took on human form and thus subjected himself to human time. In the Garden, God created a place where humans could experience, as far as was compatible with their created condition, the time of God.

Eden encapsulates the drama that determines the entire history of humanity. In this sense, Eden unfolds prior to time as we know it. True, the Sun is in its place and the Earth and Moon are making their orbits. But the first two humans existed in a state we can hardly imagine. The world was new to them. They were not anxious about the passing of the hours. They did not have a list of things to do and deadlines to meet. Edenic time was neither timeless nor timed by the ticking of a clock. Time, after all, is a uniquely human phenomenon, and we are aware of time, as the German philosopher Martin Heidegger argued, because we are aware, however dimly and uncomfortably, with our impending deaths. Without death, we would have no final limit defining what it means to have a life. We would have plenty of time to do everything we wanted to do, which means we would not feel time as a burden. Without death, we could go so far in saying, there would be no time, at least time as we understand it. We rush at the day with the knowledge, no matter how suppressed, of a basic limit set against our lives. That limit did not become real for Adam and Even until after their expulsion from the garden.[19] We should let the time of Eden measure and judge our sense of time, rather than use our clocks and workdays to understand time in that unique place.

Notice that I am not simply arguing that the time of Genesis is compressed. The concept of compression can be useful in thinking about Genesis, but it needs careful analysis. Compression denotes the way that any report of any activity will be highly abbreviated. In other words, details will be left out. Of course, reports about an event, say a car accident, typically will be not only compressed but also distorted. Bring two or more people together as witnesses of a car accident and you are likely to get two or more versions of the same event. A compressed account is not necessarily a mistaken account, though compressing any narrative (or, we should say, the compression that is the inevitable result of every narrative) should lead us to be epistemologically modest about the accuracy of even the most trustworthy eyewitness of an event. In other words, multiple accounts of the same event can be equally trustworthy yet vary in their details because they leave out different details. They also will make different kinds of connections between points on the time line of the event. Compression is an act of interpretation, not just a matter of subtraction. When something is left out, a decision must be made about how to get the narrative across the deleted details. Bridges must be built by some narrative device, even one as simple as "then," "so," or "therefore."

A compressed account of an event needs to be expanded (decompressed, if you will) by filling in the gaps in the narrative to get at the whole truth. Expanding a narrative is also an act of interpretation, since we do not know what was left out. It is tempting to treat the relationship of Genesis to evolution as a straightforward matter of narrative compression and expansion. Genesis, from this perspective, is an incomplete account of creation. Its narrative blank spaces need to be filled with information provided by evolution. Genesis, it could be argued, gives us the true structure of creation but leaves out the details

---

19. C. S. Lewis, in his great novel about the fall, *Perelandra* (New York: Scribner, 1996), connects the discovery of time with evil when the evolutionary scientist begins questioning the Green Lady. Only in logical argument does she begin to perceive a before and an after.

The Five Theses

of evolution. Now that we know more about the world than the ancient Hebrews did, we can carefully fill in the holes with biological facts without damaging the narrative structure along the way.

The problem with this approach is that it is notoriously difficult to coordinate the slow and gradual process of evolution with the days (even when figuratively interpreted as long ages) God spent creating the world. One of the advantages of my theory, in fact, is that it frees Christians from trying to do exactly that. I am not denying that there are some basic parallels between the Genesis narrative and the Darwinian account of the order of life. Genesis sounds remarkably modern by putting the light in the beginning and human beings at the end of the sequence of creation events. Vegetation comes before animals, and humans and animals are portrayed as intimately related. Nonetheless, once the reader begins moving beyond these structural similarities, differences begin rapidly proliferating. Some people think creation science (CS) is committed to proving that the Genesis record accurately reflects modern biological knowledge, but that is not the case. Theistic evolution (TE) theorists are actually more likely to make this kind of argument, because they think Genesis reflects evolutionary truth. CS thinks Genesis is right and evolution is wrong. Henry Morris, for example, has found at least twenty-five contradictions between the Bible and modern science, from the Bible putting fruit trees before fishes to putting birds before reptiles.[20] Morris thinks Genesis and biology are irreconcilable, a point he pushes hard in order to encourage Christians to side with Genesis over biology.

To get to the bottom of the problem of synchronization, let us look at one basic example, bacteria. Bacteria, or more precisely put, their ancestors, were the first forms of life on Earth. They came into being around four billion years ago, scientists say, and for about three billion years they were the dominant form of life on Earth. Their existence was not the product of, nor was it a contribution to, violence and strife in any way that does justice to those terms. They just were. So how do we place them in terms of the time of the Garden and the time of evolution? It seems reasonable to surmise that God created them for the whole planet and used them, and other building blocks of life, to create the creatures that inhabited the Garden, but bacteria were also outside

20. Morris, *Scientific Creationism*, 227–28.

of the Garden, and subjected to use by Satan as well. Getting more specific about the relationship of evolution within the Garden and evolution outside of the Garden would probably lead to more confusions and speculation than it is worth, though I welcome more discussion of this matter. Notice that I refer to evolution within and without the Garden. I should be clear that I am not arguing that there was no evolution in the Garden, subjected to God's guidance, nor that God had nothing to do with evolution outside the Garden. I will return to this question in the next thesis, when I discuss how the dome divides the good from evil, not creation from evolution, as if evolution is never creative and creation never varies!

Another practical problem that will plague intrepid thinkers who seek to synchronize the events of evolution, both good and bad, with the events of the Garden concerns the alleged ancestry of the human species. Claims to have found the fossil remains of intermediate forms between the great apes and humans, along with genetic comparisons of apes and humans, have convinced many people that the picture of human evolution is fairly complete. Actually, the fossil record for human ancestry is both incomplete and notoriously hard to interpret. Even the nomenclature that paleontologists use to categorize hominid fossils is subject to much debate. There are different genera of primates, and all of them are sometimes referred to as humans in order to indicate that human ancestry dates back five to six million years ago. The use of terms like hominid, *Homo sapiens*, archaic *Homo sapiens*, modern humans, and anatomically modern humans litter the field in unsystematic ways. Nevertheless, as Fazale Rana and Hugh Ross explain, "nearly all paleoanthropologists agree that anatomically modern humans (*Homo sapiens sapiens*) appear in the fossil record not much earlier than 100,000 years ago."[21] This is important because it points to a gap that Rana and Ross want to fill with the special creation of human beings.

Ross has a PhD in astronomy and is president of Reasons to Believe (RTB), an organization dedicated to reconciling Genesis and some limited aspects of evolutionary theory. Rana, the son of a Muslim scientist, holds a PhD in biochemistry and has published many articles in peer-

21. Fazale Rana with Hugh Ross, *Who Was Adam? A Creation Model Approach to the Origin of Man* (Colorado Springs: NavPress, 2005) 30. For a similar position that separates the creation of human beings from the evolution of hominids, see Henri Blocher, *Original Sin: Illuminating the Riddle* (Grand Rapids: Eerdmans, 1997) 39-42.

reviewed scientific journals. He is vice president of RTB. RTB believes that the fossil record is a reasonably accurate history of life on earth, including the existence of hominids before modern humans. But RTB also firmly believes that God supernaturally and miraculously created Adam from the "dust of the earth" (not from a pre-existing hominid species) just as described in Genesis 1 and 2. Adam and Eve were the first humans, and from them came the entire human race.

Rana and Ross come to this conclusion from the plethora of hominids that have been found in the fossil record. Darwinians think that humans were only one segment of the hominid population, but they were the only one to survive when the others died off. They interpret the lack of fossil evidence for humans in the period between 40,000 and 80,000 years ago as evidence of a population loss, perhaps through some environmental catastrophe, which almost made humanity extinct. RTB considers the hominids to be mere animals, denied the status of spiritual beings reserved for human beings. Though some hominids that lived millions of years ago used tools, they did not develop beyond a crude and simplistic way of life. The fossil record, according to RTB, does not display a gradual improvement and advancement in human evolution. Instead, there was a "big bang" about 50,000 years ago in which human culture appears out of nowhere. By 40,000 years ago, humans were already present in Africa, Eurasia, and even Australia. RTB argues that this is evidence for an out-of-Africa thesis that coincides with a Garden of Eden thesis. Problems with the idea of a population collapse, which some scientists argue would surely have led to extinction, lead RTB to argue that the biological record points to the special creation of Adam and Eve in one particular place in Africa at one particular time, about 50,000 years ago.

I find this argument mostly persuasive. Nevertheless, distinguishing humans from hominids is one thing; correlating their chronological co-existence on a single time scale is quite another. Given all of their biological similarities, the question of their exact relationship begs to be asked, but it also evades any simple answer. If hominids were around five millions years ago and humans only 50,000 years ago, then does that mean that God did not get around to creating human beings in a special act until evolution had already run its course? If Eden was happening while the rest of the world was evolving, what was happening in Eden for so long if so much was happening outside of Eden? If hominids are examples of Satan's attempt to mock and parody creation, how could they have evolved before God created Adam and Eve? By placing hominids prior to Adam and Eve, this position risks confirming evolution as the means by which God created humans as the crown of creation. That would lead us straight back to theistic evolution, which gives evolution as a whole a theological blessing.

We cannot squeeze evolution into the cracks of Genesis chronology, but that does not mean that we have to treat Genesis in isolation from everything else we know. We need to acknowledge that the Genesis account of creation, while utterly true and reliable, is also incomplete. That is, Genesis does not tell us everything that is going on in the cosmos, nor does it tell us everything that God is doing when (and before) God creates the world. It tells us the truth, but it does not give us every truth. The opening of Genesis is only the tip of the scriptural iceberg. The whole Bible is the necessary and sufficient revelation of God. Like all great books, you have to read straight through to the end of the Bible in order to understand the beginning. The early Church Fathers actually had a rule about this. Scripture interprets scripture, they stated. This simply means that Scripture comprises a complete whole, the sum of which is greater than its parts. If any part seems confusing, it can be illuminated by putting it in the larger context of the whole. The Bible is the first postmodern book in the sense that it refers constantly to itself, either in the form of a prophecy in one place that comes true later on, or in an allusion at one point to an earlier story or theme. Abraham is a real person in the Bible, but he is also a symbol or type, representing the man of faith for Paul, for example. One verse always leads to another and all verses together sum up the Word of God.

Even if the time of Eden and the time of evolution cannot be synchronized, theology is still faced with the task of conceiving their relationship in some constructive way. Clearly, the first thing that needs to be said is that what happened outside of Eden was dependent on what happened inside Eden, but at the same time, what happened outside of Eden was a horrible distortion of the Garden. The matter God had created was infused with the spirit of strife, greed, and disquiet. While God was governing Eden, Satan was desecrating the wider world. Satan was preparing a literal testing ground for the humans that God had created in the image of his Son. Would humans live up to their unique status, or would they become like the wild animals, driven by desire, greed, and hunger? That is the challenge Satan wanted to throw at God, and that is the question each of us still faces every day. Adam and Eve had to choose between obedience to God and pursuit of the goods of the world regardless of what God had commanded. Satan was ready for them, if they should choose to give up their paradise. Keep in mind that in the Book of Job we get a clear portrait of Satan as a tester. God permits Satan to push Job to the limits, taking away his children, his health, and his honor. Job was not the first human to be subjected to Satan's wry examination. The world itself is the stage upon which all of us must pass or fail as we struggle with the purpose of God's plan. The world is the stage of temptation because the gates of Eden were closed to us after Adam and Eve's expulsion. We cannot return to Eden, but we can go back to Genesis with a fresh perspective to determine what makes us human and what makes us suitable for our destiny with the divine.

Thesis Four: The Dome of Eden

Satan is already fallen when he enters Eden as the serpent, but the power he holds over the earth is restricted inside Eden's gate. All he can do in the Garden is appeal to human freedom in order to tempt the first humans into pride and ingratitude. Beyond the gates of Eden is another story. The world outside of Eden is an anti-world, a mockery or demonic parody of everything God wanted for his creation. But if that is true, what was Eden, and what is its relationship to the rest of the world? If that riddle can be solved, then the problem of evolution ceases to be a problem for theology.

The key to solving this riddle is the Hebrew word, *raqiya'* (sometimes transliterated simply as *raqia*). This word is hard to translate and even harder to understand once it is translated. Scholars have debated this word for centuries. The King James Version tried with *firmament*, which has entered into the English language as one of those words that everyone who has grown up on the Bible recognizes but nobody is sure what it means. Webster's defines firmament as a vault or arch, but that does not get us very far. Other translations use sky or expanse. The Hebrew *raqiya'* is found in several other places in the Bible, but first

The Dome of Eden

and most puzzling in Gen 1:6–8. In the New Revised Standard Version, which uses the word *dome* for *raqiya'*, this passage reads:

> And God said, "Let there be a dome in the midst of the waters, and let it separate the waters from the waters." So God made the dome and separated the waters that were under the dome from the waters that were above the dome. And it was so. God called the dome Sky. And there was evening and there was morning, the second day.

Of all the puzzling verses of the Bible, this is surely one of the most difficult. On a quick literal reading it seems to suggest that God placed a dome in the middle of the waters, which ended up forcing some waters on top of it.

The next passage tells us more about the function of the Dome:

> And God said, "Let the waters under the sky be gathered together into one place, and let the dry land appear." And it was so. God called the dry land Earth, and the waters that were gathered together he called Seas. And God saw that it was good. (Gen 1:9–10).

The dome is an arching vault that covers the Earth, or at least one part of the Earth. I say one part of the Earth because it is not clear what cosmology the writer of Genesis is using, just as it is not clear what the relationship is between the dry land that emerges under the Dome and the Earth of Gen 1:1 and the waste and void of Gen 1:2.[22] On the one hand, if the sky or heaven is an immense vault that rests upon the Earth, then the Earth must be flat; otherwise, the dome could not encompass all of the Earth. The land left out of the dome would then have no sky. On the other hand, if the dome was not the sky but some kind of symbol of God's protective providence and if the Earth was not considered flat, then the Dome would cover only part of the Earth, and the earth that was left out of the Dome would indeed be waste and void. Even if the Genesis writer thought the Earth was flat, he still could have conceived

---

22. Just because the same Hebrew word is used for earth in Gen 1:1 and 1:10 does not mean that the reference is identical. In my view, Gen 1:1 is indeed about the entire Earth, while 1:2 denotes something going wrong with the Earth, and 1:10 is about the emergence of a particular piece of the Earth. Some scholars indeed hold to this view, arguing that 1:1 is about the world and 1:10 is about the continents in the world. For further arguments about this issue, see the work of Paul H. Seely, which I analyze in chapter 6.

The Five Theses

of the Dome as covering only part of the Earth, with parts of the Earth left out at the fringes of the Dome.

In any case, from the perspective of the whole of the first chapter of Genesis, it is clear that the land that is under the Dome is the land upon which God created Adam and Eve. Yet even that point is complicated by the fact that in the so-called second creation narrative, God appears to create Adam first, then plants a garden "in Eden," where he puts "the man whom he had formed" (Gen 2:8). Scholars use differences like this to argue that Genesis is combining two quite different accounts of creation. I think both creation accounts are trying to get at the same point—that is, that the Garden is not the whole of the Earth and that it is a special place set apart from the rest of the world.

If these speculations seem too much, let's return to the image of the Dome. A dome is universally conceived, as I will argue in chapter 6, to function as a crown over a special place and to provide protection for that place. If this is how the writer of Genesis conceived of the Dome, then that place could only have been Eden. But why would the Garden of Eden need a cover? From what is it being protected?

Perhaps the simplest way to avoid all of these issues is to just think of the Dome as a fancy way of picturing the sky. The Hebrew word translated by the NRSV as "sky" in Gen 1:8 is translated by most other Bibles as "heaven," because the Hebrew does not distinguish between the two. The sky is merely the visible part of heaven. So the reader should not get the idea that the Dome is simply being identified with the sky. God calls the Dome sky or heaven because that is what it looks like; God is not identifying the Dome with the vague concept of the sky. Indeed, most scholars agree that the writer of Genesis thinks that God created something solid up in the heavens or as a part of the heavens, and that this solid object has something to do with the dividing of water. For example, the great Old Testament scholar Gerhard von Rad explains in his commentary on Genesis that *raqiya'* means "that which is firmly hammered, stamped." The firmament is, as best as he can describe it, a "heavenly bell."[23] After this colorful description, he has nothing more to say about the firmament, as if it is an odd embellishment to the text that can only be a distraction to serious scholarship.

---

23. Gerhard von Rad, *Genesis: A Commentary*, trans. John H. Marks (Philadelphia: Westminster, 1961) 52.

The Dome of Eden

Claus Westermann, another great Old Testament scholar, tries to make something more of the firmament by speculating about the metaphysics behind the Genesis text. Westermann argues that the creation of light is really about the creation of time, and that the creation of the firmament is really about the creation of space.[24] He thus reads Genesis through the eyes of Kant, as if the text were worried about the conditions that make perception possible. This is actually a helpful point, because the Dome does divide space, but Westermann does not ask what it divides or why. From silence to metaphysics, scholars have not known what to do with the firmament. The simplest explanation for the Dome, I will argue, is that it separated Eden from the rest of the world. Inside the Dome, God created the world as He meant it to be. Outside the Dome, Satan was hard at work to infuse that creation with the violence we now call evolution. The Dome protected God's design from the insidious imitation of evolution.

The details of my Dome Theory will be worked out in chapter 6, but for now, I want to point out some of the reasons why the Dome has not been taken very seriously as a theological concept that does something important in the text. Let's look at three camps: fundamentalist, liberal, and what we can call the literary.

Fundamentalist Christians have not missed the significance of this text, but they have focused on the wrong thing. The fundamentalist camp has gotten hung up on the water above the dome. That water, some leading CS theoreticians argue, is the source of Noah's flood. This is commonly called the water canopy theory, which I discussed above. From my perspective, the CS camp is not necessarily wrong on this issue as it is misguided. Water canopy theorists think of the Dome as a container rather than a cover, because they think the primary purpose of the dome was to hold the waters that were above it. Holding water, however, is best accomplished by something in the shape of a cup, not a dome. A dome, in fact, is particularly inept for this function, since it is built to facilitate water running off and away from what it protects, not to hold water up. A dome is like an upside down cup, and so it is hard to imaging water on top of it, although it is easy to imagine something be-

---

24. To be more precise, the firmament is about the creation of the vertical dimension of space, while the separation of land and sea is about the horizontal dimension of space. See Claus Westermann, *Creation*, trans. John J. Scullion (Philadelphia: Fortress, 1974) 43.

neath it. To use another image, domes are like umbrellas. They protect the space below from the weather. Fundamentalists need to focus their attention on what is under the Dome, rather than what is precariously perched above it. Surely the Dome had a more significant function that merely pooling a reservoir of water for future use in case God needed to cause a flood.

When liberal scholars take this passage seriously, they treat it as an example of one of the Bible's many scientific errors. Indeed, skeptics often use the firmament as an example of the Bible's mistaken cosmology. In this view, Genesis *does* portray God making something in the heavens above to hold up some water, but that just demonstrates how outdated the Bible is.

Both conservative and liberal scholars agree that Genesis is saying something fundamental about the shape of the world, but they disagree about what it is, and whether it is true. The literary camp takes an altogether different position. This camp argues that Genesis is mythological poetry or poetic myth, and thus it is not to be taken literally or scientifically. The water above the firmament, from this perspective, evokes God's majesty but is otherwise meaningless. The poet behind Genesis is striving for effect, not accurate description. Literary critics thus save the author of Genesis from the accusation that he uses outdated science at the cost of accusing him of being a second rate poet. The firmament is an unfortunate image empty of any specifiable content. Trying to discover what it really is would be as much of a waste of time as trying to figure out if the "road not taken" in the Robert Frost poem was paved or gravel.

So, all three camps can agree that the firmament is some kind of dome, but they do not take the Dome seriously. Fundamentalists focus on the water above the Dome, because that can be thought of as the likely source of the great flood. Liberals ponder the parallels between Genesis and other ancient cosmologies, concluding that the ancients were victims of a pre-scientific worldview. Finally, those who appreciate the Bible as literature find the image of the Dome somewhat poetic but hopelessly muddled. For those who are not committed to any of these three camps, the alternative is not very clear. Whether it was meant poetically or scientifically, Gen 1:6–8 does not seem to make much sense.

The Dome of Eden

It is either confusing poetry or bad science. Could the apparently misty firmament be something more?

The Dome does not make much sense, admittedly, until it is put in the context of the fall of Satan and a spiritual interpretation of biological warfare. In that context, it becomes clear that the Dome was created over the Garden of Eden as a means of protecting that particular place from the consequences of Satan's rebellion, which had already made its mark on the Earth. Satan cannot create something from nothing, so the original creation of the world was a good act with a good outcome. But we know that Satan is at work during the time of creation, because Satan (or one of his agents) ends up in the Garden disguised as the serpent. The serpent is able to tempt Adam and Eve because he has experienced the evil that the human couple so far have not. Whether the serpent is simply identified with Satan or construed as a vehicle of Satan's ploy, it is clear that Satan has been working outside the Garden to undermine God's plan. If the serpent is taken as the product of Satan's work, then there is no other conclusion than that Satan was working outside the Garden to evolve forms of life that could disrupt Eden's peace and harmony. As the Old Testament scholar André LaCocque puts it, "The serpent's action is the animal revolt against human supremacy and, beyond, against a God who selected the human animal to dominate over all other animals."[25] As the cleverest of the animals, the serpent understands that God has bypassed the animal kingdom in choosing the human species for a unique relationship, just as Adam overlooked the animals in choosing Eve as a partner and mate. The serpent is enraged and wishes to upset the cosmic order by dragging humanity down to its own level. It is tempting to equate the source of the serpent's degraded nature and the object of Satan's work outside of Eden with biological evolution, but that would be too simplistic and would not do justice to either science or theology. Evolution is torn, we could say, between God and Satan. The human heart is the battleground between good and evil in the world of free agents, but evolution is that same battleground in the natural world.

So does this mean that I think the Dome was literally . . . a dome? I think one can recognize the significance and function of the Dome

---

25. André LaCocque, *The Trial of Innocence: Adam, Eve, and the Yahwist* (Eugene, OR: Cascade, 2006) 147.

The Five Theses

without necessarily granting it the status of having been physically real, though I personally see no reason to withhold that status. Perhaps a note about the doctrine of accommodation is in order. That God needs to accommodate divine revelation to human limitations is an old idea, but it was given its clearest expression in the work of the sixteenth-century Protestant reformer, John Calvin. Calvin argued that the Bible is absolutely true in content, but its form is an accommodation to our limited reasoning and our lack of direct understanding of the divine. We have a hard enough time knowing how evolution works, so how could human reason be relied upon to fathom the mysteries of the Triune God? God's knowledge is infinite, and our knowledge is finite. God thus speaks to us like parents speak to their children: patiently, kindly, and considerately. When a mother tells her child that babies come from her stomach, she does not mean that literally, although she is certainly not lying, especially given the elasticity of the word *stomach*. Babies do come from that general area, but children are not equipped at a young age to understand all of the details pertaining to the geography of human birth. Mature Christians are even less able to understand all of the details of the heavens, let alone the earth. Sometimes the Bible develops a precise picture of historical events, while at other times it gives us a map, and maps are meant to be read differently than pictures. Stomach is an indication, not a definition. It points at something rather than describing it with any precision. When talking to young children about babies, stomach will have to do.

The doctrine of accommodation is valuable, and I have already referred to it in the discussion of thesis two. The Dome certainly could be interpreted like the stomach in the example above. It is God's way of indicating that he is in control and thus easing our anxiety. From this perspective, the Dome is a symbol of God's intentions to protect Eden from the consequences of Satan's fall. For me, those consequences are too real to be contained by a symbol, and I see no other way to understand how God could have created a good world while permitting Satan to struggle against that goodness outside of Eden. Nevertheless, symbolic interpretations of Genesis are valid within reason. I only ask the reader to hold off on making a judgment until he or she has read the next two chapters.

The Dome of Eden

Thesis Five: Christological Interpretation of the Imago Dei

The Dome, upon first considering its role in Genesis, can be puzzling, and not just to modern readers. When confronted with enigmatic texts, the Church Fathers trusted in the whole of the Bible to make sense of its many parts. They based this trust on the doctrine of providence, which taught them to have confidence in history, no matter what. Even the most apparently meaningless incidents will make sense from the perspective of the end of time. Likewise, biblical passages that appear to be obscure will reveal their meaning when placed in the context of the whole of divine revelation.[26]

The most important passage outside of Genesis that concerns the Dome is found in Ezekiel 1, where the firmament is described in terms that clearly signify a dome. The book of Ezekiel begins with a vision given to the Prophet while he was in exile in Babylon. At one point he sees four living creatures, each with four faces, who are moving with or on mysterious, gleaming wheels. Over the heads of these creatures "there was something like a dome, shining like a crystal, spread out above their heads" (Ezek 1:22). The word translated dome in that passage by the NRSV is none other than the Hebrew *raqiya'*. Could this be the same dome that appears in Gen 1:6–8?

To the typical modern reader, the opening vision of Ezekiel is once again an example of the mistaken cosmological speculations of the biblical writers. Even its most sympathetic readers often end up in exasperation. "It is quite difficult," writes one, "to put together a clear picture of what is being described; some features are confusing, even allowing for difficulties of translation, and have defied explanation."[27] The wheels that Ezekiel describes are certainly mysterious. They appear to circle the world, and their intimate connection to the four living creatures is intimated but not explained. All of this smacks of a geocentric cosmology, with the heavenly skies (and whatever wheel-like

---

26. Christopher R. Seitz, *Figured Out: Typology and Providence in Christian Scripture* (Louisville: Westminster John Knox, 2001).

27. Ronald E. Clements, *Ezekiel* (Louisville: Westminster John Knox, 1996) 11. Some scholars attribute much of Ezekiel's imagery to the Assyrian king's throne room. Margaret S. Odell, "Ezekiel Saw What He Said He Saw: Genres, Forms, and the Vision of Ezekiel 1," in *The Changing Face of Form Criticism for the Twenty-First Century*, ed. Marvin A. Sweeney and Ehud Ben Zvi (Grand Rapids: Eerdmans, 2003) 162–76.

mechanisms keep the stars rotating) circling the earth, which is firmly anchored, unmoving, at the center of the universe. The very idea of a rigid or solid sky is the lynchpin of the geocentric universe. If the earth is stationary, then the sky as a whole must be in movement around it, so that it makes sense to think of the sky as a single object of sorts. Even most of the ancient Greeks thought the sky must be composed of a substance in order to keep the stars in their same position relative to each other. A solid spherical shell held the stars firmly in place as they moved across the night sky. Remnants of this cosmology can be found today in the flat-earth defenders, who still base their understanding of Earth's shape on the idea that God created a dome above us.

I will have more to say about the connection between the Dome and the mistaken belief in a flat Earth in chapter 6, but for now it is important to note that while flat earthists are wrong about the shape of the Earth, they are not necessarily wrong about the shape of history. In its contemporary guise, belief in a flat Earth is a peculiarly pathological episode in the quixotic history of misguided attempts to resist the total triumph of modern science. In its ancient form, however, belief in a flat Earth should not be treated as a naive scientific mistake. Historically speaking, some Christians believed that the Earth is flat because they believed that the Earth is at the center of the cosmos, and they believed that the Earth is at the center of the cosmos because they believed that humans are at the center of God's plan. This last belief they based on the incarnation. If God chose this world as the stage for the incarnation, and the human species as its form, then there must be something unique about both planet Earth and human nature.

The vision of Ezekiel affirms the uniqueness of the Earth by depicting the dome in its sheltering role, and it puts humanity at the center of the cosmos by what Ezekiel sees atop the Dome. On the Dome is "something like a throne" (1:26) that looks like it is made of sapphire. On the throne is seated "something that seemed like a human form" (1:26). Some translations have "the appearance of a man" (KJV and American Standard Version, for example). Ezekiel later clarifies his vision by saying that it is God's glory that he sees: "This was the appearance of the likeness of the glory [Hebrew: *kabod*] of the Lord" (1:28). To some commentators, Ezekiel is backing down from his claim to have seen God directly by clarifying that it is God's glory that he

The Dome of Eden

saw, not God himself. The glory of God is a common phrase in the Old Testament as well as later developments in Jewish mysticism and the *kabod* is frequently distinguished by human features. To Christian ears, it is obvious what Ezekiel saw on the throne. The only person with divine status who has a human form is, for Christians, Jesus Christ.

Irenaeus, Gregory the Great, Jerome, and Theodore of Cyr were quite happy with the though that Ezekiel saw Jesus Christ sitting atop the Dome, but other theologians, following Origen, were reluctant to make this claim, mainly because they thought that the Son of God did not have a body before the incarnation.[28] This worry over a prematurely enfleshed Word of God dominates Calvin's commentary on the opening chapter of Ezekiel, although his view is admittedly nuanced. Ordinarily, Calvin interprets the Old Testament in a decidedly christological manner. "As often as God appeared under the form of man," he writes, with regard to all of the visions of God granted to the Prophets of the Old Testament, "an obscure glimpse was afforded of the mystery which was at length manifested in the person of Christ." Nonetheless, Calvin emphasizes the obscurity of Ezekiel's vision, which was intended, he says, to prevent Jews from having a complete knowledge of God before Jesus fully revealed himself. Calvin admits that the phrase "form of a man" can apply only to Christ, yet he also argues that Ezekiel could not have seen a real body. Ezekiel had a vision of the whole essence of God, not any particular member of the Trinity, because the three persons of the Trinity became evident to humanity only after the incarnation. Yet Calvin insists that Ezekiel did see what he reports. What he saw, then, was a representation of the essence of God, and the essence of God, as opposed to the second person of the Trinity, is, for Calvin, completely unrelated to human form. Only the uneducated and superstitious, Calvin suggests, imagine that God really has a body. Calvin fears, in the end, that the idea that the Word had a body before the incarnation confuses the human and the divine, which should always be kept separate. He rightly understood that the idea of a pre-incarnate body for Christ implies that it is our destiny to become divinized in the after life, body and all, but he rejected divinization as an aspect of our salvation. Nonetheless, far from being certain about his interpretation, he ends

---

28. Kenneth Stevenson and Michael Glerup, eds., *Ancient Christian Commentary on Scripture*, vol. XIII, *Ezekiel, Daniel* (Downers Grove, IL: InterVarsity, 2008) 14–16.

his discussion by admitting that what Ezekiel saw on the firmament is a "knotty problem."[29]

The problem is knotty because Calvin has to theorize about metaphysical essences in order to avoid the plain meaning (form a Christian point of view) of the text. Indeed, Christians were able to find Christ in many parts of the Old Testament due to its thoroughly anthropomorphic view of God (it repeatedly describes God in human form). Given the many bodily appearances and descriptions of God in the Old Testament, it would have been surprising if Christians had *not* thought that Moses, Abraham, and the Prophets had seen the Son and heard his voice. Old Testament theophanies were a standard trope of Christian apologetics directed at Jews, and they had a profound impact on Christian theology. Carl Griffin and David Paulsen have shown how common it was, before Origen, to interpret the pinnacle of mystical ascent, as well as the beatific vision promised to all believers in the end time, as a vision of the body of God.[30] What the Old Testament prophets saw obscurely, the eyes of faith would see clearly and fully. What greater delight could there be than to see Jesus?

That the second person of the Trinity is active in the Old Testament is not a subject of dispute for orthodox theologians. Nonetheless, as the example of Calvin makes clear, some theologians did hesitate to identify particular revelations of God in the Old Testament with anything other than divinity in general and not the person of Jesus Christ. There are two answers for this hesitation, one having to do with the corporeality of God and the other with the heresy known as Arianism.

First, the corporeality of God. Many ancient Christians could easily imagine the prophets seeing Jesus Christ because they thought Jesus was the natural form of the divine. Put differently, they had trouble imagining that God was completely without any kind of corporeal form altogether. As the great Latin theologian Tertullian said, "Nothing is incorporeal except that which is nothing."[31] If God has form, they reasoned, then God could have no better form than the body of Jesus

---

29. John Calvin, *Commentaries on the First Twenty Chapters of the Book of the Prophet Ezekiel*, trans. Thomas Myers (Grand Rapids: Eerdmans, 1948) 97 and 102.

30. Carl W. Griffin and David L. Paulsen, "Augustine and the Corporeality of God," *Harvard Theological Review* 95 (2002) 97–118.

31. Ibid., 106.

Christ. For anthropomorphites, as they came to be called, Jesus Christ was the truest way to picture God because God fit the picture of a human form. Origenists were those who followed Origen in rejecting anthropomorphism, and the two parties came into open conflict in Egypt at the end of the fourth century.[32] Origen treated anthropomorphism as a prejudice of the uneducated, since all philosophers taught that learning begins with the distinction of form and matter. The anthropomorphites in turn grew increasingly skeptical of philosophical speculation and suspected that without form, God could not be worshipped.

On this as on so many theological issues, Augustine is the decisive figure in the West for the development of an incorporeal understanding of divinity. Augustine dismissed the idea that God has a body because he equated it with human vanity (he thought only pride leads us to want God to be like us) and mental weakness (he thought only the feeble minded had trouble understanding Platonic abstractions and immaterial spiritual essences). Augustine learned from the Platonists that God, just like the highest forms of thought, transcends physical matter. True, God became incarnate in Jesus Christ, but this unique miracle happened at a particular time and could not have been witnessed by those living before it.

Second, Arianism. The christological interpretation of Old Testament theophanies also ran afoul of orthodox responses to the Arian heresy. Calvin himself suggests as much with a brief reference in his commentary to the notorious heretic Servetus. Calvin wrote his commentary on Ezekiel after he had Servetus executed for heresy in Geneva, and he mentions Servetus as supporting the idea that Ezekiel saw Jesus Christ. Calvin was convinced that Servetus was reviving an ancient form of heresy known as Arianism. To Calvin, Servetus made the Son of God a lesser deity, subordinate to the Father, and Calvin feared that a christological interpretation of Ezekiel could have played into Servetus's hands.[33]

---

32. Fred Ledegang, "Anthropomorphites and Origenists in Egypt at the End of the Fourth Century," *Origeniana Septima: Origenes in den Auseinandersetzungen des 4. Jahrhunderts* (Belgium: Leuven University Press, 1999) 375–79.

33. Servetus is probably more accurately understood as a modalist with regard to the Trinity and an adoptionist with regard to Christology. See Roland H. Bainton, *Hunted Heretic: The Life and Death of Michael Servetus 1511–1553*, rev. ed. (Providence: Blackstone Editions, 2005; orig. pub. 1953) chs. 2 and 3.

Whether Calvin was right to blame Servetus on Arius, he was right to think that Arianism raised some vexing questions about Old Testament exegesis. Arianism had been a powerful force in the early church, forcing theologians to rethink a range of difficult issues. Before the rise of the Arian heresy, it was common for theologians to interpret Old Testament theophanies as revelations of Jesus Christ. Michel René Barnes has argued that it was just this concern about Arianism that influenced Augustine to insist on God's thorough incorporeality.[34] Like Calvin's battle against Servetus, Augustine was battling Arians who portrayed the Son of God as a visible, and thus lesser, form of the divine. By thinking of Jesus Christ as the way in which we see God, the Arians had no problem with a literal interpretation of Ezekiel's vision. Indeed, they were able to do justice to the traditional exegesis of Ezekiel far better than Augustine could. To combat the Arians, Augustine had to come up with a more complex hermeneutical scheme. For Augustine, there are no direct appearances of the Son in the Old Testament. When people saw God in human form, they were seeing manifestations of the divine essence in matter that God created as an instrument to communicate himself. They were not seeing what they thought they saw.

Augustine paid a high price in biblical hermeneutics for his critique of Arian subordinationism. He gave up the long tradition of reading the concrete revelations of a divine human form in the Old Testament as glimpses provided to the Jews of their coming Messiah. Even within the Jewish community that rejected Christianity, there were ongoing debates about the why the *kabod* (God's glory) typically takes a human form in the Old Testament. Mystical strains of Judaism were especially drawn to speculate about the identity of God's glory. Jewish mystics sometimes interpreted the human form of God to be the manifestation of a primordial or heavenly Man, who is the true and full image of God. This secret Adam preceded the human Adam and provided the physical template for all of humanity.[35] The New Testament too builds

---

34. Michel René Barnes, "The Visible Christ and the Invisible Trinity: Mt. 5:8 in Augustine's Trinitarian Theology of 400," *Modern Theology* 19 (2003) 329–55. Also see Angela Russell Christman, "What did Ezekiel See? Patristic Exegesis of Ezekiel 1 and Debates about God's Incomprehensibility," *Pro Ecclesia* 8 (1999) 338–63.

35. E. S. Drower, *The Secret Adam: A Study of Nasoraean Gnosis* (Oxford: Oxford University Press, 1960). She bases her argument on Mandaean texts, defending the idea that the Mandaeans are the heirs of Jewish-Gnostic traditions.

The Dome of Eden

on the Jewish understanding of God's humanlike glory. The story of Paul's religious vision on the road to Damascus, for example, echoes the vision of Ezekiel, which suggests that the author of Acts thought Ezekiel too had seen Jesus Christ

In chapter 7 I will defend the Christology of the medieval theologian Duns Scotus, who argues that the incarnation is the foundation of the world, not an emergency and haphazard response on God's part to a world gone awry. Scotus's position is called the Primacy of Christ, and there are debates about whether he meant that the incarnation precedes creation logically or really. In my interpretation, Scotus argues that God the Father wanted God the Son to be glorified and loved by others, which is why God first gave the Word form and then created the world to be the place where the Word could find fellowship and eventually be glorified. In chapter 7 I will argue that this Christology is crucial for understanding some of the perplexities of evolution, but it is also provides a much simpler interpretation of Ezekiel 1 than Augustine's argument that Ezekiel saw a material mediation that God used to convey an accommodation of his invisible essence. Jesus is atop the Dome because the world is created for his glory, and the creatures in the world were created to worship him. He is the summit and the secret of creation. Everything in the world, including us, has a purpose that can be found in him.

One of the corollaries of the Primacy of Christ is the idea that we take the form we have because God intended to give a human form to Christ from the very beginning of time. This insight is also rooted in the Old Testament, because it is typical of Jewish thought to locate the image of God in the human body.[36] The Old Testament has not only an anthropomorphic view of God but also a theomorphic view of humanity (humans take the form they do because God has the form he has). Christians understandably give a Christological foundation to this view. Humans are created in the image of Jesus Christ in order to be friends of Jesus and to come to know and worship him. In chapter 7 I will call this the christological interpretation of the *imago Dei*, and I will argue that it is the only way to preserve and protect the uniqueness of humanity against the reductive onslaught of Darwinism. Humans are

36. Gilles Quispel, "Ezekiel 1:26: Jewish Mysticism and Gnosis," *Vigiliae Christianae* 34 (1980) 6.

not the product of chance and violence. The form we have could not have been any different than it is because we were created in the image of Jesus Christ.

Skeptics of my position will immediately cry "Anthropomorphism!" Anthropomorphism is the attribution of human qualities to nonhuman entities, and skeptics of Christianity accuse it of being thoroughly anthropomorphic. These critics argue that Christianity treats God as an agent who thinks, acts, and talks like a human being. They suspect that anthropomorphism is inherent in Christianity, and they conclude that no matter how sophisticated theologians are, Christian belief is essential naive and problematic. These critics are on to something, but they do not understand what it is. They are wrong to claim that Christians imagine that God is like us because we think of everything from a human perspective. Rather, Christians claim that God is like us because we were created to be like God. God made the world with us in mind, to become friends of the Son and to accompany him in praise of the Father forever.

If Christ is the key to the cosmos, Christ is certainly the key to understanding Genesis. Without that key, the first few chapters of Genesis read the wrong way. Many readers think Genesis is a drama that moves us to anticipate the arrival of a hero to save the day. The problem with this reading is that Jesus is not a hero in any meaningful use of that term. If Jesus is a hero, then we human beings are at the center of the drama, because Jesus is sent to the world to make up for what we got ourselves into. A christological reading of Genesis would put Jesus, not humans, at the center of the action. Christians have always believed that the Old Testament finds its fulfillment in the new, and once Genesis is read in terms of Christ, it is hard to understand it in any other way. Creation is for him, and thus it is only for us because we were made for him. Why else does God use the royal "we" when commenting on what he has done? As the Son of God, and one member of the Trinity, Jesus was creating the world, but the world was also being created *for* him. That is why humans are given the place of honor in Eden. True, Adam names the animals, which demonstrates his rationality superiority over them, but Adam is rational because he has been created in God's image and likeness, and we discover what that image is only when we turn our eyes toward Jesus. Jesus tells us why we were created when he calls his disciples friends (John 15:15). We certainly were not created to fail, set up, that is, to fall. We were created for God's glory, and God's glory is Jesus Christ, so we were created for him. If Jesus is left out of Genesis, then all we have is the first half of a typical tragedy (the fall, with the second half, the climatic resolution, coming in the New Testament), rather than decisive revelation of the truth of our origins.

five

Karl Barth on the Edge of the Gap

Because my five theses might strike some readers as a misguided attack on evolution based on a flimsy and fantastic exegetical foundation, I want to enlist Karl Barth for his support. Barth, the greatest Protestant theologian of the twentieth century, comes as close as it is theologically possible to affirming the Gap Theory, the first of my five theses, without actually doing so. Although I have been a reader of Barth for a long time, I never noticed anything all that unusual in his treatment of Genesis. However, once I developed my approach to evolution and then reread Barth, I was amazed at how close Barth comes to the Gap Theory. Even more fascinating is how closely he anticipates the other theses I presented in the previous chapter, not only the third thesis on the reality of Eden and the fifth thesis on the christological shape of the *imago Dei*, but also the fourth thesis on the Dome of Eden. Barth takes four of my theses seriously and juggles them in such a way that he comes close to solving the problem of evolution, even though he rarely talked about evolution. Yet at key points he draws back from my position, primarily because he does not accept the second of my theses concerning the fall of Satan. If my theses represent a coherent whole, then they make sense of why Barth's theology of creation seems at times so complicated and contorted. Only a dialectical theologian could perform so elaborately a conceptual dance!

Barth provides support for the conclusion even if not all of the steps of the central argument of this book. If Satan falls before God creates the Garden of Eden, and Satan is responsible for the natural evil that is built into the process of evolution, then there must be some way to conceptualize the fundamental difference between what God was doing by creating the Garden of Eden and what Satan was doing to distort and pervert God's plan for nature as a whole. That is, if Genesis gives us a gap in time, then Genesis should also give us a division in space. This is true not only for reasons of poetic symmetry and narrative coherence but also for the logical connection of time and space. What happens on one level cannot but take place on the other. The textual gap in Genesis indicates a temporal event that disrupted creation, but gaps occur across space as well as time. An equivalent gap in space, so to speak, would help us to grasp the relationship of that disruption to the goodness of nature as demonstrated by the Garden of Eden. In other words, if the so-called gap is to help solve the problem of creation and evolution, then it needs to be supplemented by a spatial principle that explains how God could have created a good (part of the) world even after the world was fallen.

The Gap Theory is beneficial for understanding evolution because it suggests that something fundamentally objectionable was distorting and corrupting nature from almost the very beginning of time. It has the drawback, however, of placing the origin of natural evil prior to the rest of the story of Adam and Eve. The textual gap is out of sync with the story of Eden, which places peace and harmony in nature before the disobedience of the first human pair and appears to put at least some of the consequences of natural evil after the expulsion of Adam and Eve from the Garden. If the sequence of the opening verses of Genesis is taken with a sufficient seriousness to generate the Gap Theory, then the fact that these verses come before the creation of the Garden of Eden must also be taken with equal seriousness. It follows that if Genesis is thought to shed light on the primal origin of natural evil, it should also alert the reader to the way in which the Garden of Eden was protected or sheltered from that evil.

If the Gap Theory is right that Gen 1:2 describes the way the world is at odds with the Garden of Eden, then it must offer some account, if it is to be coherent, of the relationship between these two states of nature. The easiest way to think about this relationship is to follow the lead of Genesis by picturing the Garden of Eden as a real, localizable place. That, according to C. John Collins, is what the text implies when Gen 2:8 says that God planted a Garden in the East and moved man there. Evidently, then, God made man in the same unnamed land (the earth outside or prior to the Garden) that God later banished him to work.[1]

---

1. C. John Collins, *Genesis 1–4: A Linguistic, Literary, and Theological Commentary*

Collins's exegesis makes sense from the perspective of the Gap Theory because the disruption of nature in Gen 1:2 implies that the Garden of Eden was not coterminous with the whole world. The Garden must have been some part of the world that was preserved from or created in opposition to the state that is described in Gen 1:2. Of course, picturing the Garden as a real place was integral to Christian theology, art, and cosmology for many centuries, but it is not an option for most Christians today. Nonetheless, commitment to the Gap Theory does not necessarily entail belief in the Garden of Eden as a real, localizable place. What it does entail is the belief that the writer of Genesis thought the Garden was real, as well as the further belief that whatever Genesis has to tell us today cannot be understood without taking its writer's beliefs very seriously. The meaning of Genesis can be uncovered only through and not around its details, even though some of those details are for the most part implausible to the modern historical consciousness.

In other words, whether Genesis is reliable as historical record does not alter the claim that only by reading it as if it were historically true can its theological meaning be ascertained. That is what Barth meant when he insisted of the first few chapters of Genesis that "all their utterances should be taken literally: not in a shallow but a deep sense."[2] K. E. Greene-McCreight calls Barth's method a plain reading of scripture, but we could also call it a deep literalism.[3] Barth looks for the meaning of the creation account in its surface details, not in hypothetical reconstructions of its various parts in the murky depths of primordial history. He also examines how Genesis fits with the rest of the Bible according to broad theological patterns, on the assumption that the Bible was edited and intended for a theological audience. According to Barth, Genesis is a saga, not a myth, by which he means that Genesis challenges, rather than simply adopts, the science and religion of its day. Barth also thought that Genesis challenges the scientific and religious assumptions of our day. If so, it should provide the guidelines for relating the doctrine of creation to the theory of evolution. It can do that

---

(Phillipsburg, NJ: P. & R., 2006) 108–12 and 120.

2. Karl Barth, *Church Dogmatics* III/1, *The Doctrine of Creation*, ed. G. W. Bromiley and T. F. Torrance, trans. J. W. Edwards, O. Bussey, and Harold Knight (Edinburgh: T. & T. Clark, 1958) 84. All parenthetical page numbers will be to this volume.

3. K. E. Greene-McCreight, *Ad Litteram: How Augustine, Calvin, and Barth Read the Plain Sense of Genesis 1–3* (New York: Peter Lang, 1999).

only if it is clear about not only the fall of nature but also the relationship between fallen nature and nature as God intended it to be.

The spatial equivalent of the temporal gap would be a division, barrier or partition that represents or pictures the divide between nature as God intended it to be (Eden) and nature as the battleground upon which Satan stakes his claim (evolution). That is, in fact, precisely what Genesis provides with the image of the firmament. For Barth, as W. A. Whitehouse has pointed out, all space is "guarded space," which suggests that the space of creation needs the strongest guard of all.[4] Modern scholars like Collins follow Calvin in arguing that the firmament is nothing more than the sky. It is an example of what Collins calls the "exalted prose" of Genesis.[5] Collins bases his interpretation on a phenomenological understanding of how the ancients would have pictured their environment, which is another way of saying that he thinks the writer of Genesis thought in concrete terms that we should interpret metaphorically today. I will follow Barth's plain reading of Genesis and argue that the firmament should be pictured today as what it was pictured then, and that it was pictured then as a dome. The description of the Dome of Eden, as I will call it, is found in Gen 1:6–8. God decrees that a canopy or dome be placed in the midst of the waters, separating them in some fashion. I am not arguing here that the Dome of Eden is a literal dome, just as I am not arguing here that the Garden was a physical place, but I am arguing that the Dome is a crucial part of the story, and its theological implications can no more be avoided than the gap between the first two verses of Genesis. Indeed, that gap only makes sense when put in the context of the Dome, just as the Dome only has a function when understood as a response to that gap. The Dome and the gap make sense of each other and thus the Gap Theory cannot be accepted or rejected aside from this relationship. I will argue that Barth is as supportive and helpful in thinking about the firmament as he is in thinking about the Gap Theory. I will also argue that, even though he does not draw the connection as well as he could, his exegesis of the

---

4. W. A. Whitehouse, "Karl Barth on the Work of Creation," in *Reckoning with Karl Barth: Essays in Commemoration of the Centenary of Karl Barth's Birth*, ed. Nigel Biggar (London: Mowbray, 1988) 49.

5. Collins, *Genesis 1–4*, 44. Also see 54, 78, 128 and 264.

Karl Barth on the Edge of the Gap

gap and the dome together form a provocative and original resource for solving the problem of creation and evolution.

Barth's precipitous handling of these explosive issues can be found in *Church Dogmatics* III/1, the first volume of the four parts of *The Doctrine of Creation*. This volume is full of exegetical asides that are easily neglected even though they demonstrate provocative insights and masterful scholarship. Barth examines Gen 1:2 and its surrounding verses on pages 102–10, and he examines Gen 1:6–8 on pages 135–41. In both cases, he is in no hurry to trace the meaning of these texts to a prehistoric context, but neither does he think that they need to be reread in the light of modern science. Instead, these texts present fundamental theological challenges that are as relevant today as when they were first written. Regarding Gen 1:2 he says that "this verse has always constituted a particular *crux interpretum*—one of the most difficult in the whole Bible" (102). He goes on to state, "Gen. 1:1 does not stand in any positive relation to 1:2" (100), which is another way of saying there is a gap between them. Regarding the firmament, Barth calls it "the first thing" in terms of the theological priorities of the opening chapters of Genesis: "The first thing—and it is on this that the saga lays all its emphasis—is the firmament which restrains and limits the menacing intermediate waters" (134). The firmament is the first thing because it is nothing more than the "disarmament of chaos and the establishment of the cosmos" (134), and he repeatedly describes it with the synonyms of boundary, division, and separation. The firmament, he implies, is God's response to whatever it was that disordered the world in between Gen 1:1 and 1:2.

Regarding Gen 1:2, Barth does not neglect using all the best available linguistic and historical tools, but he does not think that the most rigorous methodology can exhaust the meaning of any biblical text, let alone one so taxing as this. His exegetical practice is typically critical of the idea that texts are like the tip of an iceberg with most of their meaning buried beneath a sea of opaque historical claims. He trusts that a plain reading of scripture will not only make the most sense of the text but will also be the most theologically profound. Barth is relentless in his questioning of Gen 1:2, but only because he thinks it introduces a mystery that must be dwelt upon rather than a puzzle that can be solved. For his exegesis he follows the Hebrew by dividing the verse into

The Dome of Eden

its three parts: the waste and the void, the darkness upon the deep, and the wind or Spirit of God moving upon the face of the waters.

First, then, Barth examines the waste and void, which in Hebrew is *tohu* and *bohu*. Tohu means emptiness or futility, and most scholars think the second word of this pair is, in the words of Robert Alter, a "nonce term coined to rhyme with the first and to reinforce it."[6] Many modern translations follow the pattern set by the King James Version of "without form and void," but the American Standard Version has "waste and void" and others use "waste and empty." Barth notes that as early as Augustine this notorious phrase lent itself to much speculation and many interpretations. Modern scholars typically think that they can discern ancient pagan mythologies lurking beneath it. Whether they think the reference is direct or indirect, they argue that the *tohu* and *bohu* phrase is a vestige of an earlier myth that portrays God dueling in a cosmic war with evil forces. These myths grant chaos a divine status, so Genesis is itself drawn into a battle in its risky appropriation of this phrase. For believers unpracticed in biblical scholarship, the idea that Genesis is both using and trying to cover up its dependence upon a pagan myth is unsettling. For the Jewish and Christian traditions, the idea that God could have had competitors in the act of creation contradicts the very idea of the meaning of divinity, because if God exists and is truly God, then God must be omnipotent, without equal, and utterly unique.

Barth is skeptical that Gen 1:2 so completely tangles its own reference to a pagan myth that it takes a league of scholars to unravel the passage. Many modern scholars think that we can know ancient authors better than they knew themselves, but if the author of this verse was really so confused about the myth he was referring to, why did he include it at all? It would have been simpler just to skip all talk of darkness, waste, and the void and jump right into God's commanding action. The only way to account for the modern interpretation is to assume that the writer of this verse is both drawn and repulsed by the myth he is borrowing. The idea that Genesis was trying to conceal a remnant of an earlier myth that it found both compelling and embarrassing sounds peculiarly modern—it sounds Freudian, in fact, by theorizing a textual

---

6. Robert Alter, *Genesis: Translation and Commentary* (New York: Norton, 1996) 3.

Karl Barth on the Edge of the Gap

unconsciousness that is secretly controlling what the best intentions of the author cannot repress. Barth rejects the idea that the writer of Genesis was a victim of ambivalence and thus either a very sophisticated or very sloppy (not to say neurotic!) editor.

Barth also considers and then dismisses the idea that *tohu* and *bohu* represent a primeval reality out of which God creates the world. Reading the first two verses of Genesis in "the simplest way" (103), Barth says, forces the recognition that there is a real heaven and earth that have already been created, so the waste and void that follow upon that creation cannot be the source or origin of it. Even less plausible is the idea that Genesis is echoing the formless matter of Greek metaphysics. Barth's critique of these explanations ends in a dilemma. "If the raw and rudimentary state of the world depicted in v. 2 is not a reality independent of God and His work, what else can it be but God's creation? And if it is not God's creation, what else can it be but a reality independent of God and His work?" (104). Some might reject this dilemma on the grounds that it assumes Gen 1:1 is evidence of a creation *ex nihilo*. In other words, Barth is saying that either God is God, in which case the *tohu* is not really *tohu*, or the *tohu* is really *tohu*, in which case God is not God. Since Barth is quite aware of the apparent absence of the doctrine of creation *ex nihilo* in Genesis, this would be a misreading of the dilemma, which serves a more rhetorical than argumentative function in the unfolding of Barth's position. Barth uses this dilemma to intensify, not diminish, the contradictory nature of the *tohu*. Barth is saying that the *tohu* does not really belong in this narrative because it cannot really exist in the world God has made. It cannot be, and yet there it is, an interruption of God's plan that also interrupts the flow of the creation story.

If it would have been more convenient to have eliminated the mythical allusion altogether, there must have been an important reason for including it. For Barth, Genesis is not expressing a debt; instead, it is picking a fight, though it is a fight of a peculiar kind. As Barth summarizes it, *tohu* is used in the Babylonian creation myth in reference to the mother goddess Tiamat, whose body parts, sliced in half by another god, provide the foundations for heaven and earth. It is the story itself, not the Genesis reference, which is full of Freudian conflict. Far from borrowing from the Babylonian myth, Barth concludes, Genesis

The Dome of Eden

is confronting and subverting it. This reference interrupts the narrative, but that is precisely what Genesis wants to do. Rather than being merely reactive and confused, Genesis takes the offensive. The God of the Bible is not battling other gods, and the world does not pour out of their wounds. The Bible alludes to this pagan myth not out of sneaky or shoddy editing but as a way of denying it by treating it as a little more than a literary source. The reference to the myth is not that clear, in other words, because Genesis does not take the myth that seriously. Genesis is not above using the Tiamat myth for its own purposes, and that purpose is to indicate the trouble that is brewing in the world.

If the vagueness of the allusion is intentional, it follows that a historical reconstruction of the myth behind the text will not shed any light on the meaning of this verse. Verse two is not interested in the details of the myth because the chaos follows upon God's initial activity and thus has no creative role to play in the narrative. The waste and void are not the raw material for God's further production, and neither do they set the stage for action yet to come. Neither of these metaphors—material or stage—will do, because they do not do justice to the portent of something irreducibly mysterious conveyed by the verse. Verse two is attempting a delicate balancing act: it is trying not to draw too much attention to the chaos while at the same time it is not denying that the chaos is menacing. It is menacing precisely because it opens up a gap in the creation account. Barth goes right to the heart of the matter by suggesting that verse two "is in contradiction (we can only say, in glaring opposition) to the created reality of heaven and earth summarily described in v. 1, and in glaring opposition to what is later described as God's 'good' creation" (104). If Gen 1:1 is the thesis of Genesis and Gen 1:2 is the "antithesis" (104), it contributes nothing to what God has already accomplished, Gen. 1:2 thus suggests that something has gone awry in the world, and the world's being out of kilter follows immediately upon God's initial creative act while preceding God's grand declaration of "Let there be light" in Gen 1:3. What this means is that Barth locates the gap of the Gap Theory between Gen 1:2 and 1:3 as much as between Gen 1:1 and 1:2.

To substantiate his reading, Barth refers to the way the Hebrew language uses *tohu* to describe a wilderness or deserted city, or even an empty assertion. Several places in the Bible apply it to idols and those who worship them. The most important uses of *tohu* and *bohu* together occur in Jer 4:23 and Isa 34:11, where they depict the darkness, confusion, and, according to Barth, emptiness of the final judgment. From this textual evidence, Barth draws a startling conclusion: "Thus the condition of the earth depicted in v. 2 is identical with the whole horror of the final judgment" (105). Although Barth does not dwell on this point, it is nothing less that astonishing. The same horror that comes just before the end of time is present just after time's beginning. Barth thus begins his famous theology of evil as a nothingness that nonetheless has force, a theology that comes to a climax in *Church Dogmatics* III/3, here in his interpretation of Gen 1:2. "The only primal and rudimentary state which calls for consideration is that of evil, of sin, of the fall and its consequences" (108). Whatever is wrong in the world exists without any power or reality of its own because God has already denied it even as it emerges as the negation or shadow of God's actions. The waste and void lie at the furthest frontier of God's creation in a state that is impossible to describe with any clarity. That, in fact, is why Genesis reaches out to the language of pagan myth for its description of a violence that lacks any fundamental reality. The myth itself is confusing, and that serves Genesis's purposes.

Second, Barth looks at the darkness that covers the face of the deep, which only compounds the horror of the *tohu*. Barth notes that the efforts of scholars to systematically combine these two sentences have failed and been abandoned. Barth draws the conclusion that the darkness has been set beside the void without "any attempt at co-ordination," and the result is several "superimposed pictures" (105). The darkness and the deep challenge and confuse the reader because they complicate and confound each other. Like the *tohu*, the deep is most likely connected to the Babylonian creation myth, where it symbolizes the treacherous depths of the oceans and seas, an abyss that takes the figure of the monstrous. According to many ancient creation myths, but especially the Babylonian one, water is the source of the chaos that is actively opposed to the orderliness of the cosmos, represented by the stationary land. Genesis is attached to this tradition in its treatment of "the element of water as the principle which in its abundance and power is absolutely opposed to God's creation" (105). This symbolism makes obvious sense, given how ancient peoples would have been befuddled by the vastness of seas they could not navigate.[7] Psalm 107 depicts sea voyages as the equivalent of wandering in the desert, sitting imprisoned in darkness, and facing sickness and hunger. Water is not easily controlled, a fact which was made even more present to ancient peoples in their frequent battles with flooding. The Bible too teaches the danger, threat, and reality of the primeval flood, and not just with the story of Noah. Is it no wonder that one of Jesus's most startling miracles was walking on water, an awesome feat that C. S. Lewis tried to recreate in the opening of his great novel, *Perelandra*, where this prelapsarian planet permits the born again space traveler to scale large waves without any worry, while the unmoving dry lands, ironically, are the source of temptation.[8]

That the deep holds the potential for great suffering is made even more evident by the darkness that sweeps over it. This darkness is not, as Barth points out, the darkness from which light is born. Barth notes that the idea that the dark is the source of light is both ancient and contemporary. It is always tempting to try to tame the darkness by thinking that only in it can true vision come into focus. Christian mystics too have used this idea, as with St. John of the Cross and his dark night of the soul. From this perspective, the night is the time of despair, insomnia, and dread because it is a test against which faith can gain the strength to overcome its most grievous impediments. Nighttime is thus analogous to silence, with the one silencing the eyes and the other darkening the ears. Both can be crucial for clearing the mind of distractions and purifying the heart of multiple and confusing desires. Nevertheless, even in the industrial age of artificial illumination, the night retains the power of something foreign to the life-giving healing of the sun.[9] The dark that moves across the deep in Genesis is not the night through which the stars still shine their light. Barth says that nothing good can come from this darkness and that God's only relationship to it is "one of

---

7. See, for example, the magisterial work by Peregrine Horden and Nicholas Purcell, *The Corrupting Sea: A Study of Mediterranean History* (Malden, MA: Blackwell, 2000).

8. C. S. Lewis, *Perelandra* (New York: Scribner, 1996).

9. The menace of the night is captured by A. Roger Ekrich in *At Day's Close: Night in Times Past* (New York: Norton, 2006). For a more hopeful portrait, see Christopher Dewdney, *Acquainted with the Night: Excursions through the World After Dark* (New York: Bloomsbury, 2005).

Karl Barth on the Edge of the Gap

victory" (106). This is a darkness that only God can defeat and redeem. Jesus came to cast out the darkness and to be a light unto the world. The darkness, as the instincts of our ancestors confirm, is our enemy, not our friend.

Third, Barth examines the sentence of Gen 1:2 that suggests to most readers the first glimpse of the support we need to survive the depth of the darkness: "And the Spirit of God moved upon the face of the water." God, not darkness, is now moving across the water, but is help on the way? Much has been made about how this statement echoes (and thus post-dates) God's intervention at the Red Sea to ensure the success of the exodus of Israel, and Barth also observes its intriguing connections to the story of the disciples threatened by the lake of Gennesareth and the story of the flood in later chapters of Genesis. Much also has been made of the Hebrew word for Spirit, which can also mean wind or breath. The Spirit in this verse is easily understood to be moving like a bird, hovering over the water, an interpretation that was known to the Church Fathers, who thought this passage anticipated the dove Noah sends, successfully, in search of dry land in Genesis 8. Barth agrees about the connection to a bird, but thinks it resonates with the unsuccessful raven rather than the dove (Gen 8:7). We are still in the region of something menacing that precedes the light God calls forth into being. Thus, "the Spirit of Elohim is condemned to the complete impotence of a bird hovering or brooding over the shoreless or sterile waters" (107). There is no freshly plucked olive leaf to signify something positive or productive from these waters. Barth can thus agree with a statement from Hermann Gunkel's famous Genesis commentary that, "The God who creates and the Spirit which broods have really no inner relation but actually exclude one another" (ibid.). For the same reason, however, he disagrees with Gunkel and the many modern scholars who think that the birdlike motion alludes to the ancient creation myth of a world egg. The waters here provide no nest (because they are shoreless, as Barth eloquently puts it) and are sterile (notice how he applies this metaphor to the water, not the bird, but with the same affect).

The Spirit of God is looking down on the earth, the lower part of creation, and seeing it as what it is apart from God's plan. Nevertheless, that does not mean the deep lies completely outside of God's control. This state of the world is not merely a stage that the text quickly passes over, but neither is it a stage that is a necessary preparation for the rest of God's plan—and it certainly is not an autonomous reality that really threatens God's authority. God does not will it, but it has no life of its own outside of God's willing creation into being. That is Barth's complicated position on the nothingness of evil, which has baffled many commentators and forces the reader to see if Barth's position can be made more coherent than he makes it. Barth reasons that the chaos would not exist if God had not decided to create the world, so Gen 1:2 is firmly dependent on Gen 1:1. Yet God is not the direct cause of this intervening insertion of a counterproposal to God's plan. Only when God speaks, as Barth points out, do we see what God creates, and thus we discover God's nature as the one who creates in freedom and the one who creates what is good.

Genesis 1:2 thus depicts, for Barth, the state of the world bereft of God's eternal Word. "It is the world in a state in which it lacks the Word of God which according to what follows is the ground and measure of its reality" (108). The world without the gospel is the world barren and desolate. The world that God has not spoken into being falls in between the nothingness of pure evil and what Barth calls the shadow side of existence, the ugly realm that exists, as it were, "behind God's back" (ibid.). Whether Gen 1:2 depicts a shadow of the good or its complete absence is somewhat confusing in Barth's exegesis, so his use of the shadow metaphor merits some explanation. Barth uses the metaphor of the shadow to denote a particular aspect of creation, not another place beside or in addition to the world. Shadows are a byproduct of light. Shadows can be scary, but they exist only because light is illuminating an object. The shadow side of the world is all of those aspects of life that seem scary but really are not, or should not be, threatening. Disease, natural calamities, even death itself only has the power that we ourselves give to it. These are natural limits, and as such they are not quite a part of the evil realm of the fall and not quite a part of what God has created. They fall in between the work of God and the deformations of Satan. They are limits to life that motivate us to take life seriously. Ideally, our faith will allow us to see the light even in the darkness of the shadow. Shadows do not shine with light—that is, they do not exist independently of the light, which means that the light, if it is bright enough, can cast them out. We need have no fear of the ways the world tests us with the inevitable consequences of living within the limits of time and space.

The alert reader will find this development in Barth's argument to be a retreat from his attempt to do justice to the sheer interruption of Gen 1:2. After all, the tremendous amount of exegetical energy Barth has spent would suggest that this menace, this odd pause in the creation account, is more than just a nod of the head to the fact that the creation yet to be described will include some uncomfortable limits placed on life. Barth seems to acknowledge the weakness of connecting Gen 1:2 with his concept of the shadow side of creation by not only mixing his metaphors but also continuing to identify this verse with a "monstrous world" (109). It is as if no words will do it justice, but certainly the image of a shadow is too inert and passive to convey its full terror. As if to correct this misunderstanding, Barth immediately shifts his rhetoric from the shadow cast by the light to the utter darkness of finality, the past, and death. He calls Gen 1:2 the way the "world *was*," as if using the past tense is the only way to define its fundamental nullity, but it is also a "dark possibility" that continues to persist in creation (ibid.). It is, in what is perhaps his most creative description, a myth that God will not allow "to become reality" (ibid.). Every description of nature is thus mythological, for Barth, as long as it does not interpret nature in terms of the doctrine of creation. Descriptions of nature as full of strife, violence, and chance are thus objective and accurate but at the same time utterly fantastical and unreal.

Genesis 1:2 refers, then, to what the world *would have been* (the perfect conditional of the verb *to be* that leaves open the possibility that the action referred to could still re-occur in the present) if God had not spoken it into being through his Son, the Eternal Word. "In itself and as such, without the freely uttered and freely repeated Word of the grace of God, the cosmos has no real guarantee against precipitation into chaos, i.e., into a state in which it has neither existence, essence nor goodness" (ibid.). By implication, 1:2 describes what the world could yet become if silence were to have the last word. Waste, void, darkness, and the deep are made possible, paradoxically, not by God's creative action but by God's judgment. This is the way the world looks to God, and to us, when we have fallen away from God's plan. The question naturally arises at this point why Barth does not go ahead and identify the causal agent behind the face in the deep who is responsible for this desolation. He does write that, "God will not allow the cosmos to be definitively bewitched and demonised," which suggests that, at least for the time between creation and final salvation, the world truly is being bewitched and demonized (ibid.). Why doesn't Barth take the final step of concluding that Gen 1:2 is depicting a gap in the creation account that can only be satisfactorily explained by the fall of Satan? Part of the answer to this question is that he does take this step, but he does so gingerly and indirectly. Nonetheless, his hesitation is real. Barth is at the edge of the Gap Theory. He stays at the edge, I want to argue, for two reasons. The first has to do with the role of the firmament in his theology, which is not fully connected to Gen 1:2, and the second has to do with his metaphysical quibbles with the fall of Satan, which leads back to his identification of evil with nothingness.

Let me return, then, to the idea that the Gap Theory is inextricably connected to the concept of the firmament. I have proposed that what an exegete thinks of the one will shape what he or she thinks of the other. Not surprisingly, Barth has an utterly radical view of the firmament, but like his treatment of the Gap Theory, he draws back before he reaches the final, logical conclusion of his argument. Indeed, one of the least discussed aspects of his doctrine of creation is his vivid understanding of the firmament. This neglect should not be surprising. Of all modern theologians, Barth is the most modern because he is capable of being exasperatingly original upon every close reading. He is constantly surprising because he is also the most traditional of modern theologians. It is easy to overlook many pages of the magisterial *Church Dogmatics*, and overlooked pages can easily change the picture of Barth's theology as a whole. Nevertheless, it is telling that his discussion of the firmament in *The Doctrine of Creation*, which is hardly brief or marginal to his interpretation of Genesis and thus every aspect of his theology, has been passed over in silence by Barth's many commentators and followers.

Barth recognizes the reality and presence of the firmament throughout the Bible—and he even uses it as a measure of how sloppy much modern interpretation of the Bible has become. Nonetheless, he violates his own hermeneutical procedure when he draws back from a deep literalism that would find the meaning of the firmament in its details, as if it actually existed, and treats it instead as a metaphor. He hesitates to follow through in determining the precise role of the firmament in the battle over God's creative intentions mainly because he does not adequately link his exegesis of the firmament to his exegesis of Gen 1:2. He is not wrong to give the firmament a symbolic spin, but his interpretation of its function suffers from a lack of specificity. Barth's instincts are solid, but his conclusion is unsatisfactory, like a man who has spent a great deal of energy building a house that he does not want to occupy. He builds a strong case for a very real firmament only to have it collapse, at the last minute, into a figment of the Bible's imagination.

Barth begins his exegesis of Gen 1:6–8 by noting its relation to the creation of light that precedes it. "Strictly speaking, the creation of light was a pointer to what was to take place in the separation of the chaos-reality which God rejected" (133). In creating both the light and the firmament God shows that "to create is to separate" (122). The light and the darkness, however, are more severely alienated from each other than the firmament and the waters above and below. "Between light and darkness there is no third element like the firmament between the waters above and below" (123). There is an absolute and mutual exclusion between day and night. "Night is the name of the nameless and the nature of the natureless" (132). Nonetheless, Barth describes the day in terms that sound a lot like the dome: the "day includes and encloses the night," surrounding it and "encircling it like a beleaguered fortress" (131). Likewise, the firmament is created for the waters but also as a response to the remnant of the night made noticeable by its defiant return after the first day. Day and dome (like the domical rainbow that signifies the end of the flood by demonstrating, firmament-like, God's desire to uphold the cosmos) are both emblems of divine promise. "As day is the name of that for which God has given man time by making light and thus indicating and promising his decision, so heaven is the name for the space which God has given to man in creating the firmament and thus executing His decision" (134). And one final connection between 1:6–8 and the verses that precede it needs to be stated. What is "clear enough," Barth states, is that the "material connection" between the creation of the firmament and what happened before it is "the limitation of water" (135). Thus the firmament is, as I said above, the spatial equivalent of the temporal gap. Its function as a barrier is demanded by the void and waste of v. 2.

So what is the firmament? The plain meaning of the text makes it unlikely that the firmament was meant to refer to little more than the sky. Barth emphasizes the point that God creates the firmament (*raqia'* in Hebrew) in the midst of the waters in order to divide the waters from the waters, something the sky does not do. This can be confusing to picture even though the meaning is plain enough. "The waters created by God are the waters which are divided and bounded by the *raqia'*. We cannot abstract from this purpose" (136). In other words, the waters do not, in a way, precede the firmament, which is created to hold them back. Better put, the waters are what they are because the firmament is what it is. Barth says that we cannot visualize these waters, but he identifies them nonetheless. They are none other than the primeval depths that entered so disturbingly into the narrative in Gen 1:2. As he puts it, "The reference can only be to the primal flood of chaos" (ibid.). The water, as soon as we confront it, has already been confronted by God.

We cannot visualize the waters (at least the waters that are apparently above the sky) but what about the firmament? Barth notes that *raqia'* can signify a mound or a dam, and he discusses the other passages in the Bible where this word occurs. Job 37:18 says it is "strong as a molten looking glass," and Job 26:11 describes it as being supported by pillars. Ezekiel 1:22 and 10:1 refer to it as the platform resting on four creatures that supports the throne of God. Psalm 19:1 calls it the work of God's hands. Barth quotes from a biblical scholar who describes several of these formulations as "poetical hyperbole," but such images, he hastens to add, are "certainly not intended to throw doubt on the solidity of the structure" (136–37). The Bible describes the firmament as having doors or windows (Ps 78:23, 2 Kgs 7:2, 19), and the security of the earth depends on God keeping these windows shut (Gen 8:2), though, of course, God once did open them for the flood (Gen 7:11). The firmament, then, is "the creaturely guarantee of the continuance of the lower universe" (137). A later verse (v. 14) depicts the dome as the bearer of the stars, but that is a "subsequent determination" of its function (137). Clearly, the best image of the firmament is a dome, and Barth thinks that the writer of Genesis takes it literally precisely because of what it was created to do.

Karl Barth on the Edge of the Gap

The purpose of the dome cannot be fully understood without introducing another idea that will strike modern readers as equally fantastic. That is the idea of the celestial ocean. Barth investigates the celestial ocean with the same determination he applies to the firmament. The celestial ocean has long been a staple of Protestant fundamentalist apologetics because it can account for the source of the floodwaters. Barth, however, does not treat it merely as a presupposition of the flood story. He takes it seriously on its own terms. The celestial ocean is not prominent in the Bible, but it is implied in Ps 104:3, which depicts God's chambers built atop the waters, and Ps 148:4, where the waters above the heavens are commanded to praise the Lord. For Barth, the Bible treats the terrestrial waters as dangerous primarily due to their connection to the celestial waters. "Behind and above the physical danger there lurks the metaphysical danger of the upper sea held back by the *raqia*'" (ibid.). Barth definitely rejects the idea, which Calvin defended, that the celestial waters are nothing more than the clouds and atmospheric gases from which the rain descends. Calvin thought that any other interpretation of these waters was contrary to common sense,[10] but for Barth, it is common sense that needs interrogation. Barth sides with Luther, who readily accepted the mystery of water above the sky. And who but Barth could relish the debate that then ensued between the Lutherans and the Reformed over this very issue? In the Ptolemaic system, which was still operative in Reformation theological disputes of the seventeenth century, the earth was surrounded not only by a circular heaven but also by an "immense watery globe" (ibid.). Seventeenth-century Protestant theologians speculated about the usefulness of this vault for cooling the heavens and providing a protective buffer between heaven and earth. Barth refuses to take a condescending attitude toward such speculations. "Both the strength and the weakness of 17th century orthodoxy emerge at once and plainly from this presentation" (138). Its strength was its readiness to read the Bible for what it actually says. Its weakness, Barth continues, was the flip side of its strength—its rigid treatment of the Bible as a source of readymade data. These exegetes "failed to advance," Barth admonishes, "from the palpably miraculous character

---

10. John Calvin, *Commentaries on the First Book of Moses Called Genesis by John Calvin*, trans. John King, reprint 1847 by Calvin Translation Society (Grand Rapids: Baker, 1979) 39.

of these supra-celestial waters to their open secret" (138). And what is that open secret? It is, Barth avers, the idea that the heavens are closed to us—nay, the heavens are a threat to us, given our sinful condition. The *raqia'* symbolizes a supernaturally hard material that protects us from the persistent danger of the divine wrath. Genesis, for Barth, is utilizing the ancient myth of the celestial ocean, which was known by the Persians, Babylonians, Chinese, and others, to make a decidedly theological point. God is for us and with us, but our existence is precarious, even if we do not know it. But for the grace of God, the heavens stand in judgment of our deeds.

According to Barth's Christ-centered reading of the Bible, all of the Old Testament either anticipates or takes the form of the proclamation of the good news of Jesus Christ. The firmament is no exception. The firmament is a witness to God's providential control over the nature and is thus a sign of our salvation. More specifically, it is a witness to the accomplishment of Jesus Christ, who on the cross defeated all of our enemies. Barth creatively argues that it is also a witness to the way that God has decided to expose humanity "to both a finite and an infinite threat but not to both at once" (139). Even when the terrestrial waters swallow us up in floods or sea-voyages gone awry, as they did Jonah, we know that God is holding back the greater threat of eternal damnation. The celestial waters will not prevail against those whom God has chosen to protect from disasters worse than mere mortality.

As the earth's roof, the ceiling put over our head, the creation of the firmament is also at the same time the creation of heaven. By heaven Barth does not mean the place where God is, because God is not anywhere in particular (or, rather, God can be anywhere in particular because God is not limited by space). God needs no place to be, so, technically speaking, heaven does not exist until God creates the world and thus creates the place where the world will find its perfection and its eternal rest. Just as land and sea, light and darkness are created together, so are heaven and earth. The firmament thus provides not only the ceiling to the earth but also the foundation or ground for heaven. Barth sees this in predominantly spiritual, rather than material terms. The firmament is there to keep heaven in a world set apart from our own. It says no to our desires to control our spiritual destiny, to charge heaven's gate with our utopian plans for creating a heaven on earth. In

Karl Barth on the Edge of the Gap

that sense, the *raqia'* has the character of a boundary that "opposes all human pride and tumult" (140). It places heaven on a horizon that lies just at the outer edge of all human action. Heaven is open to us, but only from the divine perspective. God can cross it, but we cannot ascend to it without daring to cross the celestial waters on our own. Only in the end of time will that ocean become calm and still. This is the meaning, Barth writes, of Rev 4:6 and 15:2, which depicts the heavenly waters transformed into a crystal sea in the new heaven. The end times will entail "a complete liberation of the earth from the sea" (145), which suggests that the time leading up to the end will entail a final push of the sea against the land. The triumph of the land, which represents order over chaos, means that the celestial sea, which separates us from God, will no longer be a boundary and a barrier. It will become a still and open throughway. At this point and only at this point will the *raqia'* become "superfluous as a barrier and boundary" (141).

Implicit in Barth's exegesis of Genesis is an entire theology of the land and the seas, a geo-theology, we could call it, if that did not sound so geocentric. A geopolitical theology understands being in terms of space and space in terms of the features of the earth and not just the structures of the human mind. Barth's geo-hydro-theology is important not only in terms of the explosion of interest in theories of globalization and environmentalism in recent years but also in terms of the role water has played in Christian rites such as baptism. The only other scholars that I know who have come close to writing a theology of the sea are Catherine Keller and Carl Schmitt, and they could not be more different in how they handle a common subject matter. Keller is a contemporary theologian whose work is influenced by feminism and deconstruction, while Schmitt is the German political theorist whose reputation was compromised by his association with the Nazis. They provide extreme and opposite alternatives to Barth's position, Keller by embracing the chaos that lies beneath Gen 1:2, and Schmitt by turning it into a deadly and absolute enemy.

Keller develops what she calls a "tehomic theology" aimed at overcoming the fear of chaos that she finds in Genesis in particular and the Christian tradition more generally.[11] She blames this fear on the

---

11. Catherine Keller, *Faces of the Deep: A Theology of Becoming* (New York: Routledge, 2003) xvii. Subsequent citations given parenthetically.

doctrine of *creatio ex nihilo*, which she contrasts with the way many religions celebrate or at least acknowledge the creative power of chaos. Christianity took a wrong turn with regard to chaos, she argues, with Gen 1:2, not 1:1, because in 1:2 chaos is broached but repressed at the same time. She admits that Gen 1:2 "betrays no fear of the dark, no demonization of the deep, of the sea, its she and its dragons" (30), yet this is only evidence of how deeply repressed chaos is in the Christian psyche. The second verse of the Bible thus inaugurates a shunning of the depths of creation because it "magnifies—like a tiny well-ground lens—our fears and longings" (25). What lies beneath the depths in Gen 1:2 is not necessarily Babylonian myth but, deeper still, "the oceanic all-mother Tiamat" (28), so that Gen 1:2 is also the origin of sexism in the Christian tradition. Barth, to whom she devotes an entire chapter, especially comes under heavy criticism for sexist tendencies, but for my purposes, what is interesting is how she categorizes him as a Gap Theorist of a peculiar kind. Barth treats the biblical cover-up of mythology as, in her words, a "hermeneutical emergency" (84). Barth, Keller argues, tries to repudiate chaos by identifying it with nothingness, but he only succeeds in sublimating it instead. She charges Barth with using the language of impotence and sterility in a futile quest to disabuse chaos of its meaning—futile because nothing can never be just nothing. For all the problems and provocations of her analysis, her point about nothing is well taken, and I will return to it when I discuss one of the main reasons why Barth cannot be counted as a full defender of the Gap Theory.

Schmitt provides another way of framing Barth's discussion of the Gen 1:2. In the *Nomos of the Earth*, Schmitt tried to write a philosophical history of planet earth from the perspective of various attempts to conceptualize the world as a whole.[12] Only by understanding how people have divided the world throughout history can we begin to un-

---

12. Carl Schmitt, *The Nomos of the Earth in the International Law of the Jus Publicum Europaeum*, trans. G. L. Ulmen (New York: Telos, 2006; originally published in 1950). Schmitt's earlier treatise, *Land und Meer* (Leipzig: Philipp Reclam, 1942) has not been translated into English. For my commentary on Schmitt's relevance for theories of globalization, see Stephen H. Webb, *American Providence: A Nation with a Mission* (New York: Continuum, 2004) 153–68. I have also benefited from Christopher L. Connery, "Ideologies of Land and Sea: Alfred Thayer Mahan, Carl Schmitt, and the Shaping of Global Myth Elements," *Boundary* 2 (2001) 173–201.

derstand the origin of political boundaries and the possibilities of their future transformations. For Schmitt, the political realm is determined by the absolutely basic (and frequently deadly) distinction between friends and enemies. Without that distinction, there would be no need for political institutions. Schmitt formulated this distinction early in his career, but in *Nomos* he shows how it is grounded in our relationship to the land. Ordering the land with "fences, enclosures, boundaries, walls, houses and other constructs" gives birth to "families, clans, tribes, estates, forms of ownership and human proximity."[13] Fields cannot be planted on the sea; ships sail across it without leaving a trace. Politically construed, then, the sea is a major problem. It limits human organization, which might be why, Schmitt speculates, the book of Revelation, when it pictures a new earth and new heaven purged of sin, also says that "the sea was no more" (Rev 21:1).

Ancient myths abound about the cathartic power of the sea to wash away all evils, as Kimberley C. Patton has documented, but these myths are non-Christian in origin, and Schmitt follows the biblical perspective.[14] The oceans, for Schmitt, are threatening, because they lack the kind of geological formations that make land borders natural and necessary. Water's smooth and borderless surface represents, for Schmitt, a realm of chaos and anarchy. Empires can compete for control of the seas, but more often than not they compete against pirates as much as against other nations. For these reasons, the process of extending law and order to the sea initiated by England in the sixteenth century was a revolutionary world-historical event that established "the first *nomos* of the earth." This *nomos*, which was also made possible by the unique features of the Mediterranean, was decidedly Eurocentric.[15]

---

13. Schmitt, *Nomos of the Earth*, 42. For John Updike, the Sunday morning crowds on a summer beach are indicative of the modern yearning for a life of smooth sailing— a paradise without consequences and a sexuality without boundaries. For Updike's relationship to Barth, see Stephen H. Webb, "Writing as a Reader of Karl Barth: What Kind of Religious Writer is John Updike Not?" in *John Updike and Religion: The Sense of the Sacred and the Motions of Grace*, ed. James Yerkes (Grand Rapids: Eerdmans, 1999).

14. Kimberley C. Patton, *The Sea Can Wash Away All Evils: Modern Marine Pollution and the Ancient Cathartic Ocean* (New York: Columbia University Press, 2007).

15. Schmitt thinks that the Mediterranean Sea is unique because it is surrounded by so many cultures, languages, and peoples. The Mediterranean is a frontier from

The Dome of Eden

Schmitt acknowledges that this *nomos* no longer exists, but he despairs whether there can be another normative order for the earth, even as battles over the freedom of cyberspace—the new ocean—demonstrate just how unavoidable the pursuit of global order is.

Barth too ties human flourishing to the land and not the sea. In Genesis, he points out, humans are given sovereignty over only the plants and animals of the dry land. Indeed, the function of the firmament on the second day to delimit the water is not really complete until the first work of the third day, when the dry land emerges to separate the seas, which might be why the second is the only day that lacks God's declaration of "it was good." As Barth puts it, "The firm and habitable land is that which is properly and positively willed and intended by God. But the land has beside it the sea—assigned by the creation of the earth to its own place—as a creaturely sign (this time a near, direct and visible sign) of the existent but averted threat of the reality which by the wrath of God might reign yet by His goodness cannot reign but only threaten, being forced in its own way to praise God and work for the good of those that love Him" (142). The ocean has its place, but humanity's place is on the land. Barth thus agrees with Schmitt that the sea represents political chaos, but for Barth, the natural order of the land is guaranteed by God's authority over the seas. Political chaos emerges only when we exhibit a lack of trust in God to hold back the tide of human rebellion. Barth thus demonstrates how a geo-politics of the sea is ultimately theological, not political. Indeed, the central story of the Old Testament is how God parted the terrestrial waters to preserve the social unity of Israel—which unlike its neighbors the Phoenicians was not a seafaring people. The baptism of Jesus in the Jordan was not only a way of symbolizing his divine status (he is the same one who parted the waters of the Red Sea because he asks us to follow him through the waters of baptism). It was also a way of demonstrating God's complete authority over all water, celestial and terrestrial. These considerations

---

whose shores are launched the navigations that have both united and divided the three great monotheistic faiths (as well as uniting and dividing Catholicism and Orthodoxy). The oceans are unregulated and unrestrained, the arena of imperial delusions and piratical destruction, but this particular sea, as its name suggests, is set in the middle of the land, and is thus set apart from all other waters. The Mediterranean functions as a kind of celestial sea for Schmitt, divided already from other water and thus less of a threat than the oceans proper.

make the first chapter of Ezekiel, where the *raqiya'* upholds not water but a throne, upon which sits what seems like a human form, the most important scripture of defending a Christological reading of the Old Testament.[16]

Barth's interpretation of the dome is thus rich and varied, even as it is absolutely focused on Jesus Christ. In the end, however, he does not adequately connect Gen 1:6-8 to Gen 1:2, just as he does not fully subscribe to the Gap Theory. I quoted Barth earlier saying, with regard to the firmament and the waters, "We cannot abstract from this purpose" (136). Yet that is precisely what Barth does. Barth's exegetical riches are finally diminished by his tendency to existentialize the first few verses of Genesis. "Behind and above the physical danger there lurks the metaphysical danger of the upper sea held back by the *raqia'*" (137). By downplaying the physical function of the dome, he settles on the moral lesson that "the character of the *raqia'* as a boundary opposes all human pride and tumult" (140). Yet even at his most existential, Barth does not deny that the oceanic threat carries a physical dimension. The threat from the celestial ocean above has very real consequence because it is "a power which would completely destroy the lower cosmos as the dwelling-place of man; a power whose victory—against the Creator-will of God—would change the cosmos into chaos" (138-39). Indeed, the author of Genesis was "not thinking of allegorical or metaphysical water but of real water, as in the myth and indeed the natural science of his day, which in this respect was that of the 17th century as well" (139). The geocentric model of the Ptolemaic system has been disproved, but that does not mean that the dome must be interpreted in purely metaphorical and moralistic terms. If we are to grasp the full meaning of the dome, we must see how it challenges the science of our day, just as it challenged all the presuppositions of its own, but that is precisely what Barth does not do.

The problem is that Barth does not think that the dome has important implications for modern science. "The modern view of the sidereal world, with its reckoning in terms of millions of sun systems and thousands of light-years, and the ancient view which found instead

---

16. Barth can also describe the cross as a kind of dome that separates the chaos from creation. For this point, see R. Scott Rodin, *Evil and Theodicy in the Theology of Karl Barth* (New York: Peter Lang, 1997) 155 n. 66.

The Dome of Eden

very powerful deities, are comparable in the sense that both seem to exclude, with a kind of magical respect, the question of any purpose in this cosmic system, and especially of its relationship to the earth, and its inhabitants, i.e., the view that man is the purpose of this world" (160). If the dome was thought to be holding back the celestial ocean in the old science, a plain reading might ask what it could be thought of as holding back in the new. That is, its function remains the same even as the medium by which it fulfills this function changes. The answer to this question, of course, can only be given by returning to the identity of the waste, void, and watery deep of Gen 1:2. If that verse is understood, as Barth comes close to understanding it, to mean the transformation of nature due to Satan's fall, then the dome can be understood as an attempt to protect the Garden of Eden from the way that nature lends itself to wanton violence and cruelty. The dome is God's no, as Barth repeatedly insists, but it is a no to the dark side of evolution first before it is a no to human sloth and pride.

Here we come to the second reason for Barth's hesitancy to more fully advance toward a Gap Theory, which has to do with his theology of evil. Genesis portrays the dome as holding back a celestial ocean because something has gone terribly wrong with the world. Barth is clear about the something going wrong when he examines Gen 1:2, but he is not very clear about that when he examines Gen 1:6–8. When these two passages are read together, it is reasonable to conclude that Genesis is saying that the world is divided against itself because something, or someone, has entered into it, against God's wishes, and thus God needs to erect a protective barrier to delineate the good aspects of creation from the bad. Of course, Christian tradition refers to this something or someone as Satan, but Barth rejects the idea that Satan fell before Adam. He makes this point not in *Church Dogmatics* III/1 but in a later volume, III/3, where he discusses angels, whom he calls the ambassadors of God, and their opponents. Barth does not want to give demons any credit for being too real. He bases this reluctance on spiritual, not dogmatic grounds. "The very thing which the demons are waiting for, especially in theology, is that we should find them dreadfully interesting and give them our serious and perhaps systematic attention. In this way they can finally catch out, not bad theologians, but good."[17] That

---

17. Karl Barth, *Church Dogmatics* III/3, trans. and ed. G. W. Bromiley and T. F.

last line gives me some hope that my line of analysis is not completely without merit! Barth does say that "angels and demons are related as creation and chaos,"[18] which would suggest that his detailed exegesis of the chaos of *tohu* and *bohu* might have some relevance to this discussion of demons. Yet Barth demurs from the idea that demons are fallen angels.[19] Demons are best thought of when they are not thought of at all. Demons should be treated with a disbelief every bit as strong as the belief we give to God. This is all good spiritual advice, no doubt, but it leaves open the question of the origin of demons, or, to give them their collective name, the origins of Satan.

Barth himself does not hesitate to describe the function of demons—their work—even if he hesitates to speculate about their origin, and the reason he does not want to speculate about their origin has to do with how they work. Demons, for Barth, have no originating power of their own, but if God does not create evil, doesn't it make sense to think of demons as causal agents with regard to evil? This is where Barth's spiritual advice about evil turns into a full-blown metaphysics. Demons should be ignored because they are more closely related to nothingness than to anything real. For example, they cannot create something from nothing, as can God. Their best efforts are never anything more than mimicry. Yet mimicry has its own kind of power. Here it is important to introduce a term—mimesis—for a point of contrast. Mimesis is a literary term that means a creative imitation, as when an artist represents some aspect of the world for an aesthetic purpose. René Girard has popularized this term in an influential theory of violence that Barth actually anticipated by several decades.[20] By mimicry Barth means something different. Mimicry is a reaction to true creativity born of resentment, envy, and hate. Mimicry cannot create anything—it is like the spirit hovering over the water in Gen 1:2, which Barth depicts as

---

Torrance (Edinburgh: T. & T. Clark, 1960) 519.

18. Ibid., 520.

19. See the helpful analysis of Joseph L. Mangina, *Karl Barth, Theologian of Witness* (Louisville: Westminster John Knox, 2004) 104.

20. In a fascinating essay, Girard actually applies his theory of mimesis to evolution itself, arguing that, "The theory of natural selection seems to me quite powerfully sacrificial." René Girard with Pierpaolo Antonello, *Evolution and Conversion: Dialogues on the Origin of Culture* (London: Continuum, 2007) 96. Girard thinks within an evolutionary framework in order to subvert it.

brooding "impotently because wordlessly" (108)—but it can be very destructive. Mimicry can be defined as the imitation of creativity for the purposes of destructiveness. Barth is alert to mimicry's odd kind of creativity: "Nothingness wants to do everything too, and not only what creatures are and can do and accomplish, but also and supremely what God is and wills and does."[21] For Barth, evil is most fundamentally a proud and self-interested imitation of God, and God, in Genesis, is most fundamentally the creator of the cosmos. What would it mean for evil to imitate God's decision to create?

Barth gives a hint of an answer when he writes that evil "plays at creation" (526). The potential of applying this line of thought to evolution is rich. According to Loyal Rue, the evolutionary process is thoroughly enmeshed in deception, camouflage, manipulation, and mimicry.[22] Evolution is hardly playful in the sense of childhood innocence, but it is playful in a more sinister fashion. At one point Barth suggests that the earth of Gen 1:2 "mocks its Creator," (105), and mocking is a kind of evil playing. Nonetheless, Barth does not make the connection between evolution and the deceptive mocking of Satan, perhaps because evolution was rarely a topic of interest to him, even though he criticized theistic evolutionists for making a "deity of evolution."[23] His missed opportunity is also understandable in the light of his well-known rejection of apologetics as a legitimate form of theology. Moreover, as with his discussion of the firmament, Barth tends to existentialize evil. He places evil in human relationships, not in the natural world, though he also connects it to "the concern and struggle for daily bread" (527), which suggests that natural scarcity plays a significant role in its origins. Evil does not try to create the good out of nothing, we could say, but instead tries to create nothing out of the good. It turns the good into a history of conflict, and it makes that conflict look noble and necessary.

Barth does not want to give evil a name, although he comes very close to doing just that at one point in his exegesis of Gen 1:6–8. The chaos held back by the firmament, he writes, "threatens and will threat-

21. Mangina, *Karl Barth: Theologian of Witness*, 526.

22. Loyal Rue, *By the Grace of Guile: The Role of Deception in Natural History and Human Affairs* (New York: Oxford University Press, 1994).

23. He makes this comment in reference to Teilhard de Chardin. See Eberhard Busch, *Karl Barth: His Life from Letters and Autobiographical Texts*, trans. John Bowden (Philadelphia: Fortress, 1976) 487.

en. It is and will be a sign that creation could have been the catastrophe of the creature; that the creature had no power to avert this; and that it was God alone who averted it. Itself a creature, it cannot and will not be again a catastrophe to its fellow-creature. It cannot prevent the cosmos into which it is integrated from being the cosmos. It is subjected to, associated with, and incorporated into it" (133). Itself a creature: what is this evil that has become a part of nature even as it continues to threaten us, however muted its agency? How is it a creature like us and yet both more powerful and less powerful than us? Perhaps this is a passage worth pondering when Barth later, in *Church Dogmatics* III/3, labels evil as nothing but also insists, as Keller points out, that it is *not* nothing, that it "has its own being, albeit malignant and perverse"[24]

Barth's reluctance to give evil a proper name is why he finally sidesteps any version of the Gap Theory. He knows the legends about fallen angels, but he calls the idea of a heavenly fall, in an uncharacteristic swipe at Protestant orthodoxy, "one of the bad dreams of the older dogmatics"[25] Barth denies the fall of Satan because he thinks it "arises from a superfluous need to ground our knowledge of the fall of man upon the notion of a metaphysical prelude which it was quite inappropriately thought should be located in heaven."[26] Barth is reluctant to turn nothingness into something. He also refuses to conceive of the freedom of angels as being of the same kind as the freedom of humanity. Barth even has the audacity to assert that "the devil was never an angel."[27] This is surely taking nothingness too far—giving it too much explanatory power—given the overwhelming testimony of church tradition to the contrary. Ironically, Barth identifies the fall of Satan with improper metaphysical speculation, while his own account of the nothingness of evil is one of the great speculative achievements in modern theology.

Barth needs only a little nudge to make his account of the void and the dome coherent by bringing them into dialogue with a theology of natural evil. Evil has a name—Satan—because it is the product of the actions of an individual causal agent. Satan mimics God by trying to

24. Barth, *Church Dogmatics* III/3, 352.
25. Ibid., 531.
26. Ibid.
27. Ibid.

use his destructive power in creative ways. He divides creation against itself in order to make nature something it is not, and he disguises his actions by trying to make violence seem natural. It is this understanding of Satan's task, I am suggesting, that provides the best and only theologically coherent context for considering the theory of evolution. Barth did not connect evil to nature because, for all of his comprehensive reading and his courage in confronting modernity, he hardly ever mentions Darwin, and he never discussed evolution in any depth. The category of natural evil and its connection to evolution, however, is crucial not only for understanding how Satan works and what evolution is but also for understanding why Genesis has a gap and why God made the dome. Satan is the author of lies and a murderer, and the lie he tells most incessantly in our day is that nature must murder in order to create. The Dome of Eden demonstrates that God knows otherwise.

six

The Dome of Domes Divides the World

What is it about domes? There is no architectural form more praised, more ubiquitous, and more studied than the dome. Domes abound throughout the world, crowning most of the most important buildings. The dome can rightly claim to be the oldest human structure as well as providing humanity with its most spectacular architectural pleasures. Constructed of thatch, animal skin, or handfuls of the earth itself, a curved roof was both functional and aesthetically pleasing, in that it imitated the sky. Indeed, there must have been something deeply satisfying about making a building that looks like the very thing it was designed to protect against. The ancients thought of the sky as a giant dome that itself provided comfort and security for the earth below, yet the sky could let loose storms and floods, necessitating smaller domes, made by human hands—a shelter from shelter, so to speak.

The Romans are usually given the credit for turning the construction of domes into a science, or at least a system. With their genius for engineering, the Romans were bound to figure out a way to build domes as impressive as the sky, and they did so by making frames, or formworks, to support the great vaults of public buildings while they were under construction. They developed concrete, which was both pliant and permanent, as a suitable material for domes, and envisioned a shape, the hemisphere, that could expansively bridge enormous spaces. The Pantheon is a tribute to their ability to mimic nature with stunning results.

The half-sphere shape of a dome imitates not only the sky but also an inverted bowl, the most basic form for preparing food. Domes protected people from the weather while at the same time offering a reassurance that was intimately connected to the feeling of nourishment. Domes, because they resemble eggs, are also a symbol of fertil-

The Dome of Eden

ity in the ancient world. Some architectural historians speculate that the dome shape was so intimately associated with primitive humanity that, in Greece, more sophistical temple designers sought ways to employ sharper angles and more rectangular shapes in order to signal the progress their civilization had made. Perhaps much of the history of architectural symbolism can be understood as a conflict between the roundedness that speaks of timeless consolations and the angular that points to human ingenuity and technical know-how.

Both primitive simplicity and space-age inventiveness came together in the work of Buckminster Fuller, who used spherical geometry to design the first geodesic dome in the late 1940s. Fuller saw the dome as more than the answer to the mathematical problem of enclosing the most space with the least material. He thought that a new era of design revolutions would put an end to the dominance of right-angle, square configurations. The geodesic dome almost miraculously gets proportionally stronger as it increases in size. Builders were in the habit of thinking in terms of piling bricks or stones on top of each other. Using triangular patterns to shape a curved space, Fuller argued, would unshackle architecture from right-angle post-and-beam conventions. He hoped as well that dome houses, though hard to fit with sewer vents, windows, and chimneys, would liberate all of humankind from the outdated ideas that impede utopian thinking.

Fuller is evidence of how domes represent the highest human aspirations, and his spirit is carried on in The Eden Project, a global garden housed under several domes in Cornwall, England. This is one of the most ambitious garden projects ever conceived, and it is no coincidence that the idea of a self-sustaining landscape is connected to the figure of the dome, since Eden, for ancient Hebrews and Christians, was literally a garden beneath a dome.

Just as domes continue to evoke paradise, their ruin can be particularly moving as a symbol of the apocalypse. This accounts for the emotional impact of the A-Bomb Dome, formerly the Hiroshima Prefectural Products Exhibition Hall, which survived that nuclear explosion to become its symbol. And Hollywood could not have written a better script for the Hurricane Katrina disaster than to have tens of thousands of people streaming to the Superdome for shelter, though, tragically, they found confusion and violence instead.

The Dome of Domes Divides the World

Hollywood did write the script for a movie that challenged the way domes typically symbolize security and prosperity. *The Truman Show*, a 1998 film directed by Peter Weir and written by Andrew Niccol, has a plot taken straight out of the Garden of Eden, but with a twist. The dome in this movie provides a false protection for the Adam-like character. The action of the movie takes place in a town called Seahaven, and near the end of the movie the viewer discovers that Seahaven is set within a giant dome. Truman, played by Jim Carrey, grows up in the Omni Camera Ecosphere, a domed world that is really a stage constructed for a soap opera televised twenty-four hours a day to millions of viewers. Truman is the only person on the globed island who is unaware that he is a celebrity. All of his friends and family are actors, and they conspire to convince him that he is afraid of anything to do with water, flying, or traveling. When he finally musters the courage to sneak away on a sailboat on the open sea, he literally runs into the end of his world, a wall painted like the sky. He finds an exit door in the wall and takes his leave from the show. His perfect world was a false paradise that had made him the center of attention but left him without a life of his own. The movie is thoughtful and engaging, but its postmodern message is predictable and mundane: the comforts of home and the protection that the sacred affords us are illusory traps from which we must escape if we are to learn to think for ourselves.

While the dome enforces a false innocence on the Adam-like character in *The Truman Show*, it protects the rest of the world from the evils wrought by the stupidity of Homer's innocence in *The Simpsons Movie* (2007). Although this film does not directly refer to Genesis, let alone to technical theological discussions of the meaning of the firmament, it seems like a parody of the Garden of Eden story, especially the role played by the original Dome of Eden. After Homer dumps a silo of pig waste in the Springfield Lake, the whole town becomes toxic, and the EPA encloses it with a dome. The point of the dome is to keep America safe, but of course it does so only by imprisoning the people of Springfield. The dome is a death trap, and Homer has to save the day. Once again Hollywood has turned a sign of God's providential care into a stigma of suffocating social control.

Most cultures take the traditional route of revering, not ridiculing, domes. It is no surprise, for example, that the first architectural

The Dome of Eden

masterpiece in the Muslim world was a dome. The Dome of the Rock was built in 687 CE, a half century after Muhammad's death, on the site where Solomon had built his Temple, destroyed by Nebuchadnezzar, and Herod had rebuilt it, only to have it destroyed by the Romans. The Dome of the Rock was designed to resemble the great dome of the Church of the Holy Sepulcher, making it either a sign of the unity of the three faiths or a sign of Islam's effort to displace the other two. Its gold covered cupola gleams like a mountain top lit by the sun. For a religion without a tradition of representational art, the dome (along with the crescent) has functioned as close to a symbol as Islam has permitted. Serious apocalyptic scenarios and cheap fictional thrillers alike play on the fear that Christian or Jewish extremists might some day try to blow it up.

Surely the greatest dome in the Christian world is Hagia Sophia, the Great Church of Constantinople (now Istanbul). The original dome, built between 532 and 537, was cracked by earthquakes and rebuilt by 563. Much of that construction survives to this day. The dome rises effortlessly due to the illusionary tricks of the architects. Curved triangular-shaped stones, called pendentives, filled in the space between the arches so that they could hold the enormous weight of the dome, and forty windows circle its base, making the dome appear to float in the air. Procopius, a sixth-century Byzantine historian, described the terror felt by first-time visitors who could not figure out why the elevated dome did not simply collapse. My own experience was one of initial shock followed by an immediate recognition that the ancients were more aware of God's glory than we moderns. The ancients were fond of calling it a great helmet or crown, but Paul the Silentary, writing in the twelfth century, likened it to the firmament, and Michael Thessalonika made that analogy explicit by writing that it imitates heaven and "hardly falls short of the cosmos."[1]

The best book about the history of domes is still the 1950 volume, *The Dome: A Study in the History of Ideas*, written by E. Baldwin Smith (1888–1956). A professor of the history of architecture at Princeton University, Smith was interested in every aspect of the dome, and it is

---

1. Quoted in Joseph Bertha, "The Dome of Hagia Sophia," *Diakonia* 21 (1987) 158. Also see Kathleen E. McVey, "The Domed Church as Microcosm: Literary Roots of an Architectural Symbol," *Dumbarton Oaks Papers* 37 (1983) 91–121.

fair to say that he saw the dome as the most interesting architectural form. Smith saw his first clues to the dome's significance while examining martyriums, which were built in honor of martyrs and served as proto-types for later Christian churches. He suspected these structures had wooden domes, but that material did not survive, so he had to play detective in order to piece together the missing roofs. He set out to solve the problem of a missing roof and ended up exploring the mystery of the greatest architectural symbol. The dome was the most appropriate form for Christians to honor their dead because it evoked "an ancient and ancestral past when the gods and men lived together in an idyllic paradise on earth."[2] Every dome was but an imitation of the firmament.

Smith was convinced that the rotund shape was not only universal in its usage and importance but also primordial in its status as the first and holiest of architectural devices. He took as his key the fact that the Latin *domus* meant, in the Middle Ages, house, and was used, more particularly, to mean a sacred house, *Domus Dei*. For centuries, this word referred to any significant house, and it was only in the seventeenth century that its meaning was narrowed to a cupola roof. The domical shape, however, goes back much further than the architectural triumph of domical vaulting. The circular shelter, in the form of tents or earthen works, was the first that humans built, and that is why it occupied pride of place when it came to creating dwellings for the gods and paying respect to the ancestors. To our eyes, the rectangle seems simpler, because that is what we see all around us, but the rectangle is the result of rigid material and hard, sharp tools. Curves are more ancient, which makes the dome as much of an idea as a shape. The curvilinear plan for a house is instinctive and primitive, according to Smith, because it is the most natural way to being at one point and, with pliable materials, return to that same point having enclosed a space. Think of a bird's nest or the way children construct a tent out of blankets and chairs. Smith is arguing that the dome did not originate as a technical solution, made possible by strong building materials, to the problem of roofing large buildings. Instead, the shape of the dome was so common

---

2. E. Baldwin Smith, *The Dome: A Study in the History of Ideas* (Princeton: Princeton University Press, 195) 8.

The Dome of Eden

and ancient that it entered into history as a symbol before it became an awe-inspiring feat.

When Constantine legalized Christianity and Christians could start building churches without fear of persecution, it was natural, according to Smith, that they would have inherited and perfected the ancient domical tradition. But the pagans had no monopoly on this idea. The Hebrew Scriptures are full of domical references. Isaiah 40:22 describes God as sitting "above the circle of the earth" and spreading "out the heavens like a curtain" to live in. And Job 26:11 portrays heaven resting on pillars, as if the mountains of the earth are holding up the firmament. That is why Christians painted (or made mosaics of) so many visions of heaven on the interior of domes.[3] The picture of the earth as a flat plane covered by an arched sky was widespread in the ancient world, although sometimes it was just that—a picture but not a serious belief. Jeffrey Burton Russell has argued that the idea that educated people before the age of exploration generally believed in a flat earth is a modern fable.[4] Ptolemy's maps, for example, which assumed a curved globe, were the basis of European astronomy in the Middle Ages, and there is no evidence that the Catholic Church conspired to keep this knowledge hidden. There is, however, a conspiracy regarding this story, which Russell uncovers. Russell traces the fable of the flat earth to Darwinians who wanted to elevate Darwin by comparing his struggle against religious authorities to Columbus's effort to prove the world round. The fact that both men found plenty of support from the religious leaders of their day has done nothing to deter those anti-Christian historians who continue to portray Christianity as the enemy of science and reason.

Ancient Christians thought that the dome was central to the biblical understanding of space, but respectable theologians today never deign to inquire into the shape and material of the firmament. Refereed journals, library catalogues, and professional conferences are silent on this topic in part because the firmament exists as a solid dome only in the misty imagination of primitive peoples. To make matters worse, the ancient understanding of the domed earth survives into the modern

---

3. Karl Lehmann, "The Dome of Heaven," *Art Bulletin* 27 (1945) 1–27.

4. Jeffrey Burton Russell, *Inventing the Flat Earth: Columbus and Modern Historians* (New York: Praeger, 1997).

The Dome of Domes Divides the World

world only due to its association with groups that fanatically or jokingly insist that the earth is flat. Flat earthists are actually domical extremists. In this cosmological picture, the dome covers the whole earth, which means that the earth must be flat. What could be more embarrassing to anyone wanting to take the Dome of Eden seriously?

As a result of this embarrassment, any discussion of the firmament must take place on the margins of serious scholarship, which means, of course, the Web. Unfortunately, the Web is often a medium for quick argument rather than in-depth reflection. On the Web, the topic of the firmament is tossed around like a scoring point for debates about biblical literacy. Anti-Christian polemicists use the firmament to denounce mistaken biblical cosmology, while fundamentalist apologists struggle to reconcile the Bible and modern science. Most theologians, of course, have long given up on the topic altogether, by declaring that the Bible is pre-scientific and interpreting Genesis as poetry, not geology. The firmament, in most contemporary theology, barely exists. It hangs on in theological circles like an ornament, embellishing the Genesis story and reminding sophisticated readers of the quaint imagination of the biblical authors, but hardly deserving of more than a glancing notice.

Ironically, it might be modern science that brings back the significance of this most archaic of biblical images. Scientists have long puzzled about the increasing rate of the universe's outward expansion, and physicists have posited a dark energy to account for it. The latest thinking, however, is that the earth might be located in a kind of space-time bubble that is particularly void of matter. This domically shaped bubble would explain why things look further away than they actually are, because light is distorted in a void. The bubble of low density matter surrounding the Earth would thus make speculations about dark energy unnecessary. The problem with this new theory for some scientists is that it violates one of the chief principles of modern cosmology, namely, that there is nothing special about where the Earth is located. The Copernican principle has long been used as an argument against traditional interpretations of the doctrine of creation, because it suggests that we are in a lonely outpost in a bleak and ever-expanding universe. If the Earth is in a domically shaped zone void of matter, however, then there might be something peculiarly special about our location after all. Perhaps the Dome is still serving a function for our planet that scientists are only now beginning to discover.

Perhaps presciently, fundamentalist Christians have never given up speculation about the Dome, with one of the liveliest debates in that theological camp focusing on what is called the water canopy theory. This theory is best formulated by Joseph Dillow, who credits Irwin Moody, George McCready, Vernon Kellog, and N. I. Saloff Astakhoff for inspiration, but most of all, Henry Morris and John Whitcomb, who co-wrote the book *The Genesis Flood* in 1961. Whitcomb and Morris virtually created "scientific creationism." Whitcomb taught at Grace Theological Seminary in Winona Lake, Indiana, from 1951 to 1990. Morris (1918–2006) was a professor of civil engineering at several universities before becoming one of the founders of the Institute for Creation Research, which has done more than any other institution in gaining creationism credibility and respect. Denounced by many evangelicals as pseudo-science and virtually ignored by mainline theologians, *The Genesis Flood* marked a turning point in fundamentalist Christianity. There is probably no other theological book written in America in the twentieth century that has had such significant impact on a single Christian community. Arthur McCalla has called it a "science of the catacombs," because it originated out of sight among Christians who had become deeply alienated from mainstream America.[5] This book emboldened many fundamentalists in their rejection of liberalism's strategy of reinterpreting Genesis in order to accommodate evolution. It put into play a theory that has been much revised, amended, and debated outside of the mainstream scientific and theological world. Dillow's book, *The Waters Above*, is an updated version of *The Genesis Flood* and an attempt to answer its many critics from with the evangelical camp.[6]

Dillow's basic thesis is that a water canopy encompassed the earth prior to the flood. It acted like a thermal blanket. This canopy maintained a storm-free, perfectly mild climate that assured that the world

---

5. Arthur McCalla, *The Creationist Debate: The Encounter between the Bible and the Historical Mind* (New York: T. & T. Clark, 2006) 173.

6. Josheph C. Dillow, *The Waters Above: Earth's Pre-Flood Vapor Canopy* (Chicago: Moody, 1981). For a helpful commentary, see John C. Whitcomb and Donald B. DeYoung's review in *Grace Theological Journal* 3 (1982) 123–32. Also see John C. Whitcomb Jr. and Henry M. Morris, *The Genesis Flood* (Philadelphia: P. & R., 1961).

God created was very good. Its condensation and precipitation through the "windows of heaven" (Gen 7:11, KJV) accounts for the great flood. The water canopy theory is not easy to evaluate, because it demands a total reconstruction of modern geology and biology. Dillow assumes that Genesis is akin to a scientific textbook, and the key to his model is his interpretation of the firmament, rendered *expanse* by the translators of the *New American Standard Bible*. Dillow likes *expanse* rather than *firmament* because he rejects the idea that it is a hard, mirrorlike surface. It is, he says, simply the sky spread out. He blames the misconception that the firmament is a solid dome on the Septuagint translation of the Bible, and he dismisses the biblical passages that refer to pillars holing up the firmament as nothing more than poetry. Dillow is actually not all that interested in the firmament. What captures his attention is the waters above the expanse. He rejects the hypothesis that the division of the waters referred to in Gen 1:6-8 merely refers to the clouds in the sky being separated from the liquid water on the surface of the earth. Instead, he defends the existence of a literal liquid celestial ocean as the only way of doing justice to the text. Many scholars agree with him that that is what the text says, but Dillow thinks this ocean is the key to reinstating Genesis as good science and overthrowing evolution. The greenhouse effect, the rapid formation of an isotope of helium, changes in the earth's atmospheric pressure, sudden temperature drops, and residual amounts of water in the stratosphere all account for the various conundrums in trying to reconcile Genesis and modern science. Even the incident of Noah becoming drunk after he departed the ark receives fresh explanation. Noah was righteous, so he would not have become drunk intentionally. Instead, he was caught off guard due to the sudden change of fermentation rates brought about by the collapse of the canopy that had by that time turned to vapor.

Paul H. Seely has been Dillow's most careful critic.[7] Seely thinks that Genesis clearly supports a solid dome conception of the firma-

---

7. Paul H. Seely, "The Firmament and the Water Above, Part II: The Meaning of 'The Water above the Firmament' in Gen. 1:6-8," *Westminster Theological Journal* 54 (1992) 31-46. Seely is not a literalist. He thinks that Genesis is religiously authoritative but cosmologically prescientific. For a spirited response to an early version of Seely's position, see Stanley V. Udd, "The Canopy and Genesis 1:6-8," *Creation Research Society Quarterly* 12 (1975) 90-93. Some conservative theologians defend the water canopy view by arguing that it consisted of ice crystals that permitted light to reach the

ment and that the solidity of the dome is presupposed by the water that Genesis locates above it. Seely points out that Dillow insists on the atmospheric constitution of the firmament because he thinks this makes for a better scientific explanation for the source of the flood waters. Following Gen 1:14–17, Seely argues that the sun, moon, and stars are placed in the firmament, so that the waters above the firmament must have been above the sun. A water canopy would have been too low to the Earth to match the idea of waters lying above the firmament.

What make Seely's argument especially persuasive is that the Hebrew phrase for "above the firmament" occurs only once outside of Genesis. It is found in Ezek 1:25, where it refers to a voice that comes from above the firmament. "And there came a voice from above the dome over their heads" (NRSV). This voice comes from the one who, in the likeness of a man, sits on the dome. Christians know this man as Jesus Christ, and he exists, prior to the incarnation, above all things. Genesis appears, then, to associate a celestial sea with the heavenly realm of God. This is confirmed by other passages in the Bible, such as Exod 24:10 and Job 38:30, that depict heaven in terms of a frozen sea of crystalline structure. Especially important in this regard is Rev 4:6, which says that "in front of the throne there is something like a sea of glass, like crystal." Whether or not it is the source of the flood, the importance of the celestial sea is its association with heaven and with Jesus. The firmament divides the seas, but it divides them fundamentally. Far from being identical to a vaporous canopy encircling the earth, the firmament separates heaven and earth.

Besides debating the finer points of the celestial sea, Seely has also documented the widespread belief in the ancient world in a solid domed sky. Many ancient peoples thought the sky touched the earth at the horizon, which means they thought the earth was flat and circular.[8] Some scholars have tried to play down the abundant evidence for this belief in the ancient world. Perhaps, they speculate, the ancients thought the

---

earth. The problem with the scientific testing of canopy proposals is that they involve conditions, by their own argument, that no longer exist, so there is no way to test their atmospheric effects.

8. Paul H. Seely, "The Geographical Meaning of 'Earth' and 'Seas' in Genesis 1:10," *Westminster Theological Journal* 59 (1997) 231–55 and "The Firmament and the Water Above, Part I: The Meaning of raqia in Gen. 1:6–8," *Westminster Theological Journal* 53 (1991) 227–40.

sky was solid because they did not understand the molecular constitution of air. The word *air* never even appears in the Old Testament. The idea of gases that stretch immeasurably through space was foreign to their thought. This line of reasoning has led some scholars to speculate that the firmament was really like a holding place in the minds of the ancients—a vague or abstract container that holds the elements of the sky and the atmosphere. Seely shows that these strategies of resistance are doomed by the plenitude of the evidence. What is unique about Genesis is not its portrait of a solid sky but its depiction of a particular kind of sky. The firmament not only divides the earthly waters from the heavenly, but—and this is my concern—it also protects the earth, or, as I will argue, it protects one parcel of the earth.

Interestingly, many conservative scholars also try their best to reject the idea that the firmament was understood to be solid. They argue against scholars like Seely because they are invested in a very particular defense of the literal truth of Genesis, and they understand that a solid sky is always connected in the ancient world with the belief in a flat earth. They begin with the premise that Genesis is literally true, add the fact that the earth is not flat, and conclude that Genesis cannot have promoted the idea of a solid sky. I too think Genesis is absolutely true, but I have a solution for their worries. The firmament did not cover the whole earth. If it did so, then we would be forced to conclude that the earth is indeed flat. Instead, it covered only Eden, and thus Genesis could promote the idea of a solid firmament without implying a flat earth.

The flat earthists refer to a number of biblical passages that denote a fixed earth (1 Chron 16:30, Pss 93:1, 96:10, 104:5, Isa 45:18). They also are eager to point out the verses that refer to God making a vaulted heavens above the earth (Job 9:8, Pss 19:1, 102:25, Isa 45:12, 48:13). They are right not to rush through such passages as if they do not exist. They are wrong only when they think that the firmament covered the whole earth.

So why did the idea of a solid firmament vanish in the West? The simple answer to that complicated question is that the firmament was identified with the sky and then was connected to an outdated cosmology. The outdated cosmology that doomed the firmament is not the idea of a flat earth but the idea that that a rigid sky revolves around the

219

The Dome of Eden

earth once each day, carrying the stars with it. Before modern astronomy, people believed that something must keep the stars in their place. When Kepler discovered that the planetary motions do not conform to their being immovably fixed in a solid dome, the firmament was fated to fade from the Western imagination. Theologians began to interpret the firmament metaphorically as the expanse of air and space.

It is time to rethink, rather that to continue to forget, the firmament. Actually, whether or not one imagines this dome literally as a dome is immaterial to my thesis. It is the function of the dome, not so much its material status, that is crucial for my theory. Indeed, if Genesis had not told us that God used a dome to protect Eden and thus divide the world, theologians would have had to invent something like the dome to make sense of Satan's fall, evolution, and the goodness of creation. The dome helps us to visualize how it is that God was doing something in one place and Satan was doing something quite different in another place. The Dome divides the waters, but more fundamentally, it divides the world into two.

The Dome of Domes can divide the world into two, of course, only if Eden was a real place. The particularity of Eden has long been a subject of contentious debate among devout Christians.[9] The web is full of articles speculating about where the writer of Genesis thought it was located, but the description in Genesis of four rivers, only two of which are identifiable, has prevented the emergence of any single consensus candidate. Nevertheless, educated guesses put it in Mesopotamia, though every such guess must be ventured with the understanding that where the ancients located it is now lost to us. The word itself comes from an Akkadian term meaning plain or steppe, and the Old Testament refers to it as a region that was commonly known at that time (Gen 4:16, 2 Kings 19:12, Isa 37:12). Many ancient Near Eastern peoples believed in a specific place of perfect peace and happiness, which could suggest that Eden is a myth or that human nature is created to long for the reality that the Bible reveals.

The association of the Garden of Eden with the term paradise does not occur in the Old Testament, but was introduced by the translators of

---

9. See Arthur H. Lewis, "The Localization of the Garden of Eden," *Bulletin of the Evangelical Theological Society* 11 (1968) 169–75. Lewis's position, close to my own, is that paradisiac conditions were restricted to Eden, while the rest of the world was "natural" from the beginning.

the Greek (Septuagint) version of the Hebrew Scriptures. Nonetheless, it is an appropriate translation, given the natural abundance and spiritual riches of the garden. Just how different from the rest of the world Eden was is a matter of debate. The Book of Jubilees, an ancient Jewish text that some early Christian groups treated as canonical, states that God did not place Adam in the garden until his fortieth day. Furthermore, Genesis does not indicate whether the dust from which Adam was made was a part of Eden or the world at large. These minor points are important because they remind us not to jump too quickly to the idea that Eden simply refers to the entire earth.

There are three basic models for determining the relationship of Eden to the planet Earth. The first model simply identifies Eden with the Earth. The reason some Christians identify Eden with the entire planet are clear and understandable. God creates the world and calls it good. The original goodness of creation is crucial for the Christian understanding of God. If the world was created good, and Eden was very good, then perhaps Eden simply was the world before the fall. If so, then God must have recreated the world after Adam and Eve were expelled from the Garden. Otherwise, to what were Adam and Eve expelled? As I argued in chapter four, the idea that God changed the ontological conditions of the entire world after the fall lacks plausibility. If I am right, the world outside of Eden must have been fallen already, before the expulsion of the human pair. This does not mean that the world into which Adam and Eve were expelled was so shatteringly different from Eden that Adam and Eve did not recognize it. It was like Eden, only harder, more strenuous, and more dangerous.

The second model identifies Eden with a specific, though today unknown, locale on the Earth. This is an important position because it guards against the temptation of treating Eden as a mere myth or legend. Eden was unique, but that does not necessarily mean that it was utterly dissimilar to the rest of the world. The church fathers could debate whether Adam and Eve would have died if they had not fallen and whether they would have had sex if they had not been expelled precisely because Eden was so recognizable. But they also debated the sexual life of Adam and Eve because they thought the Garden was a trope for heaven and thought that heaven would be devoid of sex (Luke

The Dome of Eden

20:27–40).[10] These debates are fascinating primarily because they show that the Church Fathers took Eden as a revelation of what God wants from them. Eden is not the product of human fantasy; fallen human nature could not have produced a place so earthly in its loftiness. Eden is more than a simple Hebraic pastoral ideal, but less than an abstract view of perfection.

The third model identifies Eden with the mythical human longing for perfection. This model can be taken seriously by traditionally-minded Christians only if it is combined with the second model. The strength of this model indicates how Eden was both in and not in the world, occupying a zone or region of being that was like no other. If Eden was set apart, it had to have been set apart by something, and that is where the Dome comes into play. The fall was the lifting of the dome, so to speak, and the exposure of Adam and Eve to the elements of a fractured world. Adam and Eve were already a part of this world, because they were made from its dust, but now they had to become immersed in it without the intimacy of an undivided connection to God. The first people, however, were not a product of evolution, on my interpretation of Genesis, because they were created according to the model of the person of Jesus Christ (my fifth thesis). God could create them by bypassing evolution because evolution is the process whereby nature seeks the human form. In other words, evolution is nature's struggle to achieve what God planned from the very beginning. Evolution does not explain humanity. Rather, humanity explains evolution. I will have much more to say about this when I discuss Simon Conway Morris's work on biological convergences in Chapter Seven. Morris has demonstrated how evolution, far from being random and haphazard, demonstrates biological trends toward complexity, consciousness, and intelligence that peak in human nature. "Human language may, on this planet, be unique," Morris writes, "but waiting in the wings of the theatre of consciousness are other minds stirring, poised on the threshold of articulation."[11] Orthodox Darwinians make much of the idea that hu-

---

10. Many of the Church Fathers were also committed to celibacy, which led them to suspect that sexual consummation was incompatible with the holiness of paradise. See Gary Anderson, "Celibacy or Consummation in the Garden? Reflections on Early Jewish and Christian Interpretations of the Garden of Eden," *Harvard Theological Review* 82 (1989) 121–48.

11. Simon Conway Morris, *Life's Solution: Inevitable Humans in a Lonely Universe*

mans are so much like non-human animals that we are, for all practical purposes, animals ourselves. The Christian view is exactly the opposite. Animals are like us, more than we are like them. We were created in the image of God, and they were created in our image, so to speak, and the whole world was created for the glory of Jesus Christ.

While my position allows us to think of humans as the exception to the rule of evolution, the question of what the animals of Eden were is still open. As I argued in my third thesis, Eden occupied a unique space and time that cannot be schematized according to deep biological time. It follows that the animals of Eden were not the product of evolution. Here theology enters into deep speculation, but it is not unreasonable to suppose that the animals of Eden were more along the lines of prototypes or archetypes of all the animals, rather than real biological creatures. Perhaps we should say that the Edenic animals had the form and bearing that all animals will have when they are brought into a proper relationship to both humanity and God. Adam and Eve experienced the animal kingdom as it was meant to be, without a violent struggle of life against life. If the animals of Eden had been real biological creatures in our understanding of biology today, then we would be stuck with the awkward question of what happened to them after the fall. Were they expelled along with Adam and Eve? If so, did God change their natures from herbivores to carnivores? Did they get lost or consumed in the violent world outside of Eden? Did they stay in Eden, and if so, what is their relationship to the wild animals that Adam faced after the fall? These imponderables suggest that the animals of Eden were mythical creatures in the eschatological sense of myth. They were real, and yet their reality belongs to the future more than the past.

My speculations are not as eccentric as some readers might think. Michael Denton, a Senior Research Fellow at the University of Otago, in New Zealand, has recently developed the argument that "the unique forms and properties of living systems arise like those of the double helix naturally from the intrinsic properties of matter." If so, then much of the order of biology is "inherent in the fabric of nature herself."[12] In

---

(Cambridge: Cambridge University Press, 2003) 253.

12. Michael Denton, "An Anti-Darwinian Intellectual Journey," in *Uncommon Dissent: Intellectuals Who Find Darwinism Unconvincing*, ed. William A. Dembski (Wilmington, DE: ISI, 2004) 176. For a brief discussion of Denton by Morris, see Simon Conway Morris, "The Navigation of Biological Hyperspace," *International*

a recent article for the *Journal of Theoretical Biology*, Denton has developed his argument by focusing on protein folds, the basic building blocks of proteins.

Before Darwin, he observes, biologists had a Platonic model of biology. According to this view, recurrent organic forms are abstract types that are realized by biological change. Even before Darwin biologists understood that life evolves, but they attributed evolution to the law-governed unfolding of pre-determined or pre-established biological types. Biological forms were thought to exist naturally and necessarily, like atoms or crystals. Darwin changed all of that by treating forms as "contingent and mutable assemblages of matter, like the constructs of a child's erector set." For Darwin, functions generate forms, rather than forms being the basis of functions. "Even the deep homologous patterns which underlie the major body plans such as the vertebrate body plan or the pentadactyl limb, for which no convincing selectionist explanation has ever been provided, are now assumed to represent ancient adaptations entrapped by genetic inertia and perpetuated as non-adaptive features in their present-day descendents." Denton's study of protein folds has led him back to the platonic model of biology. Protein folds are robust, complex, and beautiful, and according to Denton, they can be "classified into a finite number of distinct structural families containing a number of related but variant forms." That these folds can be specified by unrelated amino-acid sequences suggests that it is highly unlikely that evolution has discovered them in multiple, independent lines of development. Since they follow what Denton calls "constructional rules," it is simpler to hypothesize a finite set of natural forms built into nature from the beginning. Denton does not speculate about the origin of these forms. Indeed, he seems to think that the best explanation is that they are eternal. It is just as plausible to imagine God creating all biological forms as part of the divine plan for the Garden of Eden as it is to envision how matter could be eternal. The important point to be learned from Denton, however, is that nature does not select forms; instead, forms are given to nature. Forms are a matter of "biochemical predestination."[13]

Journal of Astrobiology 2 (2003) 149.

13. Michael J. Denton, Craig J. Marshall, and Michael Legge, "The Protein Forms: New Support for the Pre-Darwinian Conception of Evolution by Natural Law," *Journal*

Perhaps biology is just now catching up with Augustine's identification of Eden with the realm of the Platonic forms, the immaterial thoughts or ideas of God that God subsequently used to create the material world. Eden provides the biological foundation, then, for what happens outside of it. What happened outside of Eden is the battle between God and Satan, but Satan is not a creator, so the world outside of Eden is not without evidence of God's sovereignty. The world was subjected to a horrible distortion of the Garden, but it was not hellish, because only Hell comes close to reaching the limit of divine providence. The matter God had created in an orderly fashion was infused by Satan with the spirit of strife, greed, and disquiet. Everything God created in Eden was desecrated in the wider world, which was Satan's way of preparing a literal testing ground for the humans God created in the image of his Son. The destiny that awaited humanity was an either-or: Either humans were to live up to their status of being set apart by the image of God, or they were they to become like the wild animals, driven by desire, greed, and hunger. Remarkably, isn't that still the question every one of us faces? Satan is indeed, as his portrait is clearly depicted in the book of Job, the tester. God permits Satan to push Job to the limits, taking away his children, his health, and his honor. Job was not the first human to be subjected to Satan's wry examination. The world itself is the stage upon which all of us must pass or fail as we struggle with the purpose of God's plan. The world is the stage of temptation because the gates of Eden were closed to us after Adam and Eve's expulsion. We cannot return to Eden, but we can go back to Genesis with a fresh perspective to determine what makes us human and what makes us suitable for our destiny with the divine.

---

of Theoretical Biology (2002) 328, 328, and 330. Denton refers to "biochemical predestination" as the title of a book by D. H. Kenyon and G. Steinman (New York: McGraw-Hill, 1969). Also see Michael Denton and Craig Marshall, "Laws of Form Revisited," *Nature* 410 (22 March 2001) 417; and Michael A. Woodley, "On the Possible Operation of Natural Laws in Ecosystems," *Biological Forum* 100 (2007) 475–86. Denton's narrative of Darwin's relationship to Platonic biology needs to be complicated due to the work of Robert J. Richards. In *The Romantic Conception of Life: Science and Philosophy in the Age of Goethe* (Chicago: University of Chicago Press, 2002), Richards demonstrates that Darwin was very much in debt to biological romanticism. Nonetheless, it is true that the archetypal theory of biological forms was dominant prior to Darwin because it was easy to make the connection between types and the doctrine of creation while Darwin's move away from archetypes was popular in part for just the opposite reason (it was easy to make the connection between natural selection and atheism).

The Dome of Eden

The idea that Satan and God are involved in a battle and that the world is the scene of that battle is so thoroughly a part of Christianity that it is hard to discuss in the abstract, yet it has also been the target of a sustained and systematic attack by liberal theology for over a century. Liberal theology is founded upon the premise that the more overtly supernatural elements of Christianity can be demythologized in order to leave a spiritual and moral core that can be assimilated by modern believers. Liberal Christians have abandoned the reality of Satan in part because liberal theology gives Satan little to do. If people are basically good, and oppressive economic, social, and political structures are to be blamed for the bad things people do, then Satan must be a symbol and not a real agent of evil. Darwinism actually initiated the demotion and diminishment of Satan by demonstrating how natural evils are a necessary precondition for the evolution of higher organisms. If nature is not cursed, as Genesis states, then it was logical to draw the further conclusion that humans are not cursed, either.

Fundamentalists have long connected evolutionary theory with Satan, but most people have no idea how sophisticated fundamentalists can be about this connection. Not content to defend the scientific accuracy of the Bible, Henry Morris, one of the principle founders of scientific creationism, has constructed a demonic genealogy for Darwinism.[14] He argues that it is no coincidence that Alfred Russell Wallace, who formulated the theory of evolution at about the same times as Darwin, was influenced by spiritualism, which was immensely popular in Darwin's day. Spiritualists try to contact the spirits of the dead, and many traditional Christians think they are playing with the devil. Morris draws the conclusion that demonic spirits are the true source of evolutionary theory. This will seem far-fetched to most readers, but Morris's real aim is to establish Satan as the source for the all the calamities that Darwinism has sprung on the world, including, Morris argues, the racism in Germany that led to the Holocaust. Morris assigns the immediate cause of Darwinism to spiritualism, but he traces the longer history of Darwinism back to those ancient cosmologies that place chaos at the heart of the world. Ultimately, Babylon is to be

---

14. Henry M. Morris, *The Troubled Waters of Evolution* (San Diego: Creation-Life, 1974) 72–76. Also see his fascinating book, *The Long War Against God: The History and Impact of the Creation/Evolution Conflict* (Grand Rapids: Baker, 1989).

blamed, due to its creation myth, *Enuma Elish*, which portrays watery chaos as the source of all life. This cosmology was made sacred by the Tower of Babel and spread throughout the world when God destroyed the Tower and scattered its worshippers. In his most creative turn in this narrative, Morris argues that Satan, though the father of lies, is not lying when he promotes evolution. Rather, he is a victim of self-deception. When he first rebelled against God, Satan found himself in the watery chaos of Gen 1:2, with God's Spirit hovering above him. Satan naturally concluded that this watery chaos is indeed the origin of all things, and they he has just as much right as God to rule this world.

What Morris gets right is his insistence that evolution, as understood from a Darwinian perspective, cannot be the means by which God creates the world, because it is cruel and irrational. To substantiate this point, Morris observes that it only took three days for the resurrection of Jesus, complete with a new body, so that it makes little sense to think that God would have spent eons using death to create new species. Morris is also right to treat Satan as the source of all lies about the origin of the universe. Indeed, the lie of lies is the idea that cruelty and torment are the work of God and are, therefore, necessary and good for human progress. If that is the lie of lies, then Darwinism surely can be construed as one of the chief vehicles of Satan's influence in the modern world. Nonetheless, Satan works in ways that are constrained by divine providence, which suggests that even when we see evil in the world, it is not unadulterated by grace. Mapping Satan's contributions to evolutionary theory with any precision runs the risk of confusing Satan's terrors with God's labors. God brings good out of the bad, even in nature. Analyze Satan's relationship to evolution also risks crediting Satan with too much power and thus indulging Satan's self-importance. Darwinism is morally confused about the role of evil in the world, but I do not think it helps contemporary debates to claim that Darwin (or Russell) was one of Satan's pawns.

Just because fundamentalists take the clash of Satan and God seriously does not mean that non-fundamentalists shouldn't. The chief defender today of the idea that evil is the result of a conflict between God and Satan is Gregory A. Boyd, a prolific evangelical author and pastor. A political liberal, Boyd is probably best known for speaking out against the alliance of evangelicals and conservative politics. Boyd's inclination for provocation is also on display in his theology of what he calls warfare theodicy.[15] Boyd is not content to revive theological interest in the reality of Satan. Instead, he connects warfare theodicy to a movement in evangelical theology known as open theism. Open theism is an evangelical version of what is known in liberal academic circles as process philosophy. Open theists/process philosophers argue that God does not have exhaustive knowledge of all events, past, present, and future. If God did, they claim, we would not be free. Open theism has come in for substantial criticism from other evangelical theologians, because it seems to suggest that God takes chances with the world. Indeed, Boyd's talk about God as a risk taker makes his theology congenial to the Darwinian emphasis on randomness and the lack of purpose in nature.

Boyd defends open theism by contrasting it with what he calls the blueprint worldview, though this is more of a caricature than a description of classical theism. By assigning God's will as the ultimate cause of all events, classical theism, Boyd argues, leads to passivity, pessimism, and moral sloth. If everything that happens is meant to happen, then why should we try to alter the course of history? Why should we try to improve the world? Why shouldn't we just accept everything as it is? Boyd misunderstands how classical theism, precisely by placing absolute trust in God's control of history, empowers believers to enter into history as agents of the divine plan.[16] He also misunderstands how God can be in charge of the world and still grant people the freedom to make decisions about whether they want to work with God or against God. Nevertheless, his aim is a good one. Boyd wants Christians to realize that they are involved in a cosmic battle that forces them to draw lines and take sides.

Boyd is concerned not only about Christian activism in the world. He is also worried about theodicy, or the explanation of how a loving and all-powerful God can let bad things happen to good people. For Boyd, the answer to this ancient conundrum is simple. God does not

15. Gregory A. Boyd, *God at War: The Bible and Spiritual Conflict* (Downers Grove, IL: InterVarsity, 1997) and *Satan and the Problem of Evil: Constructing a Trinitarian Warfare Theodicy* (Downers Grove, IL: InterVarsity, 2001).

16. For my defense and reformulation of the classical position on providence, see Stephen H. Webb, *American Providence: Nation with a Mission* (New York: Continuum, 2004) ch. 5.

cause any bad things in the world, period. Satan does. This is biblical and logical, but it still does not solve the problem of theodicy. Instead, it merely pushes that problem back a step. If Satan causes all the evil in the world, then why does God let Satan have that kind of power? Boyd is caught in a dilemma. In order to explain the existence of evil, he turns to Satan. But if God does not stop Satan from causing evil, then God must be either unable or unwilling to do so. Boyd sometimes implies that God is unable, because God chooses not to be all-powerful and thus is vulnerable and limited in his engagement with the world. Other times Boyd argues that God is unwilling, but that replaces one mystery (why doesn't God do something about the evil in the world) with another (why doesn't God do something about Satan).

The fundamental problem with Boyd's position is the problem with every theology that emphasizes a cosmic battle between God and Satan. If Satan really has such tremendous power in the world, then how can God truly be God? Theologies that grant Satan too much power are called dualistic, because they divide the world into two sources of absolute power, contrary to monotheism's recognition of one absolute source. Boyd tries to avoid dualism by acknowledging that God will triumph in the end. Of that, we have an absolute assurance. Yet that assurance comes in the form of hope, not certain knowledge, so Boyd still leaves the Christian living in a world dualistically divided between two powers that appear, given the inordinate amount of evil in the world, roughly equal in power. Boyd is committed to what we can call a qualified dualism, but it is still a version of dualism. Is that such a bad thing?

Dualism has a long history in Christianity, and it has long been associated with heresy, not orthodoxy. Some Christians in the ancient world believed that Satan was so powerful he must be another God. These Christians were called Gnostics (and I should note that not all Gnostics were Christians). Gnostics and other dualist groups divided the universe into a good realm and an evil realm. The good realm is purely spiritual. The evil realm is purely material. The true God is in charge only of the good realm. Satan, or the evil God, is completely in charge of the material world. The true God has no authority in the material world. He can only send secret signals to the faithful and wait

The Dome of Eden

for them to shed their bodies, at death, and thus begin the journey back to heaven.

Many beliefs follow from these premises that contradict the Bible, common sense, and reason. Jesus, according to Gnostics, did not really have a body. Otherwise, he would have been subjected to the power of Satan. He only appeared to be clothed in matter. This is called a docetic Christology, from the Greek word for "appearance." Likewise, we human beings are only apparently embodied creatures, because our true identity is attached solely to our souls. Our bodies are an illusion of Satan's wicked imagination. Death, therefore, is liberation from this world, because at that point we shed the bodies that trap us in matter and our souls are free to being their ascent to heaven. God could not have created this world, since it is a material world. Satan thus must be a creator as well as destroyer. Some Gnostics went so far as to identify Satan with the God of Israel, the God who is depicted in the Hebrew Bible or Old Testament. After all, Genesis says that God created the world. Genesis, then, must be talking about the Satanic God, not the true God. The Jews, therefore, must worship the devil, and Christians should not be reading the Old Testament.

Little of this makes much sense on any level, though that has not stopped the Gnostics from becoming the darling of religious studies professors throughout higher education. The Gnostics propagated abstract metaphysics, denigrated the body, celebrated a cult of death, and despised the Jews. Nonetheless, because they battled orthodox Christians and were in turn persecuted by some Christians once Christianity became the established religion of Roman Empire, the Gnostics are romanticized as anti-conformist rebels by academics with an anti-Christian bias. Their disappearance in Western history was a Christian achievement that should be celebrated, not lamented. Their reappearance in countless books and articles should be a cause of concern.

The Gnostics were theological rebels, but they were also sincere in their attempts to come to terms with the pervasive presence of evil in the world. Their name is used today to label any theologian who gives Satan too much prominence, which is unfortunate. Boyd, for example, is hardly a modern Gnostic. The Gnostics associated the division of good and evil with, respectively, the spiritual and the material.

The Dome of Domes Divides the World

Boyd wants Christians to be more involved in this world through social justice programs, so he hardly follows the Gnostics by denigrating the material world. Too many theologians are too quick to use the Gnostic label to warn against any reflection on the role of Satan in the world. The Gnostics were vanquished by orthodox Christians because they denied that God created the world. This denial led them to dismiss the Old Testament and to insult the gifts of creation. They were not vanquished because they thought Satan was a real presence in the world. Nonetheless, they took much of Christianity's emphasis on Satan with them when they sank into oblivion. That is something Christians to this day should regret.

Fortunately, biblical scholars are beginning to recover the quasi-dualistic cosmology of the Bible. Jon Levenson, Professor of Jewish Studies at Harvard Divinity School, argues that the Bible portrays God's omnipotence not as a static attribute but as a dramatic enactment of the divine will. God works against evil, which means that there are obstacles to God's plan. Levenson chastises those theologians who jump too quickly from the doctrine of creation to a blanket affirmation of everything that happens. The world is good, but not everything that happens in the world is good. Levenson concedes the theological tradition that God creates the world out of nothing, but he insists that chaos ensues immediately afterward—chaos survives God's creative power to wage war against God's commands. One of the great themes of the Hebrew Scriptures is divine combat, whether it is with the Leviathan in Job or with David's many enemies in the Psalms. Levenson notes that this combat is present almost from the very beginning in the primordial waters, which are confined in two places, above the sky and in the earth's seas. Far from being forgotten in the biblical witness, these primordial waters are an enduring source of conflict with God. "In Genesis 1, the waters have been not only neutralized but demythologized and even depersonalized. They have not, however, been eliminated."[17] Nowhere is the danger of the sea as representative of the violence of nature gone awry more dramatically depicted than in God's speech in Job 38:8–11:

> Or who shut in the sea with doors when it burst out from the womb?—when I made the clouds its garment, and thick dark-

---

17. Jon D. Levenson, *Creation and the Persistence of Evil: The Jewish Drama of Divine Omnipotence* (Princeton: Princeton University Press, 1988) 122.

ness its swaddling band, and prescribed bounds for it, and set bars and doors, and said, "Thus far shall you come, and no farther, and here shall your proud waves be stopped?"

The sea, as I argued in chapter 4, is the focus of much biblical reflection on the way nature taunts and derides God's design. But who stands behind these proud waves? Who wants the sea to burst forth?

The twentieth century was the most evil on record, but it was also a time when theologians were extremely modest and reticent in naming evil. That has changed in recent years. In one of the most impressive contemporary reflections on evil, David Bentley Hart borrows the passage from Job quoted above for the title of his book, *The Doors of the Sea: Where was God in the Tsunami?* The immediate context of Hart's reflections on evil is the 2004 tsunami that devastated so many coastlines in the Indian Ocean. "Far below the water's surface, however, at and beneath the ocean floor, lies a source of elemental violence so vast, unpredictable, perennial, and destructive that one might almost be tempted to think that it is itself a particularly indomitable and infernal sort of god." Hart is referring, of course, to the geodynamic fissure that permitted two tectonic plates to grate against each other. After surveying the inane things that journalists, pastors, and even professional theologians said to try to console the victims and encourage those in despair, Hart recommends silence in the face of such abysmal dangers from the deep. "Words we would not utter to ease another's grief we ought not to speak to satisfy our own sense of piety."[18] Suffering is sometimes pointless, he suggests. We should not try to console victims with spurious theories, just as we should not construct our theories from the platitudes we mouth in the face of evil. He admits that God can bring good out of anything, but God does not cause evil in order to demonstrate how much good he can bring about. Suffering can be the occasion of lessons learned and tests passed, but it can also, especially on this magnitude, be the source of a profound puzzlement that has no rational resolution.

Yet Hart's book belies his advice that the less said about evil the better. Recommending speculative restraint is not neutral spiritual advice; indeed, it is itself a common form of consolation for the ag-

18. David Bentley Hart, *The Doors of the Sea: Where was God in the Tsunami?* (Grand Rapids: Eerdmans, 2005) 2–3 and 99.

The Dome of Domes Divides the World

grieved. Moreover, Hart does not avoid the speculation that he finds so objectionable. How could he in a *book* on evil? His theorizing about the origin of natural evil is rhetorically chaste but metaphysically rooted nonetheless. Christianity, he argues, teaches that the entire cosmos is "drawn ever onward by the yearning of all things for the goodness of God." Love imbues physical as well as spiritual motion. At the same time, nature is predatory and parasitic. "Nature squanders us with such magnificent prodigality that it is hard not to think that something enduringly hideous and abysmal must abide in the depths of life." Hart concludes that Christian must embrace a "provisional dualism" that raises as many questions as it answers. The New Testament is clear that the whole world is subjugated to mutinous powers that resist God's providential governance (Col 1:16, 1 Cor 2:8, Eph 1:21, 3:10). Hart even asserts that "the solicitude shown by some Christians for total and direct divine sovereignty in all the eventualities of the fallen world is not shared by the New Testament canon." The cosmos is a scandal to faith. God's glory is hidden in nature's cruelty. Yet Hart draws back from the implications of dualism, no matter how provisional. "Evil is born in the will: it consists not in some other separate thing standing alongside the things of creation, but is only a shadow, a turning of the hearts and minds of rational creatures away from the light of God back toward the nothingness from which all things are called."[19] The use of shadow as a metaphor for evil is telling, because shadows are cast by something blocking the sun, which can bring protection and relief. Shadows are dark, but nature is more menacing than that. Nature is permeated by an active, vigorous, and cunning streak of evil that the metaphor of a shadow cannot illuminate. Satan does more than block the sun.

Hart wants a metaphysical dualism without any moral consequences. That is, he acknowledges the New Testament's portrait of a cosmic dualism but denies that it plays any constructive role in Christian thought. The reason he does this is that he is as anxious to reject the category of theodicy as Boyd is to develop one. "Hence evil can have no proper role to play in God's determination of himself or purpose for his creatures, even if by economy God can bring good from evil; it can in no way supply any imagined deficiency in God's or cre-

---

19. Ibid., 48, 50, 6, and 73.

ation's goodness; it has no 'contribution' to make."[20] Anyone who takes evil seriously must agree with these statements, yet there is something missing in Hart's rush to render evil powerless. It is certainly wrong, as Hart makes clear, to use the cross of Jesus as a means of justifying or rationalizing evil. God works through evil, but evil is not the work of God. God does not seek out evil in order to demonstrate how compassionate he is, yet God is always there, in the midst of evil, to share in the world's sorrows. In opposition to Boyd's talk of spiritual warfare, Hart emphasizes God's *apatheia*. This term does not mean that God is uncaring in his unchangeableness, but that his caring is itself unchangeable, and his caring comes out of an infinite sense of fullness and completion, so that God does not need anything outside of himself to fulfill his being. Hart thinks that God is so perfectly self-sufficient that it is impossible to imagine God being threatened by anything or anyone. We are threatened by the sea, but God is not, having long ago shut the door on all that is evil.

Hart's commitment to a privation theory of evil makes it all the more surprising when he admits, near the end of his book, that there is "a slight sympathy for Gnosticism running through" it. The Gnostics, he correctly declares, shared the "same imaginative and spiritual universe as the earliest Christians." They understood that salvation is, at root, an escape from evil, even if they did define evil as coterminous with the material world. Hart is quick to note that the Gnostics are too callous, incoherent, and boring to be of much theological use today. They took Christian angelology and demonology to fantastic and absurd extremes. Nonetheless, they looked hard enough at the world—harder than we moderns are able to stare—and knew that when they saw death, they did "not see the face of God but the face of his enemy."[21] Hart does not say "our enemy," perhaps because he thinks, as he has written elsewhere, that martyrdom is the only Christian morality.[22] But he does say about

20. Ibid., 74.

21. Ibid., 94, 95, and 104.

22. David Bentley Hart, *The Beauty of the Infinite: The Aesthetics of Christian Truth* (Grand Rapids: Eerdmans, 2003) pt. 3, ch. 4. Hart's position on violence and ontology is shaped by John Milbank, and I have found Elizabeth Agnew Cochran's critique of Milbank to be very persuasive. See her essay, "'At the Same Time Blessed and Lame': Ontology, Christology and Violence in Augustine and John Milbank," *Journal for Christian Theological Research* 11 (2006) 51–72.

evil, "whether calculating malevolence or imbecile chance," that "we are permitted to hate these things with a perfect hatred."[23]

In the end, Hart has presented an eloquent theodicy in spite of himself, indeed, the only theodicy that the Bible gives for the problem of evil. No matter how much we think humanity is responsible for its own fallen situation, humans can hardly be blamed for the cruelty of nature—and the cruelty of nature can hardly be blamed on God. Satan is the only theodicy, even when humans share the blame. God permits Satan to choose evil, but God does not cause him to do evil. This is logical and biblical, but one hears little of Satan these days. The reason why so many Christians would find these claims shocking is that they do not have a grasp of precisely what it is Satan does. The idea that Satan tempts us has been sanitized to the point where we think that temptations are good and that we should treat ourselves to moral holidays when life gets stressful. More importantly, the idea that nature is fallen has been shattered by Darwin. Genesis teaches that nature is under a divine curse. Darwin teaches that randomness and violence are the means by which nature brings forth new life. The only way to retrieve a strong doctrine of providence after Darwin is to reconstruct dualism from the ground up.

A Darwinism informed by Genesis might conclude that Satan is more active in biology than human psychology. After all, nature at its simplest is also nature at its most dangerous. The virus is a parasite that can enter a cell uninvited and instruct the genes of the cell to make the ingredients that will make more viruses. In fact, there is a swing away from sentimental forms of Darwinism to a more realistic view of nature. In a book on the relationships among genetics, psychology, and culture, Howard Bloom has argued that the God who created the world cannot possibly be the good God of Judaism, Islam, and Christianity. "Evil," he writes, "is woven into our most basic biological fabric." Perhaps it takes a secularist these days to be so honest about the evil of evolution. "Lucifer, in fact, is Mother Nature's alter ego."[24] Of course, he takes Lucifer or Satan metaphorically, but there is no reason why Christians

---

23. *Doors of the Sea*, 100.

24. Howard Bloom, *The Lucifer Principle: A Scientific Expedition into the Forces of History* (New York: Atlantic Monthly Press, 1995) 3 and 4.

should not take Satan literally and follow Bloom's lead in identifying evil with what takes place on the level of evolutionary biology.

While biology is riddled with moral terminology, it still takes a poet to fathom the depths of natural evil. One of the best is Annie Dillard, who has described the world of insects as "the devil's *summa theologica*." Dillard is the singer of nature's sordid sublime, so she naturally goes much further than most scientists in plumbing the depths of nature's cruelty. "The creator," she writes, "is no puritan." Half the world is running from the other half, and parasitism is the rent all creatures must pay for the privilege of a little piece of existence. "Wouldn't you pay it, don't you, a little blood from the throat and wrists for the taste of the air?" Nature is fecund, but only because life is driven by a terrible hunger that we too share, which makes us less than objective witnesses of nature's profligate displays of squandered energy. "Certainly nature seems to exult in abounding radicality, extremism, anarchy. If we were to judge nature by its common sense or likelihood, we wouldn't believe the world existed." It takes a poet like Dillard, who is grounded in the Christian tradition and thus agitated by the gratuitous forms that grace appears to assume in animal life, to engage nature on this level of interrogation. This is the case because good writers must love their subject matter, but to love nature is to risk losing your own subjectivity. "Evolution loves death more than it loves you or me." Even God, for Dillard, is implicated in the devilish plot of evolution's haphazard ways. "Look, in short, at practically anything—the coot's feet, the mantis's face, a banana, the human ear—and see that not only did the creator create everything, but that he is apt to create *anything*. He'll stop at nothing."[25] If evolution is another name for God, then terror and grace are indistinguishable.

Although few scientists are as eloquent as Dillard, many echo her plaintive cry. Take, for example, Nick Lane's book, *Power, Sex, Suicide: Mitochondria and the Meaning of Life*, which was short-listed for a prestigious science writing award. The title is not merely an attempt to grab the reader's attention. As a strict Darwinian, Lane accepts the dogma

---

25. Annie Dillard, *Pilgrim at Tinker Creek* (New York: Harper & Row, 1974) 229, 233, 234, 144, 176, and 135. For my discussion of Dillard, see Stephen H. Webb, "Nature's Spendthrift Economy: The Extravagance of God in Pilgrim at Tinker Creek," *Soundings* 77 (1994) 429-51. Also see B. Jill Carroll, *The Savage Side: Reclaiming Violent Models of God* (New York: Rowman & Littlefield, 2001).

that biological organisms evolve randomly and thus show no signs of purposive or goal-driven behavior. Yet he also argues that mitochondria are the source of power in life, the reason why we have sex, and evidence of how nature favors suicide for the common good. The study of mitochondria "gives striking insights into why we are here at all, whether we are alone in the universe, why we have our sense of individuality, why we should make love, where we trace our ancestral roots, why we must age and die—in short, into the meaning of life."[26] All of these big questions can be answered by entities that are so small that a billion could fit in a grain of sand. Hundreds, maybe even thousands, live in a single cell, where they keep busy moving about, dividing into two, and merging together in complex networks.

Amazingly, Lane rests all of the questions of life on biological microstructures that are one of the greatest unsolved mysteries of Darwinism. In fact, mitochondria are the most crucial missing link in the study of evolution. Lane explains that the void between bacterial cells and the kind of cells (called eukaryotic) that contain mitochondria "is greater than any other in biology." Bacteria dominated the world, according to Darwinians, for two billion years, yet they never evolved into multicellular organisms. Lane acknowledges that "bacteria will never ascend the smooth ramp to sentience or anywhere much beyond slime, here or anywhere else in the universe." The forms of life that have filled the world all stem directly from eukaryotic cells, but their origin continues to baffle biologists. The leading theory seems to be that these cells are what one scientist has called "hopeful monsters." A hopeful monster is just what it sounds like. Rather than an accumulation of incremental genetic changes, it is a macro-mutation, the "kind of thing an archetypal mad scientist might produce in the laboratory after a lifetime of dedicated and deranged failure."[27] This is putting it hopefully, of course; not even a million mad scientists working for millions of years could have pulled off the transition from bacterial to eukaryotic cells. It follows that nature is madder than even the maddest among us.

Mitochondria are involved in other puzzles as well. They produce energy by pumping protons across a membrane that is, Lane confesses,

---

26. Nick Lane, *Power, Sex, Suicide: Mitochondria and the Meaning of Life* (New York: Oxford University Press, 2005) 8–9.

27. Ibid., 27, 29, and 30.

"a bizarre way of going about things." They also help solve the mystery of sex. Sex is a mystery to Darwinians because, as Lane puts it, "the father figure is not only redundant but a waste of space and resources." Clonal or parthenogenic reproduction would be much more efficient than mating that requires two parents. In other words, why did natural selection favor sexual reproduction, which involves the costly search for a mate and the division of species into separate sexes, over organisms simply dividing into two? Lane gives a complicated answer to this question that relies on the phrase "dual genomic control," which comes down to the idea that two are better than one. Mitochondria also, to put it bluntly, commit suicide, by controlling the process called apoptasis that tells cells when to die. When cells refuse to commit suicide, cancer is the result. "In cancer, individual cells bid for freedom, casting off the shackles of responsibility to the organism as a whole." This suggests that the basis of life is a pact made among cells to accept an early death as the price of living in large communities, but as political philosophers who study Thomas Hobbes and other social contract theorists know, explaining why individuals would trade freedom for authoritarian governments is not easy. Mitochondria also "show us why our days in this firmament are numbered."[28] As they burn oxygen, tiny molecules called free radicals escape to cause damage to the cell. This process is continuous and builds up over a lifetime. That, evidently, solves the mystery of death.

Lane's book is not only an example of how Darwinism constantly runs up against theoretical and practical difficulties in formulating the origins of life. It is also an indication of how Darwinians cannot depict even the most basic molecular structures without using a moral idiom. Nature is like us, perhaps because we are so much like it. While it is still standard procedure among many scientists to use the most basic organisms as a model for understanding the behavior of the most complex organisms, it is becoming increasingly popular to read human behavior into the actions of simpler organisms. Actually, Darwinians can go up or down the evolutionary ladder because they deny the existence of a ladder altogether: all organisms manifest the same basic behavioral structures, which means that it is just as legitimate to analyze the behavior of insects on the basis of what we know about people as it is to

---

28. Ibid., 7, 6, 5, and 321.

apply what we learn about bacteria to understanding human nature. Deception, for example, is built into every level of nature, which is precisely the argument of Loyal Rue's book, *By the Grace of Guile: The Role of Deception in Natural History and Human Affairs*. For Rue, evolution is the process by which effective deceivers are rewarded with access to increasingly complex biological niches. The living world is "not unlike a spiral of espionage—deceivers apply selective pressure for better detectives, who in turn pressure for better deceivers, and so on." Rue is as attracted to insects to expound his position as Dillard. He is fascinated, for example, by an African bug that preys upon ants by pretending to be an ant. "The bug first captures a few itinerant ants and glues their corpses to its back, whereupon it strolls undetected into the ant colony for a feast."[29] Evolution paves a smooth path from ants to the Trojan horse, but if we are all such masters of deception, how do we know that we are being deceived, even when we think we are not?

Rue's position might seem cynical, but how could a Darwinian deny it? They might *want* to deny it, because the idea that nature selects for effective deception is hardly something high schools want to be teaching teenagers. Indeed, there would be nothing stopping them from denying it, because, if they are consistent Darwinians, they will not believe that honesty is always the best policy. One could even say that the denial of deception is, following Plato, the noble lie—or perhaps the ignoble lie—of biology. Some scholars interpret Plato as arguing that all political institutions must tell "noble lies" in order to maintain social stability. If Rue is right, then Darwinism is based on a noble lie about the role of deception in evolution. If Darwinians were to be honest about their belief in the foundational role of deception in motivating all biological behavior, then their theory would be even less popular than it already is. For their own survival, they must assure the public that evolution favors honesty, even as they know better. As experts in the strategies of adaptation, they will be able to make these assurances without getting caught by the unsuspecting. It is possible that evolution has selected humans who believe in honesty, because that belief helps maintain social stability, but those who understand evolution will also understand that the belief in honesty is nature's own noble lie. In fact,

---

29. Loyal Rue, *By the Grace of Guile: The Role of Deception in Natural History and Human Affairs* (New York: Oxford University Press, 1994) 83 and 133.

The Dome of Eden

no group other than politicians would be in a better position to understand the tragic necessity of the noble lie than biologists!

Some scientists recognize the evil of evolution, but then suggest that this is why Christians should celebrate evolution! Francisco Ayala is a professor of biology at the University of California, Irvine. *The New York Times* has called him the "renaissance man of evolutionary biology." He celebrates evolution because it has solved the problem of theodicy. "As floods and drought were a necessary consequence of the fabric of the physical world, predators and parasites, dysfunction and diseases were a consequence of the evolution of life. They were *not* a result of deficient or malevolent design: the features of organisms were not *designed* by the Creator."[30] Evolution, then, is theology's disguised friend. Before Darwin, God was credited with designing everything, which resulted in blaming God for predators and parasites. After Darwin, God is credited with designing nothing, which let's God off the hook of being responsible for a lot of dangerous animals and deadly microorganisms. This logic is, of courser, perverse, because it throws God out along with the dirty bathwater of theodicy. Crediting God with nothing is no way to solve the problem of blaming God for disease and death. The real solution to the problem of theodicy is found in what appears to be an unintentional slip in Ayala's comment. He argues that God does not create evil, which is good theology, but he also states that the evil aspects of nature "were *not* a result of deficient or malevolent design" (his italics). Why not? Ayala gives an argument why he thinks God did not create predators, but he gives no argument why he thinks Satan was not involved.

At this point, the weary student of biology, suspicious of scientists' ability to discern good from evil and truth from lies, might just want to take a look at how theology explains the fall of nature. As much as biology is inevitably reduced to theology in the last analysis, theologians cannot try to understand natural evil without Darwin. Evolution, after all, is both creative and destructive—even more complex than that, it is creative through its destructiveness, and its destructiveness is the source of its greatest creativity—which means that distinguishing God's labor from Satan's in nature will never be a simple affair. Making this

---

30. Francisco J. Ayala, *Darwin's Gift to Science and Religion* (Washington, DC: Joseph Henry, 2007) 5.

distinction, though, is as necessary as it is difficult. Annie Dillard demonstrates what happens when this distinction is not made. She is a great writer, but she attributes everything that happens in nature to God and thus ends up portraying God as a demonic figure. Her prose sustains a tension between what Christians expect of God and what naturalists find in nature, and that tension is the source of some great writing, but it is not good theology.

The failure to make this distinction also underscores the primary weakness of the intelligent design movement. Intelligent design theorists find themselves backed into a corner by the Christian idea of a cosmic fall. If nature is not what God intended it to be, then not everything in nature is evidence of God's handiwork. All animals, for example, are well designed, but not all animals are designed to do what God intended. God made the world and it is good, but its goodness has been perverted by sin. From an evolutionary perspective, we can admire the independence and fierceness of predators and carnivores, but from the perspective of belief in a good and merciful God, these animals are problematic at best. If intelligent design theorists attribute the design of violent animals to God, then they take the risk of blasphemy, because they are suggesting that God is the creator of evil.

Christianity holds together two beliefs that are so intimately related that they are hard to distinguish. First, all that exists is good, because God created everything, and God is good. Second, all that exists is riddled with sin and distortion, because the world is not now what God intended nor is it what it will be when God redeems it. Something else intervenes to turn things away from the divine plan. Theologians traditionally have argued that God permits evil, rather than causing it. This subtle distinction can seem to be overly speculative, but it is utterly foundational for Christian faith. Whatever the mystery of God's decision to permit evil, God does not create evil. God can bring good out of evil, but God does not do evil in order to bring out the good. This means, among other things, that evil does not have the same ontological status in the world as the good. Evil is real enough, but it is parasitical on the good. It is derivative and secondary to the world that God made.

That all things are both good and not good means that it takes wisdom to discern the different roles that God and Satan play in the world. Satan, in the words of a Bob Dylan song, comes as "A Man of

Peace."³¹ Satan is a deceiver, and he is a master of camouflage. Rather than tempting us with evil, which would be a frontal assault on the basically good tendencies of our created nature, he makes evil look like it is good. Satan's strategy makes it all the harder for us to discern God's presence in the world, because he tempts us to rationalize the evil we do with explanations about how it is really for the good. Satan works through the good to bring out evil, while God works through evil to bring out the good. Notice how these two strategies are not symmetrical. Satan tries to get us to confuse good and evil, but God keeps them absolutely separate, even when he remains present in the darkest hours in order to redeem the worst of times. Just as God works through our bad decisions to make the best of what we have corrupted, God works through nature's violence to bring good to humans and animals alike. But our bad decisions remain bad, just as evolution remains in need of redemption. Evolution can look good to us because God has worked through it to bring forth life, but God's redemptive activity should not lead us to mistake evil for the good. God is a revealer, not a disguiser. Just as we have to exercise wisdom to see through the way Satan uses the good for evil purposes, we have to be careful to distinguish the good God does from the evil that God refuses to leave unredeemed.

Design is one word for how God works through evolution, but not all designs are equal, and not all are equally good. Is there a principle that intelligent design theorists can use to exercise wisdom in discerning when and how to attribute design to God? This is a crucial test for the intelligent design movement, and its solution is not easy. It is not enough, for example, simply to say that God made good animals whose designs were subsequently distorted by Satan. Sharks and lions are well designed killers, but it is very hard to distinguish between those aspects of their design that are admirable and those aspects that are pitiable. It is not enough, then, to talk about good designs and bad designs. Everything in nature is designed, and all designs are good, in that every design points to the order that keeps anarchy and chaos at bay. It is not the idea of design that is at stake here but the use to which various designs are put. Something can be well designed but used for evil purposes. What complicates even this insight is that all biological

---

31. For analysis of this song, see Stephen H. Webb, *Dylan Redeemed: From Highway 61 to Saved* (New York: Continuum, 2006) 87-88.

organisms seem to be designed to struggle against each other in violent, competitive, and deceptive ways. That is evidence, though, not of design but of the work of Satan. The reason the good and bad in nature are so nearly indistinguishable is that the dome, after the fall, was lifted from the Garden of Eden, which placed the good creation of God and its Satanic parody in direct contact with each other, and it takes very little evil to bring down the good. The result, according to the Bible, was a monstrous and volatile corruption of nature that led God to resolve to send a cleansing flood in order to have a new start altogether.

If nature is a mixture of creativity and destruction, purpose and randomness, design and chance, sacrifice and killing, how can we make moral judgments about nature in any particular way? This question is crucial for any theological reflection on evolution, but it is also one of the most pressing cultural problems America faces today. This question is absolutely not an obscure issue in the theology of science. It is fundamental to a Christian theology of competition and any moral position on the role of force in the world. The study of economics, for example, has become increasingly Darwinized in recent years, and for good reason. Capitalism is a thoroughly Darwinian enterprise, which is why it needs religion to counterbalance and check its destructive tendencies.[32] Market competition freed from the virtues of honesty and compassion and unrestrained by a commitment to the common good might create wealth, but it will not create a good society. Capitalism works in America because it is so intimately joined with a Christian morality. Drawing the line between balanced and extreme forms of capitalism, in fact, is not unlike the problem of discerning the different moral forces at work in evolution. This should not be surprising because, as many scholars have pointed out, Darwin was greatly influenced by economic theorists like Adam Smith who portrayed the economy as an environment that selects competitive and specialized firms, forcing them to maximize profit in order to survive.

There is little use in bemoaning evolutionary theory for emphasizing the struggle of life, just as there is little use in fantasizing about the possibility that economies can grow without being competitive. Some

---

32. For an excellent discussion of the role of "extinction" in capitalism, see Tyler Cowen, *Creative Destruction: How Globalization is Changing the World's Cultures* (Princeton: Princeton University Press, 2002).

companies, like some species, simply will not survive the struggle for scarce resources, and that is not all bad. Organisms like corporations succeed by overcoming obstacles and taking advantage of the weaknesses of their competitors. Competition can be inevitable, as in international relations, joyful, as in sports, productive, as in the business world, and even miraculous, as in biology. It can also become violent in all of those arenas. Violence, however, is not always wrong, as when it is used in self-defense or in the protection of the weak. Evolution thoroughly enmeshes competition in violence, and that is evidence of the handiwork of Satan, not God, but that does not mean that all competition is wrong. Making moral judgments about nature is no different than making moral judgments about war, football, or corporate takeovers. Ethicists and theologians disagree about what constitutes a just war and whether football is too violent and how capitalism should be regulated. Judging nature will not produce a moral consensus any more than judgments about these issues, but making judgments about natural evil is still a necessary theological task.

Competition is bred into our bones, but that does not mean that we should celebrate the way evolution masses a nearly endless pile of gnawed and bloody bones in the dark recesses of deep biological time. While environmentalists writing in the tradition of literary romanticism portray nature as a peaceful refuge, Darwinism teaches us that nature is just another name for death. The fact that so many people today take evolution for granted as simply "the way it is" has led to all kinds of groundless claims about the violence inherent in human nature. If evolution is the bedrock of reality, then it must be the source of our moral norms as well as our physical origins, but what does it really promote other than a sanguine attitude toward how awful the world can be? Competition in the natural world is not always violent, but it often is. If nature cannot tell us where to draw the line between the legitimate use of force in various forms of competition and destructive acts of violence, how can we teach our children how to be ambitious and grateful, assertive and attentive, aggressive and compassionate? Some philosophers try to salvage an ethic of cooperation from evolution, but the scurry of species climbing over one another to be king of the hill hardly justifies anything remotely close to the Christian teaching on love and compassion. We humans have won the game of evolution by becoming the one species that understands how we got here, but it is a spurious victory. We compete for knowledge only to find that there is no meaning to what we find, because we owe our existence, Darwinians would have us believe, to dumb luck. Those who want to continue drawing from the endowment of Christian values, while seeing at the same time how far they can take biological theory in explaining everything about ourselves, are racing against all that is best in human nature, blindly hoping that lady luck blinks before we crash.

seven

Could Jesus Have Been an Octopus?
(Duns Scotus Replies to Darwin)

If the human body is an accident of biological history, then the Christian belief that the Son of God came down from heaven, for our salvation, and was born of the Virgin Mary, and made man, as the Nicene Creed states, is an accident of salvation history. Is that a theological problem?

Imagine the following counterfactual scenario (that is, we know this did not happen, but there is nothing in the laws of nature, as postulated by Darwinism, that suggests it could not have happened). Millions of years ago, the oceans became the seedbed for the development of the Earth's most complex organisms. Earthquakes, drought, and gargantuan predators devastate the earth's land surfaces, while marine life evolves in ways that we can hardly imagine today. Octopuses, which are the most intelligent invertebrates in our world, emerge in this counterworld as the kings of the sea, with their eight powerful arms evolving capabilities unmatched by any other creature. Their short lifespan, a limit to their learning ability in our world, lengthens in this alternative world, enabling them to develop their intelligence to unprecedented heights. They create a closed society protected by underwater fortresses. They learn to write with their ink sacks on seaweed and rocks, recording the history of their daring exploits. Their suction discs and jet propulsion movement enables them to conquer all of their sea enemies (they continue to be threatened by dangers from the land), but their struggles turn them into monsters in their own eyes and leave them with very few friends. At some point, God decides to grant souls to two octopuses and calls them into a morally demanding covenant. Their descendants have a long history of not living up to this covenant by their poor treatment of the other sea creatures, and they continue to fear the land creatures

Could Jesus Have Been an Octopus?

that they cannot see. When God decides to save them from their evil deeds and their self-loathing, he sends his son to become one of them. The Son of God becomes an octopus, dies on a hook, and ascends to the surface in order to show the entire underwater world the way out of the deep darkness of the sea and their dread of the creatures of the air.

The octopus scenario, as we can call it, might seem blasphemous to some readers, but that is not my intention. My intention is to persuade you that the octopus scenario is ridiculous, not blasphemous, but it should seem ridiculous only if Darwinism is wrong. If Darwinism is right, then the octopus scenario should sound perfectly reasonable. That, at least, is the conclusion to be drawn from the work of Stephen Jay Gould, the best-known evolutionary writer of the twentieth century. Gould famously compared evolution to a video tape that can be rewound to any point. If you rerun the tape, Gould said, you will get a different story every time. "Any replay of the tape would lead evolution down a pathway radically different from the road actually taken."[1] Evolution proceeds through pathways that are so random that life could never have evolved in the same way twice. It follows that, even though humanity has proven itself superior (so far!) to all other species in adapting to the various conditions of Earth, it just as easily could have been some other species (as well as no species at all). Our lineage of pre-historic ancestors was lucky. We look at octopuses in aquariums; they don't look at us in airtight underwater cages. If we want to eat them, we can. If they want to harm us, we can figure out ways to prevent that. That seems like the natural state of affairs, but there is nothing inevitable about what we are. With a different roll of the dice, the octopus scenario could have just as easily put them on top and buried us in an evolutionary dead-end.

Many people will respond to the octopus scenario with, "So what?" The octopus scenario might violate a widespread intuition into the naturalness of our place in the world around us, but that intuition can easily be explained as itself the product of evolution. That is, we have evolved into the kind of species that is so arrogant that we are bothered by the thought that we are purely accidental. Our adaptive ability to kill all other species leaves us resisting the idea that another species

---

1. Stephen Jay Gould, *Wonderful Life: The Burgess Shale and the Nature of History* (New York: Norton, 1989) 51.

could have just as easily ended up in our place. Perhaps that intuition was even the reason for our successful evolution. In that case, we think we are inevitable because such thoughts enabled us to evolve into the species that we are. At some point in our distant past, a genetic mutation allowed some members of a population that would one day evolve into us to think of itself as superior, even unique, among all life, and that thought was the meme (the term some Darwinians use to describe cultural units that play a role in evolution) that set our ancestors apart. A delusion, in other words, became a self-fulfilling prophecy.

If this is the case—that through an evolutionary fluke we came to think of ourselves as set apart from the animal world, and by acting on that thought we actually succeeded in mastering the animal world—then it follows that our knowledge of Darwinism might be the worst thing that has ever happened to us. Darwinism might turn out to be the theoretical Frankenstein that destroys us because it refutes our sense of our inevitable triumph and absolute uniqueness. In other words, the fluke that made us what we are can also, once discovered, work in reverse to unravel everything we have achieved. As more and more people come to believe in Darwinism, they will begin to see that people are not all that special, and the more the human species will become just another animal, neglecting its role as master (and thus caretaker) of the earth. After all, if we are not different from the other animals, why should we act better than they do?

Let's call that rather apocalyptic scenario—that Darwinism comes to undermine the confidence that enabled scientists to come up with this theory in the first place, with disastrous results—*self-defeating Darwinism*. The self-defeating Darwinism scenario probably sounds as far-fetched as the octopus scenario, but what they have in common is the fact that Darwinians do not think that species are fixed by either nature or God. A species is merely a reproductively isolated population of organisms. Members of a given species population do not necessarily share all of their biological characteristics with all of the other members of their species. It might be going too far to say that the concept of species is a fiction in Darwinism, but it is not going too far to say that the Darwinian concept of species is loose to the point of being unstable. "It follows," writes the philosopher Stephen R. L. Clark, in a stinging analysis of the species debate, "that humanity, as the common essence of the

Could Jesus Have Been an Octopus?

present species, is of no biological significance: there is no common essence, and any species might as well be many."[2] At best, human nature names an ideal, but since Darwin deflated the Platonic pretension to know the essence of things, human nature is better described as a crass generalization based on an evolutionary trajectory that just happened to end with us. Even to speak of "us" is misleading, because there is no ultimate significance to any of the features we think of as our own. Given the premise of our open-ended material malleability, it is hard to reject the conclusion that our physical constitution can and should be rearranged to fit new circumstances

The lack of a proper species definition of humanity is one of the most troubling moral consequences of Darwinism. The twentieth century is one long demonstration that confusion over the meaning of humanity is one of the primary causes of violence and cruelty in the world. In a provocative but well-documented book with the forceful title, *From Darwin to Hitler*, Richard Weikart has demonstrated that Darwinism played a critical role in contributing to the apocalyptic ruin that culminated with World War II. Indeed, *The Origin of Species* had no greater social and cultural impact than in Germany, where it was received with enthusiasm by communists and fascists alike. Although Darwin cannot be blamed for Hitler, there is no sense in denying that Hitler was a dedicated student of Darwin. The only area of contention is what kind of student he was. Weikart argues that Hitler certainly did not flunk Darwin 101. In *The Descent of Man*, Darwin repeatedly suggests that savage tribes will vanish from the world due to their lack of competitive advantages. In Weikart's words, his theory "emphasized variation within species, which implied biological inequality." Darwin all but admitted that liberal notions of human equality cannot be grounded in nature; Hitler went further than Darwin by trying to build a pagan worldview on those biological inequalities. Hitler took Darwin to mean that the various human races evolved in isolation from each other and thus are pitted in a struggle for survival and supremacy. He proposed to bring

2. Stephen R. L. Clark, *Biology and Christian Ethics* (Cambridge: Cambridge University Press, 2000) 197. I have been much influenced by this book, which is the most sophisticated critique of Darwin that I've read. The philosopher David L. Hull concurs with Clark that biology does not support the idea that humans have a common nature. See Hull, *The Metaphysics of Evolution* (Albany, NY: SUNY Press, 1990) 1–12.

moral improvement to the German people by strictly following the laws of nature, as he understood them, rather than Christian compassion, which he scorned. As Weikart writes, "Hitler embraced an evolutionary ethic that made Darwinian fitness and health the only criterion for moral standards."[3] Hitler advocated what he called a rational racism based on the latest scientific trends, which is why he was able to gain so much support from the medical community for his euthanasia program. The Darwinian argument for inequality was especially important for Hitler's struggle against the leveling ideology of communism.

Speaking of communism, it too drew much inspiration from Darwinism. Lenin's war against the Tsar recruited Darwinian materialism for political purposes. Lenin wanted to transform human nature by changing the social conditions in which people lived. Lenin was a traditionalist when it came to art, but Stalin understood that an economic revolution required a cultural revolution too. Stalin thought artists were the engineers of the human soul (he used "soul" metaphorically, of course). Under Stalin, according to the historian Orlando Figes, Soviet artists "were convinced they could train the human mind to see the world in a more socialistic way through new art forms." As good Darwinians, the communists believe that "consciousness was shaped by the environment," so they used art to recondition the machinery of the brain. Trotsky provided the eloquence to Stalin's scary policies: "What is man? He is by no means a finished or harmonious being. No, he is still a highly awkward creature. Man, as an animal, has not evolved by plan but spontaneously, and has accumulated many contradictions. The question of how to educate and regulate, of how to improve and complete the physical and spiritual construction of man, is a colossal problem which can only be understood on the basis of socialism."[4] Few Darwinians share this faith in socialism today, but Darwinians still

---

3. Richard Weikart, *From Darwin to Hitler: Evolutionary Ethics, Eugenics, and Racism in Germany* (New York: Palgrave Macmillan, 2004) 17 and 210. For an eloquent review of this book, see Edward T. Oakes, "Darwin's Graveyard," *Books & Culture* (November/December, 2006) 35. Also see Geoffrey Cantor and Marc Swetlitz, eds., *Jewish Tradition and the Challenge of Darwinism* (Chicago: University of Chicago Press, 2006).

4. Orlando Figes, *Natasha's Dance: A Cultural History of Russia* (New York: Picador, 2002) 447, 448; Trotsky quotation is on 447.

think the contradictions of human nature can be ironed out by a more controlled or improved environment.

In chapter 2, I discussed William Jennings Bryan's fear that Darwinism supported unfettered capitalism, and today many people associate Darwinism with liberal progressivism (what Bryan was defending against Darwinism), probably because (thanks to the Scopes Trial) they think it undermines religious conservatism. As all of these examples show, Darwinian theory has been able to adapt to widely disparate political and cultural movements all at the same time. This remarkable adaptive capacity demonstrates to some how easy and dangerous it is to manipulate scientific theories, while to others it suggests how intimately connected Darwinism has been and probably always will be to the social issues of the day. Perhaps Darwinism's success will also be its downfall, because any theory that is so useful to the cultural elite will never be without controversy. In any case, the record of Darwinism's political utility, as if it were designed to fit too smugly into modern assumptions and prejudices, should raise some suspicions of its scientific credibility.

Fortunately, the Human Genome Project has now established the unity of the human race (what is often called the "Out of Africa" hypothesis), and racism finds very little ideological support in legitimate expressions of political or social power in the West as well as in many other parts of the world. Credit for that achievement, however, should be given to the book of Genesis as much as to genetic research. Drawing from Genesis, Christianity, Judaism, and Islam, all traditionally taught that every single member of the human race is a descendant of the biblical Adam. Theologians varied in their estimates of when the creation took place, with the Irish Archbishop James Ussher famously calculating the date as 4004 BCE, but they agreed that humans were united in their uniqueness. Humans were simply defined as Adam's descendants. The historian David Livingstone has shown how challenges to biblical chronology and geography began to break down that consensus.[5] Who were the peoples scattered across the Earth who seemed to have histories and myths more ancient than the Bible? One answer to this question began to emerge in the seventeenth century: they were pre-

---

5. David N. Livingstone, *Adam's Ancestors: Race, Religion and the Politics of Human Origins* (Baltimore: Johns Hopkins University Press, 2008).

Adamites. The Roman Catholic Church declared this idea heretical, but it became popular because it allowed devout Christians to reconcile the existence of pre-historic peoples with a literal reading of Genesis. The exact identity of the pre-Adamites was a subject of spirited debates. Some thought they were pre-historic peoples who left some literary and archeological evidence before becoming extinct. Others, putting a racist twist on the category, thought they were the origin of those races deemed inferior by Europeans. Orthodox theologians fiercely contested the idea that God created humans several times over, in various places and at various times. By defending orthodoxy, they were also defending monogenism (the single origin of the human race) over polygenism (multiple origins). The stakes were high, since typically polygenism, which was linked to skepticism about the Bible, was used to support slavery and racism while mongenism, which was linked to religious belief, was used to promote the abolition of slavery.

Darwin is thought by most people to have solved the problem of racism because he linked all people to a common ancestor and thus posited the biological unity of the human race. In reality, his theory of evolution only complicated the question of race. His defenders often point to the evidence from his behavior on this score, and it is true that Darwin was morally unimpeachable, although in his day one could have the highest moral standards and still be contaminated by racism. That his racism was subtle and discrete, however, does not settle the question of whether it was intrinsic or extrinsic to his theory.[6] The philosopher Anthony O'Hear has made the astute observation that Darwin spoke of "savages" in racist terms in order to "palliate the horror his contemporaries might have felt at learning they were descended from apes."[7] In other words, Darwin assured his readers that they need not

---

6. For the intrinsic argument, see the excellent article by Benjamin Wiker, "Darwin and the Descent of Morality," *First Things* (November 2001) 10–13.

7. Anthony O'Hear, *Beyond Evolution: Human Nature and the Limits of Evolutionary Explanation* (New York: Oxford University Press, 1997) 134. He is glossing this passage from *The Descent of Man*: "For my own part I would as soon be descended from that heroic little monkey who braved his dreaded enemy in order to save the life of his keeper, or from that old baboon, who descended from the mountains, carrying away in triumph his young comrade from a crowd of astonished dogs—as from a savage who delights to torture his enemies, offers up bloody sacrifices, practices infanticide without remorse, treats his wives like slaves, knows no decency, and is haunted by the grossest superstitions" (440).

worry about being descended from apes because it would have been even worse to be descended from the primitive peoples of the third world. In fact, contrary to popular misconception, there is nothing in the idea of common descent that necessarily implies racial equality. One might think that Darwin would have sided with monogenism over polygenism, but he actually sidestepped this dispute by rendering the distinction irrelevant. If humanity's common ancestor is located deep into long stretches of biological time, then the human family had plenty of opportunity to grow many branches. After Darwin, the problem about race was not the problem of the one and the many (whether there was one or many origins of humanity). The problem was whether there was even such a thing as a human race, given how Darwin treated the category of a species as inherently malleable. Humans evolved like every species, and depending on what biological changes took place after the races separated from each other, evolution could indeed create differences within the human community.

It is too early to tell, then, whether Darwinism will end up boding ill or well for the prospects of human unity and global peace and prosperity. If it is hard to determine when *Homo sapiens* branched off from various precursor hominids, and how these groups, along with the great apes, are all related to each other, and if it is hard to define human nature today, then isn't it possible that it will be even harder to define humanity in the future? In 2006 the evolutionary theorist Oliver Curry of the London School of Economics stirred up the media when he predicted that humans would evolve into two separate subspecies, one privileged and the other disadvantaged. Race will no longer be a problem, he speculated—a coffee-colored skin will be the norm across all populations—but genetic modification, cosmetic surgery and sexual selection will lead to a subspecies of tall, thin, and symmetrical humans who will refuse to mate with their shorter, stockier, asymmetrical and less intelligent biological relatives. Most scientists scoff at such speculations, even while books about the evolutionary significance of computers, gene-splicing techniques and nanotechnology become bestsellers. To stall these fearmongers, biologists patiently explain that genetic innovations usually take place in small and fixed populations. Expansion and mobility suggest that humans are done evolving, that is, unless or until some catastrophe happens to minimize our numbers and change the conditions in which we live. Yet even if natural selection is no longer a factor in human evolution, human selection (genetic engineering) just might take its place, in which case we might change the evolutionary rules that Darwin discovered. We are certainly already in the position, as the title of a new book proclaims, to enhance evolution.[8] The steps humans took from alcohol to caffeine to Prozac are surely longer than any step we need to take to make neural implants to keep us fit and happy. If a few cultural elite try to become superhumans in order to leave their inferiors behind, Darwinism might become self-defeating in short time. Having won the evolutionary lottery, we just might squander our fortune and destroy ourselves, as so many lottery winners do.

That at any rate is the worst possible outcome of the self-defeating Darwinism scenario, but its likelihood is plausible only if the idea of human rights loses its luster among the cultural elite. Could that happen? Human rights are based on the notion that humans are unique, which is another way of saying that humanity constitutes a unique species. The Western tradition of equality brings together Greek, Roman, Christian, and Jewish sources, but it is hard to exaggerate the importance of Genesis, which teaches that only humans are made in the image of God. Secular humanists, however, are loath to ground anything so important in biblical revelation. As a result, they have refashioned human rights from a theological to a purely political doctrine. Humanists today admit that rights are based on little more than social conventions, but they theorize these conventions as a product of a hypothetical universal agreement. The idea is that people, at some imaginary point in time prior to social and political order, came together to give up some of their desires and interests in order to assure their own safety and welfare. This "social contract" view of human rights is as mythological as the Garden of Eden. Indeed, it is meant to replace the Bible's account of God-given human dignity with a story about how we the people

---

8. John Harris, *Enhancing Evolution: The Ethical Case for Making People Better* (Princeton: Princeton University Press, 2007). For ethical analysis, see Francis Fukuyama, *Our Posthuman Future: Consequences of the Biotechnology Revolution* (New York: Picador, 2002) and also the important collection edited by Celia Deane-Drummond and Peter Manley Scott, *Future Perfect? God, Medicine and Human Identity* (New York: T. & T. Clark, 2006). For theological analysis, see Brent Waters, *From Human to Posthuman: Christian Theology and Technology in a Posthuman World* (Basingstoke: Ashgate, 2006).

Could Jesus Have Been an Octopus?

have given ourselves rights, so that we are in debt to nothing higher than humanity. Notice, however, that Darwinism is just as hard on an original social contract as it is on a primordial paradise. Notice too that the idea of humans giving themselves rights begs the question of what constitutes humanity. If we give ourselves rights, who is the we? From a Darwinian perspective, then, there is nothing natural about human rights. In fact, human rights are profoundly unnatural, because they presuppose the very human nature that they are postulated to protect. Christianity has its own tradition of grounding human rights in nature, called the natural law theory, but if Darwinians reject the argument that nature is grounded in the order and purposes of God, then all they have left is biology. And if humans are not biologically unique, or even biologically coherent as a species, then there is no good reason to believe in something called *human* rights.[9]

Perhaps we can leave the problem of what happens to human rights when there is no agreement about what humans are to secular humanists. The problems for theology are weighty enough. What the self-defeating Darwinism scenario is to secular humanism, I am suggesting, the octopus scenario is to Christianity. If some other species had evolved to the state where they fell into sin and God chose to redeem them by becoming one with them, would that make any difference in what Christianity teaches about the nature of God or the basic features of the world that God created? Notice that I am not trying to raise what

---

9. For the problem of extending human rights down the biological ladder (or across the biological spectrum) to include many or even all nonhuman animals, see Stephen H. Webb, *Good Eating* (Grand Rapids: Brazos, 2001) 53–58. If the idea of human rights does not become extinct in the distant future, then the coming controversy over what constitutes the human species might eclipse the debate over animal rights—or, more likely, debates about animal rights will precipitate a radical rethinking of human rights. For an example of how confused Darwinians can be on the question of human uniqueness, take this paragraph from a best selling book, Neil Shubin, *Your Inner Fish: A Journey into the 3.5 Billion-Year History of the Human Body* (New York: Pantheon, 2008): "Do the facts of our ancient history mean that humans are not special or unique among living creatures? Of course not. In fact, knowing something about the deep origins of humanity only adds to the remarkable fact or our existence: all of our extraordinary capabilities arose from basic components that evolved in ancient fish and other creatures. From common parts came a *very unique* construction. We are not separate from the rest of the living world; we are part of it does to our bones and, as we will see shortly, even our genes" (43, my italics). Besides implying that uniqueness admits to degrees (it doesn't), and confusing the state of uniqueness with the compliment of being special, Shubin is blithely unaware of the reductive qualities of his argument.

is called the mind-body problem, which includes questions about personal identity and the relative independence of our minds from our bodies. I am not wondering if we could still be us even if we were in a different physical form. I am asking instead what changes would occur to the biblical drama of revelation if God had implanted souls in octopuses instead of us. To make this question work, let's agree that God is free to do whatever God wants, and furthermore, that Christians are free to speculate about what might be the case in alternative worlds without denying the dignity and uniqueness of this world. The question the octopus scenario raises for Christians is the following: Is there anything about Christianity that commits believers to think that the human body is sacred? That question is not trivial because it masks a much deeper one: If our biological form is an accident of evolution, then what does that say about the body God assumed in Jesus of Nazareth?

Surprisingly enough, that question was actually posed—and taken seriously—in the Middle Ages. Medieval theologians (or philosophers; they drew no sharp distinction between the two disciplines) applied the best standards of logic of their day to the most specific theological topics, and one of those topics was the role of the human in the incarnation of the Son of God. Unfortunately, we do not ask many of these same questions today because medieval theologians got a bad reputation beginning with the Protestant Reformation, and they have never recovered. The schoolmen (or scholastics), as they are called due to the various sects they formed, are frequently stereotyped as obstinate debaters obsessed with abstract jargon and spurious technicalities. This accusation arose when the Protestant reformers and their allies grew tired of metaphysical debates and sought instead a direct route to biblical truth. Erasmus (1466–1536) is a good example of how the scholastics fell out of favor with the most advanced philosophers and theologians of the sixteenth century. Although Erasmus never joined the Protestants, he was a great reformer, and one of his books, *The Praise of Folly* (1511) helped open the door to the Reformation. Erasmus was the greatest humanist scholar of his day, but, unlike Luther, he had no stomach for the particulars of theological debate. He tried to raise the moral and educational standards of the church and hoped that his efforts would contribute to the institutional reform that most people seemed to desire. *The Praise of Folly* mocks late-medieval Catholic superstitions as well as

Could Jesus Have Been an Octopus?

the various corruptions plaguing the church. Erasmus is especially hard on scholastic philosophy, which he portrays as a convoluted exercise of only pedantic interest. He exaggerates the obscurity of their questions, but only by a little. The schoolmen, according to Erasmus, asked, "Whether God could have taken on the nature of a woman, of the devil, of an ass, of a cucumber, of a piece of flint? And then how would the cucumber have preached, performed miracles, and been nailed to the cross?"[10] Erasmus goes on to make fun of other allegedly bizarre scholastic arguments, and he blames the divisive state of theology on the most compulsive school of late-medieval hair splitters, the Scotists.

The Scotists were followers of John Duns Scotus (c. 1266–1308), whose brilliance among medieval theologians is generally recognized to be second only to Thomas Aquinas. In recent years there has been a revival of interest in Scotus, driven in part by theologians who compare him unfavorably to Aquinas and blame him for much that has gone wrong in modern thought.[11] Among historical theologians, Richard Cross and Allan Wolter have done the most to retrieve the complexity and coherence of this Franciscan thinker, but the Subtle Doctor, as he is appropriately known, is hard reading for even the most metaphysically astute. Historically, Scotus is best known for expounding the Immaculate Conception of Mary—the idea that Mary did not inherit original sin—which was pronounced a dogma of the Roman Catholic Church in 1854. For his role in this theological development, he is also known as the *Doctor Marianus*—the Marian doctor of the Church.

Among contemporary theologians, Scotus is most frequently discussed for his univocity theory of religious language.[12] This is where he

---

10. Desiderius Erasmus, *The Praise of Folly*, trans. Charles H. Miller (New Haven: Yale University Press, 1979) 88–89. William of Occam is notorious for having argued that the Word could have become incarnate in an ass. See Heiki Oberman, *The Harvest of Medieval Theology* (Grand Rapids: Baker, 2000) 250.

11. Catherine Pickstock outlines and promotes the charges against Scotus in "Duns Scotus: His Historical and Contemporary Significance," *Modern Theology* 21 (2005) 543–74. Mary Beth Ingham mounts a credible defense of Scotus in "Re-Situating Scotist Thought" in the same issue of *Modern Theology*, 609–18.

12. See Cyril L. Shircel, *The Univocity of the Concept of Being in the Philosophy of John Duns Scotus* (Washington, DC: Catholic University of America Philosophical Studies, 1942), Thomas Williams, "The Doctrine of Univocity is True and Salutary," *Modern Theology* 21 (2005) 575–85, and Mary Beth Ingham and Mechthild Dreyer,

most significantly differs from Aquinas. For Aquinas, God's essence is unknowable, because God exists in a way that defies our understanding. The best that we can do when we try to talk about God is to use analogies drawn from human experience (this is what Thomas called the *analogia entis*, or analogy of being). When we talk about God's perfections, for example, we are borrowing terms from human usage, like power, and applying them analogically to God. Thus, God's omnipotence (God's being all powerful) is not a literal description of God. For Aquinas, God is what God does, which means not only that there are no obstacles to God's power but also that the very notion of power falls apart when applied to God. We experience power as a set of opposing forces, so that its exercise always involves a destructive moment even in its most creative expressions. God does not exercise power as one force among many. Nor does God simply possess the sum of all powers in the world. Power is not something God has, just as it is not an attribute of any divine act. God simply is powerful, because God is God, which means that God does not need to be powerful at all.

The coupling of divine mystery with analogical language is a mainstay in theology, but it is less stable than it at first appears. In fact, the analogical theory of religious language is notoriously difficult to defend or explicate, although this has not stopped it from becoming the most popular theory of religious language among contemporary theologians. If we do not know God's essence, how can we make any comparison between what we do know and what we hope to know about God? Analogies presume some kind of proportionality or similarity between two objects. Making an analogy from the known to the completely unknown is like building a bridge out into the ocean. It won't get you anywhere, unless you want to drown in the sea. For that reason, most Thomists admit that even the best analogies about God soon enough expire in the silence of mysticism or the leap of faith. Analogies are helpful aids to devotion because they permit us to praise God, but unless they begin with the presupposition that we truly know God through worship, they are not sufficient or even dependable for helping us to determine the proper attribution of human characteristics to the divine.

The Philosophical Vision of John Duns Scotus: An Introduction (Washington, DC: Catholic University of America Press, 2004) 38–51.

Could Jesus Have Been an Octopus?

Scotus cuts through the knotty problem of analogy by arguing that being is the first and most basic category of knowledge, including our knowledge of God.[13] If language about God is at all possible, we must be able to conceive that various characteristics actually belong to an entity that exists. Moreover, when we say that God exists, we are using existence in the same basic way as when we talk about anything else that exists. Analogies are crucial in understanding God, but analogies from one existent to another do not work unless they are determinations or specifications of something more basic that both existents share. Perfection terms applied to God thus mean roughly the same thing about God as they would mean when applied to humans. When we talk about the power of God, we are using *power* in the same general sense as when we talk about the power of kings and queens. God's being, Scotus argued, is not utterly different from our own; otherwise, we would not be able to attain any intellectual comprehension of God. By creating us, God gives us our existence, which means that God lets us exist (or *be*) in a way that reflects God's own being.

Most contemporary theologians are not drawn to the univocity theory of religious language because they think it is a form of idolatry.[14] Scotus, they argue, turns the idea of existence or being into a category that applies equally to God and finite creatures. As a result, they claim, God becomes one thing among many things, rather than that which transcends every single thing in the universe. The univocity theory of religious language not only fails to do justice to God but is also, according to the most fashionable contemporary theological arguments, responsible for the most deleterious developments in modern and postmodern philosophy. Members of the Radical Orthodoxy theological movement, for example, argue that Scotus makes the created order independent of God by putting its existence on the same conceptual

---

13. Wolfhart Pannenberg's *Habilitationsschrift*, originally published in 1955, makes the case that the metaphysics of analogy falls apart by the time of Scotus, who thus had no choice but to construct a metaphysics of univocal being. See Reinhard Hütter, "After Analogy? Two Recent Contributions to a Perennial Conversation," *Reviews in Religion and Theology* 16 (2009) 288–96.

14. See, for example, Hans Boersma, "Accommodation to What? Univocity of Being, Pure Nature, and the Anthropology of St. Irenaeus," *International Journal of Theology* 8 (2006) 271–75.

level of God's.[15] Once this occurs, according to this common objection, Scotus is forced to deny the way God provides the ground for all existence only by standing completely outside of existence. Everything that exists depends on God, Thomists remind Scotists, but God depends on nothing. God is ungrounded, which means that we cannot even say that God exists without heavy qualifications. God exists only analogically, and the analogy drawn from our existence obscures as much as it illuminates God's existence. By treating existence as the common ground God and creatures share, Radical Orthodox theologians claim that Scotus subjects God to conceptual analysis that is so religiously inappropriate it is akin to blasphemy. Radical Orthodoxy theologians thus claim that Scotist is responsible for the arrogance of modern philosophies and theologies that use language as a tool to encompass the divine—an arrogance that inevitably takes the mystery out of religion. The univocity theory of religious language is thus blamed for the flattened modern spiritual landscape that treats God as a marketable commodity, just as it gets blamed for postmodern claims that "language is all we have." Radical Orthodox theologians think the only way to clean up the mess Scotus has made of religious language is to retrieve the platonic metaphysics of participation that lies beneath Thomas's theory of analogy. No matter how incomplete or partial is our understanding of God, every act of knowing, according to this view, draws our minds toward God, which suggests that analogies work by helping us to learn

---

15. Pickstock argues that univocity denies the infinite distance of God from creatures, a distance that must be bridged by metaphysics of participation rather than a process that abstracts general terms from all entities, including God. Univocity thus results in an atomism wherein every entity occupies its own self-possessed space, rather than a shared space of analogy (553–60). Pickstock here follows Heidegger's argument about the need to think ontological differences, not just ontic. Her theological worry is that univocity denies the way in which all of reality is experienced as a given, that is, a gracious gift to us, which we can understand only upon a reception born of gratitude. Only if God is absolutely other can God be the source of an absolute giving that grants us access to the divine while preserving God's difference from us. There are many problems with this line of criticism, beginning with a misunderstanding of the relation between univocity and analogy, as well as a theory of giving that strains such language to the breaking point. For my alternative theology of giving, see Webb, *The Gifting God* (New York: Oxford University Press, 1996). Nonetheless, the best response to Pickstock is simply to begin a defense of univocity with reference to the Primacy of Christ.

the limits of our language which in turn sensitizes us to the inescapable depth of our relationship to the divine.

The problem with this rather conspiratorial account of Scotus's influence on the modern world is that his actual views on language are notoriously difficult to pin down, so much so that it is doubtful that philosophy this complex could have had such widespread cultural influence. For example, contrary to many Scotus detractors, he did not think that all of our concepts of God are univocal. Nevertheless, he did argue that if *some* of our concepts of God are not univocal, then *none* of them can be analogical. If there is no conceptual unity to the way in which we understand how all beings, including God, can be said to exist, then it is impossible to say that God exists at all. And if we cannot say that God exists, then the dark night of mystical unknowing becomes indistinguishable from the despair of atheistic confusion.

For Scotus, the theory of univocity follows from the idea that there is a real community between God and all living beings. Furthermore, far from imprisoning God in the literalism of conceptual analysis, Scotus replaces analogy with something like hyperbole. Concepts drawn from human experience need to be intensified before they can be appropriately applied to God. A concept like power, for example, needs to be freed of all the ways that we are mired in resentment, envy, and impotence. It also needs to be freed from our fantasies of unlimited power, wherein we do whatever we want but end up obeying only our most base desires. To apply power to God is to risk elevating and purifying a human experience that is more like the trope of exaggeration than analogy.[16] The amplification of our language, rather than the reassignment of attributes, is the natural way of speaking about God. Theories of analogy implicitly acknowledge this when they talk of taking terms like power and applying them to God only when they are used in the mode of perfection. Exaggeration in this sense does not mean assuming that God has more than what we have. Religious exaggerations maximize language morally as well as quantitatively. God is what we are taken to an infinite degree that burns away our moral limitations.

---

16. For a history of hyperbole, including its disruptive relationship to both analogy and metaphor, and the reasons for its theological neglect, see Stephen H. Webb, *Blessed Excess: Religion and the Hyperbolic Imagination* (Albany: SUNY Press, 1993).

The univocity theory of religious language is logically connected to another controversial teaching of Scotus, which is commonly called the Primacy of Christ. I will focus on this teaching because it provides a way of making sense of the octopus scenario. Scotus, of course, did not wonder if octopuses could replace humans, but he did think about the issues that this scenario raises, and his position is as simple as it is profound. Scotus argues that the Son of God did not become incarnate as a consequence of human sin. Instead, the Son of God was predestined by the Father from eternity to become incarnate.[17] The cross was a response to sin, but the incarnation was a revelation of God's eternal identity. In other words, even if the fall into sin had not happened, the incarnation would have happened anyway (and thus this view is sometimes called the "incarnation anyway" position). God created the world because God the Father decided to give form to God the Son. That form of the Son is what we know in Jesus Christ, and that is why we can apply the category of existence univocally to God and us. The reason we can know that concepts drawn from human experience can be applied directly to God is that human nature is the form that God the Father intended from eternity to give to the Son. We can talk confidently about God because God has made us to be on intimate terms with the Son. We are imperfect images of the Son, but when we talk about human perfections, we simply *are* talking about God.

How did Scotus arrive at this view of the incarnation? He was the first to systematize it, but others, like Maximus the Confessor, held something similar to it.[18] Scotus was influenced by Pseudo-Dionysius

17. To put the matter differently, Scotus asks if the incarnation made the fall inevitable. His answer is no. For excellent commentary on Scotus and a translation of some of the key texts, see Allan B. Wolter, "John Duns Scotus on the Primacy and Personality of Christ," in *Franciscan Christology*, ed. Damian McElrath (St. Bonaventure, New York: Institute of St. Bonaventure University, 1980) 139-182. For a comprehensive commentary, see Rev. J. B. Carol, O.F.M., *Why Jesus Christ?* (Manassas, VA: Trinity Communications, 1986). For an excellent and readable introduction to the topic, see Fr. Maximilian Mary Dean, *A Primer on the Absolute Primacy of Christ: Blessed John Duns Scotus and the Franciscan Thesis* (New Bedford, MA: Academy of the Immaculate, 2006).

18. See Ilia Delio, "Revisiting the Franciscan Doctrine of Christ," *Theological Studies* 64 (2003) 3–23. Delio interestingly uses the Primacy of Christ to defend a version of theistic evolution. For St. Maximus the Confessor, see *On the Cosmic Mystery of Jesus Christ,* trans. Paul M. Blowers (Crestwood, NY: St. Vladimir's Seminary Press, 2003) 100 and 125. For one of the few contemporary metaphysical theologians to de-

the Areopagite, the anonymous late-fifth- and early-sixth-century neo-Platonic theologian who defined God as the highest good that overflows itself (*bonum diffusivum sui*). Scotus took this to mean that nothing that has (or achieves) perfection wants to keep that perfection to itself. God, who lacks no perfection, naturally, but not necessarily, communicates that perfection to others. God does this naturally because it is in the nature of goodness to be self-diffusive. God does not do this necessarily, because it is a free decision that God makes. God is already in active communication within the Trinity, but God naturally wanted to widen the circle of that communication. In trinitarian language, the Father so loved the Son that the Father wanted to give something to the Son so that the Son's loveliness could be shared by others. Scotus is very clear that the love the three persons of the Trinity share with each other is not jealous or selfish. To love someone perfectly is to want them to be loved.19 From this will toward maximal love, then, comes the decision to create a world where creatures can share that love. The Father's creative gift of love to the Son is the foundation of every subsequent act of creation. God created angels and humans—and the world in which humans live—to love Jesus Christ.

Scotus concludes from this inquiry into the love of God that God did not first create humanity, watch humanity fall, and then figure out a way to save humanity from sin. God the Father first wanted to confer on the Son as much goodness as possible. God wanted the Son to be the head and crown of creation, so he determined to create a human soul for Jesus Christ, as a gift that was meant to be shared. God intended and envisioned by this audacious act of generosity the incarnation of this soul, the fellowship of other humans with Jesus Christ, and the eventual unity of all matter with the supernatural. The destiny of the world was established from this act, which grants it absolute primacy in the order of creation. Every aspect of creation is included in this par-

---

fend Scotus, although she backs off from him in the end, see Marilyn McCord Adams, *Christ and Horrors: The Coherence of Christology* (Cambridge: Cambridge University Press, 2006) 187–91. Adams comes close to substituting the material world for Christ, so that she argues that God from the very beginning intended for there to be a material world, not necessarily the incarnation (this is almost a Primacy of the World theory).

19. Wolter makes this point in *Franciscan Christology*, 142. Wolter also points out how St. Francis argued that humans are excellent because God created us in "the image of his beloved Son according to the body" (*Admonitions*, 5).

ticular creation of a human soul for Jesus Christ. Furthermore, the soul of Christ was not some amorphous creation, an empty cipher waiting to be shaped by the world yet to come. The world is the world because Jesus Christ is its foundation. Even apart from sin, humans are meant to combine the material and the spiritual, and Christ was meant to be the perfect exemplar of this combination. The unity of flesh and spirit in Jesus Christ was set in motion before the beginning of time.

The ramifications of this teaching on the Primacy of Christ are enormous. The whole cosmos was created to glorify Jesus Christ, and humans were created in the image of Jesus Christ to be his companions in the glorification of the Holy Trinity. The human nature of Jesus Christ was predestined from the very beginning to be united to the Word of God. God speaks the Word from eternity through the Son, so the Word is not a creature, and, of course, neither is the Son. The Son is one of three equal members of the Trinity. The human flesh of the Son is created, not eternal, but the humanity of Jesus is planned (intended or designed by God, if you will) before any thing else is created.[20] As Allan Wolter explains, the Primacy of Christ "makes the human nature of Christ the motif the Divine Architect was to carry out in the rest of creation . . . after his body the visible world was sculptured. The whole universe is full of Christ."[21] The humanity of the Son is the centerpiece of creation. Even animals, especially mammals, anticipate (and reflect) the incarnation in their body plans and their shared physical features. The Primacy of Christ is the most holy secret of Christianity, and it is also why the Darwinian interpretation of evolution cannot possibly be true. Jesus could not have been an octopus, because humans were modeled after him, not the other way around.

The Primacy of Christ shows that the octopus scenario is theologically untenable, and it does so by providing the metaphysical foundation

---

20. That the human form of the Son is planned by the Father from the beginning rules out the particularly pernicious idea that has seeped into modern theology that Christ assumed a fallen human nature. For a critical discussion of this idea, see Oliver D. Crisp, *Divinity and Humanity* (Cambridge: Cambridge University Press, 2007) ch. 4. Not only does Scotus provide a firm foundation for rejecting the idea that Christ was joined to fallen human nature but also Scotus shows that the only way that Christ was not so joined is if he was united with human nature before the fall, proving that human nature need not be fallen.

21. Allan Wolter, trans. and intro., *Duns Scotus: Four Questions on Mary* (Santa Barbara, CA: Old Mission Santa Barbara, 1988) 29.

Could Jesus Have Been an Octopus?

for what Simon Conway Morris has called the inevitability of humans in a lonely universe. Morris, whose work I mentioned in chapter 1, is a champion of the evolutionary concept of convergence. Morris developed his interpretation of the concept of convergence in explicit opposition to Gould's tape metaphor (the idea that the tape of evolution, once rewound, would never replay the same way). While Gould is impressed with evolution's randomness, Morris is amazed at the number of evolutionary endpoints that mimic and repeat each other. Over and over again, according to Morris, evolution demonstrates a "recurrent tendency to arrive at the same solution to a particular need." One of the examples of convergence that he uses is, interestingly enough, the similarity between the eye of the octopus and the human eye. The evolution of incredibly complex structures is hard enough to explain under the simplest of conditions, but how do scientists account for the fact that "what is possible has usually been arrived at multiple times, meaning that the emergence of the various biological properties is effectively inevitable"?[22] The camera-eye (in contrast to the simple or compound eye) is a marvel of engineering, and Darwinians have developed elaborate scenarios in the hope of showing how random genetic changes could have brought it about. Perhaps it could have, but could evolution have produced the same eye in several different biological trajectories, most notably in both vertebrates and advanced cephalopods?

The best current answer to that question involves some form of genetic determinism. Octopuses and humans last shared an ancestor about 550 million years ago. Orthodox Darwinism contends that in the course of that time, the human and the octopus lineages just happened to undergo the same development of an original eye-spot. The odds of one evolutionary lineage developing the camera eye are astronomical, but the odds of independent lineages doing so in parallel fashion must be many times those already astronomical odds. The only explanation seems to be that the gene-set humans and octopuses share related to their eyes goes back to their common ancestor, and that the ancestor had master genes that exercised control over the evolution of the eye.[23]

22. Simon Conway Morris, *Life's Solution: Inevitable Humans in a Lonely Universe* (Cambridge: Cambridge University Press, 2003), xii and xii–xiii.

23. See the studies on the Genome Research website: http://genome.cshlp.org/cgi/content/abstract/14/8/1555?ck=nck. For a careful analysis of what the similarities are between the two eyes, see Mark B. Couch, "Functional Properties and Convergence in

Scientists have in fact established common gene sequences in humans and octopuses related to the eye, but notice two things about this explanation. First, it radically challenges Darwinism by portraying evolution as the inevitable unfolding of information already present in an original genetic plan, rather than nature's selection of random mutations. This suggests that complex biological structures are more like the growth of a plant from a seed than the endpoint of a drunk's random stumble down a road. Second, it simply shifts the mystery of evolution from random change to so-called master genes. If genes are blind, how do they show so much mastery over their environments? How did genes in separate evolutionary lineages direct their organisms down nearly identical paths over millions of years?

Morris takes a multi-causal approach to the problem of biological convergences (he rejects the primacy of genetic explanation), which is another way of saying that he admits that scientists have a lot of good guesses that do not add up to a single solution to this puzzle. If convergences were the exception that proved the rules of Darwinism, that might not be such a problem, but convergences, as Morris delights in showing, are ubiquitous in nature. Morris surveys hundreds of baffling examples, including such fascinating puzzles as the convergence between the hearing of mosquitoes and mammals and the convergence between ant farms and human farming. Morris concludes that evolution appears to be more directed toward biological progress than orthodox Darwinism warrants. It is almost as if life is exploring some sort of uniform adaptational space that limits the kinds of organisms that can develop. The space for evolution is thus not unbounded. Even on just the molecular level, if the space that evolution explores were unlimited, then it would be impossible to imagine how evolution happened at all. "With twenty different amino acids and even a rather simple protein, say one hundred amino acids in length, the combinatorial possibilities in protein 'hyperspace' are very large indeed," Morris writes with a bit of understatement.[24] Far from being thrown into hyperspace, life appears

---

Biology," *Philosophy of Science* 72 (December 2005), pp. 1041–51.

24. Simon Conway Morris, "Does Biology have an Eschatology, and If So Does it have Cosmological Implications?" in *The Far-Future Universe: Eschatology from a Cosmic Perspective*, ed. George F. R. Ellis (Philadelphia: Templeton Foundation, 2002) 165. Also see Simon Conway Morris, "The Navigation of Biological Hyperspace," *International Journal of Astrobiology* 2 (2003) 149–52.

Could Jesus Have Been an Octopus?

pulled toward predetermined ends. There are trends toward consciousness, tool usage, and language development that make it look like humans are the model of evolution rather than an accidental detour.

The hypothesis that humans are the endpoint of evolution is called hominization, and Morris cannot help but accept it. "Could the story of sensory perception be one clue that, given time, evolution will inevitably lead not only to the emergence of such properties as intelligence, but also to other complexities, such as, say, agriculture and culture, that we tend to regard as the prerogative of the human? We may be unique, but paradoxically those properties that define our uniqueness can still be inherent in the evolutionary process. In other words, if we humans had not evolved then something more-or-less identical would have emerged sooner or later." [25] We, or something very much like us, seem built into the process of increasing biological complexity from the very beginning. We are both lonely and unique in the universe, inevitable and exceptional. Evolution has a direction, and we are its point.

Morris has set himself the valiant task of explaining how convergences occur, but even if he succeeds, it is clear that he will be breaking from Darwinian orthodoxy. He ends his book with an enticing comment. "None of it [biological convergences] presupposes, let alone proves, the existence of God, but all is congruent."[26] This is enticing because one of the synonyms of congruent is *design*. If all is congruent, yet Darwinism denies that nature is designed, then there must be some post-Darwinian explanation for evolution's remarkable tendency to follow what appear to be predestined channels of development. Where Darwinism falls short in explaining convergences, Scotus shines. If something like the human species, with its intelligence, its eyes, and who knows what other parts and features, is inevitable, then biology must have been conditioned from the very beginning to unfold the human pattern. That is exactly what the Primacy of Christ leads us to expect. Indeed, the Primacy of Christ can be considered the metaphysical precondition made necessary by the phenomenon of evolutionary convergences. The only way to account for the inevitability of who we are is to posit an original and eternal model of us that only God could

---

25. Morris, *Life's Solution*, 196. The examples of hearing and farming are discussed on 191 and 205.
26. Ibid., 330.

have made. We were made from dust, but that dust was the afterthought of God's decision to be a Father to his Son. And since our shape is taken from an eternal form, all creatures reflect our physical attributes to one degree or another. That is why the octopus has an eye like our own, but it is also why God could never have become incarnate in an octopus, or put differently, it is why we and not octopuses are the endpoint of evolution.

An idea that is closely related to biological convergences is the cosmological insight known as the Anthropic Principle, and the Primacy of Christ also makes theological sense of it.[27] The Anthropic Principle is not one argument but several, and different versions of it can be found on the web and in books and articles. It is basically an argument for design from the premise that too many coincidences add up to nothing else. Simply put, the universe "seems strangely well suited for us."[28] Its physical parameters, in fact, are fine tuned for life. The gravitational force, the strong nuclear force, the weak nuclear force, the expansion rate of the universe, the mass of the universe, the electromagnetic coupling constant that binds electrons to protons, the velocity of light, the distance between the stars—not only do all of these forces have to be exactly right to get life going, but they also have to be in harmony with each other! From a Scotist point of view, the fine-tuning argument makes perfect sense, except that it should be referred to as a Christropic, not Anthropic Principle. The universe, according to Scotus, was made for Jesus Christ. It is no surprise, then, that the universe strikes us as equal parts comfortable habitat and impossible outcome of countless coincidences. The world was made for Jesus, and we were made to be the friends of Jesus, so the world looks like it was made for us too.

Whether this principle is a sufficient argument for proving that God designed the universe is beyond the scope of this book. I want to note, however, that this argument is so strong that one of the most common objections to it is really quite bizarre. In order to downplay the fortuitous factors of this universe, it is becoming common among both physicists and philosophers to argue that this universe is only one

---

27. For one of the best explications of the Anthropic principle, see Michael A. Corey, *The God Hypothesis* (Lanham, MD: Rowman & Littlefield, 2001).

28. Morris, *Life's Solutions*, 327.

of many universes.[29] The multiverse theory, as it is sometimes called, imagines trillions of parallel universes bobbing about in an equally large number of hyperspace dimensions. These possible worlds are posited in order to explain the possibility of this world. The idea is that so many worlds have come into being, one after another and many at the same time in different dimensions, that it is not surprising that one of these worlds had just the right combination of physical factors to support biological life. To say that this argument is a stretch would be an understatement. Not only is there no evidence for these multiple worlds, but their theoretical existence actually makes the fine tuning argument stronger, not weaker. What are the odds that there are countless universes, many in various stages along the way toward supporting life? The idea that our universe is one among many, perhaps struggling to survive in competition with other universes, is Darwinism run amok, and it does nothing to lessen the utterly miraculous nature of life.

If the Primacy of Christ were merely useful for providing a theological justification for biological convergences and the Anthropic principle, it would be little more than a religious curiosity or gimmick, rather than a profound Christian truth. After all, those scientific theories will have to stand or fall, in the end, on scientific evidence, not theological backing, even though if they do prove to be scientifically credible, they require the theological backing that Scotus has already given us. In the remainder of this chapter I want to show how the Primacy of Christ is not a minor or dispensable part of the Christian tradition. I will do this by working out some of its implications and some of it relations to other doctrines. In particular, I will show how it contributes to the Christian understanding of angels, provides support for the Roman Catholic doctrine of transubstantiation, and helps to solve one of the most ancient objections to the Christian doctrine of creation. I also want to show how the Primacy of Christ coheres with the two best-known features of Scotus's thought, his interpretation of the Immaculate Conception of Mary and his theory of religious language. I will then briefly discuss its biblical support, especially its role in unifying the two testaments, before attending to the most important reasons why some critics reject

---

29. See John Leslie, *Universes* (New York: Routledge, 1989) and Timothy Ferris, *The Whole Shebang: A State of the Universe(s) Report* (New York: Simon & Schuster, 1997).

The Dome of Eden

it. I will conclude by showing how it makes sense of two important theological topics, the *imago Dei* and the pre-existence of Christ.

What the Primacy of Christ Explains

The Primacy of Christ might seem like a mystery, but it actually explains one of the great mysteries of the Bible, which is the creation and status of the angels. Angels have long been a puzzle in Christian theology. When were they created, and for what purpose? Some theologians think that the angels were created first, humans second, and the incarnate Word third. Yet all Christians believe that Jesus Christ is the king of the heavenly court and the head of the celestial family. The angels are not independent operators in the divine economy of grace. They did not have an original purpose that was altered when humans were created, altered again after the fall, and altered a final time after the resurrection of Jesus. The angels have always been subordinate to Jesus Christ. The angels were created to serve Jesus, which accounts also for their role in serving the faithful on earth.

Significantly, the Franciscan school of theology, in which Scotus was trained, argues that the origin of the fallen angels was a test given them over the incarnation. They were shown a vision of Mary and the Divine Child, and those who refused to worship Jesus were cursed and became demons. This tradition can be expanded to bring the Primacy of Christ in line with the role of angels in the fall of humanity. When some angels rebelled against worshipping Jesus Christ, a divine being who shared in created nature, they took it out on Adam and Eve. The demons recognized Jesus when he walked upon the earth. "I know who you are, the Holy One of God," says one (Mark 1:24). (Jesus recognized them, too.) This suggests that the angels knew the divine plan before any human beings did. Some early theologians taught that the angels fell due to jealousy of Jesus Christ, a position that was perfectly captured in John Milton's *Paradise Lost*, where Satan is sent into a rage by the worship God demands for his Son. Other theologians have argued that Satan was jealous not so much of Jesus as humans, whose role in the divine economy meant they are more exalted than the angels. Early rabbinic sources taught that the angels fell because they were jealous of Adam. "The angels noticed Adam's resemblance to God, said: 'Are there two powers in this world?'"[30] The angels understood that there was a deep physical connection between Adam and God. Adam had a form, which the angels did not, and his form reflected God's. The fallen angels tempted Adam and Eve because they could not attack Jesus directly. They saw Mary in Eve and Jesus in Adam. There is even a Jewish tradition that teaches that the serpent looked like a man because he stood upright and walked on two feet, as if, inspired by or inhabited by Satan, the serpent could not stand to be less than man. The fallen angels thought they were above the world of flesh, blood, and bone. They could not tolerate the fact that God had chosen not only Jesus but also human beings for a destiny above their own.

One could also make the case that the Primacy of Christ provides the metaphysical foundation for transubstantiation. When Jesus Christ said to the disciples that the bread and wine were his body and blood, he could literally mean what he said, because his body is the Ur-matter, as it were, the substance or essence of all matter. When we receive communion, we are doing more than remembering the life, death, and resurrection of Jesus. In communion with Christ, the Holy Spirit begins the process of transforming our bodies to more closely match his body. We were created in the image of Jesus, but to enter into heaven we must take on the glorified body that Jesus had at his resurrection. That glorified body was not something radically new that Jesus did not possess during his incarnation. The body of Jesus was already saturated with grace in the womb of Mary. As the foundation of the world and the reason for creation, the body of Jesus during his life was already full of divine perfections. That is why he could walk on water and heal the sick. He had mastery over nature because his nature was suffused with the divine. In the last supper, he gave his disciples a foretaste of matter transformed, which is to say, he gave them a foretaste of what he already was. He could give of himself in this way because he is both flesh and spirit, and his flesh is the spiritual destiny of all who call upon his name. The Eucharist is the foretaste of the heavenly banquet wherein all matter will become what God created for Jesus.

---

30. Louis Ginzberg, *The Legends of the Jews*, vol. 5 (Baltimore: Johns Hopkins University Press, 1998) 86.

The Dome of Eden

As the discussion of the Eucharist shows, the Primacy of Christ is a necessary teaching for thinking through any aspect of the Christian view of matter. The closest parallel in the ancient world to the challenge of Darwin to modern theologians is the question of how an immaterial God could have created a material world. If the cause of a thing is in some way present in its effect, as the ancients assumed, then how can pure spirit beget clunky matter?[31] This question puzzled philosophers long before Christianity came on the scene, and many, following Aristotle, concluded that matter must be eternal. Christians, however, did not have this option, because they believed that God made the world out of nothing (*creatio ex nihilo*). If matter is eternal, theologians reasoned, then it must be equal in dignity to God. It would follow that God is not unique, nor does God transcend the world in power and glory. The divinity of matter contradicts the main tenet of monotheism, which is that God is the one and only source of all that is. Some theologians, in response to the dualism of matter and God, argued that the world must have been created from God in the sense of coming out of or emanating from God's nature. The emanationist view, however, comes close to denying the reality of matter. If the world is made of the same substance that comprises divinity, then matter is ultimately spiritual, and thus immaterial. Augustine puzzled over this issue and decided that there is a difference in saying that the world is from God (*ex ipso*) and the world is of God (*de ipso*).[32] The world comes from God, but it is not made of God. This introduces a technical distinction that merely restates the problem.

The only true solution to this problem is the Primacy of Christ.[33] Matter can come from spirit, and the two are neither identical nor opposed, if and only if God from the very beginning determined to be a

---

31. For a discussion of this assumption, see Richard Sorabji, *Time, Creation and the Continuum* (London: Duckworth, 1983) and Gerhard May, *Creatio Ex Nihilo: The Doctrine of Creation Out of Nothing in Early Christian Thought* (Edinburgh: T. & T. Clark, 1995).

32. Augustine, *Concerning the Nature of Good*, in *Nicene and Post-Nicene Fathers*, vol. 4, ed. P. Schaff, trans. A. Newman (1890. Reprinted, Peabody, MA: Hendrickson, 1994).

33. For an alternative solution that relies, like Augustine, on technical wordplay rather than doctrinal explication, see Neil B. MacDonald, *Metaphysics and the God of Israel: Systematic Theology of the Old and New Testaments* (Grand Rapids: Baker Academic, 2006) ch. 3.

Could Jesus Have Been an Octopus?

divine person in human form. God created matter for himself, or, more specifically, for his Son. It is more helpful to say that he created it out of himself than out of nothing, because he created it for himself before he created it for us. Matter is not eternal, because it is a gift tied intimately to the relationship of the Father and the Son, but it is also not lacking in reality, because this gift comes from the eternal love that unites the Trinity.

The Primacy of Christ, properly understood, also explains why Scotus was so dedicated to defending and explaining the Virgin Birth as well as Immaculate Conception of Mary. If God predestined the Son to be Jesus Christ, then God at the same time must have predestined Mary to be the mother of Jesus. This can be seen from the following argument. If God made the world for Jesus, then Jesus had no need to enter into the world in the ordinary manner. Jesus Christ precedes every man and woman. God determined to create a human nature for him from the beginning of creation, so he did not need to have his humanity created in the usual way (that is, he did not need to begin as a seed planted by a man in a woman). However, God gave the Son a human soul destined to be implanted in a human body. Jesus did not *need* to be born of a woman, but God wanted to demonstrate to the world that Jesus is indeed one of us and not just a heavenly being who came down from the sky. If Jesus had not been born at all, but merely inserted into the world like a brand new object without any history or family, then he hardly could have been the incarnation of the Word. So he had to have begun life in a mother's womb. God wanted the world to know that the Jesus Christ born of a woman was the same Son of God begotten by the Father. So before the world was created, God chose a mother for the Son. God the Father is the Father of Jesus, but Mary is indeed the Mother of God incarnate (the technical term is *theotokos*, which was granted Mary at the Third Ecumenical Council at Ephesus in 431). The upshot is Mary was the first person willed after the Father decided to give the Son human form. Jesus was not the product of a chain of procreative events, and neither, in a way, was Mary. It follows that Mary was no ordinary human being. She was granted the special status of being exempt from original sin because she was the only human being willed by God before Adam and Eve even existed.[34]

---

34. Some Catholic theologians have argued, along similar lines, that the primacy of

The Dome of Eden

With so many important theological issues at stake, it is appropriate to inquire into the biblical support for the Primacy of Christ in both the Old and New Testaments. One of the great mysteries of the Old Testament concerns the way the wisdom of God was often given a quasi-personal status. This occurs in the genre known as wisdom literature, which includes Job, Proverbs, Ecclesiastes, and other intertestamental and New Testament texts. The personification of wisdom was not uncommon in the ancient Near East, but it was especially important for the Israelites as a way of addressing everyday practical problems. It also allowed the Israelites to acknowledge the universal constraints of the human condition. Wisdom, according to this tradition, was created before the world and is, in turn, the foundation of the rest of creation.[35] Psalm 104:24, for example, declares, "O Lord, how manifold are your works! In wisdom you have made them all," implying that wisdom is the agent of creation, and Prov 3:19 states, "The Lord by wisdom founded the earth." The exact status of wisdom as the representation of God's immanence in creation is debated by scholars, though the Church Fathers did not hesitate to identify wisdom with Jesus Christ. The wisdom sayings, however, have never become as integrated into Christian ethical teachings as they deserve. The Primacy of Christ lets Christians embrace these teachings wholeheartedly as the words not just of the wise old men of Israel but also of Jesus himself.

The Primacy of Christ helps to solve another puzzling feature of the Old Testament. Close readers of the Old Testament have long pondered the many passages—too many to catalogue here—that attribute bodily characteristics to God. The scholarly word for this is anthropomorphism, which refers to the depiction of the divine in human form. Perhaps the most important anthropomorphism in Hebrew Scriptures is the one I have already discussed, the appearance of God looking like a man seated on a throne above the Dome in the first chapter of Ezekiel. For obvious reasons, theologians have frequently downplayed or simply ignored the extent to which the Israelites imagined God in human terms. If God is spirit, and the incarnation is the only instance of the

---

Christ justifies granting Mary the titles of Mediatrix and Coredemptrix.

35. The literature on the wisdom teaching of the Old Testament is vast, but see James L. Kugel, *The Bible as It Was* (Cambridge: Harvard University Press, 1997) 53–57.

physical embodiment of God, then what is to be done with all the references to God's body prior to the incarnation? Some scholars argue that the Israelites always understood these references in purely metaphorical terms, but that is becoming a minority view, given how numerous and detailed they are.[36] Many passages indicate that the biblical author was reticent to describe God in human terms, rather than eager to use figurative language to render God more vivid. The revelation of God's body, when it occurred, was surprising and awkward for the biblical authors. God too could be hesitant to reveal himself in bodily form. The most dramatic example of this is found in Exod 33:12–23, when Moses asks to God to "show me your glory" and God lets him see only his back. Some theologians talk about progressive revelation, as if God first appeared in human form to the Israelites as an accommodation to their limited understanding, but that teaching is hard to reconcile with the traditional view of the authority of Scripture and any plausible reconstruction of Old Testament chronology. It is much simpler, then, to conclude that God had a body before the incarnation revealed that body to us, and that God's body was always Jesus Christ.

The wisdom teachings do not come to an end with the Old Testament. The Apostle Paul was immersed in this genre and relied on it to explicate the centrality of Christ for every Christian doctrine. Of course, highlighting certain scriptures cannot alone attest to the truth of the Primacy of Christ, since opponents of this doctrine can find other scripture that seems to deny it, but three passages from the Pauline epistles do give it striking support. First, in Ephesians, Paul writes that God "chose us in Christ before the foundation of the world to be holy and blameless before him in love" (1:4). This seems to suggest that whatever predestination means, our predestination to holiness is based on a prior predestination of Christ. Surely this is what Paul calls later in this letter "the mystery hidden for ages in God who created all things" (3:9). God had an eternal purpose that he made known in the fullness of time. Our destiny to be made holy in Christ is that eternal purpose, even though the incarnation occurs in time.

---

36. See H. Eilberg-Schwartz, ed., *People of the Body: Jews and Judaism from an Embodied Perspective* (Albany: SUNY Press, 1992) and *God's Phallus and Other Problems for Men and Monotheism* (Boston: Beacon, 1994).

A second key passage is Rom 8:29: "For those whom he foreknew he also predestined to be conformed to the image of his Son, in order that he might be the firstborn within a large family." Notice that Christians are destined to become like Jesus Christ, not the whole Trinity. Jesus was intended from the beginning to be the firstborn of a large family. We were created to join him, not the other way around.

The third passage is Col 1:15–20:

> He is the image of the invisible God, the firstborn of all creation; for in him all things in heaven and on earth were created, things visible and invisible, whether thrones or dominions or rulers or powers—all things have been created through him and for him. He himself is before all things, and in him all things hold together. He is the head of the body, the church; he is the beginning, the firstborn from the dead, so that he might come to have first place in everything. For in him all the fullness of God was pleased to dwell, and through him God was pleased to reconcile to himself all things, whether on earth or in heaven, by making peace through the blood of his cross.

The interpretation of this complex and beautiful passage pivots on the meaning of the simple pronoun, *him*. Who is Paul talking about? Is it the second person of the Trinity, or the incarnate Word? Or does this passage problematize that very distinction? Most scholars agree that the Colossians were mired in heated philosophical debates when Paul wrote to them. The Colossians were not content with Christ. Perhaps they believed in various Platonic, Gnostic, or angelic intermediaries who could supplement or take the place of Christ. Whatever their theological confusions, Paul responds with a clear definition of the Primacy of Christ. The one who is the firstborn of creation is the very same one who is the firstborn from the dead. The Jesus Christ of eternity is identical with the Jesus Christ who was raised from the dead. We can know this because Jesus Christ is identifiable as the one for whom the world was made. The Jesus Christ of eternity is not an invisible form of the Jesus Christ who was raised from the dead. They are identical because Jesus Christ is visible from the very beginning. The Triune God is invisible, but Jesus Christ is the image of the invisible God. *He* is the original image in which we are created. God thought of him first. We are the afterthought, not him.

Could Jesus Have Been an Octopus?

For all of the magnificence of Paul's explications of what came to be known as the Primacy of Christ, this teaching is not well known outside of specialized circles of professional theologians. It is important to note that Scotus did not invent the idea. Albert the Great argued for it, and Scotus had many other forerunners, going back to the patristic period. Scotus's name, however, is usually attached to it because he was extremely influential in Catholic theology up to and including the seventeenth century. After Thomas Aquinas rose to preeminence, both Scotus and his doctrine of the Primacy of Christ became marginalized and almost forgotten. Even Richard Cross, in his detailed examination of the work of Scotus, only devotes two pages to it.[37] It is worth speculating about why it has been so neglected. As far as I can tell, there are five reasons why it is so often overlooked in discussions about Christology.

First, some of its neglected status is due to concerns that it implies the eternity of creation. If God willed the incarnation from all eternity, then isn't matter, in some sense, eternal?[38] Above I argued that the Primacy of Christ shows how God as pure Spirit could create matter. Now I want to look more closely at how the Primacy of Christ determines the temporal status of matter. The eternity of matter is excluded by the doctrine of creation *ex nihilo*, and rightly so for a variety of metaphysical reasons, but the primacy of Christ, far from grounding the eternity of matter, sheds light on this Greek intuition by clarifying its strengths and weaknesses. If matter is that out of which everything is made, then the pre-existent Son is the form that gives matter its allure of eternity, because all things were made by, through, and for him. In other words, if matter appears eternal, it is because the pre-existent Son is matter's true eternity. Actually, the Greeks could not overcome a basic dualism between matter and form, imagining, as they did, that formless matter indicates a basic limit on the power of the intellect.[39] Where Christianity corrects this intuition is in disagreeing with the Greek argument that formless matter is eternal. The pre-existent Son

37. Richard Cross, *Duns Scotus* (New York: Oxford University Press, 1999) 128–29.

38. For an excellent handling of this issue, see Ilia Delio, "Is Creation Eternal?" *Theological Studies* 66 (2005) 279–303.

39. See Thomas L. Pangle, *Political Philosophy and the God of Abraham* (Baltimore: Johns Hopkins University Press, 2003) 33.

guarantees the priority of form over matter, thus guaranteeing the ultimate reliability of human perception.

Scotus anticipates this worry about the eternity of matter by arguing that God creates the world for Jesus Christ, but that the hypostatic union of human nature and divinity in Jesus Christ occurs in time, not eternity. What is crucial is Scotus's insight that God's decision to create a being who freely loves him is first focused on the creation of a material nature for the Son, not the creation of human beings. Scotus's meaning can be counterintuitive. Didn't God create the world first, and only subsequently send his Son for the sake of the world? For Scotus, the chronology of the creation is not the same as the order of God's intentions. God first desires to extend the love that is within the Trinity to a work outside the Trinity. God further desires that this love be returned. God thus decides to create the perfect creature to love and to receive love from. This creature will be the unity of the Son and a finite nature shaped especially for him. The world is created for the incarnation of the Son into this nature. The priority of God's intentions should not be confused with the chronology of God's actions in creating the world.

Second, the Primacy of Christ is probably also neglected due to confusion over the difference between redemption and salvation. If Adam and Eve had not fallen, they still would have needed to be saved, in the sense of having their human nature elevated to the point of becoming one with God. The material world was created for humanity, but humanity was created to be the friends of Jesus and to enjoy worshipping God forever. Adam and Eve needed grace, and therefore salvation, even in the Garden of Eden, as demonstrated by their vulnerability to temptation from the serpent. After the fall, humanity needed redemption, not just salvation. Redemption is the form salvation took when humans turned themselves over to sin in rebellion against God. Scotus thus rejects the classic argument that Anselm developed in *Cur Deus Homo? (Why God Became Man)*. For Anselm, the incarnation was a consequence of the fall. Humans had dishonored God, and a penalty needed to be paid, but only someone who was both God and man could pay the price for humanity's rebellion. For Scotus, the cross is the consequence of the fall, but not the incarnation. The incarnation would have happened regardless of the fall. Because of sin, Jesus Christ had to suffer and die on our behalf. That the Word became man, however, is not dependent on human sin. To suggest this is to make the masterpiece of creation into an incidental act dependent upon human failure. It is also to suggest that God did not know what he was doing when he created the world. For Anselm (and Aquinas follows him on this point), the incarnation was a reaction to events that God did not foresee (or if he did foresee them, then he took no action in advance of their occurrence, preferring to react to them instead).

Third, the idea that evolutionary forces converge in the making of the human species is most closely associated, in theological circles, with the controversial theologian Pierre Teilhard de Chardin, the French Jesuit who was trained as both a philosopher and a paleontologist (he was involved in the discovery in China of the Peking Man). I criticized Teilhard in chapter 3 as an example of theistic evolution, so I need to explain how I am using Morris's theory of convergence in a way that does not lead to the problems associated with Teilhard. In chapter 3, I drew attention to the weakness of his theology of sin. In several books that were denied publication during his lifetime, Teilhard reinterpreted Genesis as a story about the ongoing transformation of matter from disorder into organized complexity and, with humans, into spirit, which led him to deny original sin. Nonetheless, many of the points Teilhard makes sound very much like both Scotus's Primacy of Christ and Morris's idea of biological convergences. Teilhard is a philosopher given to optimistic speculations, while Morris keeps his ruminations close to the ground of biological evidence, but can Teilhard be read as a precursor to Morris and as a sympathetic exponent of the Primacy of Christ?

Probably not, but it is important to see how close Teilhard comes to Morris and Scotus and how far he goes wrong. An account of Teilhard's relationship to Scotus has been recorded in a little known book by Gabriel Allegra. Allegra was president of the Franciscan Biblical Institute in China, and in the early 1940s he had the opportunity to have a series of conversations with Teilhard. He later reconstructed those conversations for publication, and one of their chief topics was Scotus's teaching of the Primacy of Christ. Allegra was thoroughly immersed in this teaching, which he thought was the most fundamental articulation of the love of God, while Teilhard was not very familiar with it but eager to learn more about it. Allegra sums up Scotus's position by saying that "it is Christ who is the occasion, or rather the cause of the existence of the world, which in him alone has consistency." The incarnation does not merely recapitulate the various stages of human existence in order to redeem humans from sin. It recapitulates the entire cosmos, revealing the very reason for our existence. Teilhard reacts to Allegra's summation of Scotus with genuine delight and curiosity, but then Allegra questions him on the issue of original sin. Teilhard just cannot seem to get his mind around the idea that, in Allegra's words, "the sum-total of the glory of all creatures is not as intensively great as the glory of Christ" and that this glory was already established before the creation of the world. For Teilhard, glory lies in the future, not the past. The image of God is the product of forces that gradually produce a species worthy to reflect God's nature; it is not something that precedes humans and provides the template for our nature. Ever the optimist, Teilhard says that sin "does not belong to the study of the phenomenon of man." The Bible "is a sublime religious narrative of a popular character that must be implemented with the data of science." Above all, Teilhard is anxious to reject any system of thought that might be static. Evolution seems to have revealed to Teilhard a dynamic conception of religion as well as nature, which leads him think of truth as something that is dependent on a complex interplay of biological and spiritual forces. To sum up his position, he calls Christ "the great Evolver."[40] Christ is both the cause and the effect of evolution, its secret purpose and its supreme success.

Fourth, the Primacy of Christ is also controversial in some theological circles because it implies that divinization is the form of salvation. Most closely associated with Eastern Orthodoxy theology, divinization is traditionally attributed to Athanasius, the fourth-century Bishop of Alexandria. He taught that the Word "was made man so that we might be made God." The form of that statement is more shocking than it needs to be. What Athanasius meant is that the purpose of the incarnation is to enable men and women to become one with God.[41] The na-

---

40. Gabriel M. Allegra, *My Conversations with Teilhard De Chardin on the Primacy of Christ, Peking, 1942–1945*, trans. Bernardino M. Bonansea (Chicago: Franciscan Herald, 1971) 65-66, 94, 75, 76, and 81. For an example of a theological project that conflates Scotus and Teilhard, see Zachary Hayes, *The Gift of Being: A Theology of Creation* (Collegeville, MN: Liturgical, 2001) 107–15.

41. For the most comprehensive treatment, see Norman Russell, *The Doctrine of Deification in the Greek Patristic Tradition* (New York: Oxford University Press,

ture of that oneness, however, could be easily misconstrued, especially by Protestants. Protestants typically reject divinization as evidence of residual paganism in early Christian thought, though divinization should be carefully distinguished from deification, which the Roman Emperors routinely claimed for themselves. Adding to Protestant suspicions is the favorable comparison Mormons have increasingly made in recent years between the patristic doctrine of divinization and their own beliefs centered on the materiality of the supernatural. Whether Mormons cross the line from divinization to deification, the Church Fathers were careful to keep the focus on the consequences of the resurrection of the body. When we become full partakers of the divine in heaven, we will be immortal, and our bodies will be incorruptible and impassible. We will be godly and godlike. So understood, divinization is making a comeback in Protestant theology, as demonstrated by a recent collection of essays that argues that Martin Luther did not reject it, as is commonly assumed.[42]

It is worth pausing here to note that just as Weikart argues that Hitler cannot be understood without reference to Darwin, it can also be argued that Hitler cannot be understood without reference to his Satanic parodying of the divinization of man. Many scholars have demonstrated how Hitler tried to create a new, pagan religion in Nazism, but the primacy of Christ actually sheds radical light on the degree to which Hitler tried to replace Christianity, and how that process of replacement shaped his anti-Semitism. As the historian Michael Burleigh has shown, Hitler's idea of the Aryan race derived "from the age-old quest to discover what language was spoken in the Garden of Eden." Nineteenth-century philology was consumed with the search for the *Ursprache*, the original language of primordial humanity. German scholars thought they found the source in an Indo-Germanic tongue that had affinities with Sanskrit but was absolutely different from the Semitic languages that fed into ancient Hebrew. Hitler added to this quest a theological overlay when he portrayed the Aryan as "the highest

---

2004). Also see Stephen Finlan and Vladimir Kharlamov, eds., *Theosis: Deification in Christian Theology* (Eugene, OR: Pickwick, 2006).

42. Care E. Braaten and Robert W. Jenson, eds., *Union With Christ: The New Finnish Interpretation of Luther* (Grand Rapids: Eerdmans, 1998), and Tuomo Manermaa, *Christ Present in Faith: Luther's View of Justification* (Minneapolis: Fortress, 2005).

image of the Lord."⁴³ The Aryan is thus the first creation, the founder of humanity, and the prototype for all subsequent humans. The role of the state was to gather the Aryans who has been scattered through Europe and to shepherd their stock by eugenic experiments and the regulation of marriage. Hitler's Aryan ideology was an effort to rewrite Darwinism, placing racial struggle at the center of natural selection. It was also, however, an attempt to rewrite Christianity, by putting the Aryan in the place of Adam and even in the place of Christ. According to Nazi antitheology, Christ was the incarnation of the Aryan, which makes the Aryan body divine. Jews, for the Nazis, were subhuman because they were excluded from the Aryan origin and destiny of humanity.

Fifth, lastly and most bluntly, the teaching of the Primacy of Christ wounds our vanity. The origin of sin lies in our rebellion against God, and the nature of that rebellion is our attempt to pretend that we are gods. This rebellion insinuates itself into theology in subtle ways. The Primacy of Christ is denied every time we talk about the incarnation in passive terms, as if it were a mere accident compared to God's plan to create us. We like to think that we, not Christ, are at the center of the universe, and that Jesus Christ became like us, instead of getting the picture right by acknowledging that we were created to be like him. We want to think that God made the universe for us, rather than for Jesus. Indeed, one could say that the teaching of the Primacy of Christ is, of all theological doctrines, the most effective remedy for human pride. It stands as the single strongest bulwark against every ideology that would place humanity in the position of Jesus.

From the perspective of the Primacy of Christ, the theory of evolution, as it is usually formulated, is the most blatant ideology to try to usurp the honor that is due to Jesus. Evolution usurps Christ's honor because, in its theistic form, it portrays humanity as the crown of creation, and in its more secular form, it portrays humanity's biological supremacy as having been earned through a combination of struggle and chance. Many writers have argued that evolution is an affront to the dignity of humanity. G. K. Chesterton, for example, wittily retorted to Darwinism, "Man is not merely an evolution but rather a revolution."⁴⁴

---

43. Michael Burleigh, *Sacred Causes: The Clash of Religion and Politics, from the Great War to the War on Terror* (New York: HarperCollins, 2006) 107.

44. G. K. Chesterton, *The Everlasting Man* (New York: Dodd, Mead, 1925).

Could Jesus Have Been an Octopus?

The problem with this line of criticism is that humans have no basis on their own to resent being grouped with other animals. Evolution is an affront to the dignity of humanity, but only because it is an affront to Jesus Christ.

More incisive than Chesterton's oft-cited quip is the sobering statement of Karl Barth: "Adam is already Jesus Christ and Jesus Christ is already Adam."[45] Although Barth does not credit Scotus for this theological move, he gets the priority exactly right, and he does so in a Scotist manner.[46] Pope John Paul II has also spoken like a true Scotist on several occasions, as when he declared in an Apostolic Letter on the dignity and vocation of women, that *man*, whether man or woman, is "the only being among the creatures of the visible world that God the creator has willed for its own sake."[47] Humans have this great privilege because they were created to be companions of Jesus. They could be willed for their own sake because they were created for the sake of Jesus.

To conclude this chapter, I want to focus my rejection of the octopus scenario by examining two theological doctrines in the light of the Primacy of Christ. These doctrines are integral to my discussion, but so far I have treated them in a peripheral manner. The first is the doctrine of the image of God. The second is the doctrine of the preexistence of Christ.

Few biblical motifs have generated as much theological heat as the *imago Dei*. The idea that we are created in the image and likeness of God, found in Gen 1:26–27, begs for theological elucidation. Its deceptive simplicity opens up a world of questions. At first glance, the doctrine of the *imago Dei* looks like a definition of human nature, but upon closer inspection, it redirects our gaze toward God. We are the image of the divine, yet when we look closely at ourselves, we see but a mirror. What is it we see? How can we be the image of an imageless God? Without a clear picture of God, the *imago Dei* looks empty and bare.

---

45. *Church Dogmatics* III/1, 203.

46. See Stephen H. Webb, *The Divine Voice: Christian Proclamation and the Theology of Sound* (Grand Rapids: Brazos, 2004) ch. 7.

47. Pope John Paul II, *Mulieris Dignitatem* (1988) par. 7. Online: http://www.vatican.va/holy_father/john_paul_ii/apost_letters/documents/hf_jp-ii_apl_15081988_mulieris-dignitatem_en.html.

Philosophically inclined theologians have argued that the very fact that we can ask who we are provides the best clue to our divinely appointed role in the world. The fact that those who ask questions for a living have been certain that our rationality best reflects God's nature seems like a particularly severe case of wishful thinking. If the mind is image of God, then becoming enlightened by philosophy is the means of salvation.

Some scholars (most notably Theodor Nöldeke and Hermann Gunkel) have rebelled against the Enlightenment equation of the *imago* with reason by suggesting that the *imago Dei* is our physical appearance.[48] They follow the second-century Church Father Irenaeus, better known for his criticisms of the Gnostics, who was one of the few early theologians to argue that the image exists in our material bodies, which thus reveal the archetypal significance of Jesus Christ. Few respectable theologians defend this position today. Henry Morris, whom we've met in previous chapters defending unpopular and seemingly eccentric views, is a particularly eloquent defender of Irenaeus on this point, which we can call the physicalist interpretation of the *imago Dei*. "There is something about the human body, therefore, which is uniquely appropriate to God's manifestation of Himself, and (since God knows all His works from the beginning of the world—Acts 15:18), He must have designed man's body with this in mind. Accordingly, He designed it, not like the animals, but with an erect posture, with an upward gazing countenance, capable of facial expressions corresponding to emotional feelings, and with a brain and tongue capable of articulate, symbolic speech."[49] It is important not to equate Henry Morris with Scotus (or to confuse Henry with Simon Conway Morris). Henry Morris and other fundamentalists can appear to be defending the Primacy of Christ, when in reality they are defending the Primacy of Humankind. Henry Morris comes close to the Scotus position but falls short by attributing the goal of creation to the unique features of the human anatomy. After all, the

---

48. Theodore Nöldeke identified the image with the human body in 1897, and Hermann Gunkel took this position in his commentary on Genesis. See J. Maxwell Miller, "In the 'Image' and 'Likeness' of God," *Journal of Biblical Literature* 91 (1972) 289–304. For the relevant citations of Gunkel and Nöldeke, see Phyllis A. Bird, "Male and Female He Created Them: Gen. 1:27b in the Context of the Priestly Account of Creation," *Harvard Theological Review* 74 (1981) 130 n. 4.

49. Henry M. Morris, *The Genesis Record* (Grand Rapids: Baker, 1976) 4.

biological advantages of the human species could just have easily been developed by another species, like the octopus, for example. The point of creation is to honor Jesus, not humanity, though humanity shares in that honor by being made to be like Jesus. Arguing that humanity is the goal of creation is easily conflated into a theistic interpretation of evolution. The biological point of the Primacy of Christ is that God had humans in mind from the beginning of creation because God chose to enflesh the Son. Only when the Primacy of Christ is properly conceived does it work to refute the octopus scenario.

Most contemporary scholars reject both the Enlightenment and the physicalist interpretations of the *imago Dei*. Indeed, there is a consensus among both biblical scholars and theologians that a functionalist approach does the best justice to Genesis. This position argues that what we do, not what we are, reflects the divine image in which we were created. One of the best defenses of the functionalist interpretation can be found in J. Richard Middleton's *The Liberating Image*.[50] Middleton begins his argument by reflecting on ancient Near East customs that involve the dissemination of royal power. Simply put, it was common for kings to set up statues of themselves as a symbol of their rule. These statues—or images—were a reminder that the physical absence of the king did not prevent his exercise of power. Middleton argues that the author of Genesis both draws from and subverts this practice by democratizing the idea of a king's image. Genesis portrays all humans as "God's living cult statues on earth" (207). The idea that we are living statues representing the most powerful and most just king of all kings is powerful but not without problems. The Genesis creation account, for

---

50. J. Richard Middleton, *Liberating The Image: The Imago Dei in Genesis 1* (Grand Rapids: Brazos, 2005. In discussing this book, I draw from my article, "In Whose Image?" *Books & Culture* 12 (July/August 2006) 10–11. For evidence of the scholarly consensus on functionalism, see Gunnlaugur A. Jónsson, *The Image of God: Genesis 1:26-28 in a Century of Old Testament Research*, trans. Lorraine Svendsen; rev. Michael S. Cheney (Stockholm: Almqvist & Wiksell, 1988). My own views have been influenced by the important essay by Stanley J. Grenz, "Jesus as the Imago Dei: Image-of-God Christology and the Non-Linear Linearity of Theology," *in Journal of the Evangelical Theological Society* 47 (2004) 617–28 as well as the work of Robert Jenson. See, for example, Oliver Crisp, "Robert Jenson on the Pre-Existence of Christ," *Modern Theology* 23 (2007) 27–45, and Simon Gathercole, "Pre-Existence and Freedom of the Son in Creation ad Redemption: An Exposition in Dialogue with Robert Jenson," *International Journal of Systematic Theology* 7 (2005) 38–51.

one thing, portrays God as an artisan and not a king. Moreover, most scholars think that the beginning of Genesis reflects a priestly tradition that would hardly have imagined humans taking the place of, or even sharing in, God's power. Middleton is aware of these problems, but he insists that Genesis plants the seeds of a political revolution. God does not abdicate his power by transferring it to us, Middleton argues, but God does share his power with us. Genesis is "intentionally subversive literature" (186) because it allows ordinary people "to participate (as they are able) in the creative process itself" (287). The *imago Dei* provides the rationale for Israel's egalitarian social organization prior to the monarchy. It is also echoed in the Tower of Babel story, which demonstrates how God intended for political power to be diffuse rather than consolidated by imperial ambition. According to Middleton, the scattering of Babel's population should be interpreted as redemptive, not punitive. Genesis shows us how we are liberated from all forms of oppressive authority because God has chosen to share his authority with us.

Middleton is forthright about how his personal background has shaped his understanding of the *imago Dei*. He grew up white in predominantly black Jamaica, emigrated to Canada and then the United States, where he settled on "Jamericadian" as the best term to describe his cultural hybridity. His experiences of dislocation and alienation have inspired him to treat Gen 1:26–27 as something like a biblical declaration of human rights. Middleton even goes so far as to suggest that the Protestant doctrine of the priesthood of all believers can be found, in latent form, in the *imago Dei*.

Affirming the biblical warrant for depicting humanity as the ruling species is a risky position to take in these politically suspicious times. The problem for me, however, is not that Middleton grants humans so much power but that he appears to do so at the expense of God's prerogatives. Middleton thinks that God takes a big risk in inviting us to share his power. He thus ends up limiting God's power in order to explain humanity's uniqueness. This is a reversal of the traditional theological teaching that human freedom is found in submission to divine rule. In his haste to find a biblical basis for democracy, Middleton has created the *imago Dei* in his own politicized image. Democracies are very good at creating structures of shared power, but democracies do not need to be justified by assuming that God too is a democrat. We can share political power with each other not because God shares power with us but because God the Father shares his power with the Son. Political arrangements should respect the uniqueness of every human being because we all are created in the image of Jesus Christ.

Part of the problem with Middleton's position is that he has severed the anthropological implications of the *imago* from the cosmological. The ambiguity of the *imago Dei* should not incite us to run headlong into anthropological speculations about what constitutes human nature. Instead, it should lead us to contemplate the cosmological significance of Jesus Christ, who is "the exact imprint of God's very being" (Heb 1:3). The cosmological provides the foundation for the anthropological, but only because the cosmos *is* anthropomorphic (or, to say the same thing, Christomorphic). When the anthropological is separated from the cosmological, it is possible to think that the *imago Dei* can be lost altogether due to the consequences of sin. The sixteenth-century Protestant Reformers were so convinced that every part of our humanity is mired in sin that they tended to deny the ongoing vitality of the *imago*. Jesus Christ is like God, they agreed, but our fallen flesh makes us so unlike Jesus that we are not like God at all. From the Scotist perspective, no matter how sinful we are, we are still very much like Jesus, who is very much like God.

Ian A. McFarland appears to understand this linkage between anthropology and cosmology in *The Divine Image*, which can be read as a constructive counterpart to Middleton's Old Testament exegesis.[51] McFarland gets right to the point by observing that Genesis does not say that human beings *are* the image of God. That honor belongs to Jesus alone. To see Jesus is to see God (John 14:9). Nevertheless, McFarland hesitates to embrace the whole person of Jesus, including his body, as the image of God. The reason for his hesitancy is Jesus's maleness. McFarland doubts that we can separate Jesus's maleness from our understanding of his identity, yet he wants to avoid treating his gender as an independent source of our knowledge of the divine. That is, he does not want us to draw any conclusions about God from the fact of Jesus's maleness. This is a legitimate concern, but the fear of making maleness

---

51. Ian A. McFarlan, *The Divine Image: Envisioning The Invisible God* (Minneapolis: Fortress, 2005).

a source of reflection on God should not lead us to detach the *imago Dei* from the fullness of Jesus's humanity. Jesus's garment was not divided by the soldiers, who gambled for it at the foot of the cross, and neither should Jesus's body be divided by theologians for the purpose of safeguarding modern assumptions about gender. When we start picking and choosing what parts of Jesus's life we wish to follow, we run the risk of reducing Jesus to a projection of our own desires. We run the risk, that is, of making copies of Jesus that are little better than forgeries.

McFarland is keenly aware of this danger, but he is willing to risk its consequences. He argues that Jesus has not yet been fully revealed to us, so that we must be on the lookout for further clues to his identity. McFarland draws from the apophatic or negative theology that denies, in opposition to Scotus, that we can know anything directly about God's essence. What we see in Jesus is nothing less than God, he admits, but God remains beyond our knowing. The divine is both revealed and hidden in Jesus. Apophatic Christology argues not only that it takes faith to confess Jesus as the Christ but also that even with graced eyes, there is always more to Jesus than what we think we know.

So how do we find Jesus, if we do not know what we are looking for? What exegesis is for Middleton, epistemology is for McFarland. His emphasis is not so much on Jesus as the image of God as Jesus as the lens through which we see the world. He is less interested in keeping our gaze on Jesus than in figuring out where we look in the world today for his reflection. At times, this leads McFarland to treat Jesus as a blurry or poorly cropped image of God, so that we have to look elsewhere to complete the picture. In other words, we need more information—we need to expand the vision given to us in the Gospels—in order to make a proper identification of the divine. Where we need to find Jesus, it turns out, is in a myriad of practices and places, but most of all in the preferential option for the poor. When we sacrifice for the poor, we discover who Jesus really is.

Compassion for the poor is not only a worthy sentiment but also a biblical commandment. Nonetheless, one wonders if McFarland is not running from the idea that the body of Jesus is itself worthy of our ministrations. For McFarland, the body of Jesus is corporate, not individual. Jesus is the head and all humans comprise his body. We know Jesus best in other peoples' bodies, not his own. McFarland struggles against the dissolution of Jesus's identity in all of its embodied integrity, but the very fact that he has to struggle on this issue demonstrates a weakness in his theology. A more fully trinitarian account of the *imago Dei* would show us how to avoid losing Christ in our neighbors by reminding us that the best way to love our neighbors is to help them find Christ. Jesus Christ, after all, reigns in heaven, while the Holy Spirit prepares us to enter into his presence with perpetual adoration.

Like many theologians today, McFarland is worried about Christians who idolize Jesus. He wants to make faith practical, but can theologians really persuade nonbelievers that they need to believe in the *imago Dei* in order to believe in human rights? The beauty and glory of the *imago Dei* surely has to do with less mundane (and more supernatural) matters. Most theologians, if they pay attention to the human body at all, try to explain how the relationship between humans and the divine excludes any thought of resemblance. While it is true that in heaven we will see Jesus more clearly, it is just as true that when we get to heaven we will see that the incarnate Son really does resemble the Father. Otherwise, the dark glass through which we see Jesus in this life would be so impenetrable as to render us blind. The *imago Dei* assures us that there is an essential correlation between humanity and God that guarantees our basic intuitions into God's nature. The *imago Dei* is mentioned only three times in the Old Testament (Gen 1:26–27, 5:1, and 9:6). If we are to rescue it from hopeless obscurity, it must be taken both literally and christologically. Our bodies look like they do because God decided from eternity to become incarnate in Jesus Christ. We can properly imagine that God is like us because we are like God. In a world saturated with images, we are the only images that count, and we count only because we were made according to the specifications of someone else.

Russell D. Moore, Dean of the School of Theology at The Southern Baptist Theological Seminary, is eloquent about the implications of the Primacy of Christ:

> Human beings don't simply share a theoretical humanness with all the rest of humanity. They are built after the model of a Jewish Carpenter. The perfect image of God we will one day see in the glorified Christ will share with us fingernails and a blood type and eyelids and DNA. He'll wipe away the tears from our eyes,

and He'll do so with *hands*, hands that look like ours. And one can imagine there may be a couple of anti-Semites in line for the White throne Judgment whispering in horror about "how Jewish" the King looks.[52]

This level of physical detail might shock some readers, but the shock should come in recognizing that God created the world out of nothing, but he created us out of the design of the Son.

The *imago Dei* is related to a second theological theme, the pre-existence of Christ. This term, *pre-existence*, is actually something of an oxymoron. The *pre* and *exist* of *preexistence*, often pinned together by a hyphen like siblings stuck in the back seat of a long car ride, add nothing in their combination to our understanding of Jesus Christ. Jesus exists, and he exists prior to everything, so talking about his preexistence is incoherent. He certainly does not exist prior to his own existence, which the term seems to imply. Of course, theologians often retool ordinary words with technical meaning. This word, however, is neither ordinary nor precise. In fact, *preexistence* actually does not apply to anything, because nothing exists prior to Jesus saying so, and he exists like nothing else. It would be better to speak of his eternal existence than his preexistence.

If *preexistence* were merely confusing, it might be worth salvaging, but its damage extends beyond the rules of grammar. Although this word has a long history of theological use, it actually drives a wedge into the life of Jesus Christ. The *pre* of preexistence suggests, in an insidious fashion, that Christians worship a split person if not a split personality: Jesus of Nazareth the miracle worker who had a prior career as the Son of God.

The truth is that Jesus exists in a manner that befuddles the way we are cursed to divide time into before, now, and after. We *preexist* ourselves, to coin a variant of this term, because we are always looking to the receding past to discover who we are. *We* have a problem with time, not Jesus. Rather than view the existence of Jesus Christ through the prism of our fragmented sense of time, we should let the coherent wholeness of his life judge our own. The Son of God mixes together time and eternity as if they were as easily interchangeable as ketchup

---

52. This quote comes from a web commentary by Moore on one of my articles on this topic. Online: www.henryinstitute.org/commentary_read.php?cid=266.

and mustard. That is why we can hope that the rushing blurs of our lives will one day find their rest in him.

Rather than give this term a decent burial, Douglas McCready, in a recent book, tries to give it new life.[53] He explains that there are at least three interpretations of preexistence. The first is real or personal preexistence. It is one of the awkward features of this term that even heretics like Arius, who denied the full deity of Christ, could affirm his preexistence as a lesser deity created before the rest of the world. The second is ideal preexistence, which means that Jesus existed in God's mind prior to the incarnation. McCready shows how trivial this position is, because, given God's omniscience, everything preexists in the divine mind. The third interpretation, called eschatological preexistence, argues that the experience of the resurrection led Jesus's disciples to create the myth of his preexistence. Post-existence gave rise to pre-existence in order to provide balance to the story of Jesus, as if the prolonged ending of the Gospels in his being raised from death into glory required an equally elongated beginning in his coming down from heaven.

In order to combat ideal and eschatological preexistence, McCready conducts a common sense survey of the New Testament, concluding that the earliest writings affirmed personal or real preexistence. This conclusion is confirmed by Simon Gathercole, who has written what should become the standard scholarly treatment of preexistence in the Synoptic Gospels.[54] The title that Jesus most frequently gives himself in the Gospels is the somewhat mysterious Son of Man, which evades scholarly efforts at a precise definition. McCready and Gathercole agree that this designation does not offer much help in thinking about pre-existence, but to me it is utterly decisive. By calling himself the Son of Man, Jesus was alluding to the brotherhood of all humanity in his personal identity. Just as God the Father is the Father of all men, so God the Son is the Son of Man. By being the son of both God *and* man, Jesus demonstrates that God chose to be with us from the very beginning of time. Jesus Christ is not a man but *the* man, which is a crucial distinction.

---

53. Douglas McCready, *He Came Down From Heaven: The Preexistence of Christ and the Christian Faith* (Downers Grove, IL: InterVarsity, 2005).

54. Simon J. Gathercole, *The Preexistent Son: Recovering the Christologies of Matthew, Mark, and Luke* (Grand Rapid: Eerdmans, 2006).

If McCready and Gathercole are right that the earliest Scriptures affirm personal preexistence, then why do so many modern theologians deny it? According to McCready, there are two main reasons. The first is that preexistence can appear to downplay Christ's humanity. Docetism was an ancient heresy that taught that Jesus only appeared to be human. He was really a divine being who used a human body like a costume, discarding it at will. Liberal theologians in the twentieth century liked to argue that Docetism had returned as a hallmark of evangelical Christianity. They alleged that evangelical Christians overemphasize Christ's divinity at the expense of his humanity. That charge, which was rarely substantiated, provided liberals with the cover they needed to sacrifice Christ's divinity to his humanity. For liberal theology, preexistence is incompatible with a fully human Jesus.

What liberal theologians miss is how the eternity of Christ is the only guarantee of the reality and perfection of his human form. The Son of God became incarnate; he did not fill somebody else's body with the invisible spiritual fluid of divinity. He took a role in his own production. The Word does not put on flesh like a man who gets dressed in the morning, although, if we were to use this unsuitable metaphor, we would have to say that God's clothing is a perfect fit. The highest honor we can give to the humanity of Jesus is to recognize that his body is not unconnected to his identity as the Son of God. Otherwise, he would not have been resurrected in his human form.

Modern liberal theology wants to portray Jesus as just like us in order to establish his credentials as a great teacher and moral role model who inaugurated a process of revolutionary social change. The New Testament, however, does not distinguish between the message and the person of Jesus Christ. He himself is the future of the world. When the point of the world comes into final focus, we will recognize his personal features. We will be at home in the end of time because God made his home in him.

The second reason liberal theology tends to deny preexistence is that this concept smacks of metaphysical speculation. Liberalism focuses on morality more than salvation, and moralistic theologians define the divinity of Jesus by what he does, rather than who he is. This is called functional Christology, and it is predicated on the assumption that metaphysics is foreign to Hebraic thought. From this perspective, speculation about preexistence arises only when Christianity becomes mired in Hellenistic culture. What liberal theology misses this time is the way in which being and doing are intimately connected in every life, let alone in the harmonious actions of Jesus. Jesus's mission makes no sense apart from his identity as God.

The only way liberal theologians can coherently deny the doctrine of preexistence is to embrace some form of Adoptionism. Adoptionism portrays Jesus as a very good man upon whom the spirit of God descended at his baptism. Adoptionism was so soundly rejected by the early church that it is something of a straw figure, though McCready demonstrates, in a helpful survey of modern religious thought, how various liberal theologians have adopted Adoptionism, often in a cagey manner, so that the heretical genealogy of their positions cannot be easily traced.

The sad fact is that Adoptionism is not just the temptation of liberalism. Any Christology that goes too far in separating the fully human person of Jesus from the Son of God risks Adoptionism by depicting the flesh of Jesus as a mere appendage to the divine. McCready himself takes this risk by being overly anxious to distance himself from any notion of the preexistence of Jesus's human nature. "Jesus is the name we normally associate with the incarnate One, and it is incorrect to refer to Jesus' existence at any time before the annunciation to Mary" (241). He attributes any talk of the incarnation as the manifestation of a humanity in the heart of God to Platonic metaphysics, but if metaphysics is defined as the study of eternal truths, then preexistence and metaphysics go hand in hand. The Church Fathers legitimately adopted Plato as a providential gift from God. Christianity and Western philosophy are inextricably linked, regardless of attempts, from across the spectrum of modern theology, to sever their relationship.

McCready avoids adoptionism only to fall into another trap of liberal theology when he worries that "teaching Jesus' preexistent humanity would violate one of the major concerns of modern theologians, making his humanity different from everyone else's" (242). The liberal insistence that Jesus is "just like us" has been the cause of much confusion in contemporary theology. Jesus is not "one of the gang" because we are all able to be one with him. He had no need to try to be one of us because we were created to be like him.

For all of his efforts to demonstrate the consistency of the doctrine of preexistence, McCready ends up cleaving Jesus Christ into two—the eternal Christ and the Jesus bound by time. The problem comes down to the idea of personhood. Jesus does not just reveal the identity of the Son. Jesus is the proper name of the Son of God. He is the Son. That means that nothing in the incarnation that manifests Jesus's identity is alien to or an alteration of the eternal Son. Even his very flesh and bones is not an afterthought to God's triune nature.

To avoid even the appearance of Adoptionism, theologians should begin Christology with a simple principle. Do not begin with the characteristics of human flesh that are incompatible with the divine attributes and then subtract them from Jesus in order to obtain what it was about him that preexisted his human form. Instead, begin with the Father begetting the Son, and think of the human form of the Son as the first act of creation, whereby God determined to create a world full of us so that we might be friends of him.

The physical life of Jesus is thus more than an illustration of God's purposes. His body is more than a visual aid. Modern Christians have gone too far in purging the spiritual realm of all analogies with physical matter, while scientists, in the meantime, have been busy discovering just how mysterious matter really is. Many in the scientific community have been influenced by the feminist idea that the world is God's body, which veers into pantheism. The more startling truth is that Jesus is God's body, and the world is what was needed to make creatures like us whom Jesus could call friends (John 15:14).

Some readers might accuse me of downplaying the newness—the Good News—of the incarnation. That news is good because Jesus Christ is God for us, which makes sense only if we realize that we were created for Jesus. The human form is the father's gift to the Son for his glory, which was established before the foundation of the world (John 17:24). The incarnation can be understood as the fullest expression of the Son only if the entire cosmos was created by, through, and for him. The theory of evolution will never be able to explain the origin of human nature in natural terms because humanity lies as the beginning, not the end, of nature. Russell D. Moore is again enviably eloquent: "The reality is not, as the high priests of Darwin tell us, that we are animals aspiring to something great. Instead we are kings and queens who are becoming animal-like."⁵⁵ Sin, as the ancients always taught, is surrender to our lesser, animal natures, which is why the Apostle Paul could admonish the Galatians not to "bite and devour one another" (Gal. 5:15). We are most human when we act like him.

55. Russell D. Moore, "All Things Dark and Terrible," *Touchstone* (June 2007) 22. For my application of the Primacy of Christ to debates about the Mormon Jesus, see my review of Robert L. Millet and Gerald R. McDermott, *Claiming Christ: A Mormon-Evangelical Debate*, in *Reviews in Religion and Theology* 15 (2008) 426–29.

eight

An Ethics of Pets vs. the Darwinian Sublime

Many books have been written about the problem of evil, but most of them deal with the question of why bad things happen to good people. Of course, good people do not deserve to have bad things happen to them, but people who know the goodness of God can hope and trust that God will bring some good out of their suffering. Why bad things happen to animals is a question of an altogether murkier conceptual order. Animals, presumably, are morally innocent. With the exception of pets trained to be members of a human household, we do not hold animals morally accountable for their behavior. We might shoot a wild animal if it dares to attack us, but we ordinarily do not blame it for treating us as a threat. We might admire the skill of predatory animals, but we do not prosecute them for mauling their victims, just as we do not commend herbivores for leaving their neighbors alone. Animals do not have a choice with regard to their instincts; that is what makes them animals. But they do experience pain, and some animals, presumably, can experience that pain in ways that are not totally dissimilar to our own. While we should not exaggerate the brutish and competitive nature of their life in the wild, we should not blind ourselves to their suffering either.

Subjected to even the most cursory theological scrutiny, the problem of animal suffering quickly breaks down into a variety of boggling issues. If predators are the primary cause of animal pain, why did God create them? If God did create them, when did he do so? If they did not come into existence until after the fall, how did that happen? If God created them from nothing after the fall, wasn't this, in effect, an entirely new second creation? If there is no second creation, then how did the

An Ethics of Pets vs. the Darwinian Sublime

peaceful animals of the Garden of Eden become so violent after the fall? Did they just naturally turn that way, did demons intervene, or did God push them toward violence as a way of punishing humans for their sin? Do any of these options make any sense?[1]

Given these options, it is no wonder that theologians treat animal suffering as an abstruse issue that lends itself too readily to tortuous speculation. People in the pews, however, know better. They frequently face animal suffering firsthand in the lives of their companion animals. And animal suffering, just like human suffering, cries out for some kind of answer or explanation.

Theologians call any explanation of evil a theodicy, but since orthodox Darwinians want to have nothing to do with theology, they fiercely deny that their theory has any resemblance to a theodicy. They are right to be so defensive. If Darwinism did provide a theodicy, then it would be at least in part a branch of theology and thus subject to theological analysis and evaluation. Like most Darwinians, Kenneth Miller, a biologist who teaches at Brown University, wants his evolutionary theory straight, not mixed with theology. He denies not only that Darwinism seeks to explain animal suffering but also that there is even any problem in need of explanation. "Could [natural] evil really be so cruel as to require such an apology?" He thinks not. Cruelty, like beauty, he writes, is relative. Nature is not the problem; we are.[2]

Nonetheless, we too are a part of nature, and many of us are not content to set animal suffering aside as a brute fact of nature that should not be taken personally. Darwinism itself, by opening up unimaginable lengths of prehistoric time and the spectacle of millions of species falling victim to incessant biological warfare, exacerbates the problem of animal suffering by portraying nature as a machine designed to extract the maximum pain out of the animal kingdom by the most devious means. Darwinism also, however, attributes this suffering to ironbound laws of scientific necessity. Animals suffer because they have to, and when something is necessary, it is easier to accept. Even many modern theologians have taken advantage of Darwinism to clear God's name

---

1. One of the best treatments of this issue is Michael Lloyd, "Are Animals Fallen?" in *Animals on the Agenda*, ed. Andrew Linzey and Dorothy Yamamoto (London: SCM, 1998) 147–60.

2. Kenneth R. Miller, *Finding Darwin's God: A Scientists Search for Common Ground between God and Evolution* (San Francisco: HarperCollins, 1999) 245.

from the charge of animal cruelty. God does not make animals suffer; evolution does. Doesn't that make the problem go away?

To his credit, Darwin took animal suffering more seriously than many present-day members of the biological and theological guilds. As I pointed out in chapter 1, Darwin's kindliness to animals is often used by his supporters as evidence for how benign his theory is. This is the case, for example, with George Levine's book, *Darwin Loves You*. Portraits of Darwin in his youth often emphasize how susceptible he was to the pain of others, which was one of the reasons he decided not to pursue a career in medicine. In fact, he was so affected by the suffering of animals that he found himself disbelieving that God could have designed nature. We could call this the argument from squeamishness. Nature is just too gross to be the produce of a perfectly benevolent designer.

Darwin felt so strongly about animal suffering that he formulated a stark either-or in order to force his readers to make a decision about his theory. Either God or natural selection is responsible for the glut of suffering in the world. Darwin assumed that, if you had to choose between the two, any reasonable person would rather blame natural selection than God. Darwin thought that belief in God only made animal suffering all the more incomprehensible and religion all the more reprehensible. Darwin thus treated his theory as a theodicy. It solved his own personal struggle with the biological wasteland that his travels and speculations were beginning to uncover. The question is whether Darwin's theory of evolution is really so consoling. Indeed, did it work for Darwin himself?

By the standards of his own theory, Darwin should have resisted being sentimental about animals. If animal suffering is built into the fabric of nature, and if that fabric has no inherent design, then animal suffering has no discernible pattern or shape. It simply is, and thus it is not worth our grief or our anguish. That Darwin could not overcome his own sentimentality is evidence, perhaps, of how far he was from being a complete Darwinian. More than just sentimental, Darwin was an animal lover, at least when it came to the animal Victorians most loved—the dog. In the *Descent of Man*, he favorably compares the intelligence of dogs to that of "savages" and uses the common descent of all life forms to justify anthropomorphic descriptions that would make modern scientists cringe. To take one comment, Darwin attributes moral motivation to dogs: "A great dog scorns the snarling of a little dog, and this may be called magnanimity." Darwin even thought that dogs have a rudimentary form of religious piety, since they are disturbed by noises or movements even when there is nobody there. Darwin borrowed from a trope with a long literary history when he argued that the devotion of dogs is not different in kind from humanity's devotion to God. He thus interpreted dogs in religious categories, even though he had concluded that his theory invalidates religion. Darwin's sentimentalism did not stop with dogs. "All animals," he suggests, "feel wonder, and many exhibit curiosity."[3] Today's Darwinians read such passages and instinctively think that Darwin was comparing animals to humans in order to demonstrate that human behavior is reducible to its lowest biological level, but Darwin was also trying to promote animals to the rank of humanity. He kept trying to draw moral lessons from nature to the very end. In his last book, *The Formation of Vegetable Mold, through the Action of Worms* (1881), Darwin humbly knights these lowly creatures with a form of intelligence not completely unlike our own.

The worse Darwin portrayed nature's struggles, it seems, the more he compensated by empathizing with animals and even identifying with them. Stanley Edgar Hyman has argued that *On the Origin of Species* should be read as an epic poem in which anthropomorphized species heroically trek through the tragic terrain of human history. "Darwin's mystery," he writes, "is a kind of totemic brotherhood, a consubstantiality with all organic beings, resembling St. Paul's 'every one members one of another.'"[4] Darwin was not content to attribute animal suffering to pointless biological forces. He wanted his theory to provide a robust alternative to Christian theology. While claiming to be merely a scientist, with a sleight of hand he replaced the traditional morality based on human uniqueness with a new morality based on the kinship of all animals. The trick might work for some people, but it is still a trick. If the evolution of species is a struggle for existence, then an idealistic portrait of global harmony cannot come from biology. The only way

---

3. Charles Darwin, *Descent of Man* (Modern Languages edition, no date), 450. For a more detailed discussion of Darwin and dogs, see Stephen H. Webb, *On God and Dogs: A Christian Theology of Compassion for Animals* (New York: Oxford University Pres, 1998) 115–23.

4. Stanley Edgar Hyman, *The Tangled Web: Darwin, Marx, Frazer, and Freud as Imaginative Writers* (New York: Atheneum, 1962) 42.

humans can be called upon to make sacrifices for other species is if we are unique. If humans are not unique, then we might be part of one large family of animals, but that kinship does not mean that we will treat our relatives with respect. Darwin's theory, in fact, suggests just the opposite.

Darwin's keen awareness of the inner life of animals laid the foundation for a full-blown moral philosophy that is still being advanced and developed today. His idea of the kinship of all animals has had a particularly tremendous cultural influence in America, where it has provided the moral worldview for the environmental movement. Environmentalism ranges from the subversive arguments of "deep ecology," which pit nature's interests against our own, to the more tame fare of a feminist ethic of caring, which argues that women are more in tune to nature than men. The idea that unites all of these points on the environmental spectrum is that mutual dependence and interconnection are the wellspring for moral action. The more we recognize our dependence on the environment and our connections to all other organisms, environmentalists contend, the more we will be willing to act out of other-regard, rather than self-regard.

The ethic of universal kinship, with its echo of the peaceable kingdom proclaimed throughout the Bible, is a long way from the tragic necessity of animal suffering. It is, in fact, an attempt to articulate a middle way between Darwinian tragedy and Christian hope. Rather than placing the ultimate reconciliation of all things at the end of history, however, the kinship ethic claims to find its principles firmly rooted in nature. The flaw in this move is glaring. If we are a part of nature, why wouldn't we want to play by nature's rules? Only if we rule nature, which Genesis teaches under the rubric of stewardship, can we be expected to tame and discipline our natural instincts. We can exercise restraint and responsibility toward other animals only if we transcend our animal selves—especially since animals are much more endangered by us than we are by them.

Darwinism (unadulterated by Christian mercy) and Christianity (with the book of Genesis still intact) thus present two competing models of how humans should treat non-human animals. I have argued throughout this book that Darwinism has a tragic view of nature, but as Stanley Edgar Hyman suggests, the Darwinian story of evolution also takes an epic form. The categories of tragedy and epic are, of course, drawn from the world of theater and literature, which might suggest to some that they have no place in the study of biology. Then again, as I argued in chapter 1, biologists have never been able to purge metaphors and morality from their portraits of nature. In fact, literary categories are crucial for understanding the difference between a Darwinian and a Christian ethic. Hans Urs von Balthasar, the great Swiss Catholic theologian, has argued that any theory of human or natural history must utilize dramatic nomenclature. Celia Deane-Drummond, in one of the best theological books on evolution, has shown how von Balthasar identifies the genre of the epic with interpretive models of history that take a long and distant view of events.[5] Epic narratives cover a lot of ground, and the further removed the story is from the events it is narrating, the more those events appear to conform to universal laws and repeatable patterns. The perspective of the epic for von Balthasar tends toward determinism because it is resigned to impersonal forces that cannot be controlled. Applying von Balthasar's ideas to biology, it becomes immediately clear that the deep time of geology lends itself to an epic reading. Who can fathom it? Up close, animals and humans are revealed as agents with their own freedom, dignity, and mystery, but in the epic of deep geological time all organisms appear to be ruled by the same necessary laws. As a result, the differences between humans and non-human animals all but disappear, as species drift into the haze of randomness and violence.

Christianity too has a tragic view of history, but while Darwinian tragedy tends toward the epic, Christianity, with its hope in redemption, tends toward an appreciation of the comedic. Christianity teaches that humans have authority over nature, even though that authority is fleeting and easily bound, limited, and subverted. Like the best of comedic plays, history shows how humanity is its worse enemy, and human plans often end up thwarted by unintended consequences. Nonetheless, humans cross the stage of nature as dramatic characters with real purpose, freedom, and agency. Evolution is part of that drama, but it does not steal the show.

5. Celia Deane-Drummond, *Christ and Evolution: Wonder and Wisdom* (Minneapolis: Fortress, 2009). For von Balthasar's discussion of epic, see Hans Urs von Balthasar, *Theo-Drama*, vol. 2: *Dramatis Personae: Man in God*, trans. Graham Harrison (San Francisco: Ignatius, 1990) 54–59.

The Dome of Eden

Many critics of Darwinism have termed it a worldview, but few have analyzed the contours of its aesthetic relationship to nature. Darwinians view animal suffering as both tragic and epic (or as a tragedy-tending-toward-epic) because such suffering is simultaneously necessary, horrible, and beneficial. Animal suffering is necessary for the progression of life, horrible to contemplate, but ultimately beneficial for the survivors of the struggle. Tragedy is the dramatic genre that treats the horrible as pedagogically useful. The sacrifice of animals on the altar of evolution evokes and purges extreme emotions of sorrow and pity. Epic takes the long view, which encourages the observer, who is tempted to flee from horror, to stand fast. The tragic-epic experience of nature is more than a satisfaction of morbid curiosity. Persisting in the face of nature becomes, in the Darwinian worldview, a moving aesthetic experience.

I want to take this literary analysis a bit further by arguing that the paradigmatic Darwinian experience of nature can be summed up in the aesthetic category of the sublime. The German philosopher Immanuel Kant was one of the first philosophers to define the sublime as a particular kind of experience of the beautiful. In his *Critique of Judgment* (1790), Kant connected the sublime to a mental state that is rare yet profoundly important for human experience.[6] The sublime, he argued, is an experience of something so great and boundless (think of the Grand Canyon) that it transcends our categories of perception. Yet the very fact that we have this experience intimates that we are able to understand things that overwhelm us. Resisting the urge to flee the Grand Canyon as we creep up to its edge demonstrates that the power of our understanding is not futile. Our capacity for reflection tells us that our minds are up to the challenge of nature, no matter how daunting it is to comprehend. The Kantian sublime is, after the initial stirring of the soul, serene and tranquil, while what I am calling the Darwinian sublime is more awful and dreadful, yet both pertain to experiences that threaten and flatter us in equal doses. Just as Kant's speculations provided impetus to German romanticism, Darwin should be located in the great tradition of English romantic poetry, especially William Wordsworth, who also tried to synthesize the terrible and the pleasur-

---

6. Immanuel Kant, *Critique of Judgment*, trans. James Creed Meredith (Oxford: Clarendon Press, 1986).

able experience of nature. The sublime, it is important to note, does not attribute the safety and assurance that we feel when we experience nature to God; it attributes our feeling of perseverance to ourselves. We can accept animal suffering without submitting that suffering to God because we are able to turn that suffering into an ennobling and uplifting experience. Darwin invites us to see nature as an "entangled bank," the famous metaphor he used in the conclusion of the *Origin*. He wanted to place animal suffering in the context of an interwoven whole. His theory of evolution intensifies our experience of the boundless depths of natural cruelty while also fortifying the observer who might be tempted to turn away.

Christian morality looks at nature from a more hopeful and thus comedic perspective. In fact, the Bible is full of compassion for animals, from the Mosaic covenant to Noah's ark. The covenant God made with the Hebrews spelled out a variety of obligations regarding domesticated animals. The Fourth Commandment, for example, specifies that the Sabbath, the day of rest, is meant for animals as well as humans, and the prohibition of yoking an ox and an ass together reflects a deep recognition of the mutual dependence of humans and animals. Even wild animals are included in this compassion, as indicated by the regulation to let the land lie fallow in the seventh years, so that first the poor and then the wild animals can use it (Exod 23:10–11). The Old Testament Prophets often portrayed animal suffering as the one of the signs of the coming end. Joel identifies with their pain: "How the animals groan! The herds of cattle wander about because there is not pasture for them; even the flocks of the sheep are dazed" (1:18). One of the most memorable passages in the Bible imagines the redemption of the world as a return to Eden's peace and harmony: "The wolf shall live with the lamb, the leopard shall lie down with the kid, the calf and the lion and the fatling together, and a little child shall lead them" (Isa 11:6). This raises the question of whether the wolf can peacefully co-exist with the lamb and still be a wolf, rather than a lamb, but if God can change our natures while preserving our identities then animals do not raise a special theological problem. The point of this verse is that violence is not essential to any animal nature, even though it takes an act of literary imagination to see how this is so.

The Dome of Eden

The story of Noah rescuing the animals from the flood is hardly an anomaly. The rabbis developed their concept of animal compassion—*tsaar baalei hayyim*, which means do nothing to contribute to the pain of living creatures—directly from their reading of the Hebrew law and prophets. The Bible favors the peaceful animals of the lamb and the dove over the hawk and the lion. In Christianity, this preference is concentrated in the life and teachings of Jesus. The Holy Spirit descends as a dove at Jesus's baptism, and the Bible identifies Jesus as the Lamb of God in the Book of Revelation. Jesus talks about his Father's love for the sparrows (Luke 12:6, Matt 10:29), compares himself to a hen gathering her brood under her wings (Matt 23:37), and teaches that it is acceptable to pull an animal out of a pit even on the Sabbath (Luke 14:5). He even imagines a dog tenderly licking a poor man's sores (Luke 16:21).

Nevertheless, actual pets in the Bible are rare. The Bible was written by and for an agricultural community that knew the danger of wild animals and the value of domesticated ones, but most poor people had little time or money to spend on animals kept for personal pleasure alone. Yet the logic of animal compassion in the Bible can break through these social restraints in remarkable ways. When the Prophet Nathan wanted to rebuke King David, he told him the story of a poor man's lamb. "It used to eat of his meager fare, and drink from his cup, and lie on his bosom, and it was like a daughter to him" (2 Sam 12:3). A rich man steals and slaughters it, Nathan says, to which David replies, "As the Lord lives, the man who has done that deserves to die" (12:5). Of course, David is the one who has stolen something that was not his and deserves to be punished, but the story Nathan tells is effective precisely because it played on David's sympathy for a man who treated his favorite lamb just like a pet.

As I noted in chapter 5, Darwinians argue that the so-called lower life forms provide the most basic clues for how even the most complex life forms are organized. I now want to argue that from a biblical perspective, pets, not microbes, provide the clues for the nature and destiny of animals. I argued in chapter 6 that Jesus Christ is the foundation of the world, and I pointed out that this is counterintuitive to the way most theologians typically think of the incarnation as an emergency reaction to human sin. Now I want to argue that if Jesus Christ is prior to creation, then in a similar way, peaceful, domesticated animals are prior to wild, carnivorous ones. There is a primacy of pets just as there is a Primacy of Christ.

The priority of pets appears to make no sense from the perspective of evolution, of course. Domestication is a very late development in biological history. Moreover, peaceful animals are the exception, not the rule in the struggle for existence. Even domesticated animals are peaceful only to the extent that we have bred their wildness out of them. We have made them our servants, or at least bred them to submit to our authority in some way. This process is laden with risk because anytime one species exercises power over another, even in the case of humans, exploitation and abuse result. Nonetheless, breeding should not be reduced to its lowest motives. Steven Budiansky, in *The Covenant of the Wild*, has argued that domestication is a two-way process.[7] Animals choose domestication because there are significant benefits at stake. Horses would be extinct today if they had not been tamed. Budiansky calls this process "co-evolution," and it is not just certain animals that have benefited. Domesticating animals has, in a significant way, domesticated humans too. Taking responsibility for and working with various species has been a key development in what makes us human. These experiences have taught us the value of cooperation and the importance of respect for the natural world.

Darwin's love of dogs led him to reflect on the successes of dog breeding, which in turn was one of the inspirations for his theory of evolution. He saw in dog breeding a kind of model for how evolution works. The similarities between the two, however, are superficial. Pet breeding is done with an intentional and passionate purpose, motivated, at its best, by a love of animal life. Evolution, according to Darwin, unfolds without direction or plan. Pet breeding works in opposition to the way evolution advances by chance and struggle. How could pets, then, represent the origin and destiny of all animals?

The study of companion animals, which for a long time has been little more than an interdisciplinary area of study, has only recently become a field of its own. Called anthrozoology, the study of the relationship between people and animals is still seeking its identity, not least because there is no consensus on how to define, let alone study, com-

---

7. Stephen Budiansky, *The Covenant of the Wild: Why Animals Chose Domestication* (New York: William Morrow, 1992).

panion animals. Methodological anxiety has led the editors of a recent groundbreaking volume to articulate what can only be called a theology of animal studies. "Poised as we are on the brink of environmental catastrophe," they write, "the importance of establishing or reinforcing this sense of connection and identity with other lives can hardly be over-emphasized."[8] This is a field, then, with a mission. As with all theologies, anthrozoology has a story to tell about our past and a message of hope to preach about our future. Evidently, humans carry in their genes the memory of a relationship with animals that is healing and comforting. We have fallen from a more innocent and intuitive knowledge of animals, these scholars preach, but the proper study of animals today can save us from our alienation and isolation. Anthrozoology can also save the animals from human abuse by demonstrating their value as companions in life's journey.

Moral urgency is one way to get a new academic field the attention it deserves. Whether basing the study of pets on moral grounds will earn this field scientific credibility remains to be seen, but the fact is that the study of pets is an essentially moral enterprise. After all, pets are what we have made of them. We cannot remove ourselves and our obligations from this object of study. What this means in practice is that the study of companion animals is typically dominated by a psychological paradigm that tends to view pets as a function of human desire and need. The social sciences tend to treat the study of pets as really a study of human behavior, replacing the *zoo* with the *anthro*. This reduces pet keeping to a narcissistic and dysfunctional activity. Christianity has a different story to tell, as well as a different morality to defend.

Everything we know from science tells us that wild animals came before domesticated ones. The first dogs, for example, were probably adolescent or injured wolves who took the leap of joining the human circle gathered around a fire. Christianity defies this chronology by reversing the historical order of wild to domestic. Genesis teaches that the original nature of animals is peaceful, not violent, so thinking about animals according to the order of God's intentions, dogs have priority

---

8. Anthony L. Podberscek, Elizabeth S. Paul and James A. Serpell, eds., *Companion Animals and Us: Exploring the Relationships between People and Pets* (Cambridge: Cambridge University Press, 2000) 2. For the best literary and aesthetic reflection on pets, see Alice Kuzniar, *Melancholia's Dog: Reflections on our Animal Kinship* (Chicago: University of Chicago Press, 2006).

An Ethics of Pets vs. the Darwinian Sublime

over wolves. Perhaps this reversal can be seen more clearly if we imagine a spatial hierarchy of animals, with those at the top being closest to God's ordering of the world and those at the bottom being furthest away. From a Christian perspective, dogs, taken as emblematic of any animal that becomes a part of the human family, are the upper limit of the animal world. As the most domesticated species, they represent the original design as well as the destiny of all animals.

The lower limit of the animal world, from this theological perspective, would be insects. That might sound like a surprising claim, but ancient theologians and philosophers frequently puzzled over the meaning of insects. The historian Robert Grant has even suggested that the Church Fathers developed an "apologetic entomology." That is, they had to defend God from the charge of having made a whole class of animals that have no purpose other than to be annoying and destructive. They did so by adopting from the Stoics the idea that everything about the world is arranged to comfort, sustain, challenge, and instruct us. This idea came to be known as the Great Chain of Being, because it portrays all the pieces of nature as tightly interlocked. All parts of nature not only lock together but also stretch upward, vertically and hierarchically, so that the lower links serve the higher. Nature is completely full with every kind of thing that God found fit to be created and it is ordered in such a way that humanity can exercise stewardship over its vast resources. In the words of St. Basil the Great, the fourth century Doctor of the Church, "God created nothing unnecessary or lacking anything that is necessary."[9] It follows that every kind of animal serves as a useful link in the chain. Even those animals that do not serve our immediate good, Christians reasoned, must serve God's. Domesticated animals are clearly intended for our use, the ancients agreed, but wild animals too play their role, because they are meant to chasten and humble us.

Many insects, however, appear to be unchained in their vast numbers and their uselessness. Even so, the Bible reveals how God can use even the humblest of creatures to advance the divine plan. Flies were let loose in the plagues against Egypt (Exod 8:20–24), and moths, which can be so damaging to clothing, pop up repeatedly in the Bible as a

---

9. Robert M. Grant, *Early Christians and Animals* (New York: Routledge, 1999) 30 and 31. For a medieval theological treatment of insects in terms of the doctrine of providence, see William of Auvergne, *The Providence of God Regarding the Universe*, trans. Roland J. Teske (Milwaukee: Marquette University Press, 2007), ch. 2.

warning to the transitory nature of human treasure (Jas 5:2). The Bible certainly recognizes that insects can be a complete nuisance. Leviticus announces what seems to be a truism rather than a commandment: "All winged insects that walk upon all fours are detestable to you" (11:20). Nonetheless, perhaps because they are so annoying, they can also be morally instructive. Proverbs advises, "Go to the ant, you lazybones; consider its ways and be wise" (6:6). The Church Fathers also praised bees, not only for their industry and utility but also because one among them is their king (queen, we now know), which exemplifies the kingship of Jesus Christ.

Not all Christians found insects worthy of reflection. The Gnostics were a heretical movement that divided the cosmos into good (the spiritual realm) and evil (the material), and they understood salvation to be an escape from the treacheries of mundane existence. They thought an evil divinity was the creator of matter, and what could be earthier than insects? Tertullian makes fun of Marcion, one of the arch-heretics of ancient Christianity, for being afraid of bugs. Tertullian tells Marcion that there is much to learn from the labor of the smallest creatures, and that complaining about them is a sign of ingratitude and ignorance.

> Now, when you make merry with those minute animals, which their glorious Maker has purposely endured with a profusion of instincts and resources—thereby teaching us that greatness has its proofs in lowliness, just as (according to the apostle) there is power even in infirmity—imitate, if you can, the cells of the bee, the hills of the ant, the webs of the spider, and the threads of the silkworm; endure, too, if you know how, those very creatures which infest your couch and house, the poisonous ejections of the blister-beetle, the spikes of the fly, and the gnats sheath and sting.[10]

Tertullian is as interested in chastising Marcion as he is apologizing for insects.

Against the Gnostics, orthodox theologians taught that the one true God, not a lesser, inferior deity, created all things and pronounced them good, which served as a check on Christian reactions to the puzzle of insects. But what if insects were not a part of the Garden? After all,

---

10. Tertullian, *Against Marcion*, in *The Ante-Nicene Fathers*, ed. Alexander Roberts and James Donaldson, Vol. 3 (Grand Rapids: Eerdmans, 1968) 280.

An Ethics of Pets vs. the Darwinian Sublime

the Garden was lush, food was abundant, and Adam and Eve did not have to struggle for their supper. In fact, most Christians found it hard to imagine that God populated the Garden of Eden with insects and their like. Insects were a sign of the fall, not only by their destructiveness but also by their origin. Most people believed, until modern science proved otherwise, that worms and insects were generated by filth and carrion. This alleviated God of the burden of being accused of making such creatures, although Augustine was quick to point out that if filth has generating qualities, it is only because God permitted it. Augustine, who like Tertullian was convinced that even the harmful aspects of the world must be beneficial to us, if only as penalty for our pride, confessed to ignorance about insects. "I admit that I am ignorant as to why mice and frogs were created, or flies or worms, but I see that all things in their kind are beautiful even though because of our sins many seem hostile to us."[11] The ethical imperative for Christians regarding even the lowliest of animals is to seek out their beauty even when they are most repulsive to us.

Insects provide a test case for how far Christians can go in imagining Eden as a real place that was, nonetheless, a paradise. Put differently, insects lie at the lower limit of the Christian capacity to imagine the animal kingdom as a good product of divine providence. I have argued all along that it makes little sense to think of God creating new creatures after the fall or changing the ontological conditions of how nature works. Rather than saying that certain kinds of animals, like insects and predators, were not in the Garden, it is better to think of the animals of Eden as nonviolent prototypes of what their biological correlates became. Adam and Eve certainly would not have experienced the fear of being the victim of predation in the Garden, a fear which is one of humanity's oldest and most terrible.[12] That we refuse to be reduced to meat indicates just how viscerally we grasp our own uniqueness. The Bible responds to this anxiety by assuring us that the Lord is the good shepherd, though in the comforts of our homes we forget that shepherds are trained to battle and defeat animals that prey on their flocks (John 10:11–12). Wolves belong in a sheep hold as little as a snake belongs in

---

11. Quoted in Grant, *Early Christians and Animals*, 33.
12. See David Quammen, *The Man-Eating Predator in the Jungles of History and the Mind* (New York: Norton, 2003).

Eden. Humans have domesticated wolves over the centuries, turning them into dogs, so the idea that God can tame lions in the world to come (Isa 11:6) should not be beyond our imagination (it wasn't beyond Isaiah's). Moses fought poisonous snakes in the wilderness with a bronze pole that had the image of a serpent on it (Numbers 21:4-9), and Jesus spent time in the wilderness before his ministry began, where "he was with the wild beasts" (Mark 1:13). That same verse says that the angels waited on him, so presumably he calmed the wild animals by exercising his rightful authority over them.[13] Revelation acknowledges the role of predation in the economy of salvation by portraying Christ not only as the lamb but also as the lion (Rev 5:5, following in the line of Judah, Gen 49:9), capable of devouring every enemy.

True, the serpent was in the garden, and serpents are predators, but the serpent entered the Garden from the world outside of it. Nonetheless, placing the serpent and all other wild animals outside of the Dome should not be taken to mean that they are completely outside of God's providential care. The Bible is clear that God loves and watches over all animals. The book of Job, in fact, is the most moving and provocative reflection on God's providential relationship to animals in all of world literature.[14] The images of untamed animals are meant to test the limits of our understanding of both God and nature. Some of the most disturbing images come in chapter 39. God, speaking from a whirlwind in order to demonstrate that he is the master of every natural phenomenon, makes it very clear that the crouching of goats when they give birth, presumably in pain, is something he knows all about (39:3). God goes on to ask Job if he understands why the Ostrich "deals cruelly with its young, as if they were not its own" (v. 16). Of the hawk, God says, "Its young ones suck up blood; and where the slain are, there it is" (v. 30). Elsewhere God says he provides the prey for the ravens (38:41).

---

13. For criticism of the idea that Mark represents Jesus as a new Adam in his relationship to wild animals, see John Paul Heil, "Jesus with the Wild Animals in Mark 1:13," *Catholic Biblical Quarterly* 68 (2006) 63-78.

14. For a reading of Job that is similar to mine, see Eleonore Stump, *Faith and the Problem of Evil: The Stob Lectures of Calvin College and Seminary, 1989-99* (Grand Rapids: Stob Lectures Endowment, 1999) 1-41, and the careful summary and criticism of Stump's position by John R. Schneider, "Seeing God Where the Wild Things Are: An Essay on the Defeat of Horrendous Evil," in *Christian Faith and the Problem of Evil*, ed. Peter van Inwagen (Grand Rapids: Eerdmans, 2004) 226-62.

An Ethics of Pets vs. the Darwinian Sublime

Job anticipates by centuries the Darwinian argument that God could not possibly have created animals that eat their young in all manner of ghastly ways.

Job's descriptions of animal power and cruelty can seem to be anticipations of the Darwinian Sublime. God appears in the sublimity of a whirlwind and appears to want Job to marvel at nature's magnificent indifference to the standards of biblical morality. The Darwinian Sublime, however, admires natural evil because there is no choice to do otherwise. It leaves the observer of nature feeling mentally, though not physically, superior to the cruelties that only humankind can try to fathom. The sublime in Job is of another order. All of the descriptions of animal power in Job are meant to humble the human heart and enlarge our understanding of God's majesty. They are meant to leave us trusting that God is in charge of nature and thus nature has a purpose, no matter how purposeless it seems.

Identifying nature in all of its gory with God's intentions would be a hasty misreading of Job. Job clearly presents God as exercising providential governance of wild animals. Their ways are hidden to us, but not to God. Wild animals, thus, are not really all that wild. They appear wild to us, but not to God, and God's reality is the one that counts. This is the opposite of the Darwinian Sublime. The point of God's speech from the whirlwind is that God sees wild animals in the same way God sees us: with sympathy and understanding. Put in Christian terms, God looks at wild animals through the eyes of Jesus, who suffered an animal-like death on the cross. The wildness of the animal kingdom defies our sensibility, but not God's. God governs the wild animals, which means that they cannot be wild in any absolute sense. Their wildness is not what animals ultimately are, just as it is not what animals originally were. Wild animals appear to be viciously persecuting an agenda contrary to God's plan, but Christians have faith that God's plan will triumph and that even the wildest of animals will someday be servants of God's intentions.

Even the Leviathan, a monstrous water creature that some scholars identify with the crocodile, is not beyond God's providential reach. The section on the Leviathan in Job chapter 41 makes some startling claims about God's relationship to wild animals. The chapter begins with a taunt: "Can you draw out Leviathan with a fishhook, or press down its tongue with a cord?" (v. 1). God goes on to ask, "Will it make a covenant with you to be taken as your servant forever?" (v. 3) That verse is significant because it implies that the destiny of the Leviathan is to be embraced and tamed by God. The next verse is also crucial: "Will you play with it as with a bird, or will you put it on leash for your girls?" (v. 5). The author of this text is now having quite a bit of fun at the expense of his readers, but the meaning is clear. To God, the Leviathan is nothing more than a pet. If more evidence of my interpretation is needed, look at Ps 104:25-26. Here the Psalmist shows that the most fearsome creature to us is little more than an amusement to God. "Here is the great immeasurable sea, in which move creatures beyond number. Here ships sail to and fro, here is Leviathan whom thou hast made thy plaything." This passage is rhetorically effective, but it is not an exaggeration. It is a moving portrait of a God who seeks companionship even from violent animals. All animals are meant to be in communion with both God and us. In fact, it is significant that the only wild animal that Genesis specifies that God created is the sea monsters (Gen 1:21). Sea monsters, of course, would have been no threat to Adam and Eve or their Garden. It is as if Genesis is saying that sea monsters were not in the beginning really monsters, because they could not harm anyone. They could only be monstrously free in the deep seas, much to God's delight. All animals, from the perspective of Genesis, even those that appear cruel to us, are joyful to behold when seen from the perspective of what God intended them to be.

Job is daring *not* because it portrays the wildness of animals. It is daring because it couples that portrait with the insistence that these animals are still under the watch of God's providential care. Job is the most daring book in the Old Testament because it strives to push God's providence beyond all human boundaries. We do not understand why God permits so much violence in the natural world, or how that violence ultimately fits into the divine plan, any more than we understand why God permits so much human evil in the world. In both cases, Satan is the immediate cause of evil, but God let's us know that, far from being passive, he is taking sides. God providentially rescues meaning from the meaningless events in our lives and the disasters that befall us. God can do this with animals too. The doctrine of providence should not be confused, however, with the doctrine of creation. God creates all good

An Ethics of Pets vs. the Darwinian Sublime

things, and God can work through all things, whether they are good or evil, but God's ability to redeem evil does not mean that God creates evil.

Listen more closely to the whirlwind and it becomes clear what God is and is not saying. God takes credit for all the fantastic spectacles of nature in order to chastise Job and his friends for presuming to know too much about the reasons behind God's actions. Job, the hero of the book, is inflicted by natural disasters and evil of all sorts. God is saying that even if we find natural evil baffling, God can use those disasters and that evil in ways that transcend our understanding. He is not saying that he is directly responsible for the cruel things that animals do. He does not cause their cruelty, though he can help them make the best of their situation. Notice, for example, how God insists that he is the one who provides prey for the raven. There is an echo of this in other passages in some of the psalms, where the singer praises God for all of nature's wonders, including lions. "The young lions roar for their prey, seeking their food from God" (Ps 104:21). These passages are not saying that God approves of predatory behavior, nor are they saying that God does not side with the victims of violence, whether it is caused by humans or other animals. These passages say that God feeds the hungry, even when the hungry are predators! In other words, even when bad things happen to innocent animals, God is still in charge. God does not relinquish his control over nature just because it is fallen, and God does not abandon wild animals just because they are predators.

Although some theologians argue that Job anticipates the modern environmental movement by accepting and celebrating nature in all of its interconnected complexity, this is an anachronistic and misguided reading. Job is not conveying a gentle message of ecological harmony. Job is proclaiming the almost terrifying majesty of God, not the consoling balance of nature. Keep in mind that Job is not rationalizing the sorry state of nature. God, in speaking from the whirlwind, is not explaining to Job why nature must be the way it is. Indeed, the entire book of Job is a diatribe against the kinds of explanations, like Darwinism, that make nature's cruelties tragically necessary. Job is a stop sign for any attempt to speculate about God's responsibility for evil because God is not so responsible. Recall that the story of the book concerns Job's friends' assurances that God must be punishing Job for something he did. This response is not commended by the text, nor is it acceptable to God. The source of evil is mysterious, God says; be careful when you look for that source, because you might not be pleased with what you find. The Book of Job is certainly not saying that the wildness of nature is the way things should be, nor is it saying that this is the way things will always be. God is asserting his power to work through things as they are to make them what they should be.

Lest we forget the most important part of the context for the book, Satan plays an essential role in this story. Although scholars debate the place of this text in the ongoing development of how Israel understood Satan, the book is clear that it is Satan, not God, who initiates the testing of Job. Some readers are surprised to see that God and Satan are on speaking terms! The text cautions us not to exaggerate their relationship. "One day the heavenly beings came to present themselves before the Lord, and Satan also came among them to; present himself before the Lord" (Job 2:1). Satan appears to be sneaking into God's presence along with a host of angels. God then asks Satan, "Where have you come from?" (2:2). This question indicates that Satan is not at this time under God's providential control. Satan has his own realm of temporary authority. Satan replies that he has been walking the earth, which is, after all, his terrain for trouble making. When God wonders if Satan has considered how blameless Job is, Satan senses an opportunity to test God as much as Job. Satan wants Job to curse God. In other words, Satan wants Job to attribute the natural calamities that befall him to God. Any interpretation of this book's poetic passages about animals that concludes that God wants animals to be turned against each other plays into the hands of Satan. That interpretation is exactly what Satan wants. He wants us to blame God for evil.

I am not saying, by the way, that the death of animals is always an instance of evil. Theologians have long debated the relationship of death to sin, and that debate is hard enough when it is limited to the death of human beings. It gets only harder when animals are considered. Just as it is possible, God willing, that we can face death with dignity, animals have their own coping mechanisms and natural consolations. What is death to animals that hibernate for long stretches of time, like the snapping turtle that buries itself in mud beneath ice-covered lakes and takes no breath for several months? Death could have been a part of animal life in the Garden of Eden without disrupting its happiness for humans and animals alike.

Even under the conditions of evolution the life of animals is not always violent. Animals experience an innocence and playfulness that we can only envy. They are saved from the some of the most vicious aspects of the fall because they are not burdened with the freedom to make bad decisions. Many of the Psalms recognize that even the wildest animals are endowed by their creator with a capacity for praise, and when the Prophets pictured the New Jerusalem, they could not imagine it shorn of animals (see for example Zech 2:4 and Ezek 1:5, 10). Nonetheless, it was a commonplace of ancient Christian and Jewish teaching that animals have no inclination toward the good, just as angels have no inclination for evil. To the ancients, this maxim explained why God created humans, because neither animals nor angels could satisfy God's desire to be worshipped by free, rational agents. This maxim is not true, however, to the Christian witness about animals (nor does it explain how some angels could have turned their back on the good). The Christian tradition is full of stories about saints befriending and taming wild animals. According to tradition, St. Francis even tamed a wolf and asked it to cease attacking both humans and other animals.[15] These stories would not resonate so deeply with us if we could not hold some animals to some level of accountability and admire animals for their natural tendency toward the good.

Portraying nature as utterly godless does not do justice to God. Likewise, romanticizing nature does not do justice to animal suffering. Of all English poets, perhaps William Blake was the most sensitive to the gulf dividing heaven and hell. His best friend during his last years was Henry Crabb Robinson, who recorded their conversations. According to Robinson, Blake once said that the elegance of Wordsworth's nature poetry is proof for atheism, because nature is the work of the devil. Blake then said something about nature that is wiser than a shelf full of romantic poetry. "Whoever believes in nature disbelieves in God."[16] Blake was deeply influenced by Gnosticism, especially in its Manichaean variety. While traditional Christians cannot go as far as Blake went in

---

15. See Helen Waddell, *Beasts and Saints* (Grand Rapids: Eerdmans, 1995).

16. Quoted in Matt Cartmill, *A View to a Death in the Morning: Hunting and Nature through History* (Cambridge: Harvard University Press, 1993) 123.

attributing nature as a whole to Satan, they can learn to see the nature's evils in that dark light. They can learn to listen as the Apostle Paul did to nature's many sounds of suffering. "We know that the whole creation has been groaning in labor pains until now" (Rom 8:22). Nature too needs to be reborn.

To understand the destiny of animals we need to return to the biblical account of their origin. The *locus classicus* of all Christian discussions about animals is the story of the Garden of Eden. Many people find it hard to imagine that the Garden of Eden was a real place where evil had no foothold because they cannot imagine, as Darrel Falk puts it, "grass-eating lions, vegetarian hawks and anteaters that did not eat ants—all because there was no death on the earth during the Garden of Eden era." Where Falk makes his mistake is in thinking that Eden was identical with the whole earth. Falk is a professor of biology at Point Loma Nazarene University, and he has written elegantly (perhaps too elegantly!) about how evolution can be interpreted from a Christian point of view. Like many theistic evolutionists, he thinks that it is obvious that death must have been part of life on Earth before Adam's fall. If death is the way of nature, and nature is God's good creation, he reasons, then there should be no problem for Christians believing that evolution is how God created Adam and Eve.

Christians often thank God for nature's sustenance, but what would it mean to thank God for evolution? If we are the product of evolution, then our hands are so covered in the blood of animals that it is difficult to know how we could ever rejoice in our salvation. What would we do in heaven with the memories of animal suffering from our experiences on earth? How could we enjoy paradise when it is paid for not only by the blood of Jesus in his infinite sorrow but also by the blood of countless animals? Like a lot of Christian biologists, Falk is too complacent when it comes to evolution's terrible trajectory. He dismisses the idea that God works against evolution, so to speak, in order to battle chance and strife with order and harmony. "More likely," he says, "what we see in biology is just God working in ways that characterize who he is."[17] It is common at this point in the books of theistic evolutionists to introduce the idea of the cross as the place where God

---

17. Darrel R. Falk, *Coming to Peace with Science: Bridging the Worlds between Faith and Biology* (Downers Grove, IL: InterVarsity, 2004) 201 and 208.

An Ethics of Pets vs. the Darwinian Sublime

and evolution meet, but what does the agony of Jesus' death have to do with the strife of speciation? On the cross the Son chooses to be judged in our place, so that we might have life abundantly. Evolution sacrifices animals involuntarily and for no better purpose than that more death can come into the world.

In order to sustain the Christian dream of a peaceful consummation of history, the Garden of Eden must be given more attention that it usually receives among theologians. If the world is saturated in death, to the point where death is the essence of nature, as Darwinism teaches, then it is hard to give any concrete meaning to the idea of a new heaven and a new earth depicted in Rev 21:1. Gary Anderson, an accomplished Old Testament scholar, has demonstrated how the Christian and Jewish faiths were thoroughly enmeshed in the story of Adam and Eve.[18] The Israelites imagined that paradise was regained at Mt. Sinai, while Christians believe that Jesus Christ is the new Adam and his mother, Mary, is the new Eve. Anderson points out that there were several ancient traditions in both Judaism and Christianity that portrayed Adam and Eve in the Garden as immortal and angelic. Origen, one of the most distinguished Church Fathers, taught that the coat of skins God gave Adam and Eve when they were expelled was nothing more than human flesh to clothe their fallen souls (Gen 3:21). The first couple's original skin, according to this argument, would have been akin to the glorious garment—our resurrected bodies—that all Christians hope to put on when they enter into heaven. The earliest Christian liturgy reenacts this drama by having the postulant stand naked, exposed to shame, before baptism, after which the new garment they are given to wear is meant to symbolize the act of "putting on immortality" (1 Cor 15:53). The baptismal rite begins with an exorcism because it is at this stage in the liturgy that men and women enter into their full stature as creatures created in the image of God. Postulants who are entering into baptism can expect Satan to be at his most active, precisely because the source of his rebellion is envy of both Jesus Christ and those created to look like him.

If Adam and Eve were clothed in celestial glory in the Garden, then the animals too must have been indescribably embodied. A story in the

---

18. Gary A. Anderson, *The Genesis of Perfection: Adam and Eve in Jewish and Christian Imagination* (Louisville: Westminster John Knox, 2001).

ancient rabbinic literature says that, after Eve gave the fruit to Adam, she gave it to all the other animals, "so that they too might be subject to death."[19] Stories like that support my contention that we should not think of these wondrous beings as animals at all, but as prime examples or primordial originals of all the creatures that have left their traces in the fossil record. Here is where we reach the limits of theological speculation about the nature of animals and the meaning of animal suffering. Yet this line of inquiry is not pure speculation. Something happened after the loss of Eden that accelerated the plunge of the animal kingdom into strife, turmoil, and death. The Bible tells us that ten generations intervened between Adam and Noah, and during that time span, the direction that natural and human history took was very disappointing to God. As Genesis says, "Now the earth was corrupt in God's sight, and the earth was filled with violence" (6:11). Many readers instinctively think the word *earth* in Gen 6:11 is being used as a poetic device to mean the human, not the natural world, but there are no good reasons to make that interpretation. The very next verse states unequivocally, as if to answer this query, "And God saw that the earth was corrupt; for all flesh had corrupted its ways upon the earth" (6:12). Genesis is clearly suggesting that the violence was not limited to humans alone. In the interval between Adam and Noah, the whole world had degenerated into a violent and wicked place. The ancient rabbinical tradition emphasizes this point. "For the animals of the time were as immoral as the men: the dog united with the wolf, the cock with the pea-fowl, and many others paid no heed to sexual purity. Those that were saved were such as had kept themselves untainted."[20] Animals were mixing with each other in unlawful and dangerous ways, just as humans were descending into a spiral of gluttonous and promiscuous violence.

Boundaries were being broken. Categories were becoming confused. Animals that were meant to be kept apart were coupling with each other. A Jewish text, Midrash Rabba (26:9), blames the corruption of flesh on same gender marriages as well as sexual liaisons between humans and animals. According to the Bible, sexual immorality was not

19. Louis Ginzberg, *The Legends of the Jews*, vol. 1, trans. Henrietta Szold (Charleston: Bibliobazaar, 2007) 66. This is the origin of the story of the bird of paradise, which is the one animal that did not eat of the forbidden fruit and thus was granted permission to live in paradise forever.

20. Ibid., 125.

An Ethics of Pets vs. the Darwinian Sublime

limited to animals and humans. The sixth chapter of Genesis tells the story of the sons of God who took the daughters of man for their wives. The story of the Nephilim, as they are called, is one of the most mysterious and fantastic in the whole Bible, though it has New Testament support.[21] Many ancient commentators thought they were fallen angels, but some theologians rejected this interpretation on the ground that angels are not embodied and thus cannot have sex. Clues to their identity can be found in two ancient apocryphal texts that are additions to but not part of the Old Testament. The book of Enoch calls the offenders angels and says they acted out of lust. Their coupling with humans produced giants. These giants in turn "began to sin against birds and beasts and reptiles and fish" (Enoch 2:7). Bestiality is a particularly grievous symptom of the fall, I want to note, because it turns Adam's proper intimacy with the animals of the Garden, as exemplified by his naming them, into a shambles. The book of Jubilee also attributes bestiality to the unlawful coupling of angels and humans. "And lawlessness increased on the earth, and the way of life of every creature became corrupted—men, cattle, wild animals, and birds alike, everything that lives on earth; corrupt were the ways of all of them and of the whole natural order; and they began to devour one another" (Jubilee 5:2–3).[22] The violence between humans, between humans and animals, and between animals, was a result, it appears, of sexual lust gone awry.

Today we think that God asked Noah to save the animals because people cannot live without them. Although the affluent do not use them to work the land anymore, many people cannot go a meal without eating some kind of meat. Prior to the flood, however, the directive from God to eat only plants and fruits was still in effect (Gen 1:29). Even

---

21. Most scholars think that Jude 6 is a reference to Gen 6:1–4. Jude is reminding his readers about the fate of the wicked. "And the angels who did not keep their own position in heaven, but left their proper dwelling, he has kept in eternal chains in deepest darkness for the judgment of the great day." The Greek word for proper dwelling, *oiketerion*, is found in only one other place in the New Testament, 2 Cor. 5:2. There it refers to the form that we will be given in heaven. Jude is clearly passing onto his readers the story of the fallen angels. The next verse of Jude refers to the sexual immorality of Sodom and Gomorrah, which was also a case of illicit relations between angels and humans. Jude is thus solid evidence that the early Christians read Genesis 6 as a story about rebellious angels who had sex with human women.

22. These texts can be found in H. F. D. Sparks, ed., *The Apocryphal Old Testament* (Oxford: Clarendon, 1984).

The Dome of Eden

the beasts were told to eat only green plants (Gen 1:30). Only after the flood did God give permission to Noah to consume animal flesh: "Every moving thing that lives shall be food for you; and just as I gave you the green plants, I give you everything" (Gen 9:3). This permission, however, comes with a restriction on consuming blood and the warning that now, at this point in history, "The fear and dread of you shall rest on every animal of the earth, and on every bird of the air, on everything that creeps on the ground, and on all the fist of the sea; into your hand they are delivered" (Gen 9:2). Rather than imagining that Noah saved the animals *for* their value to humans, then, it is more faithful to the Bible to think that they were saved *from* something. They were saved from the flood, of course, but they were also saved from each other. God was angry not just at humans and fallen angels, but also at the animals. He was so angry that he blotted out everything that moved (Gen 7:23). He asked Noah to save the clean animals (Gen 7:2), which suggests that God wanted to start over with the animal population. Somehow, the animal population had been as disturbed by invaders just as much as human society had been ruined by the fallen angels.

Can we be more specific than that? Evolution is a wild dance not only between chance and natural selection but also between God and Satan. After the fall, the work God was doing in the Garden came into conflict with the ways of the world. Angels under the influence of Satan violated the descendants of Adam and Eve. Could it also be that animals under the influence of Satan violated the descendants of the Garden creatures? Whatever the merit of these speculations, the fact is that strife and struggle had became the order of the day after the days of Eden had come to an end. God was enraged, and not just at humanity, but God did not start the world all over from scratch. God did not create a totally new human race, nor did God create animals all over again. God saved what he could and destroyed the rest, and he compromised with Noah, permitting animal sacrifices as a means of controlling and purging (in the Aristotelian sense of catharsis) the human desire for bloodshed. God wanted to destroy all evil, but that would have meant destroying all living beings, so God decided to accommodate violence by letting some animals go wild and permitting, in a very controlled ritual, some animals to be slain for food.

C. S. Lewis captures the theological meaning of the role of the animals in the flood story in *The Last Battle*, the seventh and final novel in *The Chronicles of Narnia*. At the end of yet another great battle, the survivors are thrown into a barn, much like the stable where Jesus was born. There they encounter a fake Aslan, the antichrist of the novel. They also find Aslan himself, who stands ready to pass a final judgment on all living creatures he summons to meet him.

> As they came right up to Aslan one or other of two things happened to each of them. They all looked straight in his face, I don't think they had any choice about that. And when some looked, the expression of their faces changed terribly—it was fear and hatred: except that, on the face of the Talking Beasts, the fear and hatred lasted only for a fraction of a second. You could see that they suddenly ceased to be *Talking* Beasts. They were just ordinary animals. And all the creatures who looked at Aslan in that way swerved to their right, his left, and disappeared into his huge black shadow.

To the call of "Further in and higher up!" the dogs lead the way, of course. The animals that are not loyal to Aslan return to their dumb state and soon vanish into nothingness as an endless sea covers the land. Aslan/God/Noah has separated the clean animals from the unclean, and the ones that seek the company of others, just like the humans who seek God, are welcomed into the heavenly community of the saved.

Ending this chapter with a fable, even if it is by C. S. Lewis, might be considered a cop out, so let's return one last time to the problem of natural evil. The relationship between the problem of natural evil and the problem of human evil has been much debated, but Darwinism, because it seeks to explain human behavior as a product of natural developments, conflates these two sets of problems into one. That gives some theologians the hope that solutions to the problem of human evil can also apply to the problem of natural evil. One of the classic defenses of human evil is the "free will" defense, which holds that God had no choice but to permit human evil as the price to be paid for granting humans freedom. John Polkinghorne has come up with a similar defense of natural evil, which he calls the "free process" defense. This position argues that a world full of complex, conscious life necessarily entails natural evils like earthquakes and disease.[23] Evolution, in other words,

---

23. John C. Polkinghorne, *Science and Providence: God's Interaction with the World*, new ed. (Templeton Foundation, 2005) 77–78.

is required if God is to achieve the purpose of creating a causally open world with all of its risks and responsibilities for humans. The immediate objection to this position is that it is hard to imagine how God could *not* have come up with a better way of creating the conditions for human freedom than evolution. More significantly, the "free process" argument upon closer examination can be seen to be just a sub-set of the "free will" argument. The evolutionary process is posited as a necessary precondition for the full exercise of free will. Natural evil is one more kind of evil (in addition to human evil) that God must permit in order to test humans and enjoy their freely chosen worship. Even if that were true, it would do nothing to justify God's treatment of animals. Why should animals be thrown into a world full of so much suffering just so we humans can be forced to make more decisions?

The only "solution" to the problem of natural evil is the same twofold solution to the problem of human suffering and human evil. First, evil must be attributed to Satan, not God. (This is sometimes called a "free will defense of a higher order" because just as human sin is explained by reference to human freedom, natural evil is explained by reference to the freedom of the angels.) Second, salvation must be such that it will more than compensate for all suffering experienced on Earth. What this says about nature is that evolution itself must be redeemed from Satan's distortions. This follows from a principle that Neil Messer, in one of the very best books on evolution and religion, formulates: "There is no aspect of the world or of human life that is in principle untouched by God's saving activity in Christ; Christians are committed to the attempt to re-envision every aspect of the world and human existence through the lens of Christ."[24] Not untouched does not mean caused: God can identify with the pain and suffering of the victims of evolution through the cross of his Son without being the cause of the Darwinian aspects (chance and struggle) of evolution. Messer appends an appropriate name to the problem of imagining the redemption of evolution. He calls it the Triassic question. The timescale of evolution is so long, and the incarnation of Jesus Christ is so brief, that it is hard to envision how the latter could have anything to do with the former. Yet that is what we are called to do if the Lordship of Jesus is not bound by

---

24. Neil Messer, *Selfish Genes and Christian Ethics: Theological and Ethical Reflections on Evolutionary Biology* (London: SCM, 2007) 213.

time any more than it is bound by space. In his descent into hell during Holy Saturday Christ set free the holy souls who had died before his advent (1 Pet 3:18–20). By defeating death he also broke the chains of evolution, thus liberating all life from the deadly struggle for survival.

nine

The Nature of Naturalism

What is more dangerous, nature or naturalism? That might sound like comparing apples and oranges, or better, apples and pesticides, since nature is another word for reality and naturalism is a theory about how to protect reality from unwanted theological infestations. Nature can be dangerous, but its danger is hard to measure. In any case, humans have done pretty well in making the best of nature, to the extent that environmentalists think we pose more of a threat to nature than nature does to us.

What about naturalism? One might wonder if anyone other than philosophers and theologians should worry about naturalism. After all, epistemological debates about how best to go about knowing the world are hardly the stuff of everyday concerns. While naturalism alone is not much of a problem, I want to suggest that when it is coupled with Darwinism it becomes a threat of enormous proportions. Naturalism is more dangerous to human survival than nature.

Naturalism is a philosophical position that treats the physical world as a closed system. A closed system is one that is impervious to any outside forces. So naturalism necessarily denies the possibility of supernaturalism. Naturalists argue that there is no super-nature, that is, a nature that is superior to the physical world that we inhabit. This is a circular argument, because appealing to the physical world to disprove the supernatural begs the question of how to define matter. One cannot simply say that it is obvious that nature is all we have, since there are many people who experience nature as sacred in some way—probably more than there are pure materialists. Even many post-Christian and post-theistic naturalists strive to fashion a worldview that portrays nature as suffused or saturated with mystery. In fact, I will argue that naturalism is self-contradictory, because it attempts to transcend nature

The Nature of Naturalism

in order to capture the meaning of nature as a whole, which makes it a species of theological argument.

Sometimes the kind of naturalism that I am talking about is called metaphysical naturalism, to distinguish it from a more modest version called methodological naturalism. Methodological naturalism argues that the study of the physical world works best when the possible truth of supernatural causes or influences are bracketed and ignored. Methodological naturalism is epistemologically pragmatic. It does not make any absolute judgments about the reality of the supernatural. That does not mean that methodological naturalism is always neutral about religion. Naturalism as a method can be used to interpret religious and moral values in terms of their physical origin and impact. These interpretations typically challenge the self-understandings of religious believers. Nevertheless, methodological naturalism, in some of its versions, is open to arguments about whether religion can best be explained by reference to the natural world. It does not simply assume that religion must be explained exclusively in this way. Metaphysical naturalism, by contrast, does not argue against the supernatural. It begins with the assumption that the supernatural is unknowable and that what is unknowable must not exist.[1]

Methodological naturalism has some problems of its own, especially when it is applied to non-physical phenomena like moral principles and supernatural events. It is also problematic when it is turned into a dogmatic rule that excludes any reflection on the limits of scientific knowledge or its moral and religious implications. Metaphysical naturalism, however, is a problem of another order. Methodological naturalism was already common in the sciences before Darwin, but Darwin turned the naturalistic method of the sciences into a metaphysical principle. The great Protestant theologian Charles Hodge was the first to clearly understand and analyze Darwin's commitment to metaphysical naturalism in his 1874 book, *What is Darwinism?* Hodge realized that Darwin ruled the supernatural out of bounds on principle, not on the evidence. Furthermore, by elevating the scientific method to a metaphysical program, he made naturalism appear to be the inevitable

---

1. For excellent critiques of naturalism, see Cornelius G. Hunter, *Science's Blind Spot: The Unseen Religion of Scientific Naturalism* (Grand Rapids: Brazos, 2007), and Terence L. Nichols, *The Sacred Cosmos: Christian Faith and the Challenge of Naturalism* (Grand Rapids: Brazos, 2003).

worldview for the advancement of knowledge and the progress of the sciences. For the cultural elite, naturalism, thanks to Darwin, became the nature of the world.

The story of Darwin's transformation of naturalism is complicated, but the outline is clear. In the seventeenth century, nearly every scientist, from Newton to Boyle, was determined to keep science and religion together. Scientists were committed to thinking through the way in which the concept of God continued to be a necessary hypothesis for making sense of the world. By the end of the nineteenth century, nearly all of the leading scientists had agreed to get rid of the God hypothesis. More was involved in this transformation than Darwinism, of course. One significant factor was the practical problem of a growing volume of knowledge that made it extremely difficult for scientists to remain literate about theological debates. Even in philosophy and theology, the idea of the unity of knowledge was given up as an impossible ideal at best or an impediment to progress at worst.

Darwin's influence on the course of naturalism, however, should not be underestimated. Before Darwin, the laws of nature were taken to be a reflection of the laws of God. For example, Adam Sedgwick, one of the great nineteenth century British geologists, could not imagine formulating a system of natural laws without believing that God had ordained those laws. After all, every law implies a law giver. Sedgwick found it impossible to think about nature without also thinking about God. After Darwin, most scientists found it impossible to think about nature unless they imagined nature empty of the divine. Scientific law was reinterpreted to mean a pattern in nature that absolutely precludes divine influence. Much of the clash over evolution, then, was between two forms of science. "The vituperation is best understood when it is seen, not simply as a clash between science and religion, but as one between two antagonistic scientific epistemes: one with a deep theological commitment, the other with none."[2] One could even argue that science was transformed more than religion in the conflicts over evolution.

Darwinism portrays nature as rife with danger, yet I want to argue that metaphysical naturalism is more dangerous than nature by far. We live in an environment that is largely human made. Nature in its raw,

---

2. Neal C. Gillespie, *Charles Darwin and the Problem of Creation* (Chicago: University of Chicago Press, 1979) 18.

wild form hardly exists for most people today. The decrease in wilderness can be bemoaned and, to some extent, slowed, but it cannot be denied. The nature that impacts us is the world of institutions and ideas, and that world is increasingly void of religious influence. Metaphysical naturalism (hereafter I will just call it naturalism for short) demeans the world by stripping it of any inherent value. That, however, is not its most dangerous effect. By leaving nature bare of meaning, it opens a vacuum to every kind of effort to restore nature's standing in the human world. These attempts are inevitably inhuman in their morality, because nature alone cannot sustain the moral environment required to defend the integrity and uniqueness of the human species.

Ominously, the Darwinian definition of the natural world, despite its many problems, is becoming more pervasive in higher education. As academic specialties become narrower, Darwinism becomes more universal. Darwinian encroachment on other fields—what James Barham, has called "theory creep"[3]—is led by young Ph.D.s wanting to revitalize moribund disciplines, and Darwinism has taken such deep roots in the social sciences that it is probably beyond eradication. Economists once relied on rational choice theory to depict economic actors as calculating machines, but now they have turned to Darwinism to put economics on a more scientific footing, although the emphasis on self-interest remains the same.[4] The secret to Darwinism's invasive success—to follow its own circular logic—is its adaptability. It is so elastic and malleable that it can explain anything and everything, often in contradictory ways. Darwinism can tell us why mothers kill their babies and why mothers do not kill their babies, why people are selfish and why people are altruistic, why competition is more fundamental than cooperation and why cooperation is more fundamental than competition, and so on. Darwinians overcome the scientific flaws in their theory by turning it into a philosophical program with unlimited methodological potential, and then use the evidence of its scholarly respectability as confirmation of its scientific veracity.

---

3. James Barham, "Why I am Not a Darwinist," in William A. Dembski, ed., *Uncommon Dissent: Intellectuals Who Find Darwinism Unconvincing* (Wilmington: ISI, 2004) 178.

4. Geoffrey M. Hodgson, *Economics and Evolution: Bringing Life Back into Economics* (Ann Arbor: University of Michigan Press, 1997).

That naturalism is not an adequate foundation for morality has been brilliantly demonstrated by J. Budziszewski, a philosopher at the University of Texas at Austin. Budziszewski is a natural law theorist, which means that he grounds morality in nature as it is interpreted by the Christian tradition. Nature means something very different to Darwinians than to natural law theorists. Darwinians are forced to read moral law straight from the evidence of natural behavior. Natural law theorists make a distinction between created and fallen nature, and argue that it is only nature as God intended it to be that serves as a source of morality.

Budziszewski's argument against naturalism is as devastating as it is simple. After discussing Darwinian theories about how aiding one's relatives, who share one's genes, develops traits of altruism that get passed down to later generations, he moves in for the kill. "If kin selection happens, then it might explain the tendency to help out other people. It might even explain why we approve of the tendency. The problem is that it can't explain whether we ought to approve of it. After all, the fact that we developed one way rather than another is an accident. We might have turned out like guppies, who eat their young instead of helping them."[5] The Darwinian will retort that it is true that we might have turned out like guppies, but we didn't. We are humans with a certain level of compassion built into us by evolution. That, however, is an observation, not an argument. Darwinism might be able to explain why we have the moral sentiments that we seem to possess, but a Darwinian cannot recommend, on Darwinian grounds, that we keep, cultivate, and strengthen those sentiments. On Darwinian grounds, it might be helpful for our species if many humans practice compassion, but there is no reason why any individual should feel an obligation to do so. This lack of obligation should especially hold true for those who are committed to a Darwinian theory of nature. The more Darwinian you are, the less you will treat human nature as unique, and thus the less you will endorse moral values for anything other than their social utility.

---

5. J. Budziszewski, "Phillip Johnson Was Right: The Rivalry of Naturalism and Natural Law," in *Darwin's Nemesis: Phillip Johnson and the Intelligent Design Movement*, ed. William A. Dembski (Downers Grove, IL: InterVarsity, 2006) 250.

It was not inevitable that Darwin's discoveries would lead him into these theological and moral quandaries. It is not even inevitable that his investigations would lead him to atheism. Take the case of Alfred Russel Wallace. A paper that Wallace wrote in 1855, before Darwin had published his theory, prompted Darwin to publicize his own ideas, less Wallace gain the credit. Wallace came to the theory of natural selection independently of Darwin and grew more religious afterwards, not less. Darwin admits in his autobiography that he lost the ability to read poetry after his scientific breakthrough, but Wallace decided that natural selection alone could not explain everything in the universe. Wallace thought that natural selection implies some kind of agency and that natural history thus has an author and a plot. Wallace would undoubtedly be better known today if he had not taken such a dramatic religious turn. His religious views, I should note, were not conventional. He was a spiritualist, not a traditional Christian, which has kept him from becoming a hero to Christian theists or the intelligent design community. Nonetheless, he spent his later years not only living in Darwin's shadow but also trying to repair the breech that Darwin's version of natural selection wrought between religion and science.[6]

Darwin's own relationship to religion is complicated and much debated in the secondary literature. One of the great ironies of modern Darwinism is that it wants to keep evolutionary theory free from theological deliberations in spite of the fact that Darwin himself lived in a time when such compartmentalization was impossible. One can almost say that for many scientists evolution simply must be true if for no other reason than that these scientists must be right in their determination not to be bothered by theology. Darwin had no such hang-ups. In Darwin's day, science was not a profession set apart from other ways of knowing, with ironclad rules designed to reinforce its segregation. Natural theology was everywhere, and Darwin's theorizing would not have been possible without it. According to Arthur McCalla, "Natural theology was particularly influential in England, where the Anglican Church sought in reason and empirical evidence a means of confirming the truth of revelation independently of both Catholic tradition and

---

6. Michael Shermer, *In Darwin's Shadow: The Life and Science of Alfred Russel Wallace: A Biographical Study on the Psychology of History* (New York: Oxford University Press, 2002).

Puritan Biblicism."[7] Darwin was raised in a household where skepticism of orthodox Christian was rampant, but given the theological climate he could not help but be shaped by the religious questions of the day.

The questions Darwin asked of nature were the same that theologians were asking, though his answers, eventually, were quite different. He was theologically informed and literate at a level relative to his day that would be surpassed only by professional theologians in these postmodern times. He had doubts about religion as a young man, and they grew, by the time he was forty, into a settled skepticism that left no room for revelation as a source of truth. When he married, his father advised him to keep his doubts from his wife, Emma, in order to avoid unnecessary marital strive. Throughout his marriage he tried, unsuccessfully, to assure Emma that his biological ideas were not morally repugnant.

Darwin recognized that his theory had moral implications, and he knew that these implications would determine its reception by the wider public. As his great-great-grandson Randal Keynes has written in a moving portrait of Darwin's family life, "Charles saw that his own radically different theory of human origins would stand up only if he could show that morality could have been derived by a natural process from animal life." The strange sexual lives of organisms convinced him that nature was not ordered by the wisdom of God. Indeed, he realized that his theory made nature look more like Satan's handiwork than God's. He put this in a letter to the botanist Joseph Hooker, who was his closest friend: "You will perhaps wish my barnacles and species theory al Diabolo [to the Devil] together, but I don't care what you say; my species theory is all gospel." Losing his beloved daughter, Annie, in 1851, when she was ten, was the point at which there was no return for Darwin to religion. Darwin had written about disease and death before, but, as Keynes observes, "When he returned to the theme in his scientific writings during the years after Annie's death, he wrote about in a new way." He kept his grief private, but her death cast a dark shadow on his understanding of nature. While thinking about the odd sexual life of the jellyfish, he wrote to Hooker, "What a book a Devil's Chaplain might write on the clumsy, wasteful, blundering low and horridly cruel

---

7. Arthur McCalla, *The Creationist Debate: The Encounter between the Bible and the Historical Mind* (New York: T. & T. Clark, 2006) 14.

works of nature!"⁸ To the extent that his theory left open the possibility of belief in God, it was a God who takes no interest in individuals and, indeed, appears to enjoy the squandering of life in the pursuit of mindless gain. Darwin's God looks a lot like the devil, just as he feared that the truth about nature could only be written by the devil's chaplain.

Darwinian naturalism, then, has something to say about more than nature. Naturalistic explanations of religion are almost as old as religion itself, but Darwinians seem particularly unable to leave religion alone. Evolutionary psychology is the general name given to social scientists that endeavor to explain mind and culture in adaptive terms, but given the increasing dependence of the entire field of psychology on biology, giving psychology an evolutionary label can seem redundant.⁹ Evolutionary psychologists who write about religion can be divided into two camps, the reconcilers and the reducers. The reconcilers try to understand how religion and science might peacefully co-exist while the reducers try to explain religion completely in terms of biology. On the face of it, this might seem like the distinction between good and bad Darwinian cops that I discussed in chapter one. That is, it might seem like the reconcilers are more sympathetic to religion than the reducers and thus have more to contribute to Christian theology, but in reality both groups are equivalent to the "bad cops" of chapter one. Most Darwinian attempts to reconcile religion and evolution end up trivializing religious faith, which can be much more condescending, and much harder to argue against, than trying to reduce faith to its biological components.

The reductionist camp needs to be divided further into two groups, the adaptionists and the non-adaptionists. Most of the early Darwinian theories of religion treated it as a function of adaption. Humans developed religious ideas just like they developed erect posture, language, and the opposable or prehensile thumb, that is, so that they and their genetic offspring could survive. With this assumption, Darwinians set

---

8. Randal Keynes, *Darwin, His Daughter, and Human Evolution* (New York: Riverhead, 2001) 49, 142, 243, and 243.

9. For a blistering critique of this field, see Susan McKinnon, *Neo-Liberal Genetics: Myths and Tales of Evolutionary Psychology* (Chicago: Prickly Paradigm, 2006). Also see Hilary Rose and Steven Rose, eds., *Alas Poor Darwin: Arguments Against Evolutionary Psychology* (New York: Harmony, 2000).

out to categorize, measure, and analyze the various benefits that religion incurs, from providing personal comfort to justifying social order.

Some social scientists still study these benefits, but the adaptionists have increasingly loss favor in the academy to the non-adaptionists, who argue that religion arises as a byproduct of fitness enhancing mechanisms and does not itself contribute directly to evolutionary success. Some non-adaptionists will admit that religion might confer some advantages to believers, but they insist that religion did not arise to solve universal cognitive puzzles about the meaning of life, the order of the cosmos, or the source of moral convictions. They even reject the idea that religious beliefs arose as a mistaken attempt to provide pseudo-scientific explanations of physical processes, like why it rains on one piece of land but not another, and they certainly have no tolerance for the idea that religion arose out of a natural sense of mystical awe or wonder at the universe. For the non-adaptionists, religion is a cultural mutation that took on a life of its own, like junk DNA that has no function other than to go along for the biological ride.

The non-adaptionist camp has become increasingly sophisticated over the years, and is closely associated with the emergence of a new area of studies called the cognitive science of religion. This study is scientific because it seeks to discover the causal mechanisms that account for the visible manifestations of religion, and it is quickly gaining credibility with a new journal, *Journal of Cognition and Culture*, a new institute, Institute of Cognition and Culture, and an annual meeting organized by the International Association of the Cognitive Sciences of Religion.[10] Its theoretical starting point has been developed by the cognitive anthropologist Pascal Boyer.[11] Boyer has formulated what he calls a theory of "minimal counterintuitiveness," which is really a fancy way of saying that religious beliefs violate common sense as well as the laws of nature, but they do so by a small, not wide margin. Religious beliefs that are too odd or bizarre might grab out attention, but we would not remember

---

10. See Jesper Sørensen, "Religion in Mind: A Review Article of the Cognitive Science of Religion," *Numen* 52 (2005) 465–94.

11. Pascal Boyer, *The Naturalness of Religious Ideas: A Cognitive Theory of Religion* (Berkeley: University of California Press, 1994) and *Religion Explained: The Evolutionary Origins of Religious Thought* (New York: Basic, 2001). Also see Scott Atran, *In Gods We Trust: The Evolutionary Landscape of Religion* (New York: Oxford University Press, 2002).

them and pass them along to future generations, because they are too far afield from the rest of our knowledge. Religious beliefs that are just a little bit off from reality, on the other hand, have a way of insinuating themselves deep into our consciousness. There is, then, an optimal level of deviation, although this has proven impossible to quantify.

Boyer has put a modern spin on one of the oldest, and most superficial, theories of religion: namely, that the stories and claims of religion are orally transmitted because they are species of the rhetorical trope of hyperbole.[12] As any rhetorician knows, a good exaggeration has to have a kernel of truth to be memorable; otherwise it will be immediately dismissed as ridiculous and absurd. A good exaggeration, however, has *only* a kernel of truth, which is another way of saying that a good exaggeration is a successful lie. Religious beliefs and ideas, for Boyer, are like good exaggerations. We could reduce his theory to the following: individuals who lie boldly get caught, while individuals who tell white lies gain our admiration; likewise, religions that keep their distortions close to the ground of common sense and societal expectations can get away with murder. That this theory has no empirical support has not deterred its many supporters, but its theoretical flaws should give them something to think about. As Gregory Alles and others have noted, if the minimally counterintuitive were so memorable and so easily absorbed into our background knowledge, we would hardly have any background knowledge at all.[13] Why isn't all of our knowledge simply saturated with the counterintuitive, and if it were, then how could we distinguish between proper intuitions and basic beliefs and the exaggerations that violate them? In other words, why did ancient peoples distinguish between what we recognize today as folk psychology and folk physics and their mystical and religious beliefs? And if religious beliefs that are simply too hard to remember disappear, why is Christian theology so complicated? Besides, Boyer's definition of minimally counterintuitive seems awfully culturally conditioned. Some religions gloat in the fantastic and unreal, while others, like the monotheistic

---

12. For a survey of these theories, see Stephen H. Webb, *Blessed Excess: Religion and the Hyperbolic Imagination* (Albany, NY: SUNY Press, 1993).

13. See Gregory D. Alles, "The So-Called Cognitive Optimum and the Cost of Religious Concepts," *Method & Theory in the Study of Religion* 18 (2006) 325–50. Also see Lluis Oviedo, "Is a Complete Biocognitive Account of Religion Feasible?" *Zygon* 43 (2008) 103–26.

faiths, are much more historically grounded. Boyer's definition of religion sounds suspiciously like it is meant for an audience that enjoys debunking Jewish, Christian, and Muslim beliefs.

Boyer's theory actually only accounts for why religious beliefs are remembered and retold. How they emerge in the first place is explained by what cognitive theorists, led by Justin Barrett, call HADD, which stands for hyper-active agency detection device.[14] This made-up term refers to a made-up mechanism that is supposed to be part of the human mind. The idea is that ancient humans, in order to survive in a hostile world, had to be quick at detecting menace and threat in their environments. Even today children have dreams about being chased by wild animals, so imagine how scary that must have been to our oldest ancestors. HADD is the cognitive apparatus that leads us to be wary of motion in our immediate environment. Only those who were good at scrutinizing their surroundings for predatory threats would survive to pass on their genes to another generation. Moreover, it would have been far better to have an overly sensitive detection device—detecting too much motion rather than too little—than one with a slow or sticky trigger. HADD not only detects motion but also makes inferences about the sources of motion, and once again, it is better to be imaginative and broadminded about such inferences than skeptical and stingy. When children try to find faces in the clouds they are playing with this agency generating inferential process and thus recapitulating, according to this theory, the origin of religious belief.[15] Thus, the very same evolutionary mechanism that led ancient hominids to suspect that a lion was making the bushes shake also led pre-historic peoples to think that there must be an agent causing the rains to fall and the sun to rise.

As with minimal counterintuitiveness, it is hard to imagine what would count as evidence for these claims, but it is even harder to imagine why HADD did not devolve into paranoia or why the positing of supernatural agents became mired in costly rituals and sacrifices that have nothing to do with detecting motion. It is even hard to imagine why HADD experiences would be so inferentially rich, because if primi-

---

14. Justin L. Barrett, *Why Would Anyone Believe in God?* (New York: Rowman & Littlefield, 2004).

15. This is basically the hypothesis of Stewart Elliott Guthrie, *Faces in the Clouds: A New Theory of Religion* (New York: Oxford University Press, 1995).

tive peoples spent too much time speculating about the unknown agent behind mysterious movements, they would have been too exhausted to mate, hunt, and gather firewood—and thus would have become prey more than predator. Maybe primitive people were more sophisticated about making inferences than this theory suggests. Perhaps the simplest way to criticize HADD, however, is to turn it against evolutionary scientists themselves. Could it be that cognitive scientists have inadequate HADDs? Even in pre-historic times there must have been people who did not like the mental effort required to make inferences from inexplicable physical phenomena to unseen agents. We could speculate that these people would have died out if it had not been for the protection they were given by their more HADD worthy peers. In fact, atheism itself can be explained as a byproduct of detection inadequacy. Barrett himself, who believes in God, leans in this direction by arguing that theism is more natural than atheism. "As odd as it sounds," he writes, "it isn't natural to reject all supernatural agents."[16] Atheists are inferentially impoverished, hampered by their causal minimalism. Their inference-defeaters (whatever it is in the brain that checks our tendency to get swept away by the myriad possibilities of plausible inferences), we could say, are set way too high. The question, then, is not why some people make more inferences than others, but why some people make fewer inferences, and how we tell which of those inferences are worthy of belief. At the end of the day, as fun as evolutionary speculations can be, they do not give us much guidance for deciding what is really true.

The reducers get all of the respect in the academy, but in the popular press, the reconcilers sell most of the books. The number of religiously-minded scientists and scientifically-minded religious who are working on the reconciliation of Darwinism and Christianity is legion. The difficulty of their task is demonstrated not just by their numbers but also by the strenuousness of their efforts. Reading these books is a wearisome exercise in plodding through wishful thinking and the sloppy eradication of logical distinctions. Many do not try to correlate the specifics of evolution with Christian doctrine. Instead, they repeat various mantras, in the hope that verbal assurances will alleviate tempers and bring about good will. Their rhetorical strategies range from

---

16. Barrett, *Why Would Anyone Believe in God?* 108.

insisting that Darwinism is not as bad as you think it is to complaining that Christians misunderstand biology worse than you could imagine.

I suppose that one should applaud the deterioration of disciplinary boundaries that stifle interdisciplinary work, but some books about religion by scientists make me long for the good old days when scientists did their thing and left religion to the experts.

Joan Roughgarden is a case in point. She is a professor of biology at Stanford University and an active Episcopalian. She assures her readers of her book, *Evolution and Christian Faith: Reflections of an Evolutionary Biologist* that she "simply would not participate in evolutionary biology if I thought it somehow undercut Christian faith or was in any way immoral or destructive to our shared humanity." I will let her strongest argument against intelligent design speak for itself: "My favorite marvel is a chameleon's tongue, several body lengths long, which sticks out in a flash to catch bugs far away. How could this possibly evolve? A medium-sized tongue would be useless, because a lizard couldn't get close enough before the bug flew away. So, how does a chameleon's tongue get to be so long? Offhand, I don't know, but appeal to an 'intelligent designer' is simply a cop-out, a way to avoid doing the hard work of figuring out whether there are relatives with medium-sized tongues, what else tongues are used for, what fossil tongue lengths are, and so forth." Besides putting *intelligent design* in scare quotes in order to sequester a term that might pollute her steady stream of elegant prose, Roughgarden has no argument to make. She assumes that doing the math on the probability of an intelligent designer is *not* hard work. She is also admitting that no amount of hard work will solve the problem of the lizard's tongue, since she and many others have being doing this work for years and they still have no idea how it could have evolved. Roughgarden does make one original contribution to the evolution debates. She argues that, "If intelligent design succeeds as a movement, Christianity will be hurt. Intelligent design says the facts of nature offer a better testimonial to God than the Bible does. It will substitute science for the Gospels."[17] This argument is the flip side of those scientists who

17. Joan Roughgarden, *Evolution and Christian Faith: Reflections of an Evolutionary Biologist* (Washington: Island, 2006) 10, 91, and 98. She has one other observation worth quoting, regarding the anomaly of homosexuality from a Darwinian point of view: "If one insists that competition is the only way to succeed evolutionarily, then homosexuality seems a waste of time and likely some sort of mistake or disease" (114).

The Nature of Naturalism

claim that intelligent design will destroy biology. That absolutely no intelligent design theorists has come even close to saying such a thing has not impeded the confidence of her assertion.

Another example of a reconciler is Ursula Goodenough's *The Sacred Depths of Nature*. Goodenough is Professor of Biology at Washington University, author of a best-selling textbook on genetics, and past president of the American Society of Cell Biology and the Institute on Religion in an Age of Science. She is also the daughter of Yale historian of religion Erwin Goodenough (1893–1965), who once wrote, in defense of *Religionswissenschaft* (the scientific study of religion perfected in German universities) that "science itself is a religious exercise, a new religion."[18] Her father tried to make the study of religion scientific, but she tries to make the study of science religious. Her credentials are impressive, but her conception of religion amounts to nothing more than a sentimentalizing of scientific observations. Her purpose is to develop a planetary ethic based on a vaguely religious appreciation of the natural sciences. For example, the first chapter, which covers the origins of the earth, ends with some banal generalizations about mystery and long quotations from a Christian hymn and Lao Tzu. The implication is that it does not matter what religion you look at, because they all say something positive about mystery.

The mystery of religion, for Goodenough, is not the transcendence of the divine within the material universe but the complexity of a material universe that leaves no room for transcendence of any kind. Identifying herself as a non-theist, she accepts scientific reductionism and rejects any notion of design or purpose in nature. Yet somehow, the accidental nature of the universe inspires, rather than terrifies her. She never explains how humans can learn to be grateful for nature. "My emotions are the result of neuro-transmitters squirting on my brain cells." We are no more than a part of nature, but we should be glad to be blessed by these ties that bind us to our death. "The continuation of life reaches around, grabs its own tail, and forms a sacred circle that requires no further justification, no Creator, no superordinate meaning of meaning, no purpose other than that the continuation continue until the sun collapses or the final meteor collides. I confess a credo

---

18. Erwin R. Goodenough, "Religionwissenshaft," *Numen* 6 (1959) 85.

of continuation."[19] No matter how redundantly she writes of continuation, her prose cannot conceal the nothingness toward which her ethic strives.

Scientists are known for their rigor and honesty, but books likes this exemplify what we can call the Darwinian's theological dilemma. Darwinians find themselves in a theological dilemma because they must think like theologians, even though they know little or nothing about theology. (Or worse, what they do know about theology is wrong.) They must think like theologians because Darwinism is a worldview with ethical implications. More than that, it is a worldview that has made a bid to become a substitute for religion. Thoroughly consistent Darwinians are thus obligated to work out the details of this worldview substitution. From the very beginning of Darwinism, evolutionary biologists argued, on theological grounds, that the biblical view of creation could not be true, in order to bolster the plausibility of their own theology of creation. Yet Darwinians are so unsympathetic to theology that they always sound less than intelligent when they talk about the moral underpinnings of their worldview. Actually, they sound worse than unintelligent or uninformed. Using the rhetoric of religion to sanction this bleak view of relentless fecundity crawling toward final annihilation is either bad theology or, more likely, a terribly dishonest form of atheism.

Theologians too go to great lengths to join the reconciling crowd by affirming the Darwinian status quo. John Haught, Director of the Georgetown University Center for the Study of Science and Religion, is one of the most prolific and careful theological responders to Darwin. His work uses the metaphor of depth to explain how Darwin and Christianity can meet without conflict or competition. Haught is insistent in distinguishing his exploration of evolution's depths from the more targeted activities of the intelligent design community. By talking about depth, however, Haught leaves the surface of evolution untouched. He does not want theological claims to interfere with scientific practices. Haught finds design in nature, but only at a spiritual level so deep than it is undetectable by empirical observation. ID theorists are thus guilty of wanting "premature metaphysical gratification." This

---

19. Ursula Goodenough, *The Sacred Depths of Nature* (Oxford: Oxford University Press, 1998) 47 and 171.

The Nature of Naturalism

comment sounds like Haught is chastising ID theorists not for being wrong on an intellectual level but for being covetous on a moral level. ID theorists, from Haught's moralistic point of view, desire up front what they can only have after an appropriate waiting period. In Haught's words, they discern theological explanations too early in "what should be a prolonged journey toward the depths of design."[20] This might seem like a rhetorical quibble. If Haught too seeks design beneath evolution's obscurity, then the precise biological level at which design becomes apparent should be a friendly and productive debate. Appearances of agreement, however, are deceiving. Haught is really stretching the metaphor of depth out of any recognizable shape. He does not really mean that design resides in the deep murky underbelly of evolution. He means to say that design belongs to another conceptual dimension of nature altogether.

In order to explain his metaphor of depth, Haught argues that interpretations of nature are analogous to the act of interpreting literature. Disagreement over how to interpret classic works of literature is, arguably, what makes a book a classic. Nature is like a literary classic in its rich and productive ambiguities. For Haught, evolutionary naturalists are readers who are not wrong in their interpretations. Instead, they are just superficial. Meanwhile, ID theorists are like people who enjoy spoiling the movie for those who haven't seen it by revealing the ending. If only both sides of the debate would recognize that there are multiple meanings to the text of nature, then the debate would go away.

The problem with this "reading" of the act of interpretation is that it is ensnared in postmodern relativism. Postmodernists argue that a classic text has no single meaning. Multiple readings can thus contradict each other without any of them being wrong—or any of them being right, either. No reading is deeper than any other because all depths are relative. To fathom how illogical this is, imagine a postmodernist pool party where there are multiple depths to dive into, even though there is no water in the pool.

Unfortunately for Haught, the concept of depth is a comparative one. There must be a consistent standard to take its measure. It does not make sense to say that the depth of the shallow end of the pool is just

---

20. John F. Haught, *Deeper than Darwin: The Prospect for Religion in the Age of Evolution* (Boulder, CO: Westview, 2003) 89 and 89.

as deep as the depth at the deep end. Moreover, the depth of something will shape how we perceive its surface features. Otherwise, its depth will be merely another surface, not its deep meaning. If I know that the water in the deep end is too deep for my kids to swim in, I will treat it very differently from the water at the shallow end. If a phenomenon truly has depth, then its depth will be glimpsed through its surface, and when you get to its depth, the surface will never look the same. For postmodernists texts have nothing but multiple surfaces, so that even the most profound interpretation does not plumb the text for its true message. Yet if books just aren't that deep, why keep reading them, and why argue over what they mean?

Haught, in effect, develops a logically incoherent account of his own metaphor of depth. ID theorists are actually much more consistent on this point. ID theorists do not offer an alternative perspective of biology, as if nature can be looked at in different ways without those differences being compared and evaluated. ID theorists press the biological evidence as far as it will go by making logical inferences about intelligent design on the basis of probability analysis. They might be wrong, but they are not developing one reading of nature among many equally possible alternatives. They are after the truth about what lies at the foundation of evolution. So, of course, are Darwinians. Both camps think they have reached the bottom of evolution, and there is no reconciliation between the two. One camp has found purpose, intelligence, and ultimately God, while the other has found a bottomless pit of coincidence, luck, and violence.

Even a philosopher with no theological bones to grind understands that the argument over intelligent design comes down to basic and mutually exclusive moral convictions. In *Living with Darwin*, Philip Kitcher, the John Dewey Professor of Philosophy at Columbia University, dismisses the usual scientific complaints about ID. The charge that ID theorists do not perform experiments is little more than rhetorical whining, Kitcher argues, because neither do many astronomers, theoretical physicists, and other kinds of scientists. Furthermore, scientists should know better than to "believe that there is a magic formula, an incantation they can utter to dispel the claims of intelligent design." The chant of testability ignores large swaths of scientific theory not easily subjected to experimental trials. Kitcher even admits that Darwinism is attractive to so many scientists precisely because they have already ruled out the relevance of God's providential handiwork. "Darwin's thesis that natural selection has been the main agent of evolutionary change has won vindication by attrition." In other words, scientists believe in natural selection because "nothing else is known as a potential agent for evolutionary changes." And Darwinians maintain their convictions even though, "if they were to try experimenting on the natural selection of organisms with relatively long generation times it would take the lives of thousands of successive investigators to provide even the slightest chance of even the first steps toward experimental success." At the end of the day, he warns that "intelligent design can easily inspire a dogmatic overreaction."[21] He is especially careful not to blame the ills of scientific education in America on ID.

So how does he muster a case against intelligent design? His argument comes down not to a scientific defense of Darwin but a theological case against the doctrine of providence. First, he admits that "animal suffering isn't incidental to the unfolding of life, but integral to it" in the perspective of evolution. Second, he argues that "there is nothing kindly or providential about any of this, and it seems breathtakingly wasteful and inefficient." Evolution, that is, shows no signs of having been planned. Third, if God exists and evolution is true, then God must be whimsical at best or callous at worst, and who wants to believe in a God like that? The bottom line is that Kitcher just cannot fathom why God would have created the world through evolution. "There is every reason to think that alternative processes for unfolding the history of life could have eliminated much of the agony, that the goal could have been achieved without so long and bloody a prelude."[22] A just and merciful God would not create a world where countless numbers of creatures suffer in order that one species, Homo sapiens, can emerge to fulfill his plan.

Kitcher thinks Darwinism invalidates the monotheistic religions, but he does not think that all religions are doomed to extinction. To make his point, he divides religions into two basic kinds, providential and spiritual. In opposition to the emphasis on a transcendent and all-

---

21. Philip Kitcher, *Living with Darwin: Evolution, Design, and the Future of Faith* (New York: Oxford University Press, 2007) 9, 79, 81, 81, and 99.

22. Ibid., 123, 125, and 127.

powerful God in providential religions, spiritual religions "don't require the literal truth of any doctrines about supernatural beings." Spiritual religions inspire you to think kindly of others without requiring you to believe that there are any ultimate rewards or punishments for your actions. They are anything you want them to be, as long as you do not want them to give you something that you do not already have. How these religions will emerge and what will sustain them is, Kitcher admits, something of a mystery. He puts his hope in the possibility that science itself will show the way:

> The history of inquiry shows that our horizons have often expanded to encompass things previously undreamed of in anyone's natural philosophy. Whether inquiry will ever disclose anything that can satisfy the religious impulse, that can merit the title of "transcendent," is doubtful, and we can be confident that, even if this remote possibility is realized, it will not approximate any of the stories our species has so far produced. It would be arrogant, however, to declare categorically that there is nothing that might answer to our vague conception of the transcendent—there is too much that we do not yet know.[23]

So the purposeless meandering of evolution, which somehow both nurtured and killed our longing for the transcendent, might yet show us something radically new that will not be as satisfying as the religions of old but could prolong the day when we will have to reckon with our hopelessness—or something like that.

The question naturally arises whether keeping an anemic form of religion on life support is better than letting religion go altogether. Kitcher acknowledges that his concept of spiritual religion is so unstable that it might collapse into cosmopolitan secular humanism, although it does not seem to have occurred to him that cosmopolitan secular humanism is already the form that spirituality takes these days. What makes Kitcher so interesting is that he is a self-reflective Darwinian, which is rare enough, but he is also honest about the muddles his Darwinianism gets him into. He distances himself from his Darwinian colleagues who "are hectoring, almost exultant that comfort is being stripped away and faith undermined; frequently, they are without charity. And they are always without hope." He wishes there were role models today of stoic

23. Ibid., 132 and 152.

skepticism equal to figures like David Hume or T. H. Huxley. In their place are scholars buoyed by tenure and engaged in interesting research projects. The academy is almost enough of a community endowed with a higher purpose to provide a substitute for the church. Kitcher knows the weight of that *almost*.

> It is crushingly obvious that those most excited by the secular vision—those who celebrate the honesty of spurning false comfort—are people who can feel themselves part of the process of discovery and disclosure that has shown the reality behind old illusions. Celebrations of the human accomplishment in fathoming nature's secrets are less likely to thrill those who have only a partial understanding of what has been accomplished, and who recognize that they will not contribute, even in the humblest way, to the continued progress of knowledge.[24]

Is it any wonder that nearly all the committed Darwinians of the world are university and college professors? For many academics, the life of the mind, properly rewarded, coupled with a sense of service to higher learning, can take the place of the life of worship and the pursuit of holiness.

So the sad conclusion of Kitcher's book is that Darwinism must be its own reward. Darwin is inevitably disillusioning, but it offers as compensation the excitement of being on the side of those who disillusion, rather than those who are disillusioned. Darwinians have a choice between lying to themselves about the despairing implications of their theory and lying to everyone else in order to make their theory publicly acceptable. Scientists who give everything they have to the cause of evolutionary explanation can feel the satisfaction of expanding the world's knowledge base only if they ignore the deleterious social and moral consequences this knowledge entails.

Kitcher ends his book with the predictable glance at the possibility of finding consolation in the arts, but he also, less expectedly, suggests that social welfare policy might need reviving in the wake of Darwin's destructive march through Western culture. "The democracies that have most fully appreciated the enlightenment case, that have been the most successful in the transition to secularism, are those in which there are social networks of support." Precisely because Darwinism promotes

---

24. Ibid., 154 and 156.

a ruthless and individualistic version of capitalism, it is incumbent on nation-states to expand their social services. Since the intellectual deposit of Darwinism is so impoverishing, we need to reinvest in social safety nets and economic planning. "We should look more carefully at the causes of the pain, the harsh competitiveness of American life," Kitcher writes, without a trace of irony.[25] One of those causes, of course, would be Darwinism itself. At the end of Kitcher's Darwinian road lies some form of socialism. This is humanity's last best hope to demonstrate its dignity by contradicting the truth of evolution.

Perhaps the score of Darwinian books, like this one, that enthusiastically seek to demystify traditional religion while mystifying contemporary sentiments (that is, elevating current opinions and prejudices to the level of religious faith) are but the last nervous spurts of Darwinian energy as it succumbs to its own hopelessness. Perhaps it takes someone who is skeptical of both Darwinism and religion to plumb the depths of this hopelessness. "If Darwin's theory of evolution were true, there would be in every species a constant and ruthless competition to survive: a competition in which only a few in any generation can be winners. But it is perfectly obvious that human life is not like that, however it may be with other species."[26] The late David Stove, one Australia's finest philosophers, wrote these words shortly before his death in 1994. Stove was a fierce and polemical critic of intellectual charlatanism in any guise. He was also firmly convinced that all existing species have evolved from a common ancestor. He just did not think that Darwin did a good job of explaining how this happens. Darwinism cannot account for Darwin's own leaps of creative hypothesizing after his visit to the Galapagos Islands, nor can it account for his anguished reservations about the moral implications of his own work. Not just Darwin himself, but all people, from all apparent indications, stubbornly refuse to live down to their biological origins. Human beings just do not fit their evolutionary profile. This is surely why many people do not believe in Darwin. His theory just does not make sense of their experiences.

Stove argues that most Darwinians know this, which is why they work so hard to convince us that we are wrong about ourselves. That

25. Ibid., 163 and 166.
26. David Stove, *Darwinian Fairytales: Selfish Genes, Errors of Heredity, and Other Fables of Evolution* (New York: Encounter, 1995) 3.

is, they have developed elaborate scenarios to explain why human beings do not feel like they are the product of evolution, even though they are. Stove analyzes three such theories. The first is what he calls the cave man theory. It admits that people do not act in a Darwinian manner today, but it insists that they used to, long, long ago. The cave man story posits a brutal existence that we escaped when we learned the value of marriage, cooperation, and compassion. But where did these values comes from, if only the strongest survive? The cave man story is as commonplace in Darwinian circles as it is absurd. Stove notes that, "If Darwin's theory of evolution is true, no species can *ever* escape from the process of natural selection."[27] A better objection to the cave man theory, however, is simply its lack of evidence. Human beings and civilization are interdependent. Humanity emerged with culture, not against it. If there really had been a brutal period of a war of all against all, social bonding could never have developed. The cave man theory, in fact, is just another version of the social contract theory, popularized by Thomas Hobbes, John Locke, and Jean-Jacques Rousseau. These political philosophers theorized a state of nature in order to explain the structure and significance of government. Whether they really believed that a violent state of nature had actually existed in the ancient past is an open question, but nobody believes in the state of nature argument today—nobody, that is, except Darwinians.

The second and third theories are what Stove calls the hard man and soft man approaches. These are similar to what I called the good and the bad Darwinian cops in chapter one. The hard men of Darwinism simply deny that humans properly interpret their own experience. They deny most of human reality. According to the hard Darwinians, "a hospital among human beings is *inconceivable*, like a hospital among flies." Yet, since such hospitals exist, along with many other examples of social welfare and religious charity, they exhort their fellow human beings to come to their senses and avoid doing so much harm in the name of doing good. Hospitals and such are both impossible and injurious, which amounts to an obviously absurd position that hardly deserves analysis. The soft men of Darwinism try to ignore, rather than resolve the contradictions between their theory and the evidence of human experience. Soft Darwinians do not think that they are responsible for the moral

27. Ibid., 4.

and political implications of Darwinism. Indeed, they do not think anyone is responsible for those implications. They think that, since those implications are complicated and most likely unacceptable, they should just go away. The soft Darwinians throw up their hands to the whole sorry problem, which is not such a bad strategy. "Utter helplessness almost always has something very appealing about it, and intellectual helplessness is no exception to this rule," Stove observes.[28] While the hard men of Darwinism pose as wise old sages who see through the surface of civilization to its ugly depths, the soft men do not have the strength of their ugly convictions. Better put, they do not want to think too carefully about their convictions less they discover how ugly they are. The only conviction they openly embrace from Darwinism is the idea that everyone and everything belongs to a single family tree, an idea they dig out of its evolutionary setting in order to exhort their fellow human beings to try harder to be nice to each other.

To return to the nature of naturalism, we can conclude with Stove that hard Darwinians are likely to be political reactionaries, while soft Darwinians provide the backbone to the environmentalist movement. That Darwinian naturalism can result in two completely contradictory views of nature is not prima facie evidence of its conceptual flimsiness, but it should make anyone a bit suspicious. Because the cynicism of the hard Darwinians is difficult to sustain, the more likely course of Darwinian naturalism is to end up justifying a warm and fuzzy view of nature. Darwinism was born out of an ambivalent relationship to the romantic and idealistic views of nature that it tried to supplant, so perhaps it is not surprising that interpretations of Darwin can be so promiscuous and contradictory. A plain reading of Darwinian theory can hardly leave anyone with the impression that it can provide the conceptual foundation for ecological visions of nature's wholeness, but such is the vicissitudes of history. Environmentalists talk about nature's balance, but if they are Darwinians, they should really talk about evolution's triumphs, because what balance nature has is attributable to the way some species and plants gain control over their environment and thus over each other. Technically defined, balance is the ratio of prey to predator, but that ratio only looks constant because evolution moves so slowly. What looks like harmony to us is only the intermittent peace

---

28. Ibid., 11 and 19.

established by the mobilization of militant organic forces. Evolution, in fact, is more effective in the elimination of species than in their creation. Animals and plants that do not fit the ever-changing ecological dynamic are cast aside and wiped away.

Nevertheless, few people are content with such a harsh view of nature, so Darwinians cooperate in inventing a romantic version of naturalism that functions as a substitute for traditional religious faith. In the new world of environmentalism, Darwinism is used to legitimate the natural order by insisting that nature knows best, even though nature has no purpose and no design. Take, for example, the work of Edward O. Wilson, a professor of biology at Harvard University, who, in logical leaps that are anything but gradual, begins with the struggle for life and ends up with biophilia, the love for all living things.[29] Wilson evokes wonder at the amazing number of ways that our species is bound to other species, and all species to each other, but he can do so only by lapsing into periodic bouts of amnesia regarding the way that this bonding, according to his own biological theory, is one of competition and violence, not mutual love and admiration. Wilson's biophilia leads him to a deep ambivalence regarding humanity. According to the Bible, what sets humans apart from other animals is God's decision to call us out of our animal nature and into a relationship with the absolute. Nothing sets humans apart in Wilson's world except our ability to abstract from our dependence on nature a feeling of warmth for our competitors that has no evidentiary basis in nature itself—no evidentiary basis other than the fact of our evolutionary triumph over all of nature, which affords us the luxury of feeling kindly in a condescending way to the victims of our success.

In his quest to discover a Darwinian ethic that can inspire the task of rejuvenating our post-Darwinian experience of nature, Wilson erases the human in order to affirm the natural. Along those lines naturalism gives way to fascism, as the French philosopher Luc Ferry has documented in an important study of the political consequences of European romantic movements.[30] The deeper ecology goes the more

---

29. Edward O. Wilson, *Biophilia* (Cambridge: Harvard University Press, 1986).

30. Luc Ferry, *The New Ecological Order*, trans. Carol Volk (Chicago: University of Chicago Press, 1992). Also see Boria Sax, *Animals in the Third Reich: Pets, Scapegoats, and the Holocaust* (New York: Continuum, 2000).

totalitarian it becomes. The Nazis, for example, continued and intensified the anti-humanistic strain of German Romanticism that promoted the protection of the environment and the rights of animals at the expense of human uniqueness. Growing morality from the soil is always a bloody task. The ever eloquent Marilynne Robinson puts her finger on the strange confusions of Darwinian naturalism. "If, as the Darwinists assure us, there is only the natural world, then nothing can be alien to it, and our arrangements, however extravagantly they depart from the ways of other creatures, can never be called unnatural. It is certainly one of the oddest features of a school of thought that denies human exceptionalism as its first premise that it finds so much of human behavior contrary to nature—and objectionable on those grounds."[31] The nature of naturalism is the denial of the human, and what could be more dangerous—for humans—than that?

---

31. Marilynne Robinson, *The Death of Adam: Essays on Modern Thought* (Boston: Houghton Mifflin, 1998) 68.

Conclusion

Given so many contested issues and troubling terrains in the debates over evolution and creation, it might be helpful to step back and ask how we should talk about the more general relationship between science and religion. There are, it seems to me, three broad possibilities, and we can think about them in terms of stories with their own genre, plot, main character, and ending. The first is the scientific battle for liberation from religion, the second is the mutual indifference of the two, and the third is the return of religion as the guarantor of the value of science.

The first story is a bit dated today, but there are still those who like to tell it, like the Darwinian bad cops I discussed in chapter 1. Pitched in a heroic mode, it follows the standard linear plot of rags to riches as it traces the career of science, the main character, in its triumph over its antagonist, religion. It ends happily with the promise that technology can make us happy. Western civilization is defined in terms of an inevitable drumbeat of progress that is made possible only by liberation from the restraints of theological dogma. The story of scientific advancement and theological obscurantism, which has its origins in Protestant polemics against Roman Catholicism, comes so naturally to so many people in the academy today that they forget it is just a story, and a pretty fabulous story at that. In many circles of the cultural elite, this story carries as much weight as the Christian story once did. Indeed, to be admitted into the circle of the cultural elite requires belief in evolution as a process without purpose, just as it once was taken for granted that to be a respectable member of society was to believe in God. From a sociological point of view, speaking the language of evolution has become the substitute for theological literacy in terms of demarcating the sophisticated from the uneducated and the enlightened from the reactionary.

The Dome of Eden

The idea that science and religion are opposed to each other is actually a fairly recent development in human history. Indeed, the most recent scholarship in the history of science emphasizes how the identity of science is inextricably intermingled with the history of Christianity.[1] Probably the best that can be said about the position that science and religion are inherently opposed is that this opposition is but one stage in a much longer political struggle between church and state. In other words, this debate will not be solved for hundreds of years, and it will be solved only by the kind of gradual cultural shifts that will accelerate, restrain, or even reverse the process of secularism that has marginalized religion by transferring many of its goals and responsibilities to the state. The worst that can be said about this story is that, if it were to become the dominant narrative of the cultural elite, it could end with the defeat of science, not its triumph. What, after all, motivates individual scientists to dedicate themselves to the pursuit of knowledge, and what provides the rational justification for the trust the rest of us put in this enterprise? Throughout most of Western history, the quest to understand the natural world was a product of the religiously grounded motivation to improve the human condition. Likewise, people could be confident that scientific investigations of nature were worthwhile because they shared the monotheistic worldview that nature is orderly and that the source of that order is a trustworthy and benevolent deity.

Taxonomy, the most basic and thankless scientific task, illustrates this important question of scientific motivation. Collecting, naming, and organizing things—anything, from banana labels to dachshund paperweights—seems to be built into human nature. At least, that's what the Bible tells us. The first task God gave Adam was the naming of the animals. God "brought them to Adam to see what he would call them" and "the man gave names to all cattle, and to the birds of the air, and to every animal of the field" (Gen 2:19–20). Far from being an ancient myth with no contemporary relevance, the story of Adam's task has inspired and shaped human endeavor throughout the centu-

---

1. See, for example, Peter Harrison, *The Bible, Protestantism, and the Rise of Natural Science* (Cambridge: Cambridge University Press, 1998), which shows how the scientific reading of nature is in debt to Protestant theories of a non-symbolic reading of the Bible as well as his most recent book, *The Fall of Man and the Foundations of Science* (Cambridge: Cambridge University Press, 2007), which shows how belief in an original paradise and its environment of perfect knowledge shaped scientific ambition.

ries. Modern science got its start in the golden age of exploration, when collectors began cataloguing exotic plants and animals in the hope of restoring Adam's complete knowledge of the world. Some sixteenth-century scholars, like Benito Montano (1527–1598), gave Hebrew names to the places Columbus discovered, because they assumed that the Bible must contain all the words we need to understand the New World. Others realized that there were more things to know and to be named than they ever imagined. Francis Bacon exhorted gentlemen of means to build gardens "with rooms to stable in all rare beasts and to cage in all rare birds . . . so you may have in small compass a model of the universal nature made private."[2] Adam's sin, Christians believed, not only expelled the first couple from the Garden. Plants and animals too had been dispersed, but now scholars could imagine a return to paradise by achieving universal knowledge.

If God were to bring all the animals before man today, the line would be too long. This scene could only take place on the computer, which is exactly what the new Encyclopedia of Life proposes. This remarkable project aims to gather descriptions of every species known to science on a single Web site. Harvard biologist Edward O. Wilson has been the driving force behind the encyclopedia, and his enthusiasm for it is unbounded. "It's going to have everything known on it," he has said in various Web interviews, "and everything new is going to be added as we go along." Nearly two million species are known, but scientists estimate that ten times that many are yet to be discovered. Most of these unknown species are bacteria, fungi, and insects. We can name them because we know, or want to know, everything about them.

Call it what you will—an electronic ark, the final chapter in the book of nature—the Encyclopedia of Life is the culmination of Adam's task. Wilson's own specialty is the study of ants, and he hopes that putting all 14,000 known species on the Web site will stimulate others to add all the unknown ones, a number that might be as high as 25,000 additional species. This is a good example of how naming becomes obsessive (it becomes an end in itself) when it has no ultimate purpose. Our ancestors were inspired to name the animals by the idea that the world is

---

2. Francis Bacon, "Counsels for the Prince," *The Essays*, ed. John Pitcher (New York: Penguin, 1985) 263. For more on Montano and Bacon on collecting, see Kevin Rushby, *Paradise: A History of the Idea that Rules the World* (New York: Carroll & Graf, 2007) ch. 8.

The Dome of Eden

a good and orderly gift from God. Adam named the animals as an act of husbandry and stewardship, but Genesis also portrays Adam's task as a quest for companionship. Right before God parades the animals before Adam, he says, "It is not good that man should be alone; I will make him a helper as his partner" (Gen 2:18). The next verses states, "So out of the ground the Lord God formed every animal of the field and every bird of the air." The Israelites were an agricultural people, so it should not be surprising that this sacred text portrays the animals as the first companions of man. It should also not be surprising that Adam did not find among the animals "a helper as his partner" (2:20). At this point in the Genesis story God creates the woman to be flesh of the man's flesh. Animals, Genesis teaches, are a good part of a divinely sanctioned order, but we are not one of them. We can name them because we know that we have a destiny that transcends the animal world.

The current frenzy for naming has a different basis. Post-Darwinians name the animals because we know that we are the same as them, not different. We share the same biological structure, and, more importantly, we share the same precarious existence on the environmentally troubled planet Earth. Indeed, much of the hype for the Encyclopedia of Life concerns the claim that only by naming every species can we hope to preserve them from extinction. Yet there is no reason to think that this quest for absolute knowledge will lead to the protection of animals rather than their exploitation. Wilson is a champion of biodiversity and the love of nature for its own sake, yet even he admits that the Encyclopedia of Life will accelerate the discovery of new plant and animal species for the purpose of genetic-enhancement research, crop productivity, and pharmaceutical advancements. If knowledge is power and humans are one animal among many, what will keep us from using this knowledge to lord our power over all other animals?

Can science continue to flourish as a collective pursuit for the good of everyone without a dose of idealism about the ennoblement of humanity and a boost in confidence about the correspondence between a uniquely rational humanity and the orderly structures of nature? The distinction between technology and science is often drawn by those who want to preserve the purity of investigation from the practicalities of application, but this distinction is itself theoretical with little basis in scientific practice. Science is practiced in institutions, whether govern-

Conclusion

mental, corporate, or educational, and there is no guarantee that these institutions are or will continue to be benign servants of the common good. Science is only as good as the scientists who practice it, and they are only as good as the human nature they share. Science is all about a promise of expanding possibilities, but all promises can be broken, and few promises are devoid of deceit. Science could lead to discoveries that will deplete Earth's natural resources and tear humanity apart as easily as it could lead to discoveries that will bring world peace and prosperity.

The second story is actually a story about two stories, the plots of which are only tangentially related to each other. The story of two stories is like a postmodern novel with no heroes, no clear ending, and a jumble of juxtaposed narratives that never quite intersect or merge into each other. In one story God is the main character and in the other evolution leads the way, and many people are content to leave these stories travelling on parallel tracks, never to meet this side of the eschaton. This narrative strategy is tempting for both secular Darwinians and committed Christians, but both groups should resist it like the devil. For Darwinians, it lets them excuse themselves from debates about the moral and metaphysical foundations of their theory, and they can do so by appealing to philosophy itself, or at least postmodern trends in philosophy. Many postmodern philosophers think of science as a sociologically prescribed set of practices and habits that needs no rational explication or defense. Influenced by Ludwig Wittgenstein's discussion of "language games," these philosophers describe science as a coherent set of actions comprising a distinct linguistic community with its own rules and regulations, which function as a grammar to determine proper speech for that community. From this perspective, theological interventions into scientific debates are not wrong (there is no right and wrong) as much as they are merely garbled; they just do not make sense. Theologians might as well be speaking in tongues when they try to talk to scientists about their presuppositions. Science, it follows, has no more need for philosophical justification than football, cooking, or card playing.

That conclusion can be appealing to scientists who are suspicious of any governmental or philosophical oversight of their practices, and there is good reason for this suspicion. For the most part, science works best unfettered by special interest groups pleading their case for a piece of the laboratory pie. It would be naive, however, to think that this suspicion of external influence is unrelated to the status scientists have obtained through their many achievements. There are immense economic and political forces at work granting the sciences the prestige that serves to marginalize theological worries about Darwinism. Those very same forces, however, are also constantly pressuring the sciences to contribute to the economic, military, and medical industries of the modern nation-state. Indeed, the story of two stories provides no rational resources that scientists can use to defend themselves from any external intrusion. True, science is a human practice, and thus it never escapes the foibles and fetters of human vanity, greed, and ambition. But if it is not more than that, then there is no reason why it should be granted a special place in our society, immune to market forces, ideological demands, and philosophical and theological debates.

Christians too should resist the story of two stories, even though it looks friendlier than the Protestant/Enlightenment story of progress over irrational and superstitious forces. Like any story, this one can be told in various ways. One way we can call Catholic and the other Protestant. The Catholic way could be very orthodox but is usually deeply problematic. The Catholic version begins with Thomas Aquinas's distinction between primary and secondary causes. For Thomas, God's causal relationship to the world is primary because it is continuous and comprehensive, upholding the whole universe, but it does not supplant or disrupt the secondary causation in the world that is the object of scientific study. This distinction, in the hands of some postmodern theologians, can end up providing the framework for the use of two separate languages to describe reality, one related to the primary causation of God and the other given over to the laws regulating secondary causes. From this perspective, religious language looks like it is referring to causal relations (God as an agent directing the course of events and responding to prayer, for example), but it really isn't. The "two languages" story assumes that God's work in the world is utterly mysterious, because God's agency is completely unlike anything we have ever directly experienced. God is unique, the cause of all causes, but not a cause that can be specified in any detailed way. If God's causal efficacy in the world were detectable, that would be a scandal for religion, since it would reduce God to one cause among many causes, rather than the cause that sustains every cause. When motivated by the desire to protect the mystery of God, the Catholic version of the story of "two stories" is an admirable and even necessary theological task. Too often, however, the story of "two stories" is used to smother pressing and unavoidable questions about how God acts in the world.

The Protestant version of the "two stories" story is quite a bit simpler. Let me describe it with a quotation from the accomplished historian, Edward Larson: "Perhaps the most significant development in the relationship between science and American religion over the past two centuries within the religious community has been the disengagement of mainline Protestantism from the science and religion dialogue."[3] This disengagement was rationalized in various sophisticated ways, but it basically takes the form of indifference. When I was being trained in Protestant theology in undergraduate and graduate school, for example, I remember taking great pride in the fact that Protestant theologians simply did not enter into the debate over evolution. We were trained to extract meaning from texts, not argue about what constitutes a fact or how to find facts in the first place. Evolution was somebody else's problem.

In its most sophisticated form, the Protestant story of "two stories" treats the Bible as a narrative that has literary but not metaphysical meaning. This is typically called narrative theology. Francesca Murphy argues in her book, *God Is Not a Story*, that this school reduces theology to the modest task of describing Christian beliefs rather than arguing for their truth.[4] Narrative theologians analyze the grammatical structure of the Christian story on the assumption that the Christian narrative is a world unto itself, but they are skeptical of attempts to turn that narrative into a worldview that can be evaluated by universal rational criteria. Nonetheless, if God is one and the world is one, then there should be one true view of the world, even if that one true view is hard to put into words. Besides, even though some theologians are content to treat Christianity as one story among many stories, each with their

---

3. Edward J. Larson, *The Creation-Evolution Debate: Historical Perspectives* (Athens: University of Georgia Press, 2007) 42.

4. Francesca Aran Murphy, *God Is Not a Story: Realism Revisited* (New York: Oxford University Press, 2007).

own internal logic and grammar, most scientists (and most educated people in general) are not willing to treat science as just another story about the world. Narrative theologians thus give science the last word on what the world objectively is. As a result, God's relationship to the world is evacuated of any intellectual or social relevance. Scientists tell us how the world works, and religious believers have to fit their notion of God into that framework. The result is a determinism that does not do justice to science (especially quantum physics) and a fatalism that does not do justice to religion (especially Christianity's emphasis on a free decision for faith).

In sum, postmodernism can protect science from metaphysical arguments and protect theism from science only by relativizing the claims of each. Note how internally inconsistent this is. If science is only one sociological game among others, then there is no assurance that its truth-claims take precedence over other groups playing similar games. After all, theologians and philosophers also play their language games, and one of those games consists in examining the rules, meaning, and value of the sciences. If there is no game of games—that is, a game that is played the outcome of which determines how we should think about games in general—then every game is as good as any other and no game can outbid any other. Scientists can plead that it is the nature of their game to be set aside from political, economic, and theological scrutiny, but theologians can point out that it is the nature of their game to bother scientists with their questions and arguments. Without criteria for what constitutes knowledge and how the disciplines fit together, only custom—or administrative fiat—can separate these players from interfering with each other. Yet this whole discussion is unnecessary because the story of stories is an attempt to lay out the rules for how every intellectual game is to be played, even if those rules amount to a set of barriers that promote mutual indifference. The conclusion must be drawn that there is no way *not* to tell one story, even if the story is that of two very different stories.

If the story of scientific triumph over religious prejudice and the story of a world that has no single story both fail to do justice to the interplay of faith and reason, then it might be time to return to the story of theology as the queen of the sciences. This is the classic story of an underdog that makes a comeback against all odds. It is unlikely,

Conclusion

perhaps, but there has been a resurgence of talk about theology finding its rightful place in the academic world, and many theologians, led by the example most prominently of Nancey Murphy and George Ellis, think that place is at the top of a hierarchy of languages each of which is necessary for describing the complexity of nature.[5] Theologians of this type argue that scientific language is incomplete in its efforts to describe the emergence of genuine novelty and creativity in natural processes. Science does a perfectly adequate job of mapping causal trajectories, but causation is less like a linear chain than a web of many layers. Science looks at things as closely as possible but ends up positing objects that no eye can see, while theology tries to discipline our religious imaginations with the thought of a power that pervades and sustains every object, from the universe as a whole down to the smallest molecule. That sounds vaguely formulated, but that is where this position now stands, mainly due to its inherent complexity but also to this carefully enforced rule in writing about Darwinism for respectable publications: You can poke as many holes into Darwin's theory as you want, as long as you don't make a gap wide enough for someone to drive intelligent design through it. A corollary follows. The more holes you poke, the more you must distance yourself from the intelligent design movement. Even showing sympathy for that movement could bring the wrath of the self-appointed boundary police (those who patrol the border between science and religion) down on your head. Thus, the number of theologians, philosophers, and scientists who argue that Darwinism cannot account for the creative purposefulness of evolution are growing, yet their writings have not congealed into a coherent movement because of what they are so insistent on denying (that evolutionary theory requires an intelligent designer).

A recent book by a group of process philosophers, edited by the renowned religious thinker John Cobb, is on the cutting edge of evolutionary theory but for that very reason is a good example of this quan-

---

5. See Nancey Murphy and George F. R. Ellis, *On the Moral Nature of the Universe: Theology, Cosmology, and Science* (Minneapolis: Fortress, 1996). For a critical reflection, see Robert John Russell, "The Theological Consequences of the Thermodynamics of a Moral Universe: An Appreciative Critique and Extension of the Murphy/Ellis Project," *CTNS Bulletin* 18 (1998) 19-24, and Philip Clayton, "Hierarchies: The Core Argument for A Naturalistic Christian Faith," *Zygon* 43 (2008) 27-41.

dary.[6] As systems of thought, process philosophy and Darwinism have a lot in common. Both develop a dynamic account of nature and a subsequent ethics of interconnectedness. In both, relations matter more than individuals. In reality, however, few philosophical schools have more at stake in rejecting Darwinism in order to insure their own survival. Process metaphysics, which dates back to the work of the mathematician and logician Alfred North Whitehead, posits some form of agency (what process thinkers call "subjectivity") to every object in nature, and it sees goal-directed activity in even the most micro of events. If the sole agent of evolution is the inert workings of natural selection, then process philosophy has nothing to add to Darwinism. When process philosophers try to conceive of the essence of natural processes, they are trying to do more than describe a random stumbling through a biological space unshaped by purposive agents. Purposeless evolution puts process philosophy out of business.

Darwinism has always been metaphysically weak, if not confused, and process thought has always been the most metaphysically robust and confident of modern philosophical systems. It was only a matter of time, then, that Whitehead and Darwin would go at it, but the result is less exciting that it could have been. In his editorial contributions to the volume, Cobb at times speaks as if the problems of Darwinism are purely rhetorical, due to a bit of well-meaning exaggeration on the part of Darwin's defenders. "The problems highlighted in this book," he writes in the preface, "are certain assumptions and overstatements in the post-Darwin development of evolutionary theory" (viii). What Cobb calls neo-Darwinism, by which he means the synthesis of Darwin's original theory with modern genetics, is typically expressed, he argues, in "tight and extreme formulations" (ix). In other words, if Darwinians would just lighten up their terminology, everybody could get along. This is disingenuous because most of the contributors to this volume are trying to reintegrate science and religion by gutting Darwinism's core assumption about the lack of purpose in nature. The consensus in these essays, with the exception of the biology professor Francisco Ayala, who seems out of place, is that Darwinism is beholden to a mechanistic metaphys-

---

6. John B. Cobb, Jr., ed. *Back To Darwin: A Richer Account of Evolution* (Grand Rapids: Eerdmans, 2008). See my review in *Reviews in Religion and Theology* 16 (2009) 252-55.

ics that cannot do justice to the way evolution really works. The result is a challenge not just to the metaphysical backing of Darwinism but also to "much empirical evidence" (ix) that is neglected by Darwinism's "extreme formulations."

Process philosophers find agency, purpose, and meaning everywhere they look in nature, and most of all they find the old boundaries that "protected" science from religion to be at best obsolete and at worst an impediment to empirical research. For example, Jeffrey Schloss, Distinguished Professor of Biology at Westmont College, expertly surveys the problem of determining what directionality is and how alleged trends like complexity might be measured. He then looks at size, energy expenditure, and life history trends (parental investment, for example) to argue that evolution shows evidence of "contingency constrained by necessity [which] is what produces telos" (348). He concludes that the cosmos is not empty but rather ambiguous, which suggests that the reasons religion provides for hope are not contrary to the evidence of nature. The key term for many of these thinkers is "emergence," which suggests increasing levels of creativity, rationality, and individuality that cannot be explained by relying on what happens at the lowest levels of biological change. Process philosophers insist that all organisms are active agents of evolutionary change, something hyper-Darwinians refuse to admit, and they argue that agency must be understood from the perspective of its fullest development, not its most passive examples. All of these arguments could be developed in a way that is sympathetic to intelligent design theory, yet this book and many like it continue to gain their entrance into respectable academic circles by refusing to be associated with the intelligent design community. The intelligent design debate is really about the sufficiency of methodological naturalism, and as such, it should expand in the future to include all scholars interested in broadening the Darwinian horizons.[7]

Whether theology eventually retakes its place as queen of the sciences or merely takes a seat at the academic table of respectable worldviews, the third story of theology's triumph could be as advantageous for science as it would be for religion. That Darwinians and secularists have

---

7. For an extremely helpful essay on this topic, see Philip J. Jacobs, "An Argument Over Methodological Naturalism at the Vatican Observatory," *Heythrop Journal* 49 (2008) 542–81. Jacobs raises the point that a univocity theory of religious language calls into question strong versions of methodological naturalism (550).

a story to tell about culture, the West, and the whole of human history should remind us that debates about evolution are ultimately arguments between competing narratives about what we are, where we come from, and what we are destined to become. Scientists have an important voice in the social construction of any such grand narrative, but the idea that scientists can monopolize not only knowledge about nature but also the evaluation of that knowledge is hubris of a very unscientific nature. On what grounds, under whose authority, or with what skills do scientists claim to know the limits of their own enterprise, let alone its historical trajectory and metaphysical assumptions? As Christopher B. Kaiser has written, "A thick description of natural science inevitably leads to theological questions and cultivates a thick description of nature, humanity, history and God."[8] Naturalism is not natural; religion is. Naturalism is a recent metaphysical development, while all cultures—with the possible exception of contemporary Europe's attempt to reinvent itself as a secular culture bereft of religious memories—have been deeply immersed in religion of one kind or another. Taking a long view of history, Darwinism might be, as Steve Fuller ruminates, "the last gasp of what Karl Popper called 'historicism,' a cluster of 19th-century theories that would grant history a measure of necessity comparable to what physics strives for, at least in terms of using our knowledge of the past, combined with general principles, to determine both what must and what cannot happen in the future."[9] Darwinians are the biological equivalent of those who think that to understand anything we need only put it in its historical context. If Fuller is even half right, then Christians need to go all out in defending human freedom and dignity not only for the sake of Christianity but also for the sake of science.

Let me end with a story to illustrate the dangers of Darwinism but also to explain how Darwinians can be so nice about their not-so-nice theory. Picture the Greco-Judeo-Christian heritage of the West as a bank account, an enormous sum of money that is set aside as an endowment, and imagine that people have been drawing from it for centuries in order to sustain the highest moral ideals of compassion for others and

---

8. Christopher B. Kaiser, *Toward a Theology of Scientific Endeavour: The Descent of Science* (Burlington, VT: Ashgate, 2007) 1.

9. Steve Fuller, *Science vs. Religion? Intelligent Design and the Problem of Evolution* (Malden, MA: Polity, 2007) 127.

respect for human dignity. Of course, like all large sums of money, this endowment can be misspent, but it has also funded all of the great moral achievements of Western history. Now suppose that there are two kinds of people in the West that dip into this endowment. We will call one group orthodox Darwinians and the other group religious traditionalists. Religious traditionalists are those who try to put something back in the endowment from which they draw. They treat their withdrawals as loans and feel a bit guilty if they do not reinvest in the original sum. In other words, they want the endowment to grow. Orthodox Darwinians draw from the endowment just like everyone else, but they think they do not need Greco-Judeo-Christian standards and values. They draw from the endowment somewhat secretly and sheepishly, and if they are caught taking any money out they deny that they even know the bank exists. They publicly work for the depletion of the endowment. They think it is a burden to have so much moral wealth on hand, so they squander it freely and do not put any money back into this account, and they hope that someday it will be empty. Indeed, they hope that some day the whole bank with go bankrupt. Orthodox Darwinians are nice people living in a basically good world, full of hope and ideals, but it is a world that their ideology did not make, and it is a world that their ideology cannot sustain. When the Greco-Judeo-Christian endowment in the West runs dry, overdrawn and undervalued, orthodox Darwinism will be all that the West has left. That will be a day of reckoning, when we will see what Darwinism is really worth.

Index of Names

Adams, Marilyn McCord, 263n18
Allegra, Gabriel, 279, 280
Alles, Gregory D., 333
Alter, Robert, 186
Anderson, Gary A., 143n4, 222n10, 317
Anselm, 278
Aquinas, Thomas, 258, 277, 279, 354
Aristotle, 56–58, 111, 272
Arnhart, Larry, 85
Atran, Scott, 332n11
Attfield, Robin, 52n55
Augustine, 138, 150, 153–55, 176–78, 225, 272, 309
Avise, John C., 27n23
Ayala, Francisco, 240, 358

Bacon, Francis, 351
Baer, Jonathan R., 75n11
Bainton, Roland H., 176n33
Balthasr, Hans Urs von, 301
Barham, James, 327
Barnes, Michel René, 177
Barr, Stephen M., 107n18
Barrett, Justin L., 59n65, 334, 335
Barth, Karl, 11, 143, 181–208, 283
Beatty, John, 65n77
Beecher, Henry Ward, 77
Behe, Michael, 110, 112–15
Benedict XVI, Pope, 2, 107
Berry, R. J., 8, 9
Bird, Phyllis A., 284n48
Blake, William, 315
Blocher, Henri, 145n6
Bloom, Howard, 235
Boersma, Hans, 259n14
Bouteneff, Peter, 154
Bowler, Peter J., 69n1, 78
Boyd, Gregory A., 227–31, 234
Boyer, Pascal, 332–34

Browne, Janet, 26n21
Bryan, William Jennings, 71–74, 88–91, 251
Budiansky, Steven, 305
Budziszewski, J., 328
Burleigh, Michael, 281, 282
Burnham, Terry, 85n29

Calvin, John, 171, 174–77, 184, 197
Carol, J. B., 162n17
Carroll, Scott P., 47n50
Cartmill, Matt, 315n16
Chesterton, G. K., 24, 282
Christman, Angela Russell, 177n34
Clark, Stephen R. L., 130n43, 248, 249
Clayton, Philip, 357n5
Clements, Ronald E., 172
Cobb, John, 357, 358
Collins, C. John, 182–84
Copernicus, 13
Corey, Michael, 95, 96, 268n27
Couch, Mark B., 265n23
Cowen, Tyler, 243n32
Crick, Francis, 16
Crisp, Oliver D., 264n20, 285n50
Cross, Richard, 277
Cunningham, Conor, 20n10
Curry, Oliver, 253
Custance, Arthur C., 143n3

Darrow, Clarence, 70, 71, 73, 74, 84, 88, 90
Davies, Paul, 16n5
Dawkins, Richard, 26, 27, 28, 30–33, 35, 46, 49
Dean, Maximilian Mary, 262n17
Deane-Drummond, Celia, 93n1, 301
Delio, Ilia, 262n18, 277n38
Dembski, William A., 110, 111, 118

363

Index of Names

Dennett, Daniel C., 26, 28–30, 31–33, 35, 46
Denton, Michael, 113, 223, 224
Dewey, John, 82, 83
Dillard, Annie, 236, 239, 241
Dillow, Joseph, 216, 217
Dobzhansky, Theodosius, 23
Dorrien, Gary, 77, 83n25
Dose, Klaus, 15
Drower, E. S., 177n35
Drummond, Henry, 81
Dylan, Bob, 241

Ekrich, A. Roger, 190n9
England, Richard, 60n69
Erasmus, Desiderius, 256

Falk, Darrell, 316
Ferry, Luc, 347
Figes, Orlando, 250
Fiske, John, 80
Foley, Robert A., 18n8
Forsyth, Neil, 137n46
Fortey, Richard, 16
Francis, Mark, 77n15
Freud, Sigmund, 45, 46, 67
Frost, Robert, 169
Fuller, Buckminster, 210
Fuller, Steve, 62, 117, 360

Gathercole, Simon, 285n50, 291, 292
Galton, Francis, 71
Giberson, Karl, 41n43
Gillespie, Neal C., 79, 326
Ginzberg, Louis, 271n30, 318n19
Girard, René, 205
Goodenough, Ursula, 337
Goodwin, Brian, 24n18
Goss, Phillip, 124n36
Gould, Stephen Jay, 18n8, 50, 105, 115, 247
Graff, Gerald, 23
Grant, Robert, 307
Gray, Asa, 79, 100
Greene-McCreight, K. E., 183
Gregersen, Niels Henrik, 53

Grenz, Stanley J., 285n50
Griffin, Carl W., 175n30
Gunkel, Hermann, 191, 284
Guthrie, Stewart Elliott, 334n15

Hagopian, David G., 123n35
Haig, David, 63
Ham, Ken, 129, 131
Harris, John, 254n8
Harrison, Peter, 350n1
Hart, D. G., 88n33, 89n34
Hart, David Bentley, 232–35
Hasker, William, 100n12
Haug, Matthew C., 47n49
Haught, John F., 98n8, 106n15, 338–40
Hayes, Zachary, 280n40
Heidegger, Martin, 159
Heidel, Alexander, 144n5
Hobbes, Thomas, 238, 345
Hodge, Charles, 325
Hodgson, Geoffrey M., 327n4
Hoeveller, J. David, 76
Hofstadter, Richard, 32
Holloway, Carson, 85n30
Horden, Peregrine, 190n7
Hull, David L., 54n58, 249n2
Hunter, Cornelius, 42n44, 325n1
Hütter, Reinhard, 259n13
Huxley, Julian, 70
Hyman, Stanley Edgar, 299, 300

Ingham, Mary Beth, 257n11
Inwagen, Peter van, 95
Israel, Charles A., 75n11

Jackelén, Antje, 140n1
Jacobs, Alan, 153n10
Jacobs, Philip J., 359n7
Jastrow, Robert, 20
Jenson, Robert, 285n50
John Paul II, Pope, 106, 283
Johnson, Monte Ransome, 57n62
Johnson, Phillip, 84, 110
Johnston, George Sim, 106n16
Jones, John E., III, 116

Kaiser, Christopher B., 360
Kant, Immanuel, 58, 59, 66, 302

Index of Names

Kazin, Michael, 73n8
Keller, Catherine, 199, 200, 207
Kelly, Henry Ansgar, 149n7
Keynes, Randal, 330
Kitcher, Philip, 340-44
Kohn, David, 62, 63
Koonin, Eugene V., 50n52
Koons, Robert, 49
Korsmeyer, Jerry, 108-10
Kugel, James L., 274n35
Kuzniar, Alice, 306n8

LaCocque, André, 128, 170
Lane, Nick, 236-38
Larson, Edward, 71, 75, 355
Lehmann, Karl, 214n3
Levenson, Jon, 231
Levine, George, 298
Ledegang, Fred, 176n32
Lennox, James G., 65n77
Levine, George, 31, 32, 33, 34
Lewens, Tim, 60n67
Lewis, Arthur H., 220n9
Lewis, C. S., 140, 160, 190, 320, 321
Livingstone, David, 251
Lloyd, Michael, 297n1
Luther, Martin, 197

Machen, J. Gresham, 86-90
Mangina, Joseph L., 205
Marsden, George, 74n9
Marx, Karl, 45, 46, 67
Masani, P. R., 97n6
May, Gerhard, 272n31
Mayr, Ernst, 7, 47n49, 51-53, 55, 65, 66, 69
McCalla, Arthur, 59, 216, 329
McCready, Douglas, 291-94
McFarland, Ian A., 287-89
McKinnon, Susan, 331n9
Mencken, H. L., 70
Mendel, Gregor, 70
Messer, Neil, 322
Meyer, Stephen C., 17n7, 110
Middleton, J. Richard, 285-87
Midgley, Mary, 55, 98
Miller, J. Maxwell, 284n48

Miller, Kenneth R., 23, 297
Miller, Stanley, 15
Millstein, Robert L., 56n61
Milton, John, 270
Montano, Benito, 351
Montgomery, Scott L., 25n19
Moore, Aubrey, 60n69, 82
Moore, James R., 78n16
Moore, Russell D., 289, 290, 294
Morris, Henry, 124, 125, 161, 216, 226, 227, 284
Morris, Simon Conway, 12, 13, 17, 18, 19, 222, 223n12, 265-67, 279
Murphy, Francesca, 355
Murphy, Nancey, 357n5

Nagel, Thomas, 116n30
Nichols, Terence, L., 325n1
Niebuhr, Reinhold, 99
Nietzsche, Friedrich, 61, 88
Nöldeke, Theodore, 284

Oakes, Edward T., 250n3
Oberman, Heiki, 257n10
O'Brien, Graham J., 14
Odell, Margaret S., 172n27
O'Hear, Anthony, 34n35, 77, 252
Olson, Randy, 119
Origen, 154, 176, 317
Ospovat, Dov, 60n68
Oviedo, Luis, 333n13

Paley, William, 59, 60, 78, 79
Pangle, Thomas L., 277n39
Pannenberg, Wolfhart, 259n13
Patton, Kimberley, 201
Paul, Diane B., 32n31
Pendergast, Richard J., 140n2
Peters, Ted, 109n19
Phipps, William E., 79
Pickstock, Catherine, 257n11, 260n15
Pinker, Steven, 84
Pius XII, Pope, 106
Plato, 111, 225, 239, 249

Polanyi, Michael, 118
Polkinghorne, John, 321

365

Index of Names

Pollan, Michael, 130n42
Popper, Karl, 51, 52

Quammen, David, 309n12
Quispel, Gilles, 178n36

Rad, Gerhard von, 167n23
Ramm, Bernard, 155
Rana, Fazale, 17, 18, 162, 163
Reed, Annette, 149
Richards, Robert J., 24, 34n34, 59n64, 225n13
Rifkin, Jeremy, 96
Roberts, Jon H., 78n16
Robinson, Marilynne, 27, 348
Rodin, R. Scott, 203n16
Rolston, Holmes, 98n8
Ross, Hugh, 162, 163
Rose, Michael R., 44
Roughgarden, Joan, 336
Rue, Loyal, 206, 239
Ruse, Michael 54n58
Rushby, Kevin, 351n2
Russell, Jeffrey Burton, 214
Russell, Norman, 280n41
Russell, Robert John, 22n12, 96, 97, 99, 357n5

Sanford, J. C., 18
Scafi, Alessandro, 153
Schloss, Jeffrey P., 118, 119, 359
Schmitt, Carl, 199–202
Schneider, John R., 310n14
Schönborn, Christoph Cardinal, 107, 108
Scotus, John Duns, 11, 12, 178, 257–64, 268, 270, 273, 277
Sedgwick, Adam, 326
Sedley, David, 111n21
Seely, Paul, 217–19
Seitz, Christopher R., 172n26
Shermer, Michael, 329n6
Shircel, Cyril L., 257n12
Shubin, Neil, 255n9
Smith, Adam, 243
Smith, E. Baldwin, 212, 213
Smith, Quentin, 96n5
Sober, Elliott, 56n60

Sorabji, Richard, 272n31
Sørensen, Jesper, 332n10
Southgate, Christopher, 95
Spencer, Herbert, 32, 77, 78
Stove, David, 27, 344–46
Stump, Eleonore, 310n14

Teilhard de Chardin, Pierre, 105, 106, 206, 279, 280
Tertullian, 175, 308, 309
Thomson, Keith, 111
Tipler, Frank J., 112n24

Udd, Stanley V., 217n7
Updike, John, 201n13

Wallace, Alfred Russell, 226, 329
Walsh, D. M., 53n56
Waters, Brent, 254n8
Webb, Stephen H., 72n7, 116n30, 201n13, 228n16, 236n25, 242n31, 255n9, 260n15, 161n16, 283n46, 285n50, 295n55, 299n3, 333n12
Weikart, Richard, 249, 250, 281
Wells, Jonathan, 16, 70n3
West, John G., 84, 85n30
Westermann, Claus, 167
White, Andrew Dickson, 71
Whitcomb, John, 216
Whitehead, Alfred North, 358
Whitehouse, W. A., 184
Wiker, Benjamin, 34n35, 252n6
Wilberforce, Samuel, 74
Wildman, Wesley J., 101n13
Williams, Mary B., 54n58
Williams, Patricia A., 153n9
Williams, Thomas, 257n12
Wilson, David Sloan, 35–41, 63, 64
Wilson, Edward O., 347, 351, 352
Wittgenstein, Ludwig, 353
Wolter, Allan B., 262n17, 263n19, 264
Woodward, Thomas, 113n26

Yong, Amos, 22n12

www.ingramcontent.com/pod-product-compliance
Lightning Source LLC
Chambersburg PA
CBHW021339300426
44114CB00012B/1001